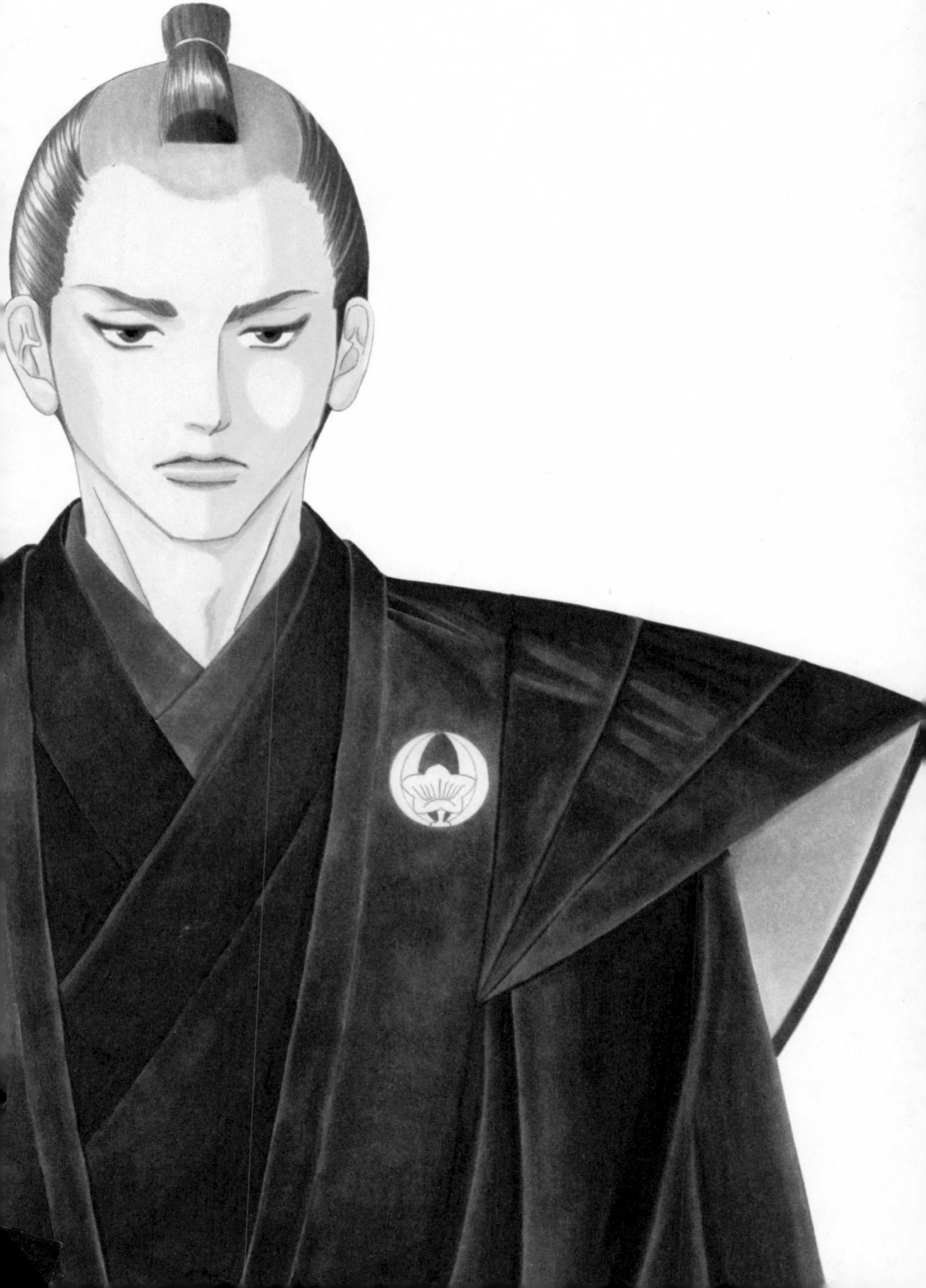

TABLE *of* CONTENTS

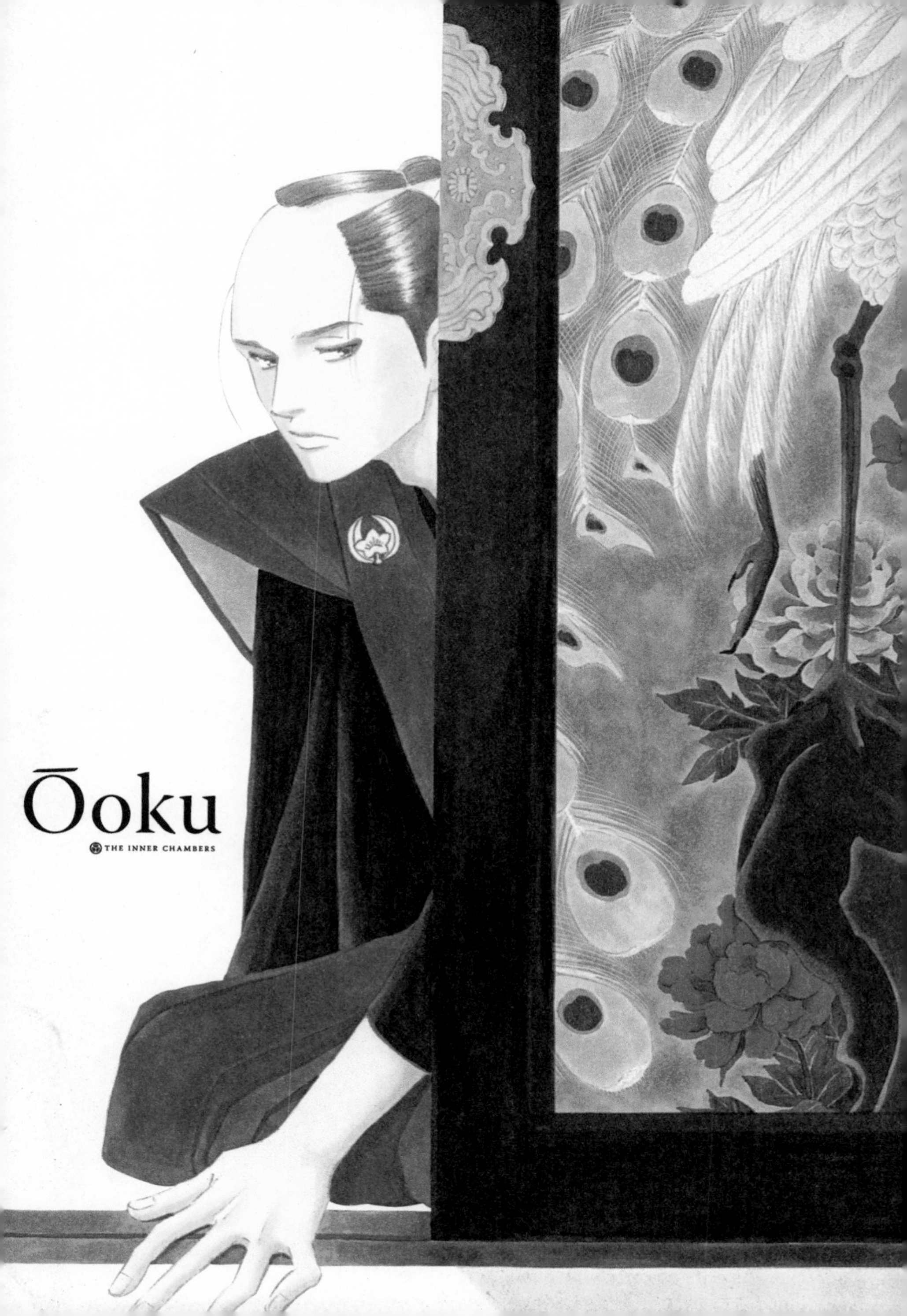
Ōoku
THE INNER CHAMBERS

All who serve inside the Ôoku, the Inner Chambers in the deepest interior of Edo Castle, must seal with blood the following oath—

“Never shall I speak of things I have seen or heard inside the Ôoku, nor of anything else that doth take place therein, to my parents, or to my brothers or sisters, or to any other person beyond its walls.”

—from *The Ōoku Code*

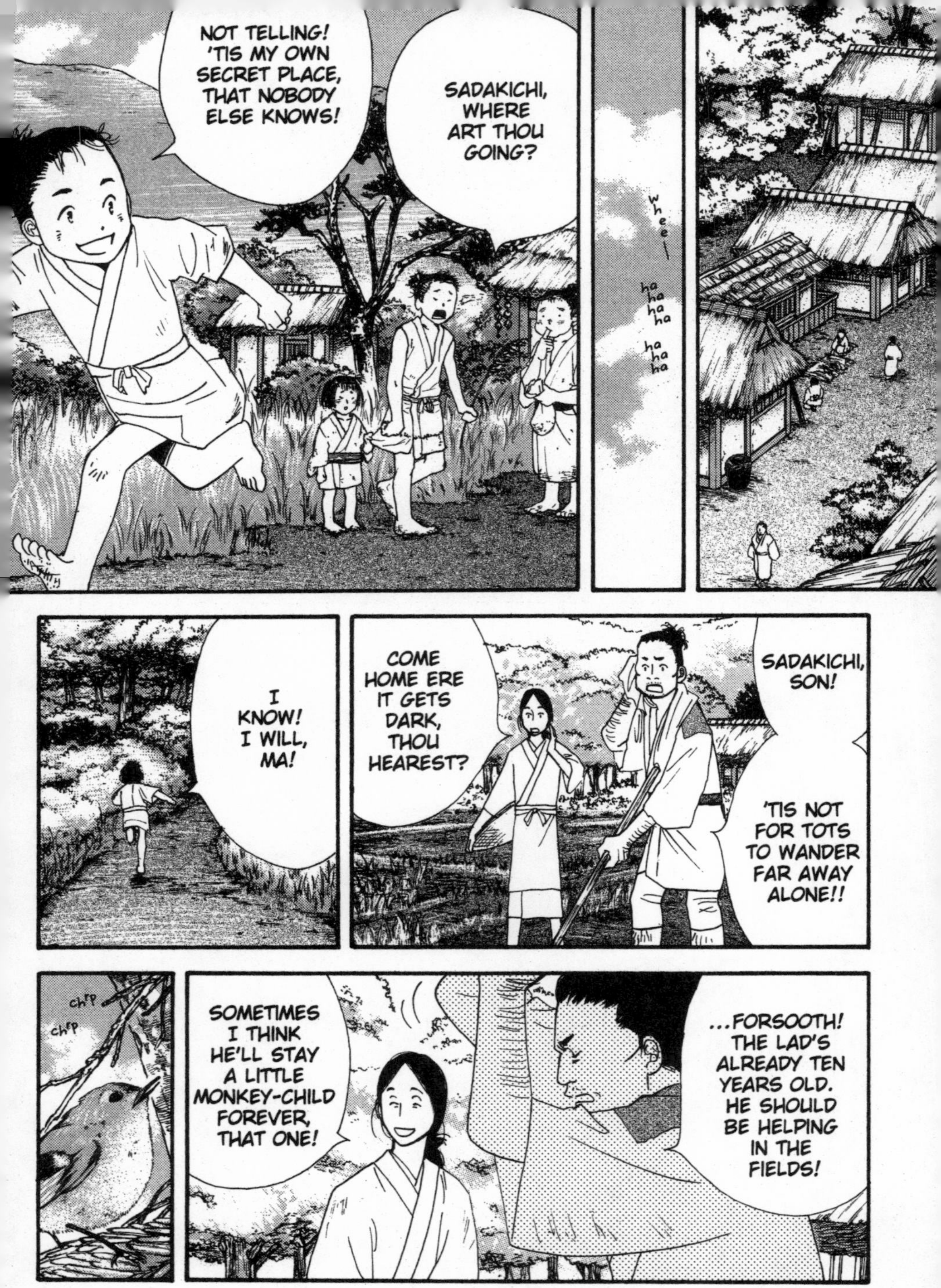
whee—
ha ha ha ha
ha ha ha
SADAKICHI, WHERE ART THOU GOING?
NOT TELLING! 'TIS MY OWN SECRET PLACE, THAT NOBODY ELSE KNOWS!
SADAKICHI, SON!
'TIS NOT FOR TOTS TO WANDER FAR AWAY ALONE!!
COME HOME ERE IT GETS DARK, THOU HEAREST?
I KNOW! I WILL, MA!
...FORSOOTH! THE LAD'S ALREADY TEN YEARS OLD. HE SHOULD BE HELPING IN THE FIELDS!
SOMETIMES I THINK HE'LL STAY A LITTLE MONKEY-CHILD FOREVER, THAT ONE!
chirp
chirp

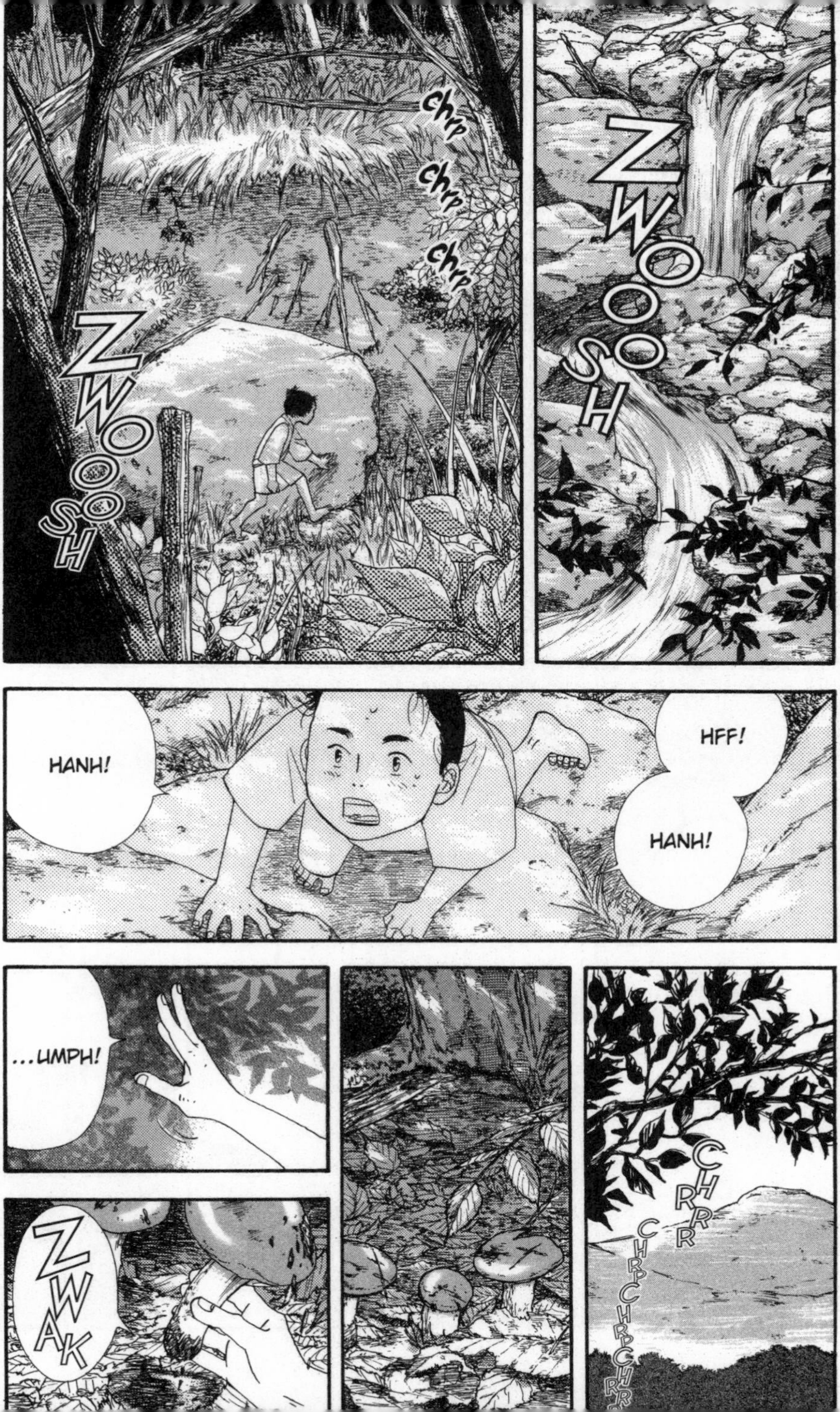
ZWOOOSH
chrp chrp chrp
ZWOOOSH
HFF!
HANH!
HANH!
CHRR
CHRPCHRPCHRR
...UMPH!
ZWAK

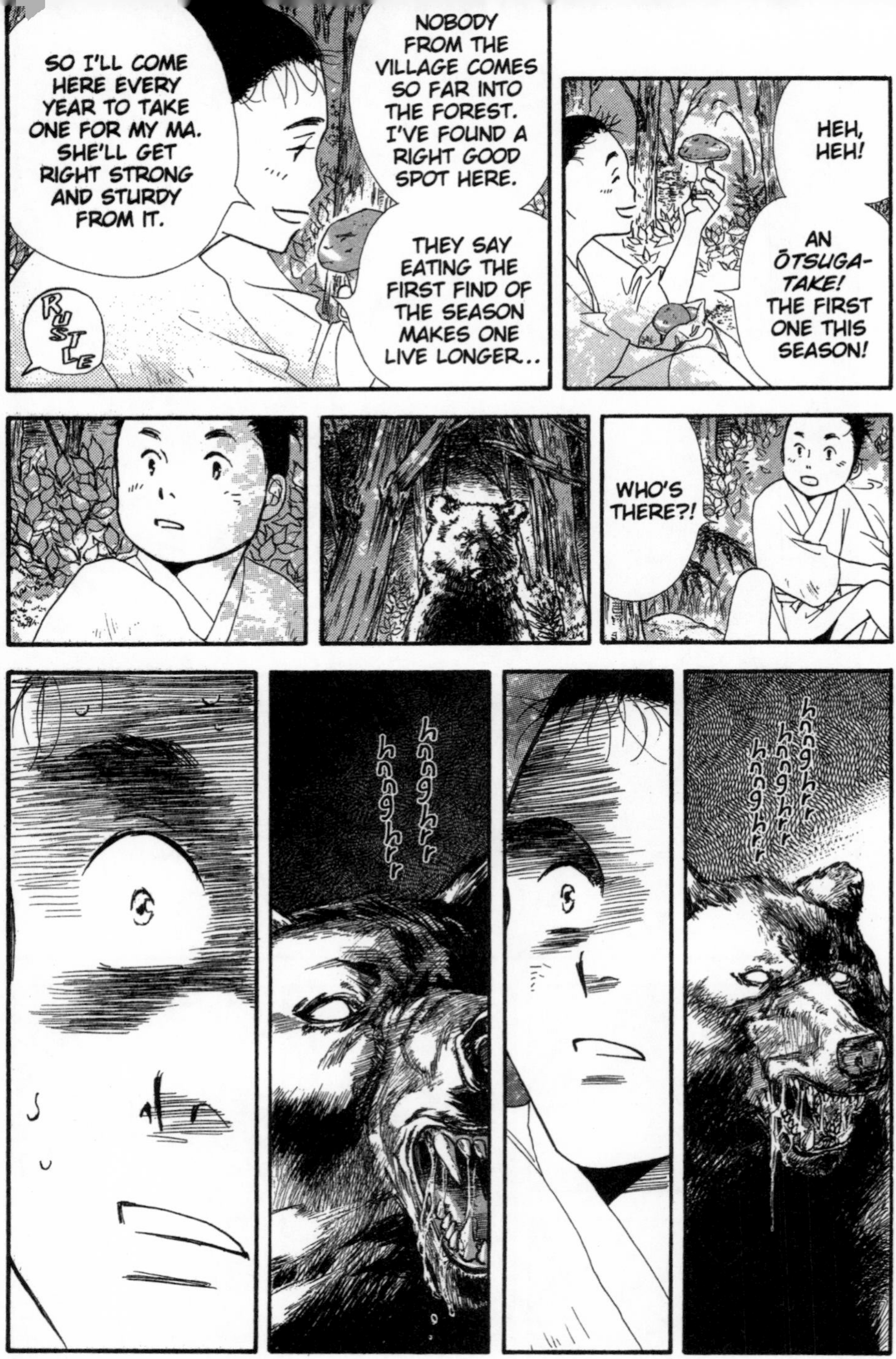
HEH, HEH!
AN ŌTSUGA-TAKE! THE FIRST ONE THIS SEASON!
NOBODY FROM THE VILLAGE COMES SO FAR INTO THE FOREST. I'VE FOUND A RIGHT GOOD SPOT HERE.
THEY SAY EATING THE FIRST FIND OF THE SEASON MAKES ONE LIVE LONGER..
SO I'LL COME HERE EVERY YEAR TO TAKE ONE FOR MY MA. SHE'LL GET RIGHT STRONG AND STURDY FROM IT.
RUSTLE
WHO'S THERE?!
hnnghrr
hnnghrr
hnnghrr
hnnghrr
hnnghrr

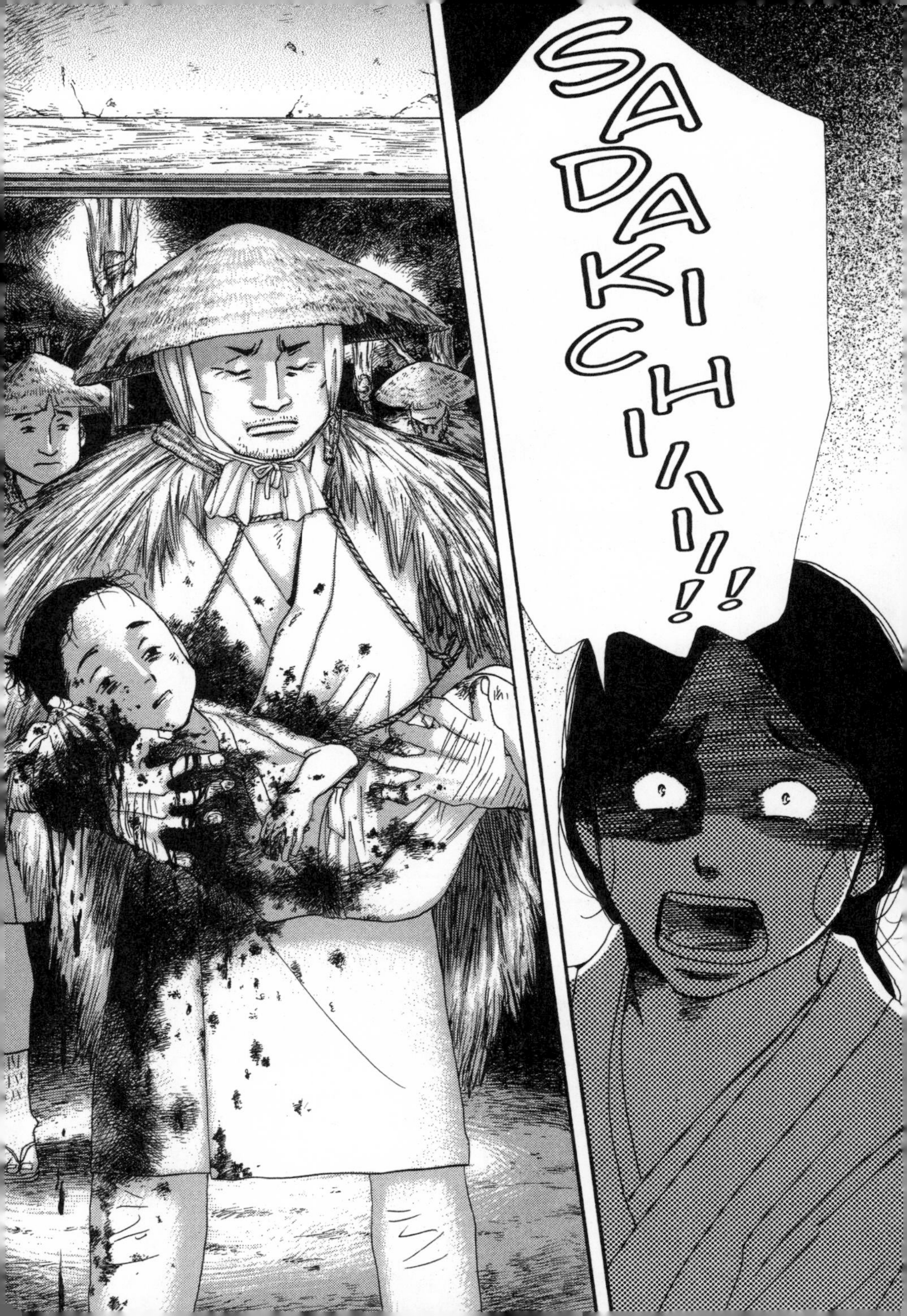
SADAKICHIIIII!!

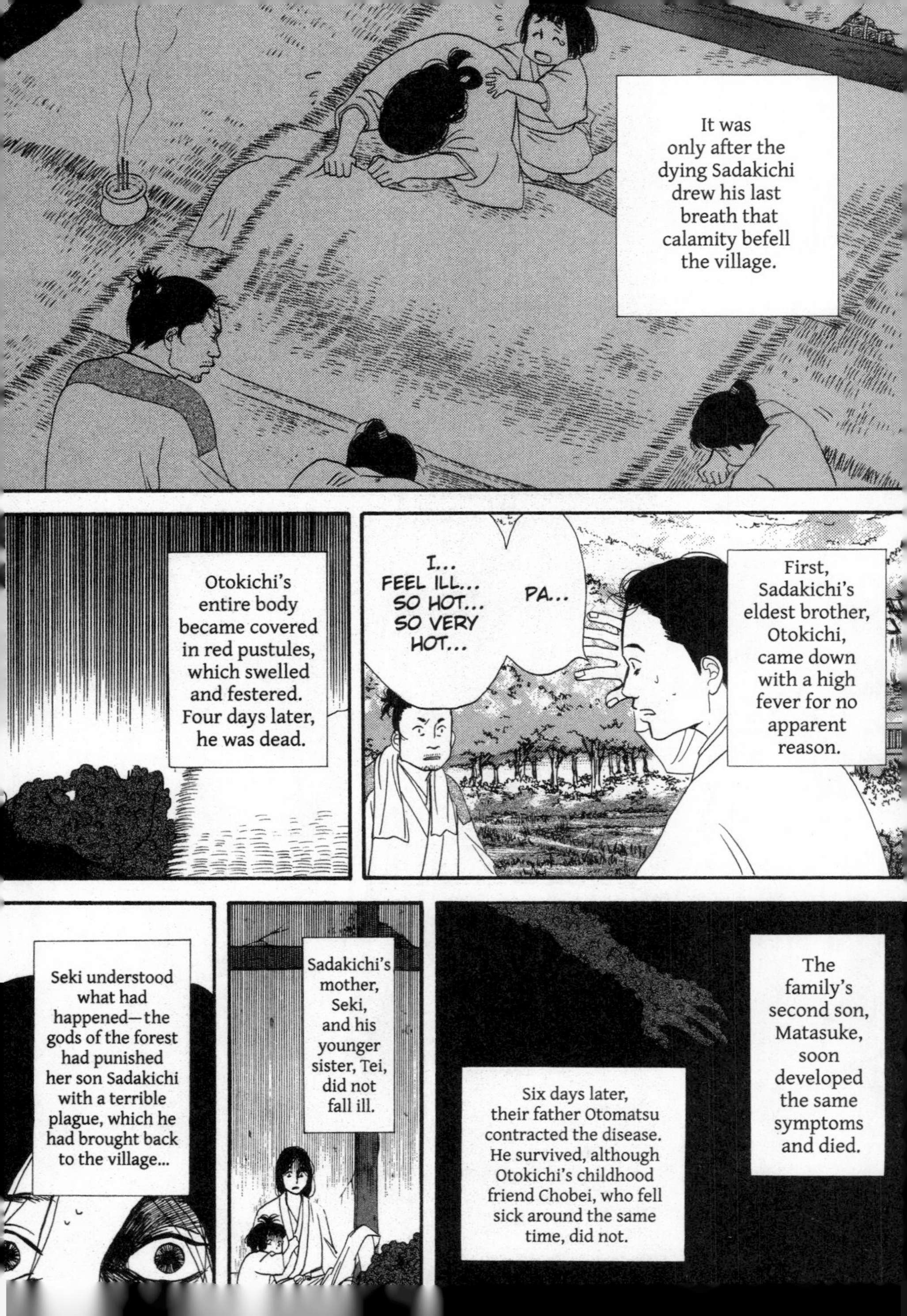
It was only after the dying Sadakichi drew his last breath that calamity befell the village.
First, Sadakichi's eldest brother, Otokichi, came down with a high fever for no apparent reason.
PA...
I... FEEL ILL... SO HOT... SO VERY HOT...
Otokichi's entire body became covered in red pustules, which swelled and festered. Four days later, he was dead.
The family's second son, Matasuke, soon developed the same symptoms and died.
Six days later, their father Otomatsu contracted the disease. He survived, although Otokichi's childhood friend Chobei, who fell sick around the same time, did not.
Sadakichi's mother, Seki, and his younger sister, Tei, did not fall ill.
Seki understood what had happened—the gods of the forest had punished her son Sadakichi with a terrible plague, which he had brought back to the village...

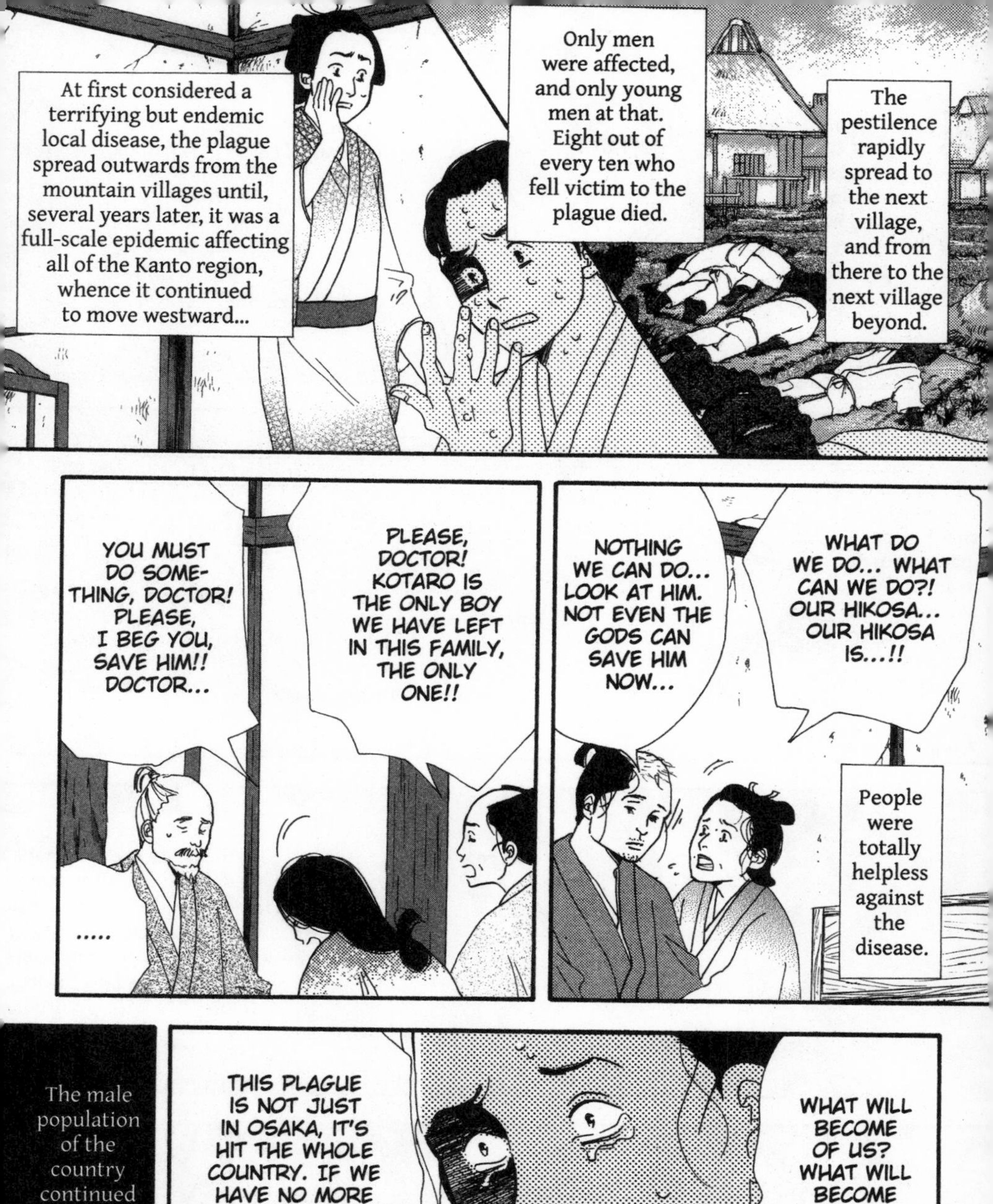
The pestilence rapidly spread to the next village, and from there to the next village beyond.
Only men were affected, and only young men at that. Eight out of every ten who fell victim to the plague died.
At first considered a terrifying but endemic local disease, the plague spread outwards from the mountain villages until, several years later, it was a full-scale epidemic affecting all of the Kanto region, whence it continued to move westward...
WHAT DO WE DO... WHAT CAN WE DO?! OUR HIKOSA... OUR HIKOSA IS...!!
NOTHING WE CAN DO... LOOK AT HIM. NOT EVEN THE GODS CAN SAVE HIM NOW...
People were totally helpless against the disease.
PLEASE, DOCTOR! KOTARO IS THE ONLY BOY WE HAVE LEFT IN THIS FAMILY, THE ONLY ONE!!
YOU MUST DO SOME-THING, DOCTOR! PLEASE, I BEG YOU, SAVE HIM!! DOCTOR...
.....
WHAT WILL BECOME OF US? WHAT WILL BECOME OF THIS WORLD...?!
THIS PLAGUE IS NOT JUST IN OSAKA, IT'S HIT THE WHOLE COUNTRY. IF WE HAVE NO MORE BOYS LEFT IN THIS WORLD, WE ARE ALL DOOMED. THIS WORLD WILL END...!!
The male population of the country continued to decrease at a frightening rate.

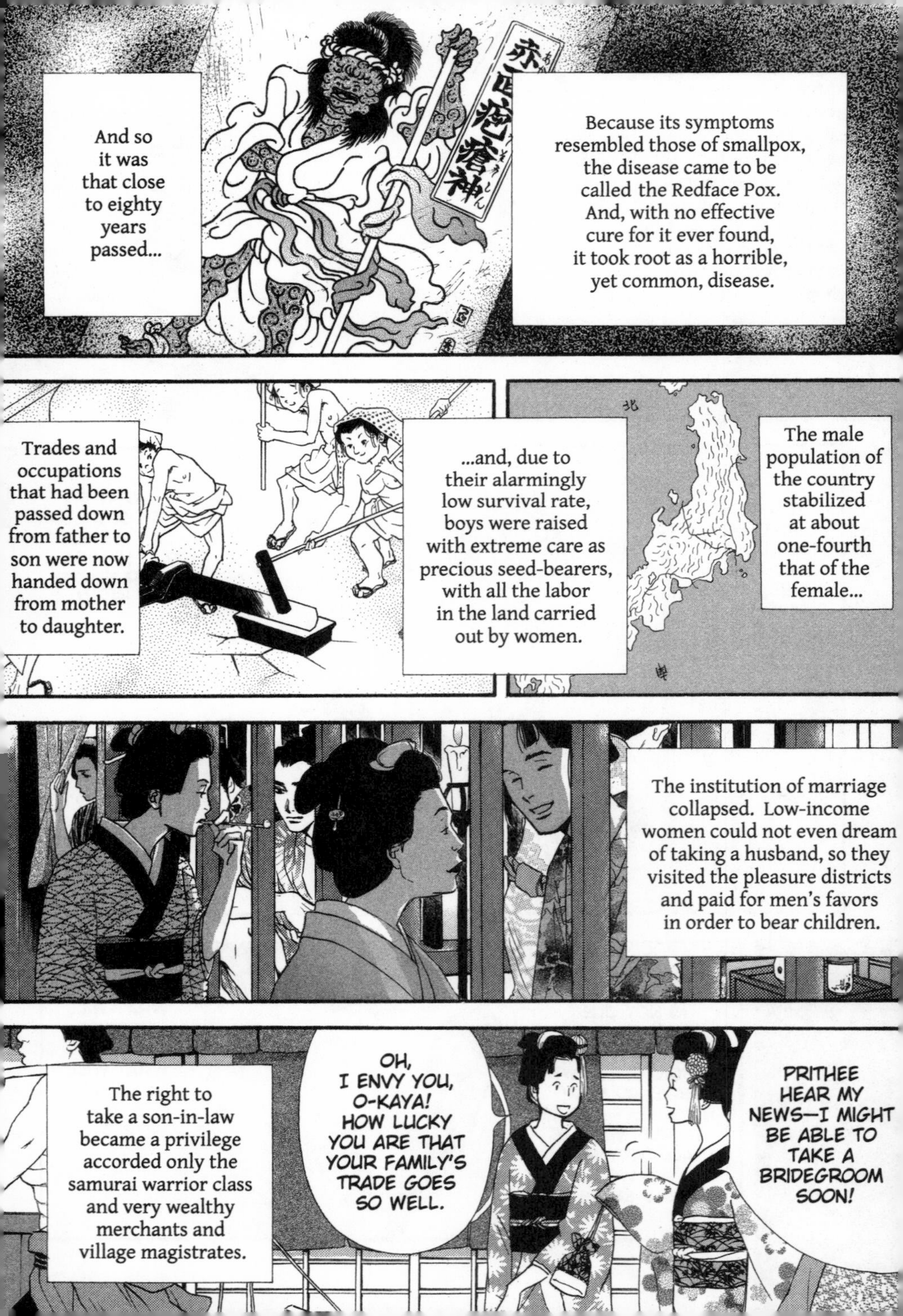

Because its symptoms resembled those of smallpox, the disease came to be called the Redface Pox. And, with no effective cure for it ever found, it took root as a horrible, yet common, disease.
赤面疱瘡神
And so it was that close to eighty years passed...
北
The male population of the country stabilized at about one-fourth that of the female...
...and, due to their alarmingly low survival rate, boys were raised with extreme care as precious seed-bearers, with all the labor in the land carried out by women.
Trades and occupations that had been passed down from father to son were now handed down from mother to daughter.
The institution of marriage collapsed. Low-income women could not even dream of taking a husband, so they visited the pleasure districts and paid for men's favors in order to bear children.
PRITHEE HEAR MY NEWS—I MIGHT BE ABLE TO TAKE A BRIDEGROOM SOON!
OH, I ENVY YOU, O-KAYA! HOW LUCKY YOU ARE THAT YOUR FAMILY'S TRADE GOES SO WELL.
The right to take a son-in-law became a privilege accorded only the samurai warrior class and very wealthy merchants and village magistrates.

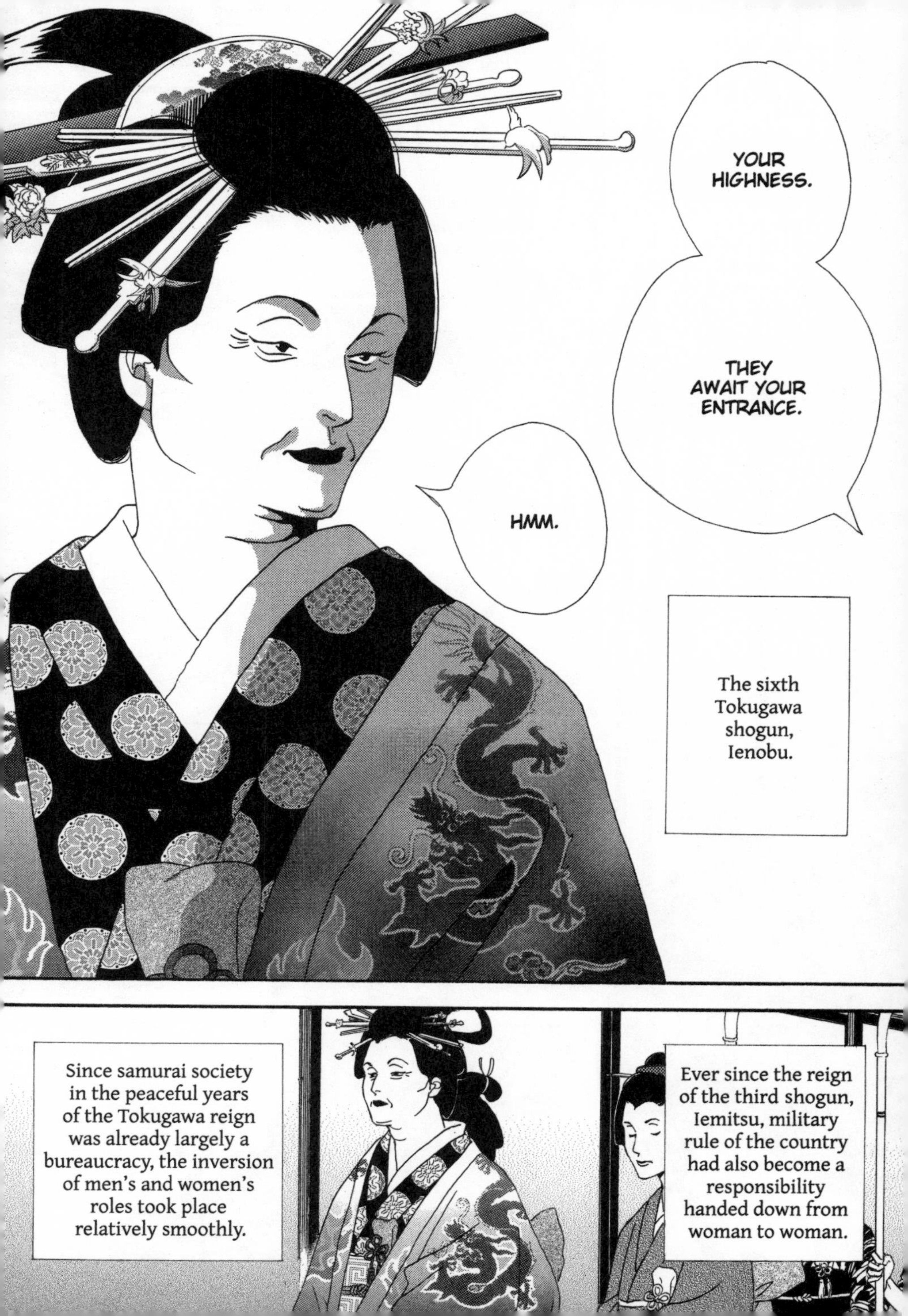
YOUR HIGHNESS.
THEY AWAIT YOUR ENTRANCE.
HMM.
The sixth Tokugawa shogun, Ienobu.
Ever since the reign of the third shogun, Iemitsu, military rule of the country had also become a responsibility handed down from woman to woman.
Since samurai society in the peaceful years of the Tokugawa reign was already largely a bureaucracy, the inversion of men's and women's roles took place relatively smoothly.

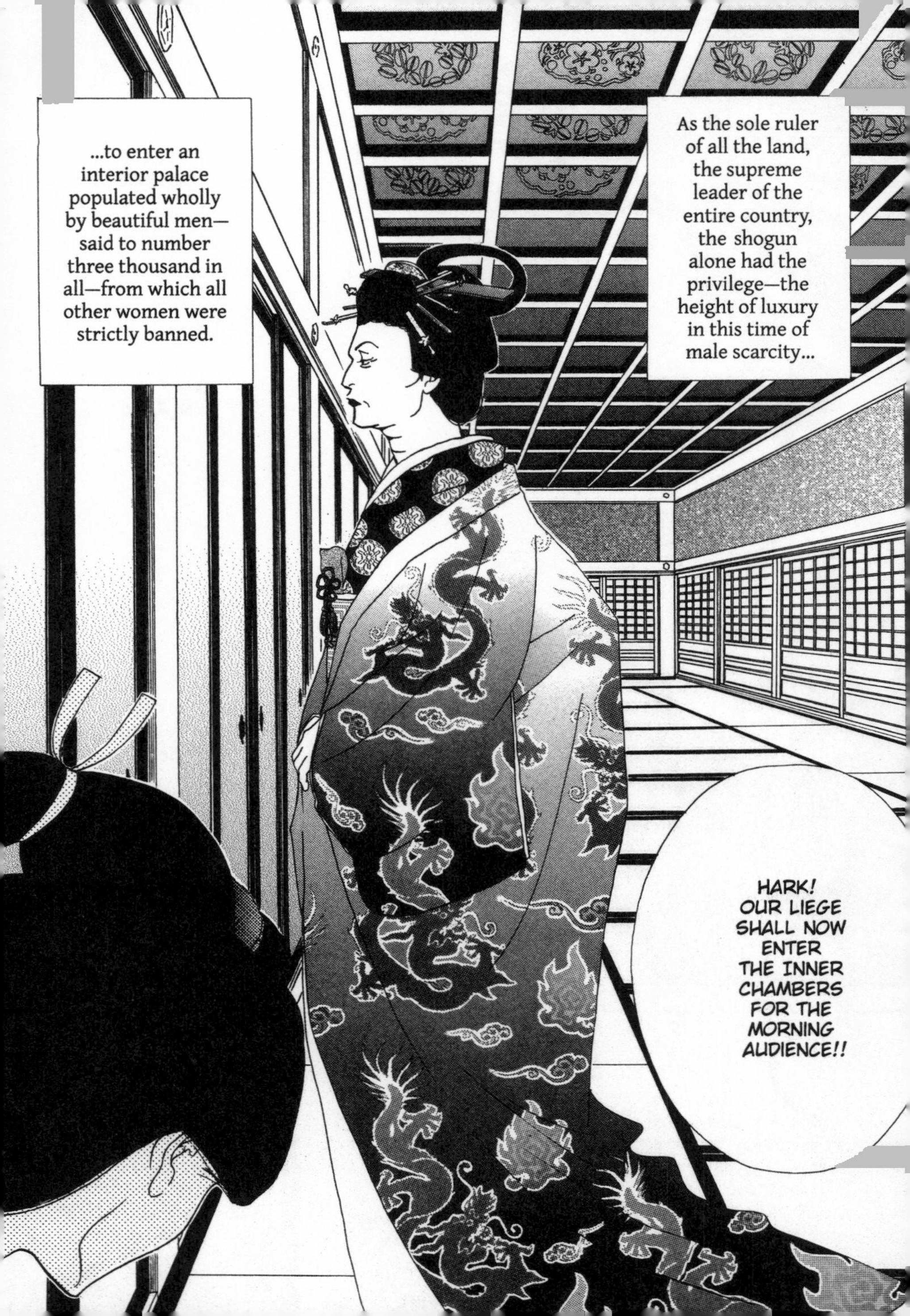
As the sole ruler of all the land, the supreme leader of the entire country, the shogun alone had the privilege—the height of luxury in this time of male scarcity...
...to enter an interior palace populated wholly by beautiful men—said to number three thousand in all—from which all other women were strictly banned.
HARK! OUR LIEGE SHALL NOW ENTER THE INNER CHAMBERS FOR THE MORNING AUDIENCE!!

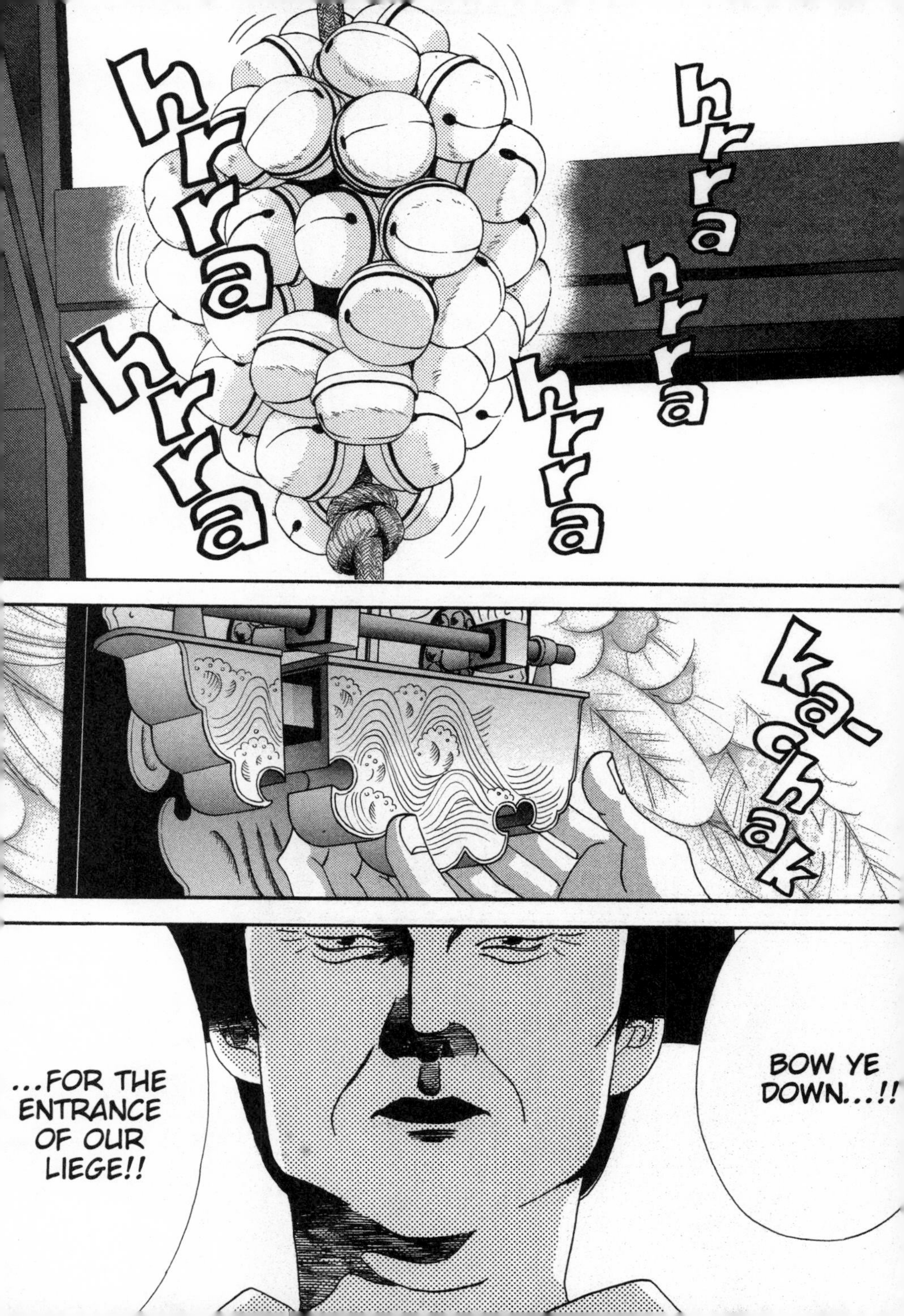
hrra hrra
hrra
hrra hrra
ka-chak
BOW YE DOWN...!!
...FOR THE ENTRANCE OF OUR LIEGE!!

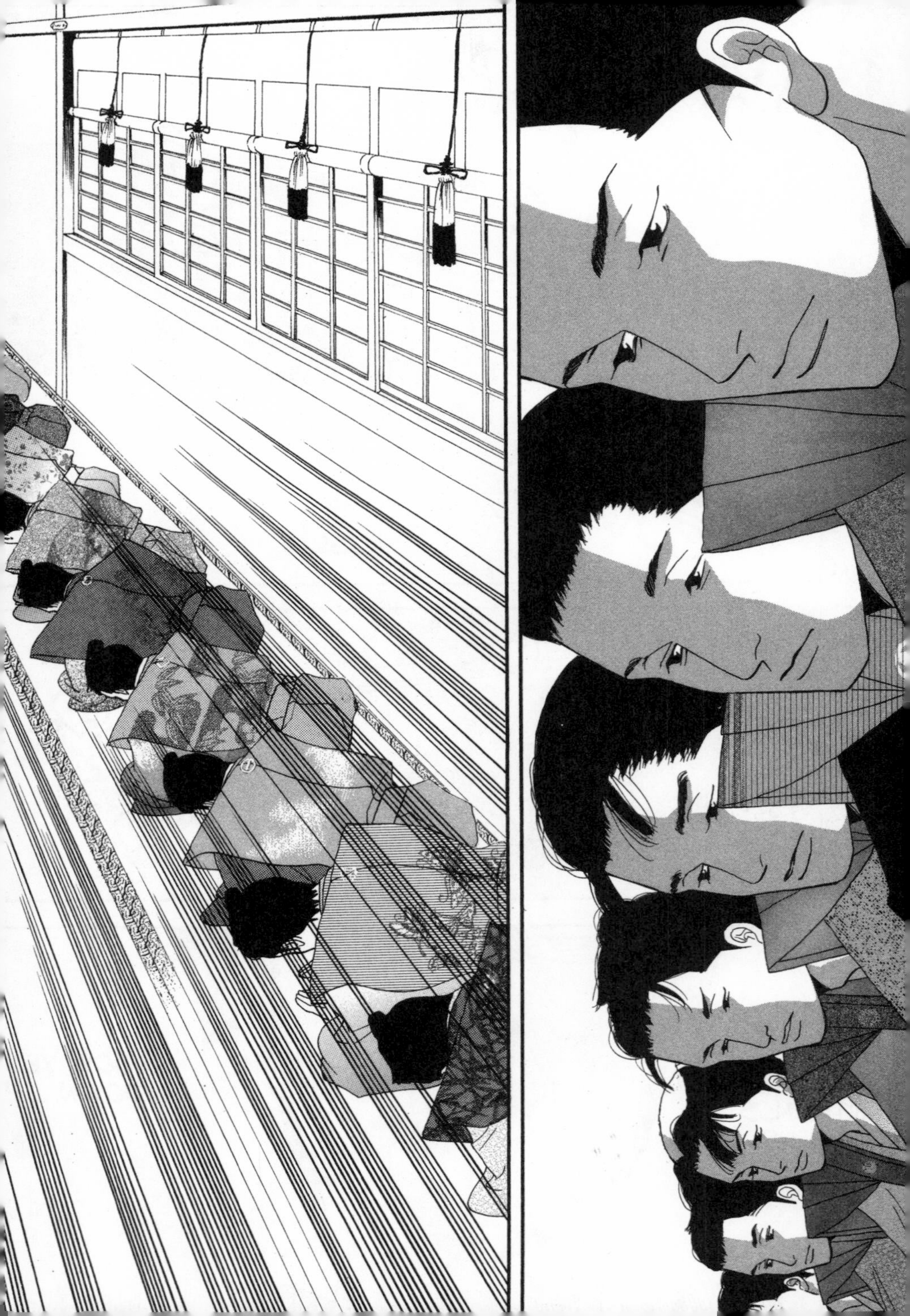

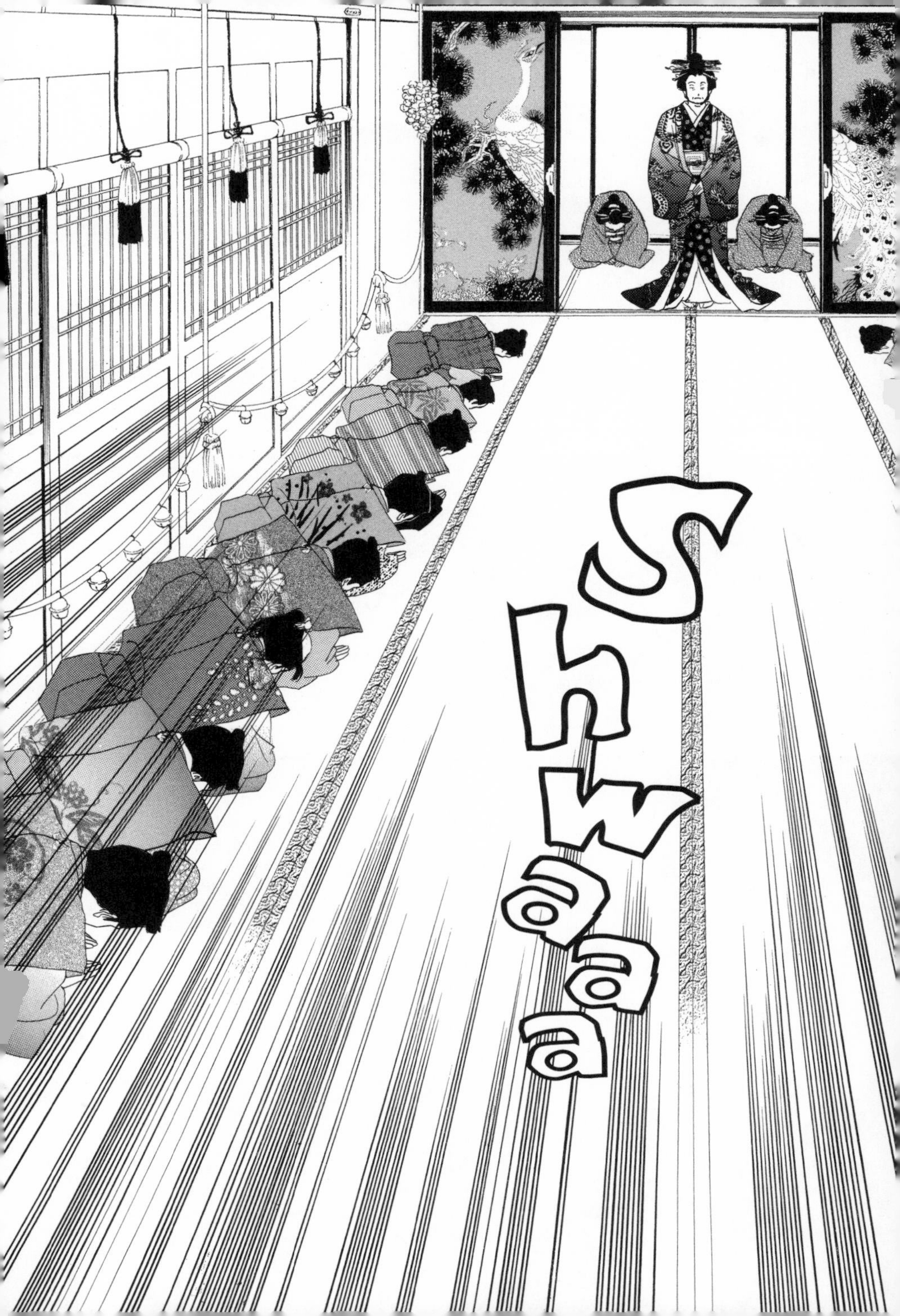
Shwaaaa

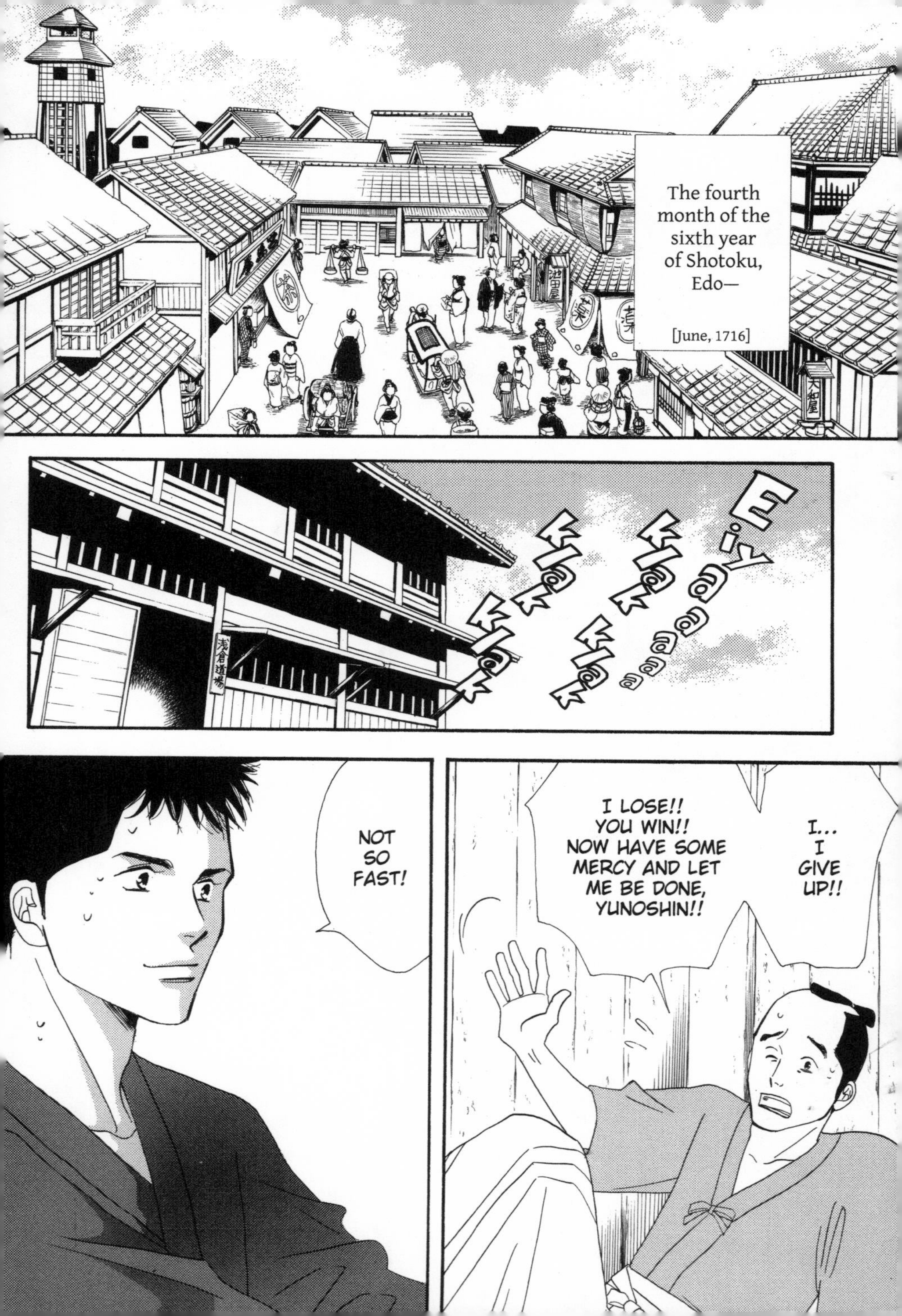
The fourth month of the sixth year of Shotoku, Edo—
[June, 1716]
EiYaaaaaaa
Klak Klak
Klak Klak
I... I GIVE UP!!
I LOSE!! YOU WIN!! NOW HAVE SOME MERCY AND LET ME BE DONE, YUNOSHIN!!
NOT SO FAST!

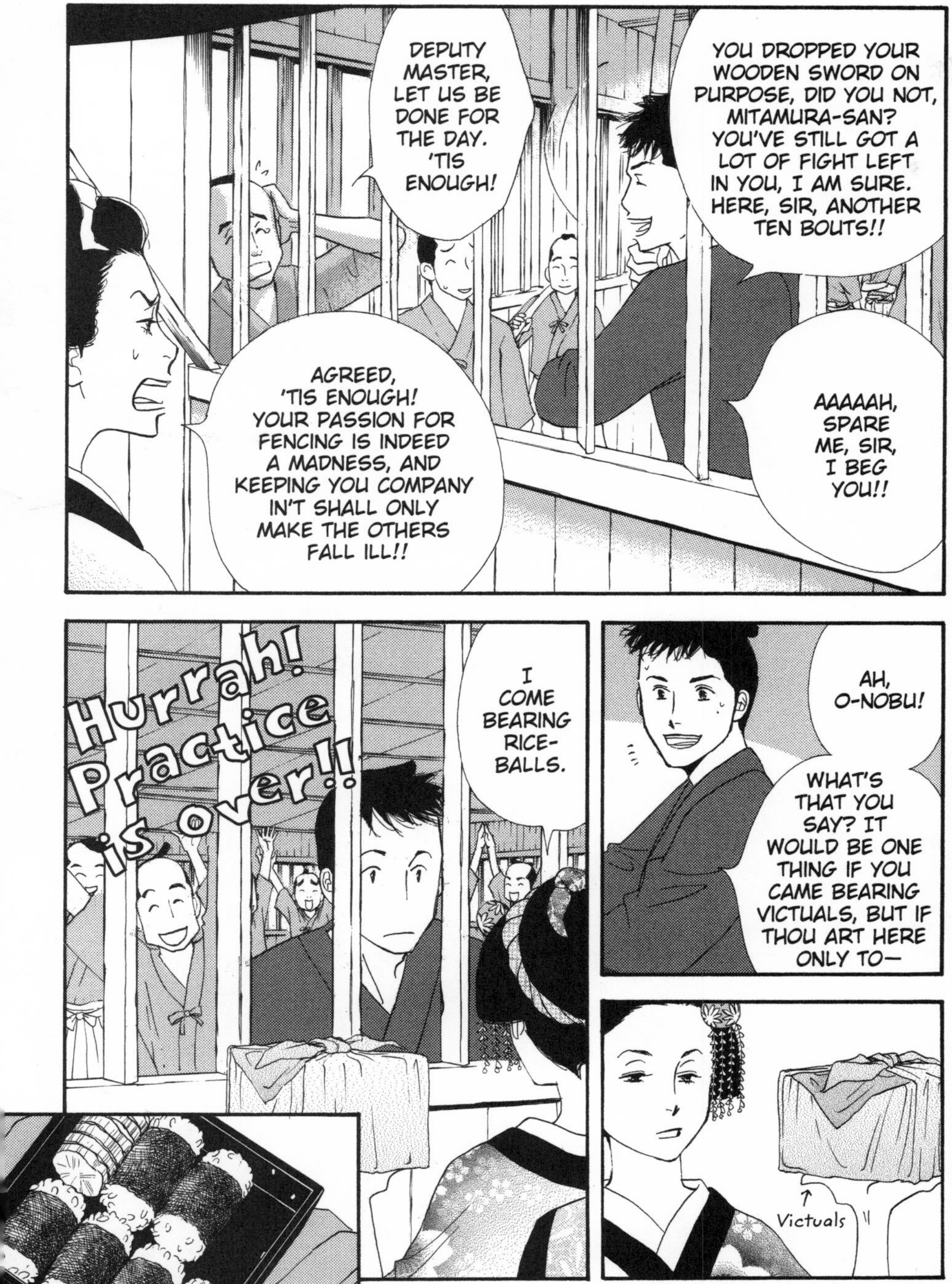
YOU DROPPED YOUR WOODEN SWORD ON PURPOSE, DID YOU NOT, MITAMURA-SAN? YOU'VE STILL GOT A LOT OF FIGHT LEFT IN YOU, I AM SURE. HERE, SIR, ANOTHER TEN BOUTS!!
DEPUTY MASTER, LET US BE DONE FOR THE DAY. 'TIS ENOUGH!
AAAAH, SPARE ME, SIR, I BEG YOU!!
AGREED, 'TIS ENOUGH! YOUR PASSION FOR FENCING IS INDEED A MADNESS, AND KEEPING YOU COMPANY IN'T SHALL ONLY MAKE THE OTHERS FALL ILL!!
Hurrah! Practice is over!!
I COME BEARING RICE-BALLS.
AH, O-NOBU!
WHAT'S THAT YOU SAY? IT WOULD BE ONE THING IF YOU CAME BEARING VICTUALS, BUT IF THOU ART HERE ONLY TO—
↑ Victuals

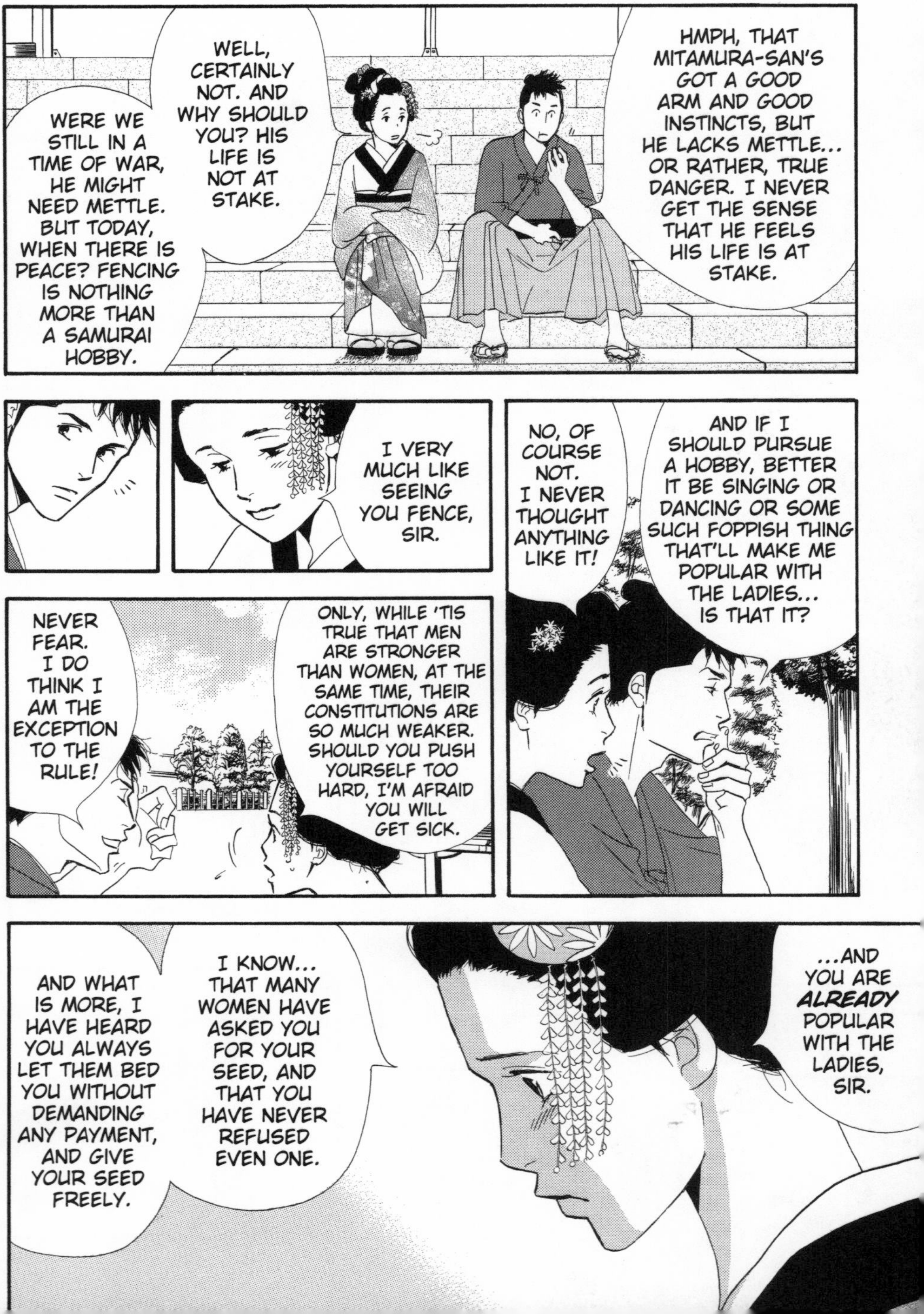
HMPH, THAT MITAMURA-SAN'S GOT A GOOD ARM AND GOOD INSTINCTS, BUT HE LACKS METTLE... OR RATHER, TRUE DANGER. I NEVER GET THE SENSE THAT HE FEELS HIS LIFE IS AT STAKE.
WELL, CERTAINLY NOT. AND WHY SHOULD YOU? HIS LIFE IS NOT AT STAKE.
WERE WE STILL IN A TIME OF WAR, HE MIGHT NEED METTLE. BUT TODAY, WHEN THERE IS PEACE? FENCING IS NOTHING MORE THAN A SAMURAI HOBBY.
AND IF I SHOULD PURSUE A HOBBY, BETTER IT BE SINGING OR DANCING OR SOME SUCH FOPPISH THING THAT'LL MAKE ME POPULAR WITH THE LADIES... IS THAT IT?
NO, OF COURSE NOT. I NEVER THOUGHT ANYTHING LIKE IT!
I VERY MUCH LIKE SEEING YOU FENCE, SIR.
ONLY, WHILE 'TIS TRUE THAT MEN ARE STRONGER THAN WOMEN, AT THE SAME TIME, THEIR CONSTITUTIONS ARE SO MUCH WEAKER. SHOULD YOU PUSH YOURSELF TOO HARD, I'M AFRAID YOU WILL GET SICK.
NEVER FEAR. I DO THINK I AM THE EXCEPTION TO THE RULE!
...AND YOU ARE ***ALREADY*** POPULAR WITH THE LADIES, SIR.
I KNOW... THAT MANY WOMEN HAVE ASKED YOU FOR YOUR SEED, AND THAT YOU HAVE NEVER REFUSED EVEN ONE.
AND WHAT IS MORE, I HAVE HEARD YOU ALWAYS LET THEM BED YOU WITHOUT DEMANDING ANY PAYMENT, AND GIVE YOUR SEED FREELY.

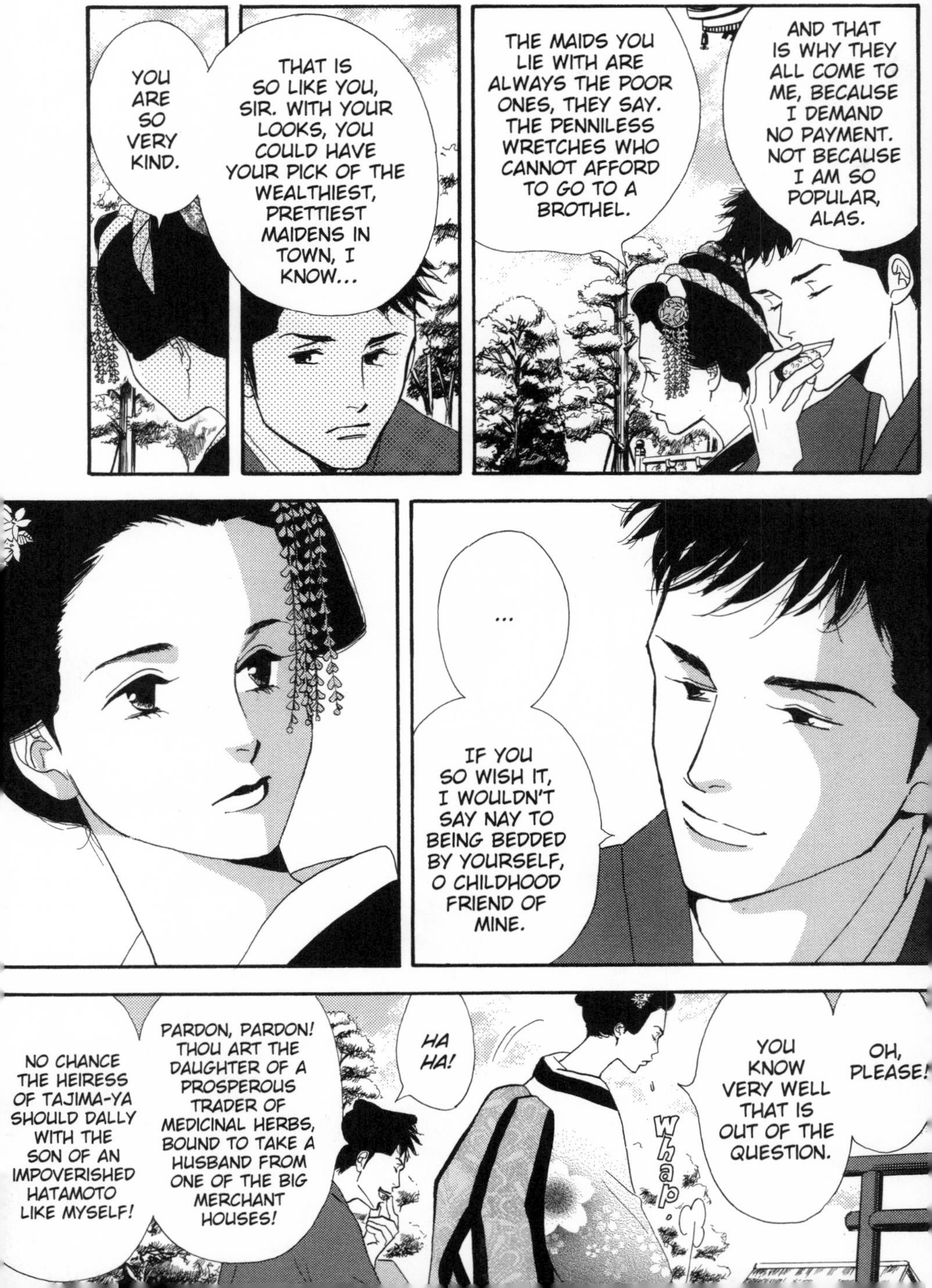
THE MAIDS YOU LIE WITH ARE ALWAYS THE POOR ONES, THEY SAY. THE PENNILESS WRETCHES WHO CANNOT AFFORD TO GO TO A BROTHEL.
AND THAT IS WHY THEY ALL COME TO ME, BECAUSE I DEMAND NO PAYMENT. NOT BECAUSE I AM SO POPULAR, ALAS.
THAT IS SO LIKE YOU, SIR. WITH YOUR LOOKS, YOU COULD HAVE YOUR PICK OF THE WEALTHIEST, PRETTIEST MAIDENS IN TOWN, I KNOW...
YOU ARE SO VERY KIND.
...
IF YOU SO WISH IT, I WOULDN'T SAY NAY TO BEING BEDDED BY YOURSELF, O CHILDHOOD FRIEND OF MINE.
OH, PLEASE!
YOU KNOW VERY WELL THAT IS OUT OF THE QUESTION.
Whap.
HA HA!
PARDON, PARDON! THOU ART THE DAUGHTER OF A PROSPEROUS TRADER OF MEDICINAL HERBS, BOUND TO TAKE A HUSBAND FROM ONE OF THE BIG MERCHANT HOUSES!
NO CHANCE THE HEIRESS OF TAJIMA-YA SHOULD DALLY WITH THE SON OF AN IMPOVERISHED HATAMOTO LIKE MYSELF!

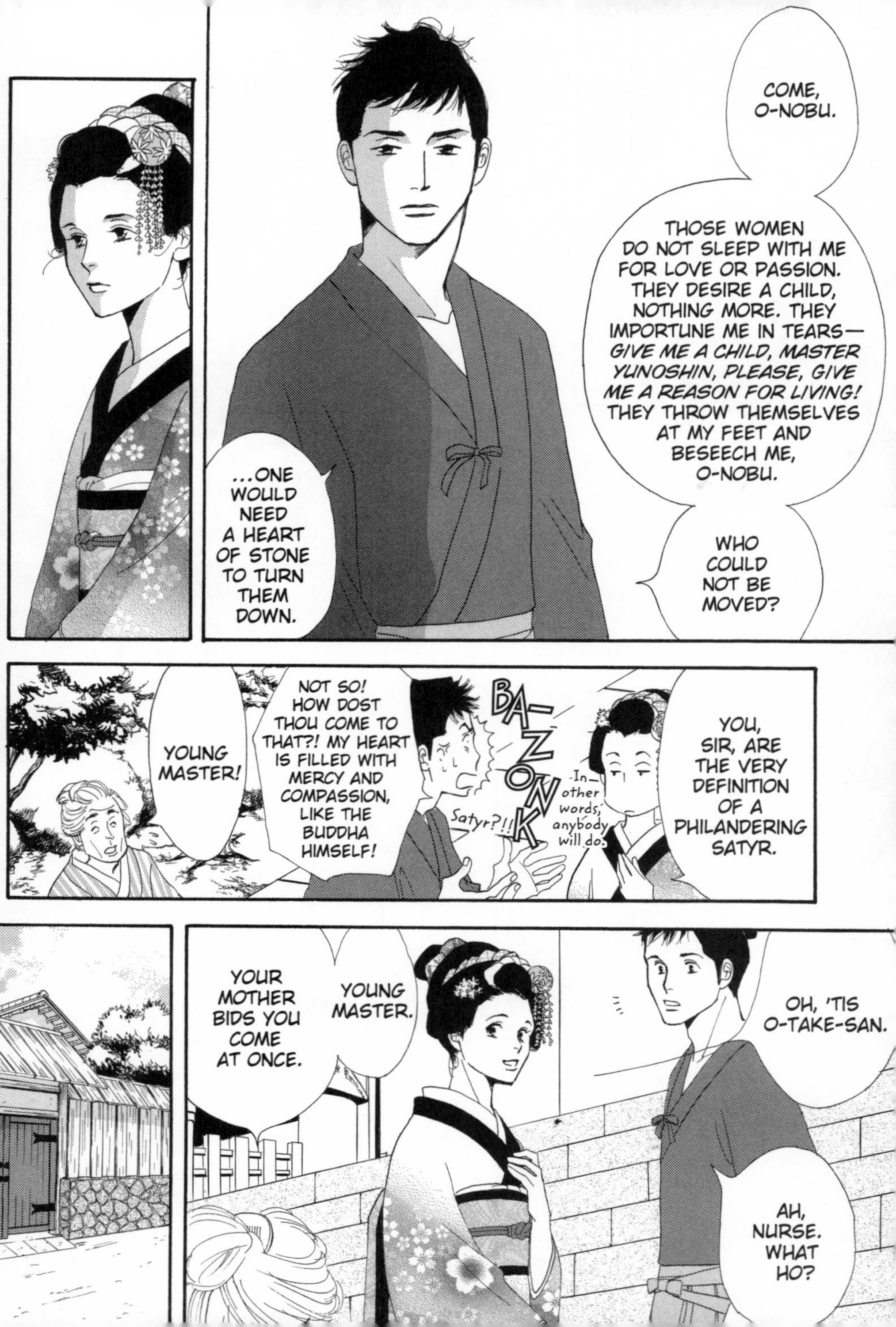
COME, O-NOBU.
THOSE WOMEN DO NOT SLEEP WITH ME FOR LOVE OR PASSION. THEY DESIRE A CHILD, NOTHING MORE. THEY IMPORTUNE ME IN TEARS—*GIVE ME A CHILD, MASTER YUNOSHIN, PLEASE, GIVE ME A REASON FOR LIVING!* THEY THROW THEMSELVES AT MY FEET AND BESEECH ME, O-NOBU.
WHO COULD NOT BE MOVED?
...ONE WOULD NEED A HEART OF STONE TO TURN THEM DOWN.
YOU, SIR, ARE THE VERY DEFINITION OF A PHILANDERING SATYR.
-In other words, anybody will do.
BA-ZONK
Satyr?!!
NOT SO! HOW DOST THOU COME TO THAT?! MY HEART IS FILLED WITH MERCY AND COMPASSION, LIKE THE BUDDHA HIMSELF!
YOUNG MASTER!
OH, 'TIS O-TAKE-SAN.
YOUNG MASTER.
YOUR MOTHER BIDS YOU COME AT ONCE.
AH, NURSE. WHAT HO?

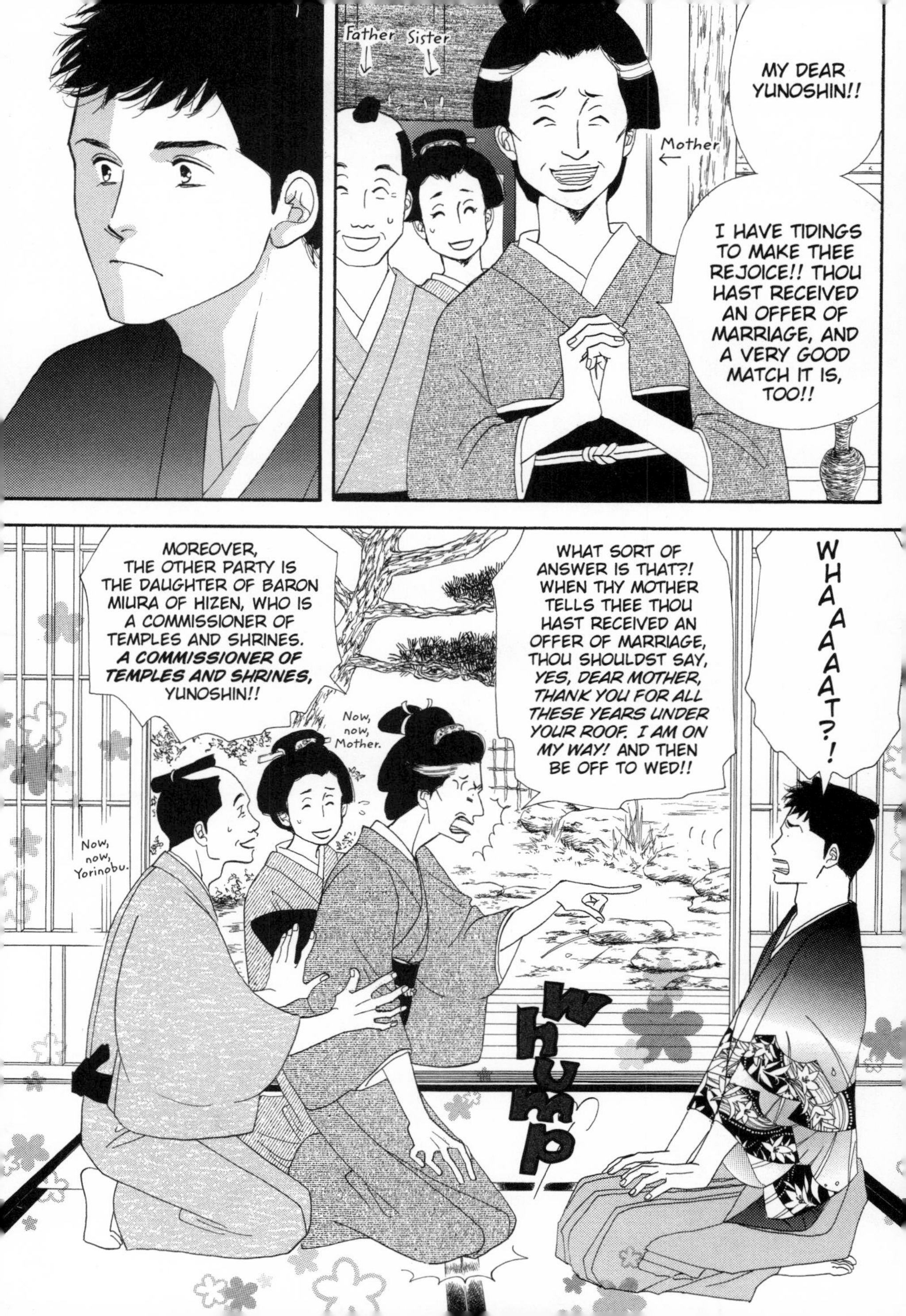
MY DEAR YUNOSHIN!!
I HAVE TIDINGS TO MAKE THEE REJOICE!! THOU HAST RECEIVED AN OFFER OF MARRIAGE, AND A VERY GOOD MATCH IT IS, TOO!!
Mother
Sister
Father
WHAAAAAT?!
WHAT SORT OF ANSWER IS THAT?! WHEN THY MOTHER TELLS THEE THOU HAST RECEIVED AN OFFER OF MARRIAGE, THOU SHOULDST SAY, YES, DEAR MOTHER, THANK YOU FOR ALL THESE YEARS UNDER YOUR ROOF. I AM ON MY WAY! AND THEN BE OFF TO WED!!
MOREOVER, THE OTHER PARTY IS THE DAUGHTER OF BARON MIURA OF HIZEN, WHO IS A COMMISSIONER OF TEMPLES AND SHRINES. A COMMISSIONER OF TEMPLES AND SHRINES, YUNOSHIN!!
Now, now, Mother.
Now, now, Yorinobu.
whump

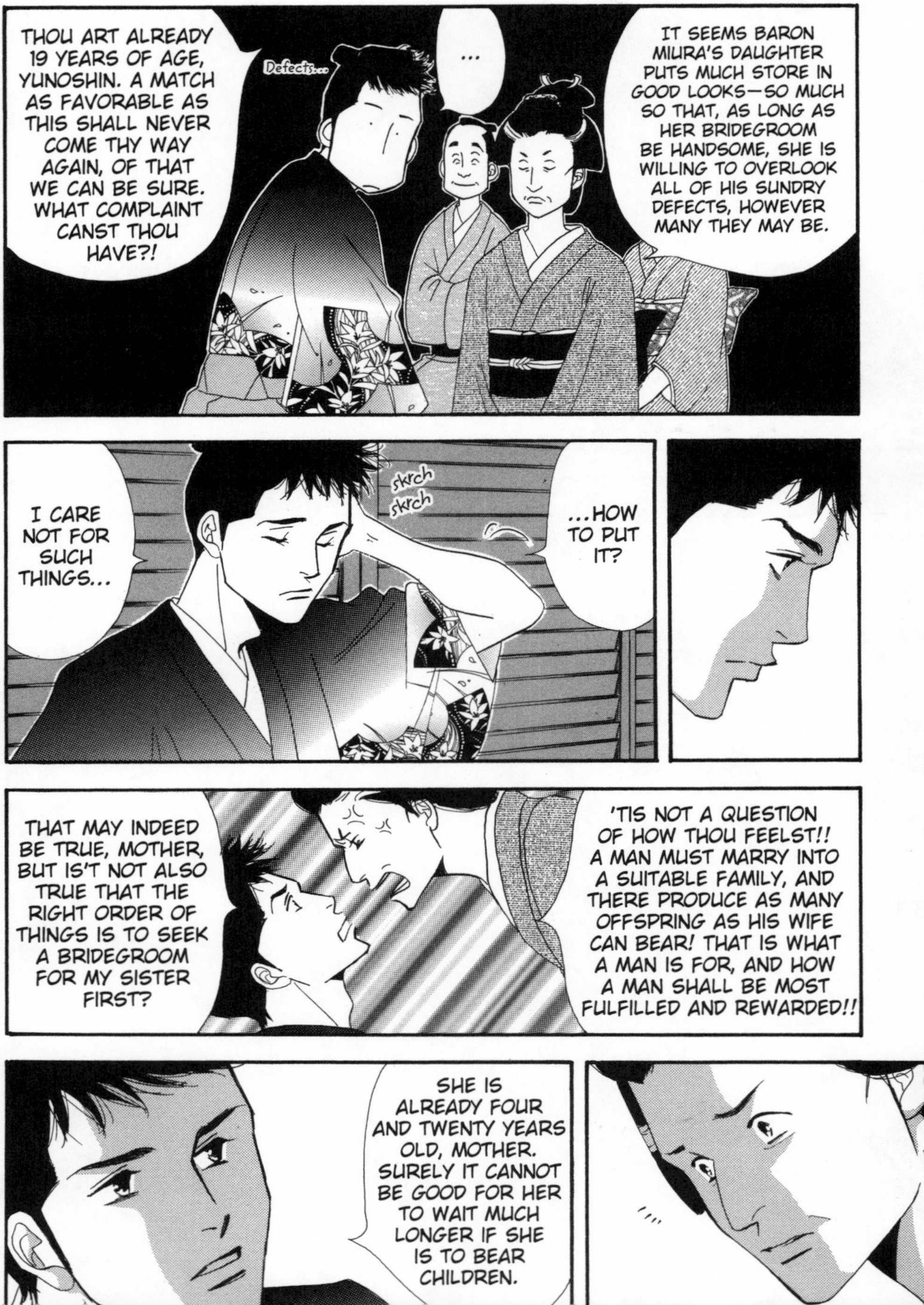
IT SEEMS BARON MIURA'S DAUGHTER PUTS MUCH STORE IN GOOD LOOKS—SO MUCH SO THAT, AS LONG AS HER BRIDEGROOM BE HANDSOME, SHE IS WILLING TO OVERLOOK ALL OF HIS SUNDRY DEFECTS, HOWEVER MANY THEY MAY BE.
...
Defects...
THOU ART ALREADY 19 YEARS OF AGE, YUNOSHIN. A MATCH AS FAVORABLE AS THIS SHALL NEVER COME THY WAY AGAIN, OF THAT WE CAN BE SURE. WHAT COMPLAINT CANST THOU HAVE?!
...HOW TO PUT IT?
skrch skrch
I CARE NOT FOR SUCH THINGS...
'TIS NOT A QUESTION OF HOW THOU FEELST!! A MAN MUST MARRY INTO A SUITABLE FAMILY, AND THERE PRODUCE AS MANY OFFSPRING AS HIS WIFE CAN BEAR! THAT IS WHAT A MAN IS FOR, AND HOW A MAN SHALL BE MOST FULFILLED AND REWARDED!!
THAT MAY INDEED BE TRUE, MOTHER, BUT IS'T NOT ALSO TRUE THAT THE RIGHT ORDER OF THINGS IS TO SEEK A BRIDEGROOM FOR MY SISTER FIRST?
SHE IS ALREADY FOUR AND TWENTY YEARS OLD, MOTHER. SURELY IT CANNOT BE GOOD FOR HER TO WAIT MUCH LONGER IF SHE IS TO BEAR CHILDREN.

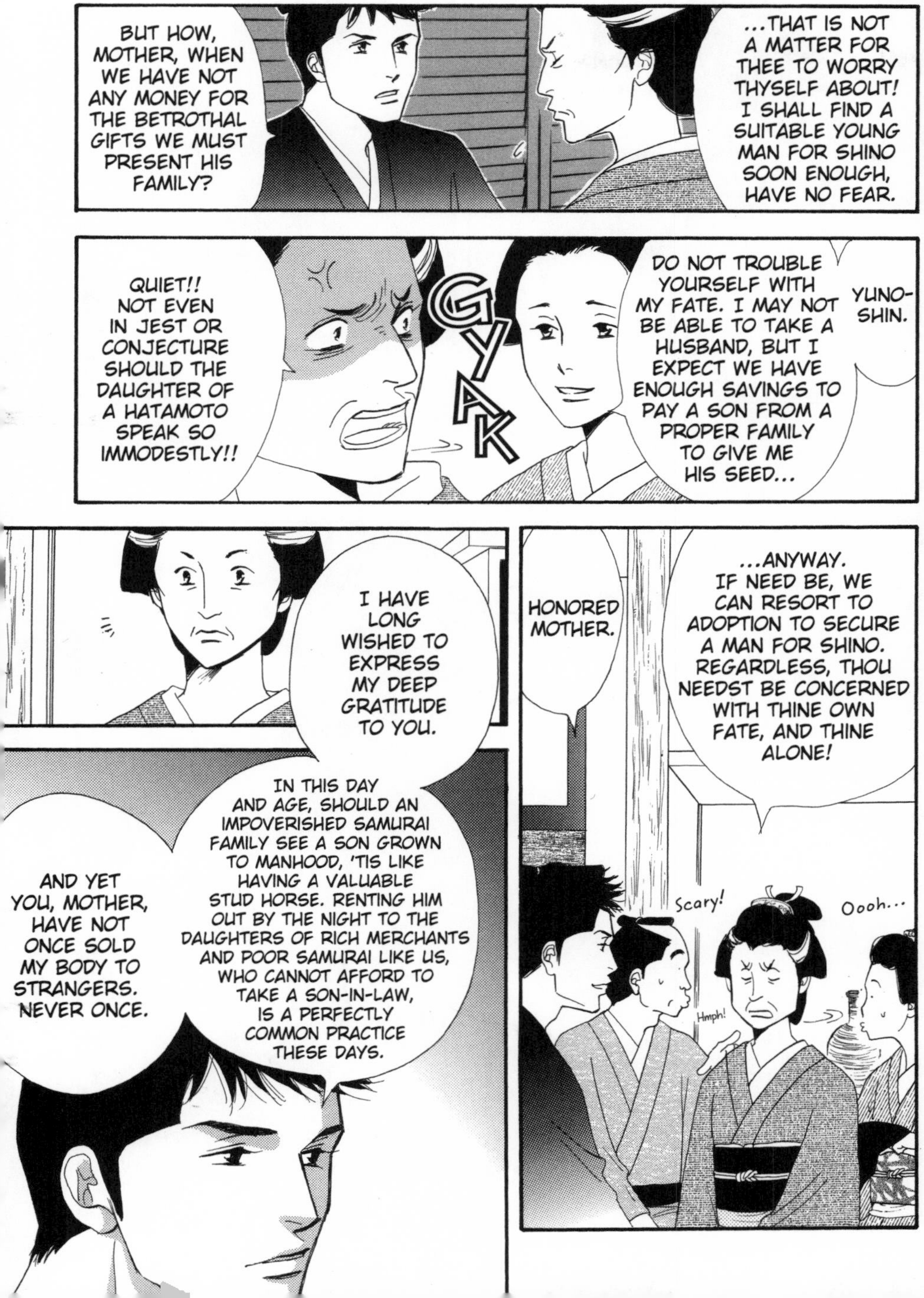
...THAT IS NOT A MATTER FOR THEE TO WORRY THYSELF ABOUT! I SHALL FIND A SUITABLE YOUNG MAN FOR SHINO SOON ENOUGH, HAVE NO FEAR.
BUT HOW, MOTHER, WHEN WE HAVE NOT ANY MONEY FOR THE BETROTHAL GIFTS WE MUST PRESENT HIS FAMILY?
YUNO-SHIN.
DO NOT TROUBLE YOURSELF WITH MY FATE. I MAY NOT BE ABLE TO TAKE A HUSBAND, BUT I EXPECT WE HAVE ENOUGH SAVINGS TO PAY A SON FROM A PROPER FAMILY TO GIVE ME HIS SEED...
GYAK
QUIET!! NOT EVEN IN JEST OR CONJECTURE SHOULD THE DAUGHTER OF A HATAMOTO SPEAK SO IMMODESTLY!!
...ANYWAY. IF NEED BE, WE CAN RESORT TO ADOPTION TO SECURE A MAN FOR SHINO. REGARDLESS, THOU NEEDST BE CONCERNED WITH THINE OWN FATE, AND THINE ALONE!
HONORED MOTHER.
Oooh...
Scary!
Hmph!
I HAVE LONG WISHED TO EXPRESS MY DEEP GRATITUDE TO YOU.
IN THIS DAY AND AGE, SHOULD AN IMPOVERISHED SAMURAI FAMILY SEE A SON GROWN TO MANHOOD, 'TIS LIKE HAVING A VALUABLE STUD HORSE. RENTING HIM OUT BY THE NIGHT TO THE DAUGHTERS OF RICH MERCHANTS AND POOR SAMURAI LIKE US, WHO CANNOT AFFORD TO TAKE A SON-IN-LAW, IS A PERFECTLY COMMON PRACTICE THESE DAYS.
AND YET YOU, MOTHER, HAVE NOT ONCE SOLD MY BODY TO STRANGERS. NEVER ONCE.

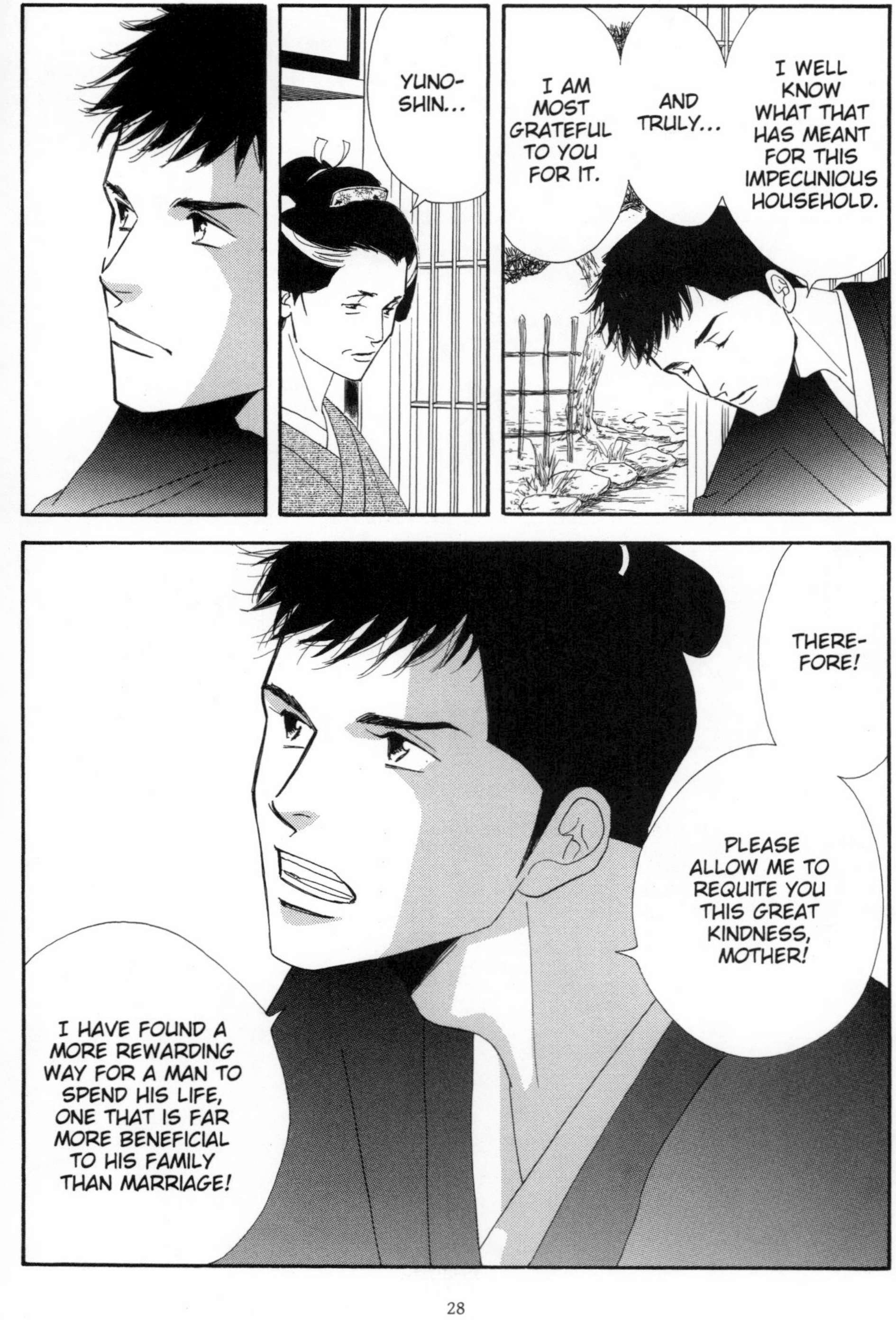
I WELL KNOW WHAT THAT HAS MEANT FOR THIS IMPECUNIOUS HOUSEHOLD.
AND TRULY...
I AM MOST GRATEFUL TO YOU FOR IT.
YUNO-SHIN...
THERE-FORE!
PLEASE ALLOW ME TO REQUITE YOU THIS GREAT KINDNESS, MOTHER!
I HAVE FOUND A MORE REWARDING WAY FOR A MAN TO SPEND HIS LIFE, ONE THAT IS FAR MORE BENEFICIAL TO HIS FAMILY THAN MARRIAGE!

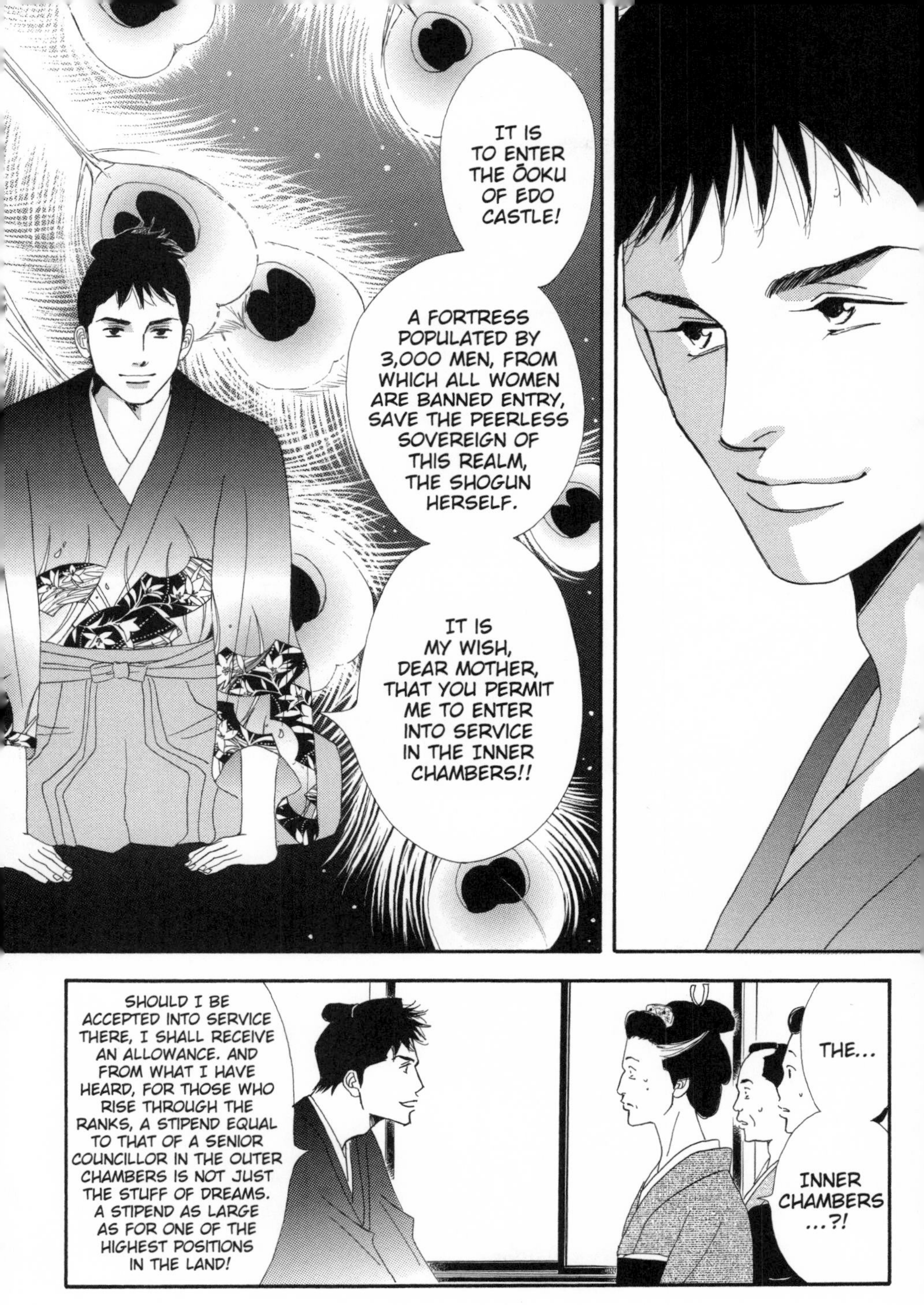
IT IS TO ENTER THE ŌOKU OF EDO CASTLE!
A FORTRESS POPULATED BY 3,000 MEN, FROM WHICH ALL WOMEN ARE BANNED ENTRY, SAVE THE PEERLESS SOVEREIGN OF THIS REALM, THE SHOGUN HERSELF.
IT IS MY WISH, DEAR MOTHER, THAT YOU PERMIT ME TO ENTER INTO SERVICE IN THE INNER CHAMBERS!!
THE...
INNER CHAMBERS ...?!
SHOULD I BE ACCEPTED INTO SERVICE THERE, I SHALL RECEIVE AN ALLOWANCE. AND FROM WHAT I HAVE HEARD, FOR THOSE WHO RISE THROUGH THE RANKS, A STIPEND EQUAL TO THAT OF A SENIOR COUNCILLOR IN THE OUTER CHAMBERS IS NOT JUST THE STUFF OF DREAMS. A STIPEND AS LARGE AS FOR ONE OF THE HIGHEST POSITIONS IN THE LAND!

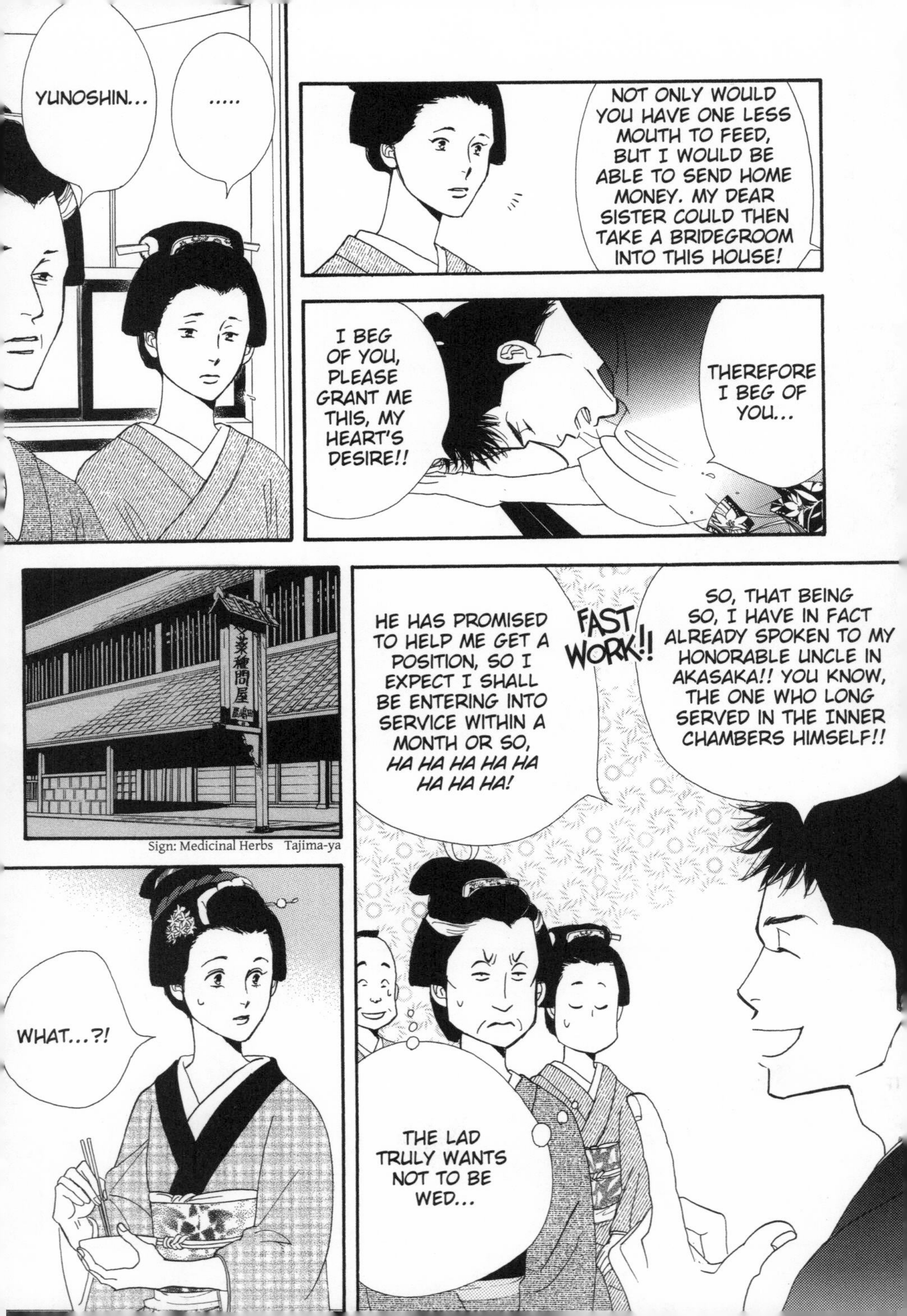
NOT ONLY WOULD YOU HAVE ONE LESS MOUTH TO FEED, BUT I WOULD BE ABLE TO SEND HOME MONEY. MY DEAR SISTER COULD THEN TAKE A BRIDEGROOM INTO THIS HOUSE!
THEREFORE I BEG OF YOU...
I BEG OF YOU, PLEASE GRANT ME THIS, MY HEART'S DESIRE!!
YUNOSHIN...
.....
SO, THAT BEING SO, I HAVE IN FACT ALREADY SPOKEN TO MY HONORABLE UNCLE IN AKASAKA!! YOU KNOW, THE ONE WHO LONG SERVED IN THE INNER CHAMBERS HIMSELF!!
FAST WORK!!
HE HAS PROMISED TO HELP ME GET A POSITION, SO I EXPECT I SHALL BE ENTERING INTO SERVICE WITHIN A MONTH OR SO, *HA HA HA HA HA HA HA HA HA!*
THE LAD TRULY WANTS NOT TO BE WED...
Sign: Medicinal Herbs Tajima-ya
WHAT...?!

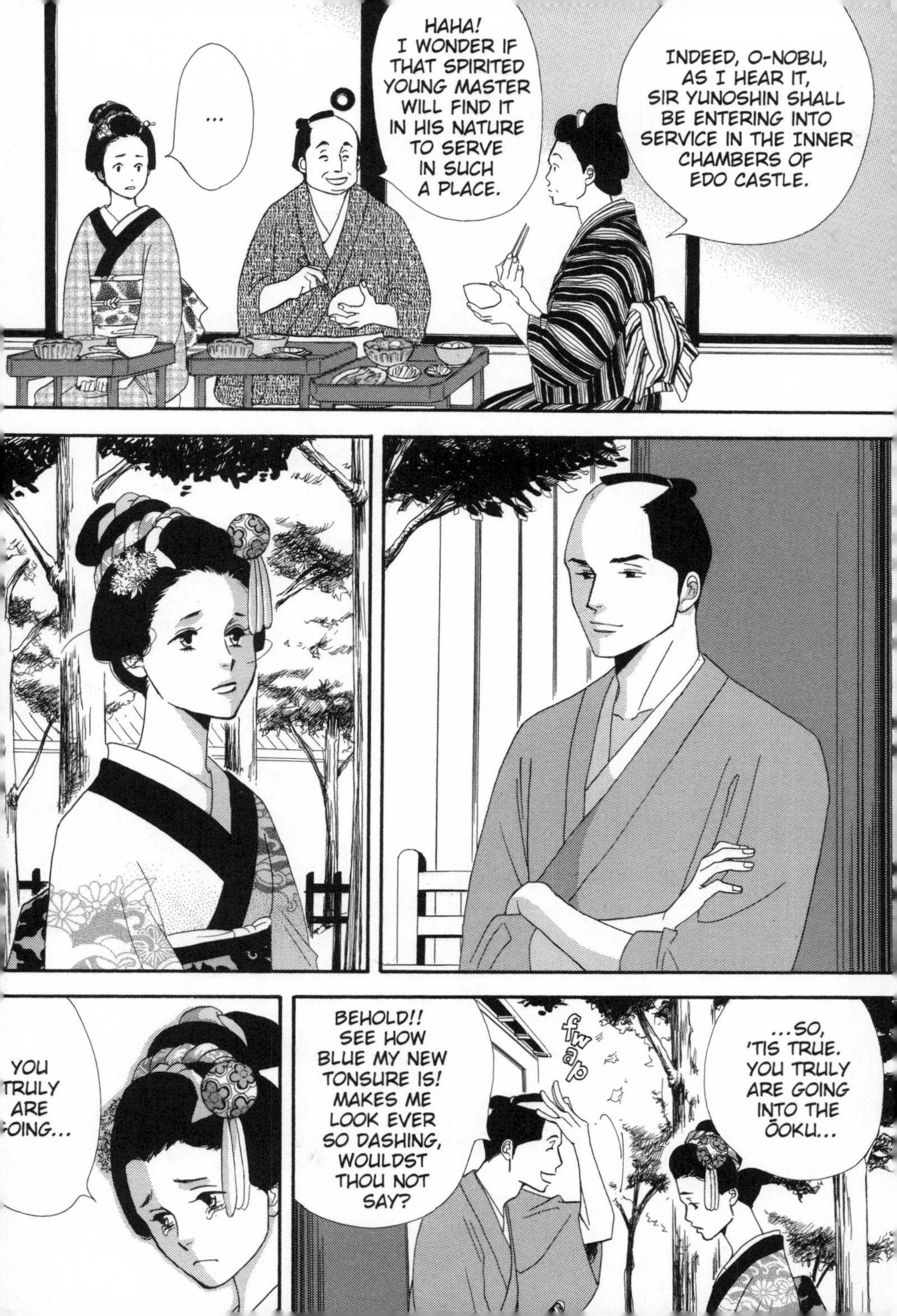
INDEED, O-NOBU, AS I HEAR IT, SIR YUNOSHIN SHALL BE ENTERING INTO SERVICE IN THE INNER CHAMBERS OF EDO CASTLE.
HAHA! I WONDER IF THAT SPIRITED YOUNG MASTER WILL FIND IT IN HIS NATURE TO SERVE IN SUCH A PLACE.
...
...SO, 'TIS TRUE. YOU TRULY ARE GOING INTO THE ŌOKU...
fwap
BEHOLD!! SEE HOW BLUE MY NEW TONSURE IS! MAKES ME LOOK EVER SO DASHING, WOULDST THOU NOT SAY?
YOU TRULY ARE GOING...

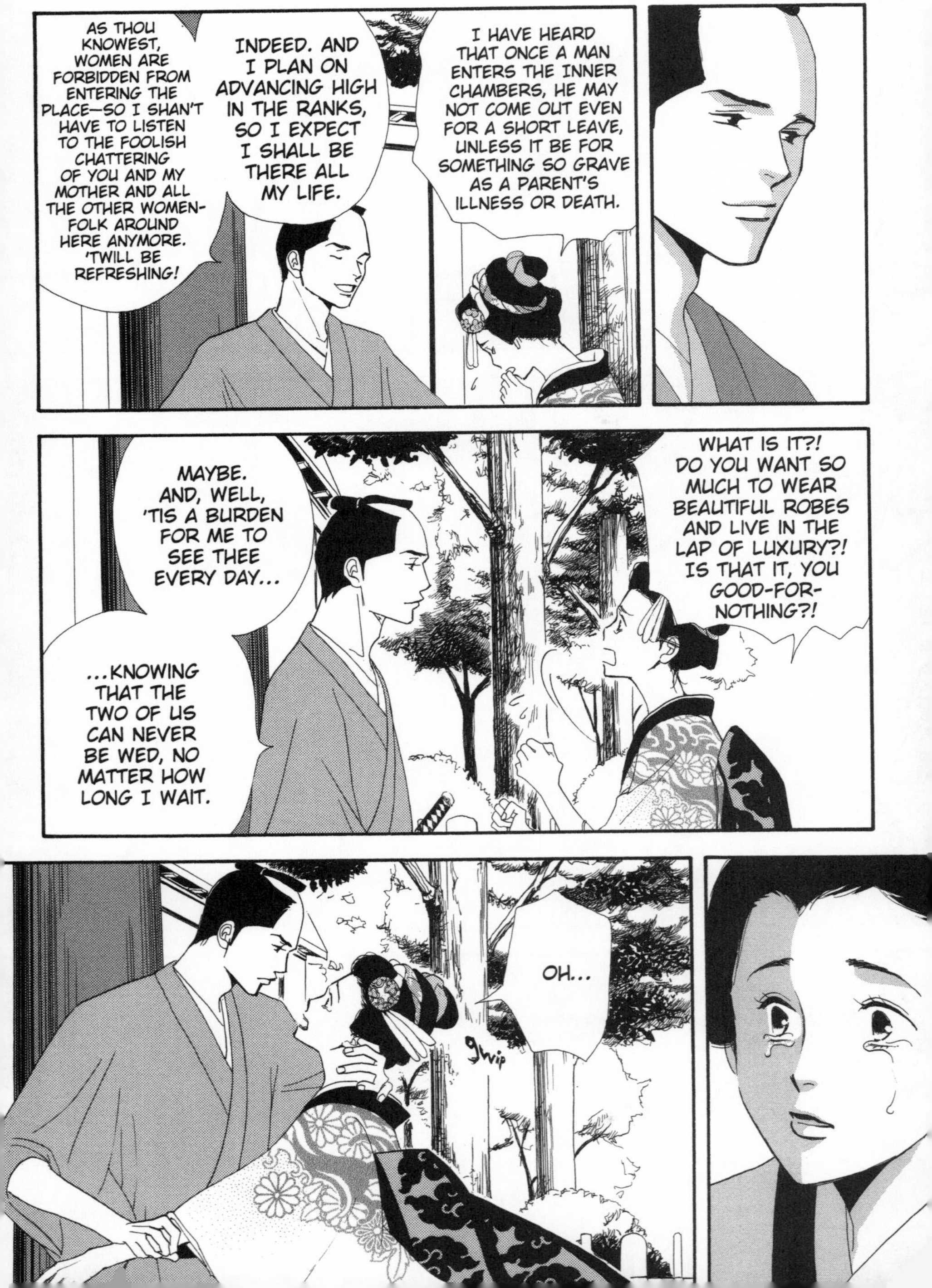
I HAVE HEARD THAT ONCE A MAN ENTERS THE INNER CHAMBERS, HE MAY NOT COME OUT EVEN FOR A SHORT LEAVE, UNLESS IT BE FOR SOMETHING SO GRAVE AS A PARENT'S ILLNESS OR DEATH.
INDEED. AND I PLAN ON ADVANCING HIGH IN THE RANKS, SO I EXPECT I SHALL BE THERE ALL MY LIFE.
AS THOU KNOWEST, WOMEN ARE FORBIDDEN FROM ENTERING THE PLACE—SO I SHAN'T HAVE TO LISTEN TO THE FOOLISH CHATTERING OF YOU AND MY MOTHER AND ALL THE OTHER WOMEN-FOLK AROUND HERE ANYMORE. 'TWILL BE REFRESHING!
WHAT IS IT?! DO YOU WANT SO MUCH TO WEAR BEAUTIFUL ROBES AND LIVE IN THE LAP OF LUXURY?! IS THAT IT, YOU GOOD-FOR-NOTHING?!
MAYBE. AND, WELL, 'TIS A BURDEN FOR ME TO SEE THEE EVERY DAY...
...KNOWING THAT THE TWO OF US CAN NEVER BE WED, NO MATTER HOW LONG I WAIT.
OH...
gwip

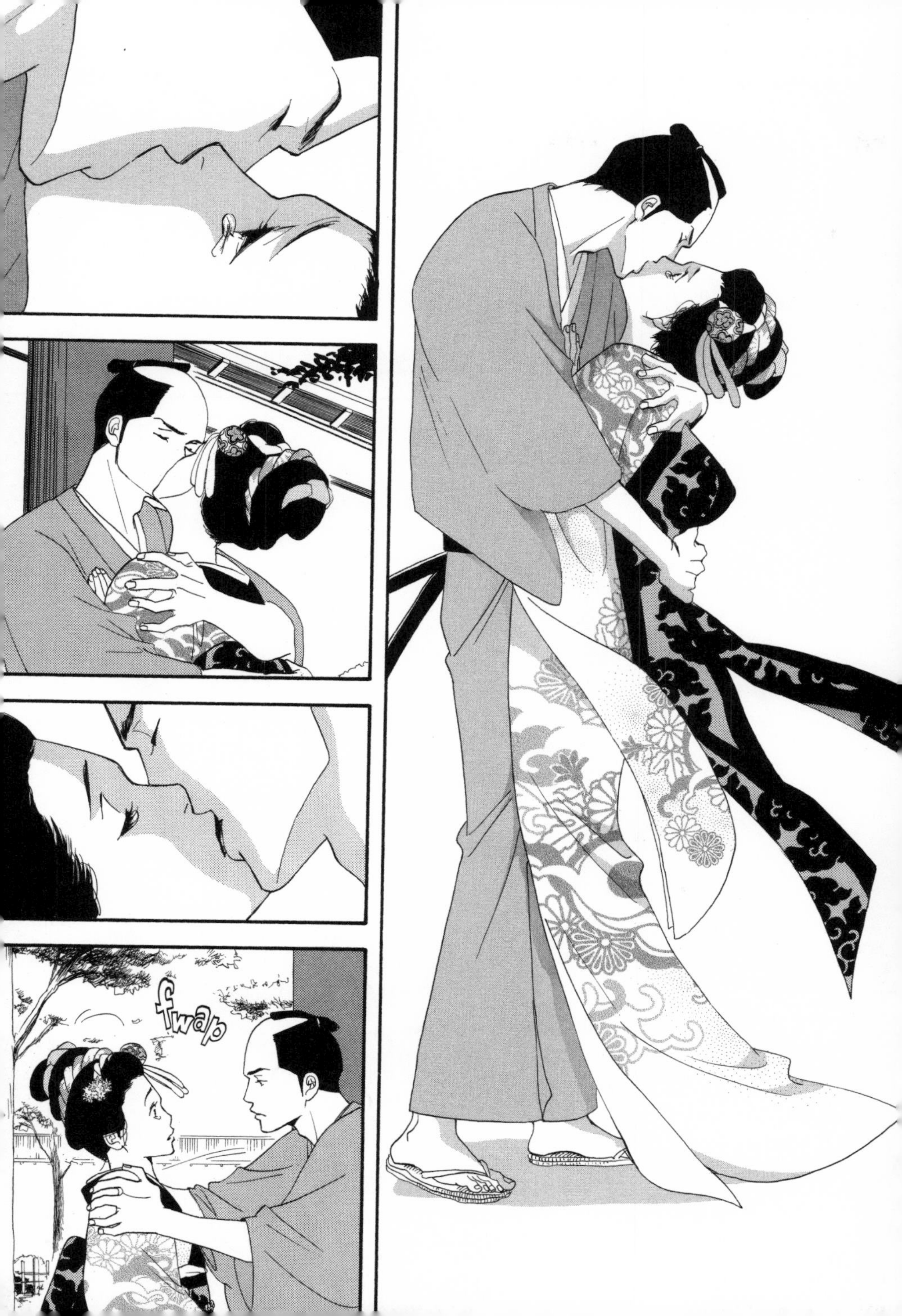
fwap

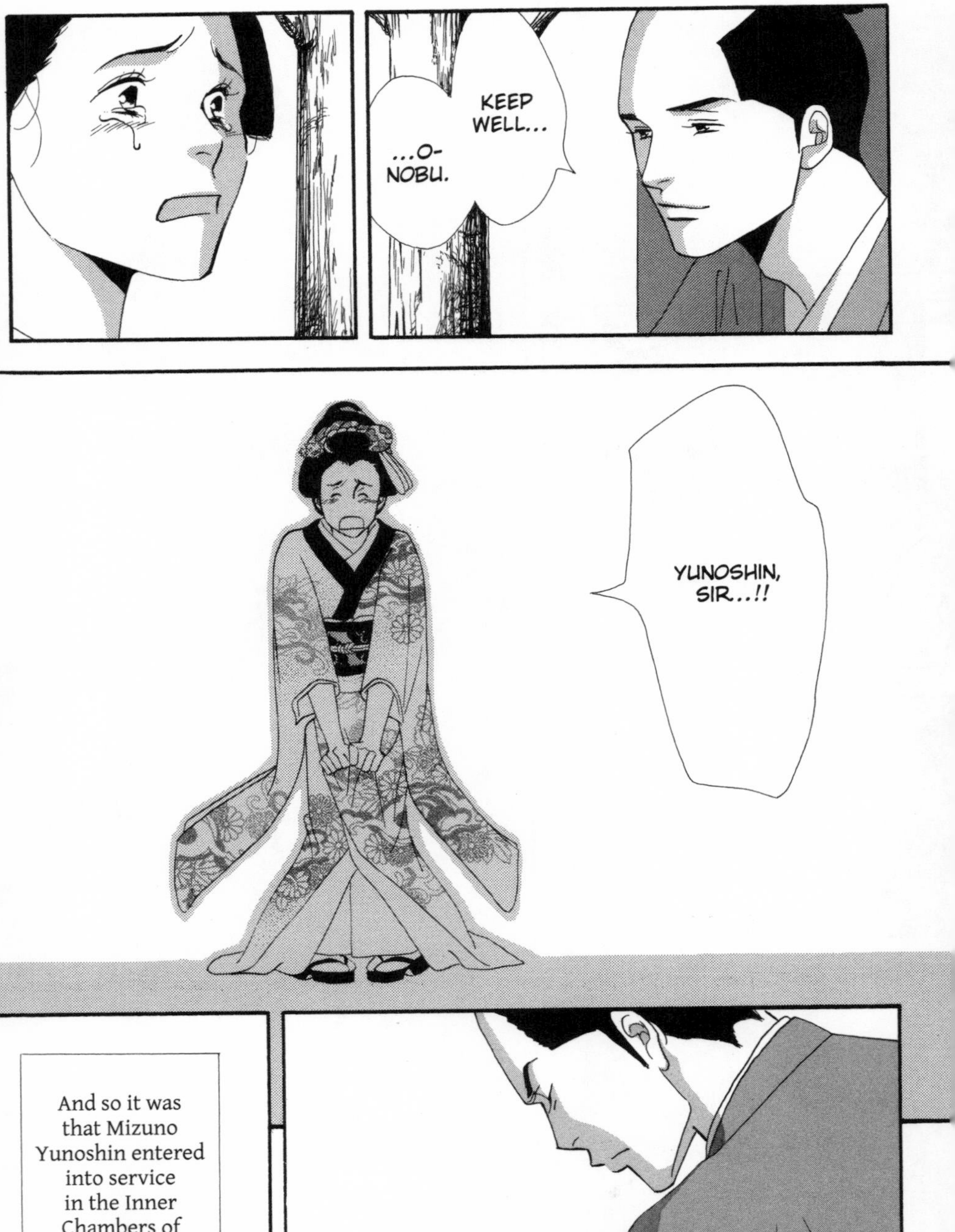
KEEP WELL...
...O-NOBU.
YUNOSHIN, SIR...!!
And so it was that Mizuno Yunoshin entered into service in the Inner Chambers of Edo Castle.

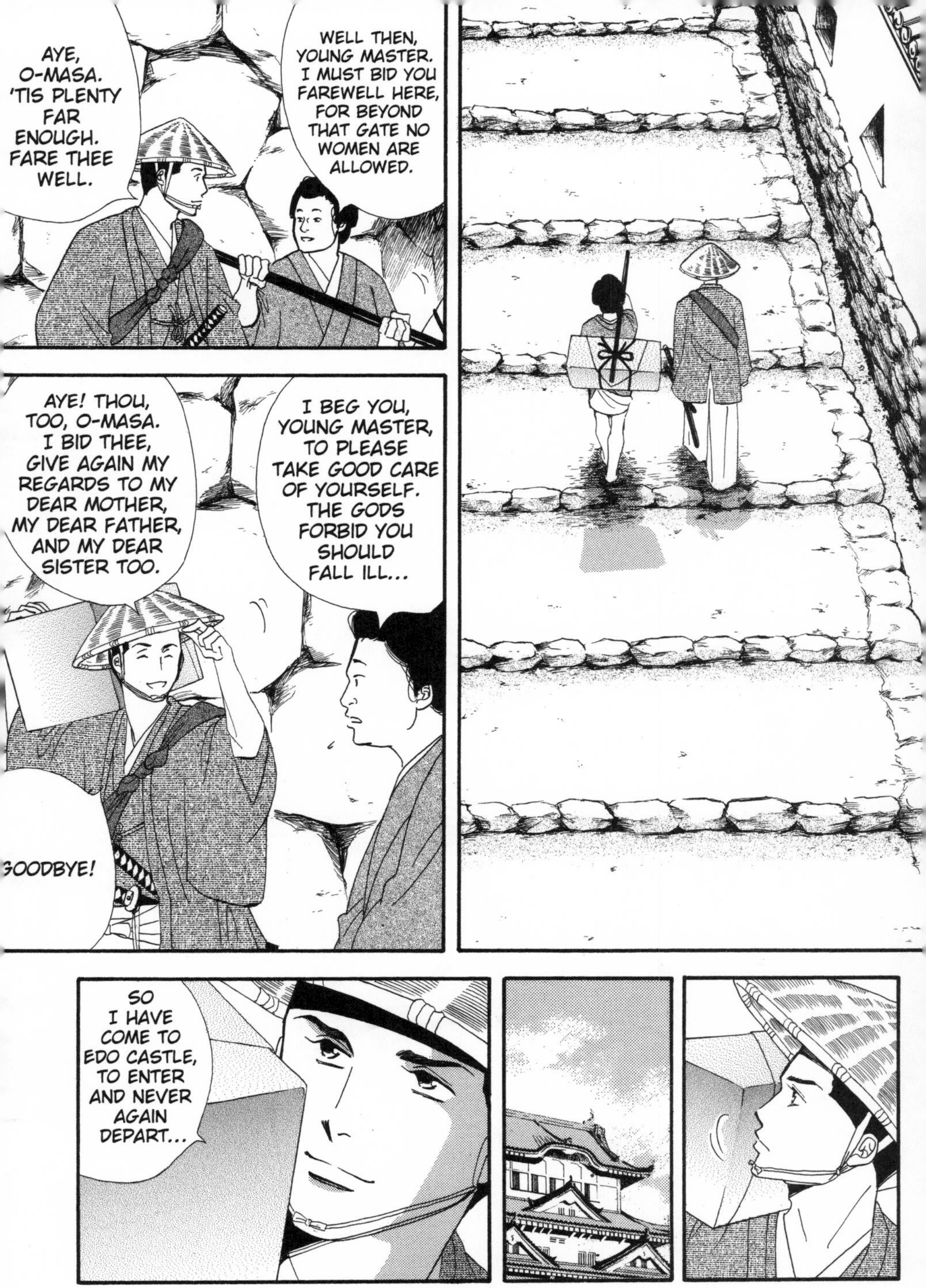
WELL THEN, YOUNG MASTER. I MUST BID YOU FAREWELL HERE, FOR BEYOND THAT GATE NO WOMEN ARE ALLOWED.
AYE, O-MASA. 'TIS PLENTY FAR ENOUGH. FARE THEE WELL.
I BEG YOU, YOUNG MASTER, TO PLEASE TAKE GOOD CARE OF YOURSELF. THE GODS FORBID YOU SHOULD FALL ILL...
AYE! THOU, TOO, O-MASA. I BID THEE, GIVE AGAIN MY REGARDS TO MY DEAR MOTHER, MY DEAR FATHER, AND MY DEAR SISTER TOO.
GOODBYE!
SO I HAVE COME TO EDO CASTLE, TO ENTER AND NEVER AGAIN DEPART...

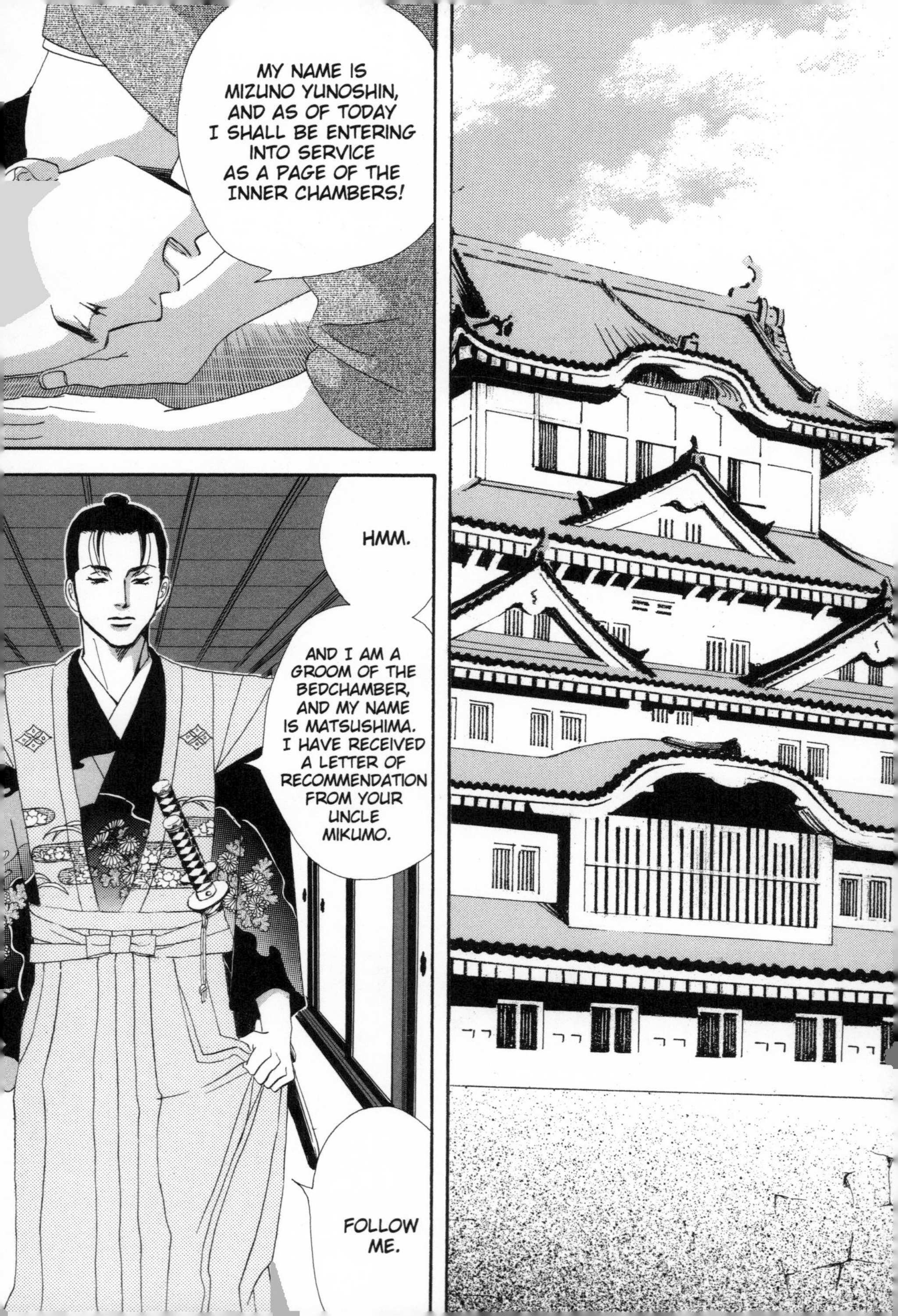
MY NAME IS MIZUNO YUNOSHIN, AND AS OF TODAY I SHALL BE ENTERING INTO SERVICE AS A PAGE OF THE INNER CHAMBERS!
HMM.
AND I AM A GROOM OF THE BEDCHAMBER, AND MY NAME IS MATSUSHIMA. I HAVE RECEIVED A LETTER OF RECOMMENDATION FROM YOUR UNCLE MIKUMO.
FOLLOW ME.

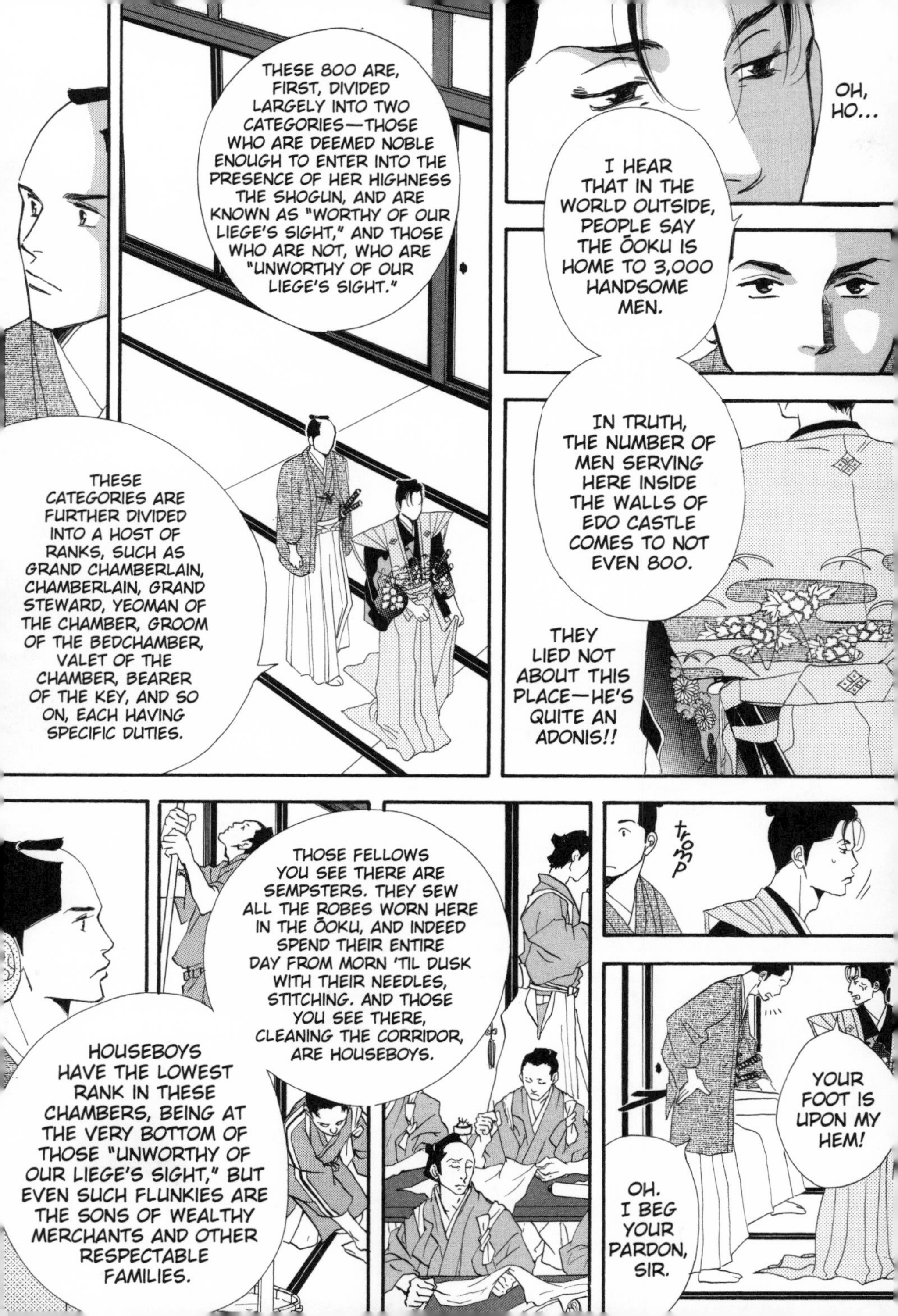
OH, HO...
I HEAR THAT IN THE WORLD OUTSIDE, PEOPLE SAY THE ŌOKU IS HOME TO 3,000 HANDSOME MEN.
IN TRUTH, THE NUMBER OF MEN SERVING HERE INSIDE THE WALLS OF EDO CASTLE COMES TO NOT EVEN 800.
THEY LIED NOT ABOUT THIS PLACE—HE'S QUITE AN ADONIS!!
THESE 800 ARE, FIRST, DIVIDED LARGELY INTO TWO CATEGORIES—THOSE WHO ARE DEEMED NOBLE ENOUGH TO ENTER INTO THE PRESENCE OF HER HIGHNESS THE SHOGUN, AND ARE KNOWN AS "WORTHY OF OUR LIEGE'S SIGHT," AND THOSE WHO ARE NOT, WHO ARE "UNWORTHY OF OUR LIEGE'S SIGHT."
THESE CATEGORIES ARE FURTHER DIVIDED INTO A HOST OF RANKS, SUCH AS GRAND CHAMBERLAIN, CHAMBERLAIN, GRAND STEWARD, YEOMAN OF THE CHAMBER, GROOM OF THE BEDCHAMBER, VALET OF THE CHAMBER, BEARER OF THE KEY, AND SO ON, EACH HAVING SPECIFIC DUTIES.
tromp
YOUR FOOT IS UPON MY HEM!
OH. I BEG YOUR PARDON, SIR.
THOSE FELLOWS YOU SEE THERE ARE SEMPSTERS. THEY SEW ALL THE ROBES WORN HERE IN THE ŌOKU, AND INDEED SPEND THEIR ENTIRE DAY FROM MORN 'TIL DUSK WITH THEIR NEEDLES, STITCHING. AND THOSE YOU SEE THERE, CLEANING THE CORRIDOR, ARE HOUSEBOYS.
HOUSEBOYS HAVE THE LOWEST RANK IN THESE CHAMBERS, BEING AT THE VERY BOTTOM OF THOSE "UNWORTHY OF OUR LIEGE'S SIGHT," BUT EVEN SUCH FLUNKIES ARE THE SONS OF WEALTHY MERCHANTS AND OTHER RESPECTABLE FAMILIES.

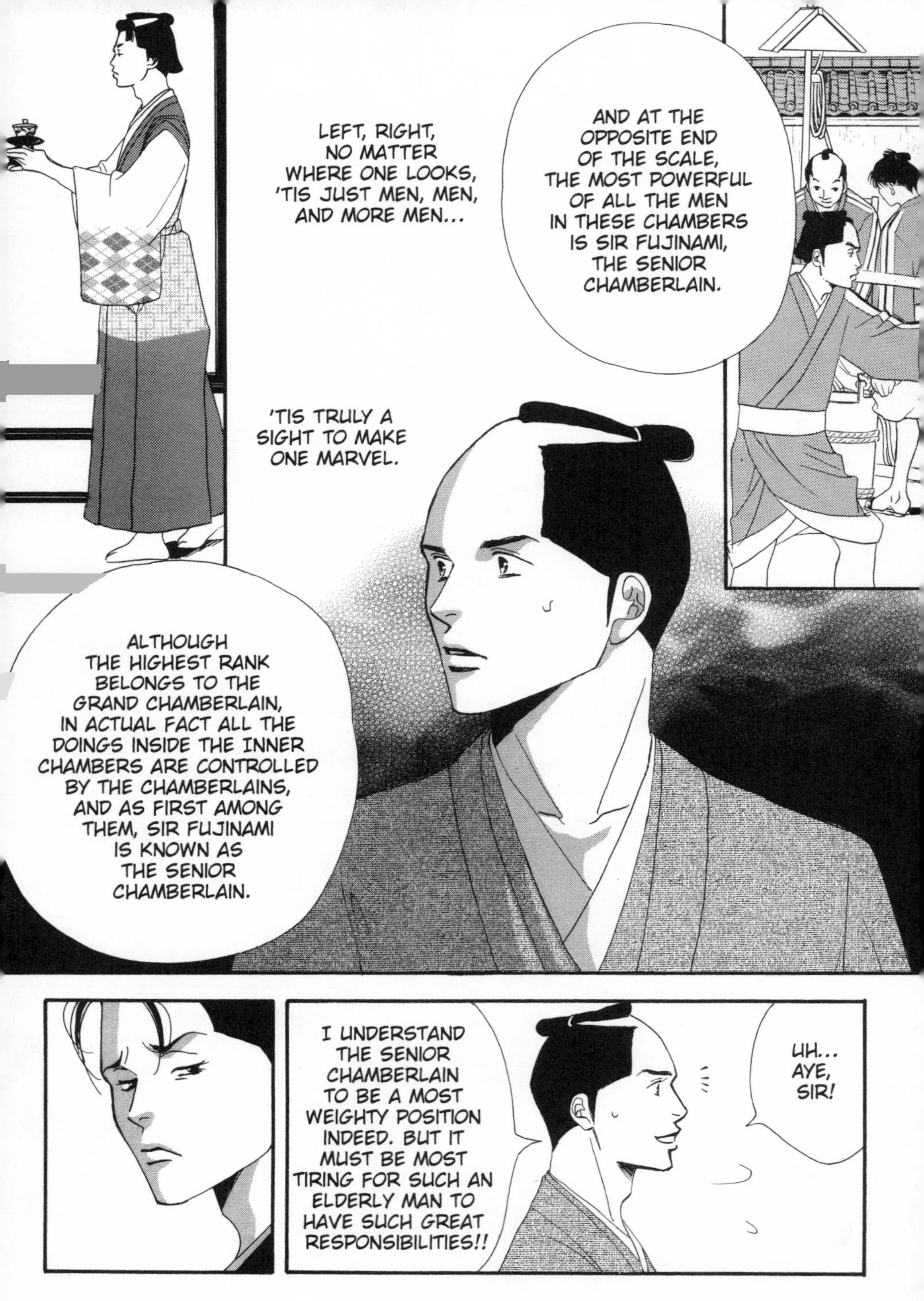
AND AT THE OPPOSITE END OF THE SCALE, THE MOST POWERFUL OF ALL THE MEN IN THESE CHAMBERS IS SIR FUJINAMI, THE SENIOR CHAMBERLAIN.
LEFT, RIGHT, NO MATTER WHERE ONE LOOKS, 'TIS JUST MEN, MEN, AND MORE MEN...
'TIS TRULY A SIGHT TO MAKE ONE MARVEL.
ALTHOUGH THE HIGHEST RANK BELONGS TO THE GRAND CHAMBERLAIN, IN ACTUAL FACT ALL THE DOINGS INSIDE THE INNER CHAMBERS ARE CONTROLLED BY THE CHAMBERLAINS, AND AS FIRST AMONG THEM, SIR FUJINAMI IS KNOWN AS THE SENIOR CHAMBERLAIN.
UH... AYE, SIR!
I UNDERSTAND THE SENIOR CHAMBERLAIN TO BE A MOST WEIGHTY POSITION INDEED. BUT IT MUST BE MOST TIRING FOR SUCH AN ELDERLY MAN TO HAVE SUCH GREAT RESPONSIBILITIES!!

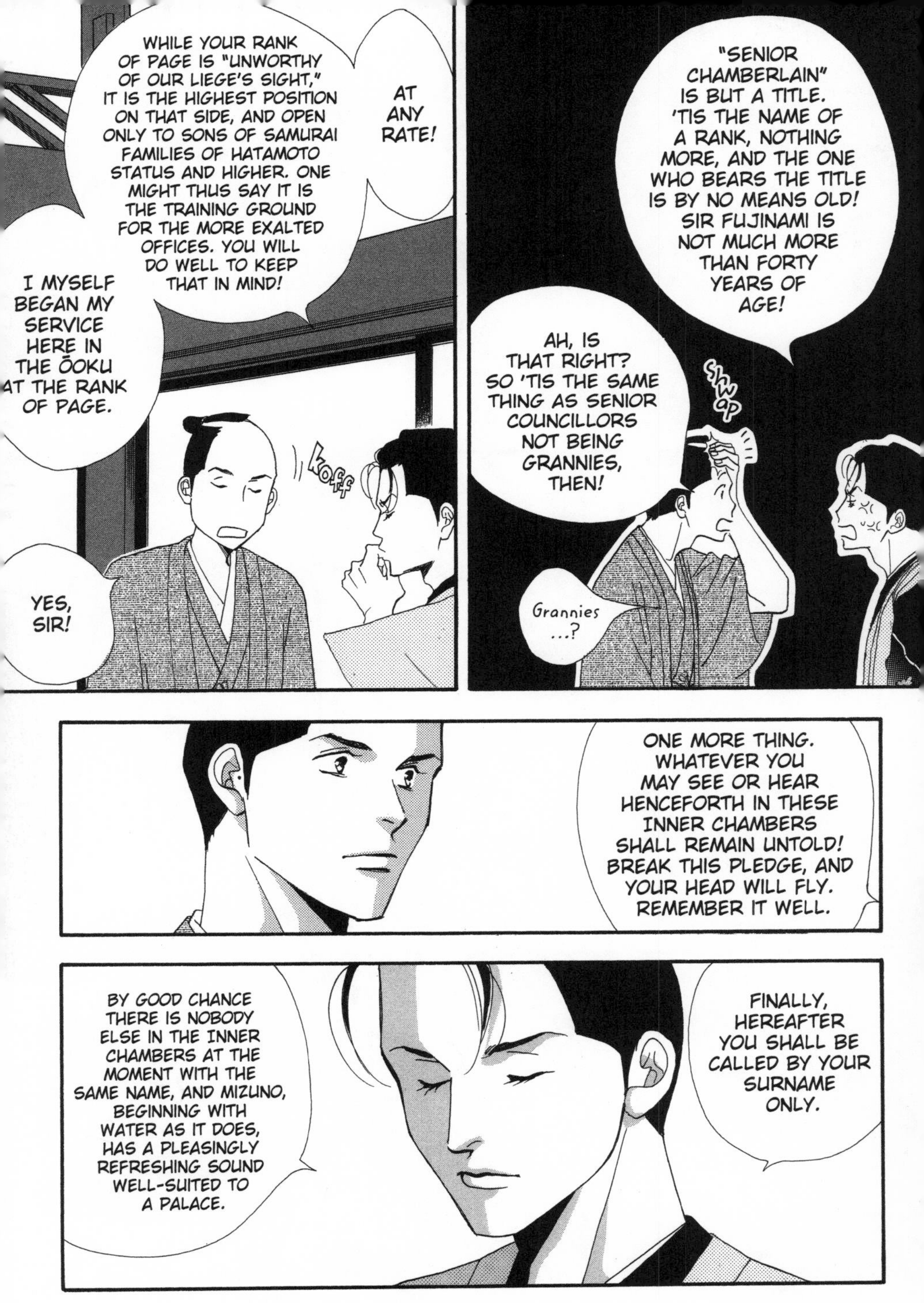
"SENIOR CHAMBERLAIN" IS BUT A TITLE. 'TIS THE NAME OF A RANK, NOTHING MORE, AND THE ONE WHO BEARS THE TITLE IS BY NO MEANS OLD! SIR FUJINAMI IS NOT MUCH MORE THAN FORTY YEARS OF AGE!
AH, IS THAT RIGHT? SO 'TIS THE SAME THING AS SENIOR COUNCILLORS NOT BEING GRANNIES, THEN!
shwap
Grannies ...?
AT ANY RATE!
WHILE YOUR RANK OF PAGE IS "UNWORTHY OF OUR LIEGE'S SIGHT," IT IS THE HIGHEST POSITION ON THAT SIDE, AND OPEN ONLY TO SONS OF SAMURAI FAMILIES OF HATAMOTO STATUS AND HIGHER. ONE MIGHT THUS SAY IT IS THE TRAINING GROUND FOR THE MORE EXALTED OFFICES. YOU WILL DO WELL TO KEEP THAT IN MIND!
I MYSELF BEGAN MY SERVICE HERE IN THE ŌOKU AT THE RANK OF PAGE.
koff
YES, SIR!
ONE MORE THING. WHATEVER YOU MAY SEE OR HEAR HENCEFORTH IN THESE INNER CHAMBERS SHALL REMAIN UNTOLD! BREAK THIS PLEDGE, AND YOUR HEAD WILL FLY. REMEMBER IT WELL.
FINALLY, HEREAFTER YOU SHALL BE CALLED BY YOUR SURNAME ONLY.
BY GOOD CHANCE THERE IS NOBODY ELSE IN THE INNER CHAMBERS AT THE MOMENT WITH THE SAME NAME, AND MIZUNO, BEGINNING WITH WATER AS IT DOES, HAS A PLEASINGLY REFRESHING SOUND WELL-SUITED TO A PALACE.

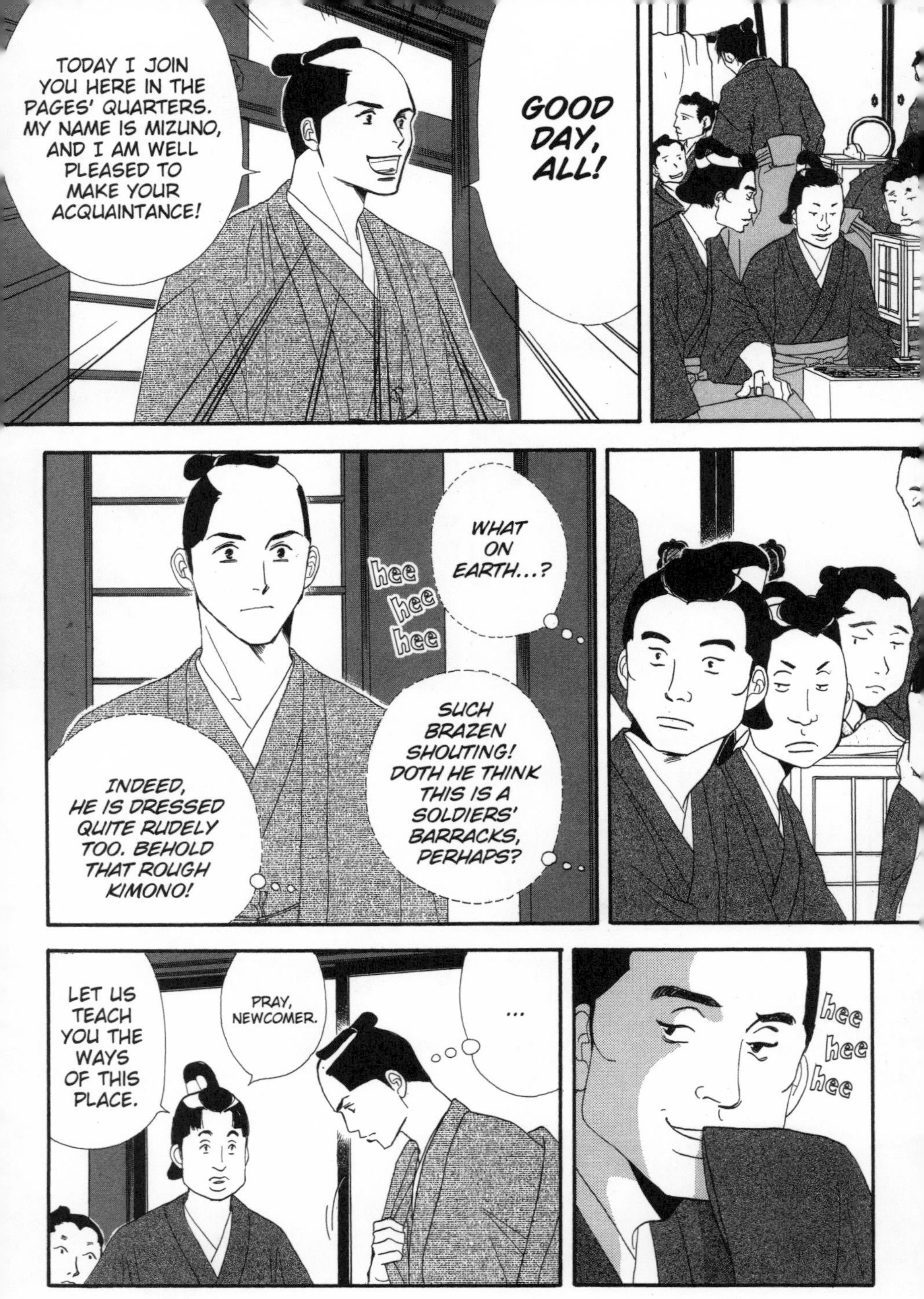
GOOD DAY, ALL!
TODAY I JOIN YOU HERE IN THE PAGES' QUARTERS. MY NAME IS MIZUNO, AND I AM WELL PLEASED TO MAKE YOUR ACQUAINTANCE!
WHAT ON EARTH...?
hee hee hee
SUCH BRAZEN SHOUTING! DOTH HE THINK THIS IS A SOLDIERS' BARRACKS, PERHAPS?
INDEED, HE IS DRESSED QUITE RUDELY TOO. BEHOLD THAT ROUGH KIMONO!
hee hee hee
...
PRAY, NEWCOMER.
LET US TEACH YOU THE WAYS OF THIS PLACE.

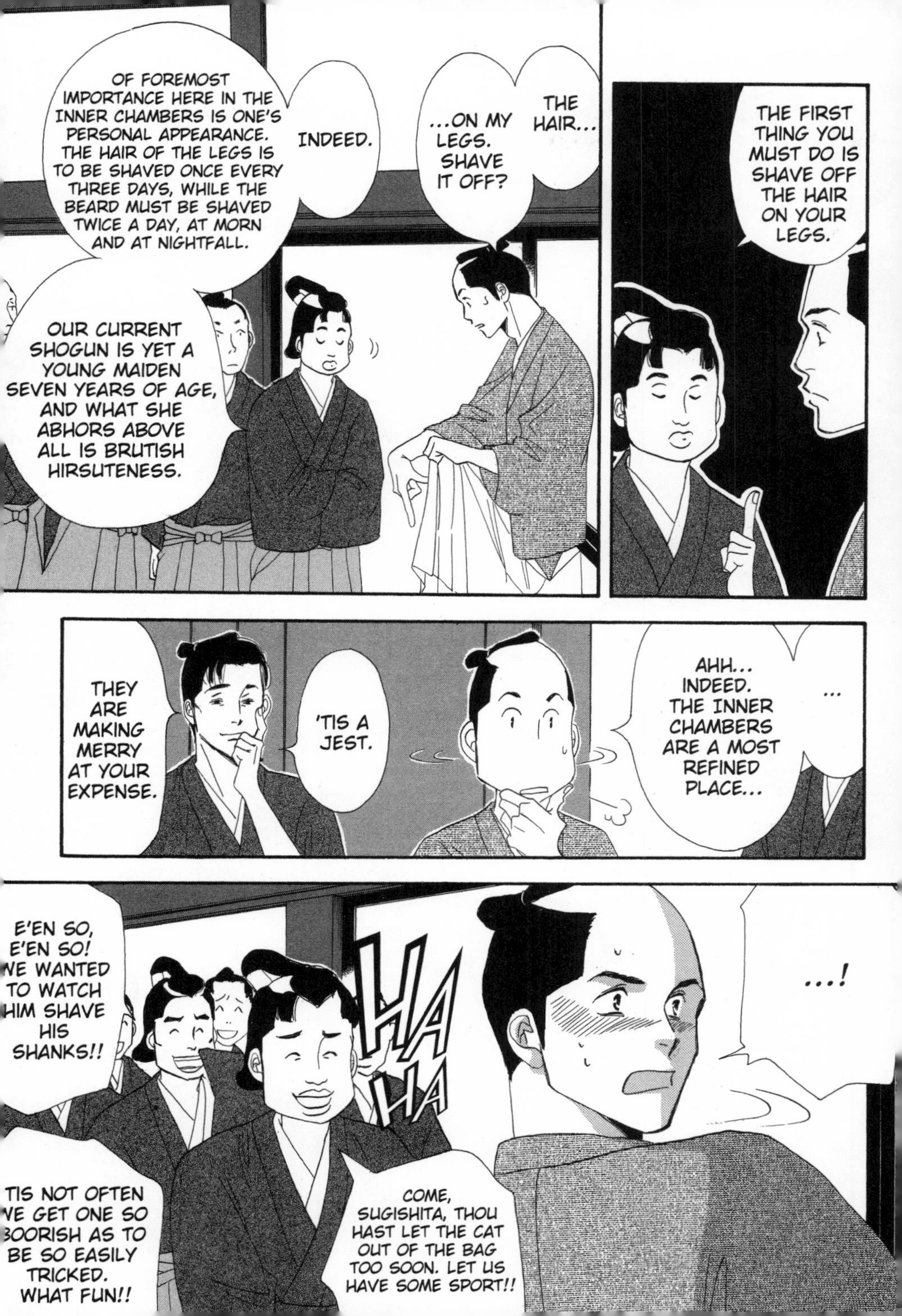
THE FIRST THING YOU MUST DO IS SHAVE OFF THE HAIR ON YOUR LEGS.
THE HAIR...
...ON MY LEGS. SHAVE IT OFF?
INDEED.
OF FOREMOST IMPORTANCE HERE IN THE INNER CHAMBERS IS ONE'S PERSONAL APPEARANCE. THE HAIR OF THE LEGS IS TO BE SHAVED ONCE EVERY THREE DAYS, WHILE THE BEARD MUST BE SHAVED TWICE A DAY, AT MORN AND AT NIGHTFALL.
OUR CURRENT SHOGUN IS YET A YOUNG MAIDEN SEVEN YEARS OF AGE, AND WHAT SHE ABHORS ABOVE ALL IS BRUTISH HIRSUTENESS.
...
AHH... INDEED. THE INNER CHAMBERS ARE A MOST REFINED PLACE...
'TIS A JEST.
THEY ARE MAKING MERRY AT YOUR EXPENSE.
...!
HA HA HA
E'EN SO, E'EN SO! WE WANTED TO WATCH HIM SHAVE HIS SHANKS!!
COME, SUGISHITA, THOU HAST LET THE CAT OUT OF THE BAG TOO SOON. LET US HAVE SOME SPORT!!
'TIS NOT OFTEN WE GET ONE SO BOORISH AS TO BE SO EASILY TRICKED. WHAT FUN!!

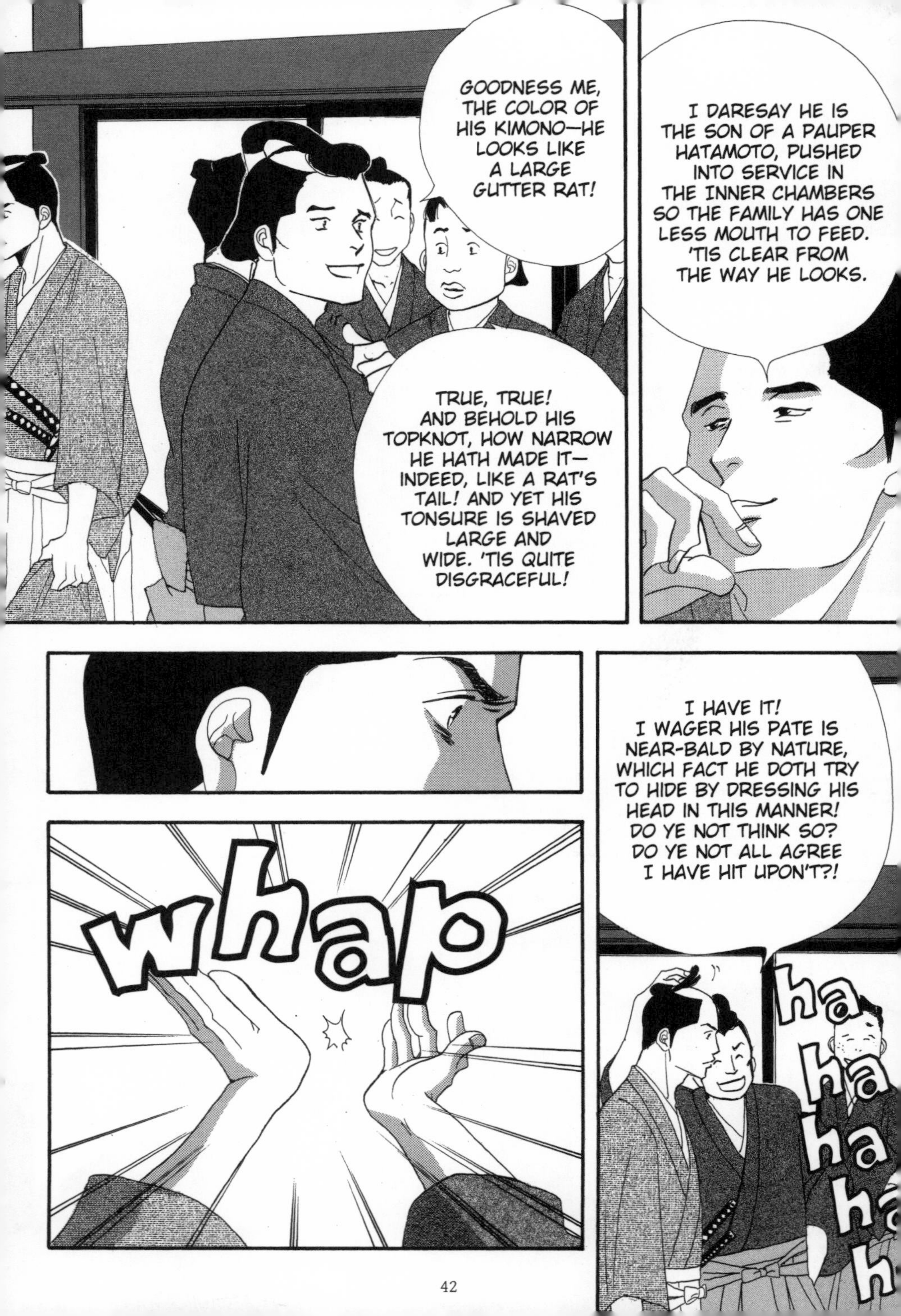
I DARESAY HE IS THE SON OF A PAUPER HATAMOTO, PUSHED INTO SERVICE IN THE INNER CHAMBERS SO THE FAMILY HAS ONE LESS MOUTH TO FEED. 'TIS CLEAR FROM THE WAY HE LOOKS.
GOODNESS ME, THE COLOR OF HIS KIMONO—HE LOOKS LIKE A LARGE GUTTER RAT!
TRUE, TRUE! AND BEHOLD HIS TOPKNOT, HOW NARROW HE HATH MADE IT—INDEED, LIKE A RAT'S TAIL! AND YET HIS TONSURE IS SHAVED LARGE AND WIDE. 'TIS QUITE DISGRACEFUL!
I HAVE IT! I WAGER HIS PATE IS NEAR-BALD BY NATURE, WHICH FACT HE DOTH TRY TO HIDE BY DRESSING HIS HEAD IN THIS MANNER! DO YE NOT THINK SO? DO YE NOT ALL AGREE I HAVE HIT UPON'T?!
ha ha ha ha ha ha
whap

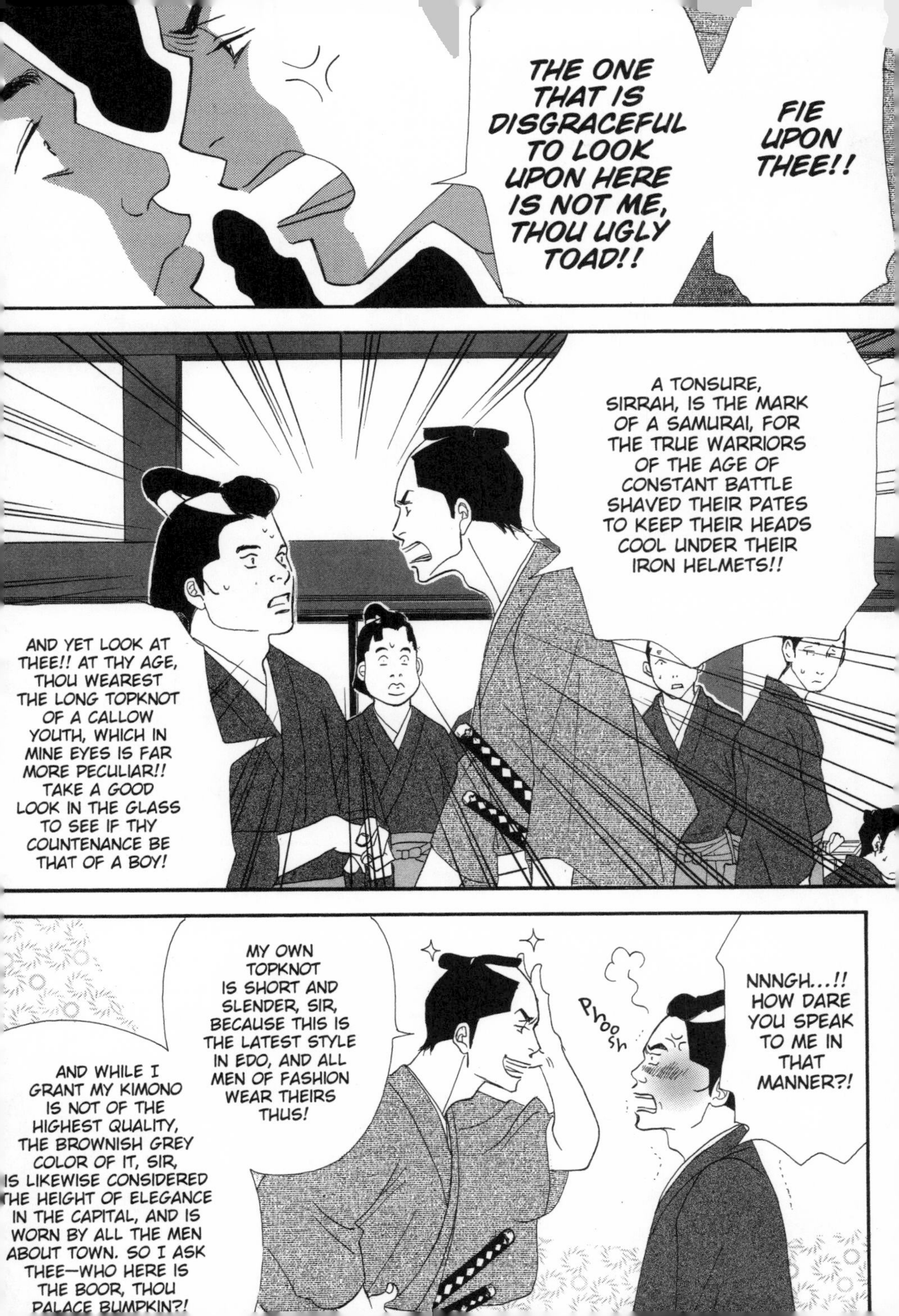
FIE UPON THEE!!
THE ONE THAT IS DISGRACEFUL TO LOOK UPON HERE IS NOT ME, THOU UGLY TOAD!!
A TONSURE, SIRRAH, IS THE MARK OF A SAMURAI, FOR THE TRUE WARRIORS OF THE AGE OF CONSTANT BATTLE SHAVED THEIR PATES TO KEEP THEIR HEADS COOL UNDER THEIR IRON HELMETS!!
AND YET LOOK AT THEE!! AT THY AGE, THOU WEAREST THE LONG TOPKNOT OF A CALLOW YOUTH, WHICH IN MINE EYES IS FAR MORE PECULIAR!! TAKE A GOOD LOOK IN THE GLASS TO SEE IF THY COUNTENANCE BE THAT OF A BOY!
NNNGH...!! HOW DARE YOU SPEAK TO ME IN THAT MANNER?!
Phoosh
MY OWN TOPKNOT IS SHORT AND SLENDER, SIR, BECAUSE THIS IS THE LATEST STYLE IN EDO, AND ALL MEN OF FASHION WEAR THEIRS THUS!
AND WHILE I GRANT MY KIMONO IS NOT OF THE HIGHEST QUALITY, THE BROWNISH GREY COLOR OF IT, SIR, IS LIKEWISE CONSIDERED THE HEIGHT OF ELEGANCE IN THE CAPITAL, AND IS WORN BY ALL THE MEN ABOUT TOWN. SO I ASK THEE—WHO HERE IS THE BOOR, THOU PALACE BUMPKIN?!

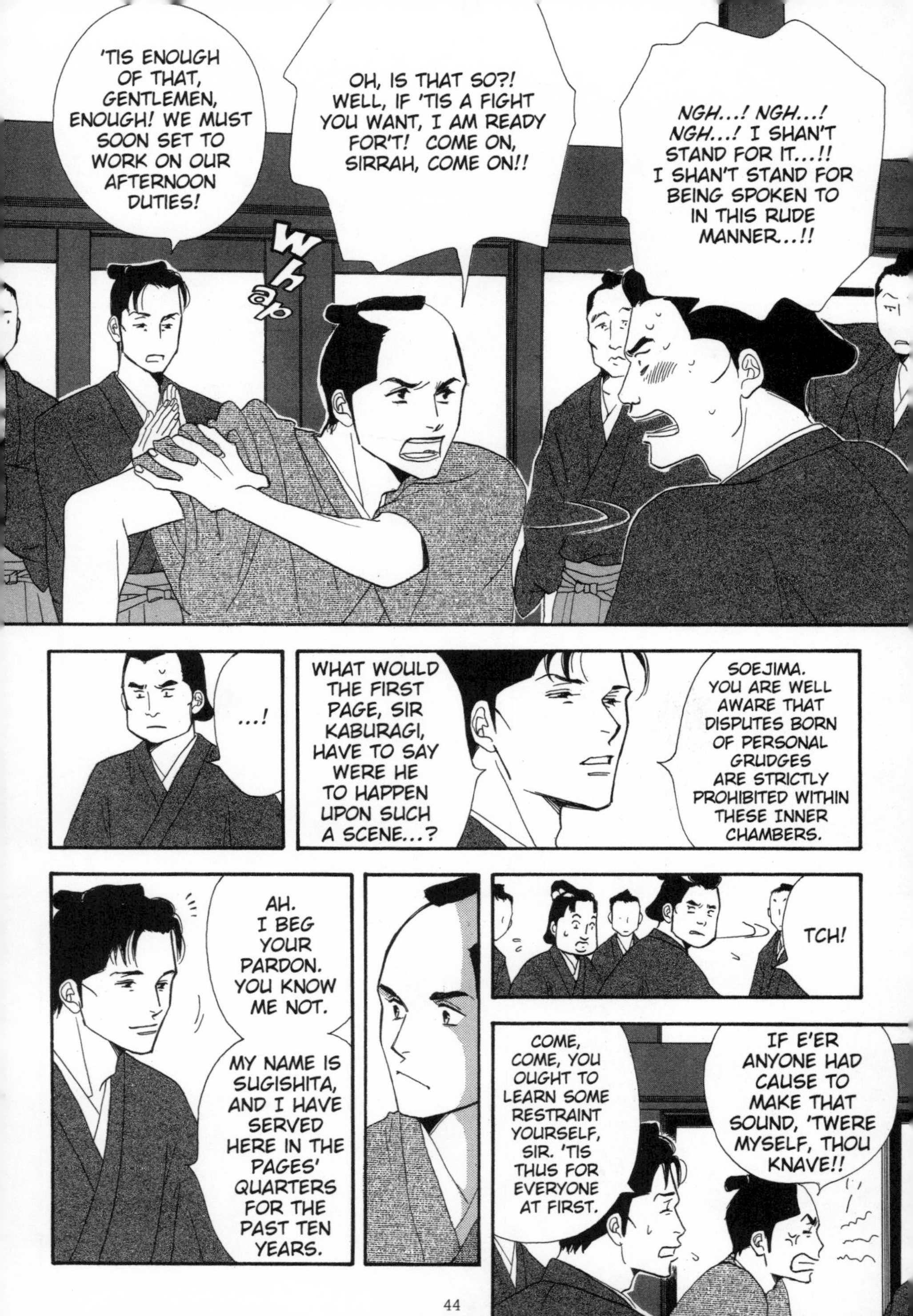
NGH...! NGH...! NGH...! I SHAN'T STAND FOR IT...!! I SHAN'T STAND FOR BEING SPOKEN TO IN THIS RUDE MANNER...!!
OH, IS THAT SO?! WELL, IF 'TIS A FIGHT YOU WANT, I AM READY FOR'T! COME ON, SIRRAH, COME ON!!
'TIS ENOUGH OF THAT, GENTLEMEN, ENOUGH! WE MUST SOON SET TO WORK ON OUR AFTERNOON DUTIES!
Whap
SOEJIMA. YOU ARE WELL AWARE THAT DISPUTES BORN OF PERSONAL GRUDGES ARE STRICTLY PROHIBITED WITHIN THESE INNER CHAMBERS.
WHAT WOULD THE FIRST PAGE, SIR KABURAGI, HAVE TO SAY WERE HE TO HAPPEN UPON SUCH A SCENE...?
...!
TCH!
IF E'ER ANYONE HAD CAUSE TO MAKE THAT SOUND, 'TWERE MYSELF, THOU KNAVE!!
COME, COME, YOU OUGHT TO LEARN SOME RESTRAINT YOURSELF, SIR. 'TIS THUS FOR EVERYONE AT FIRST.
AH. I BEG YOUR PARDON. YOU KNOW ME NOT.
MY NAME IS SUGISHITA, AND I HAVE SERVED HERE IN THE PAGES' QUARTERS FOR THE PAST TEN YEARS.

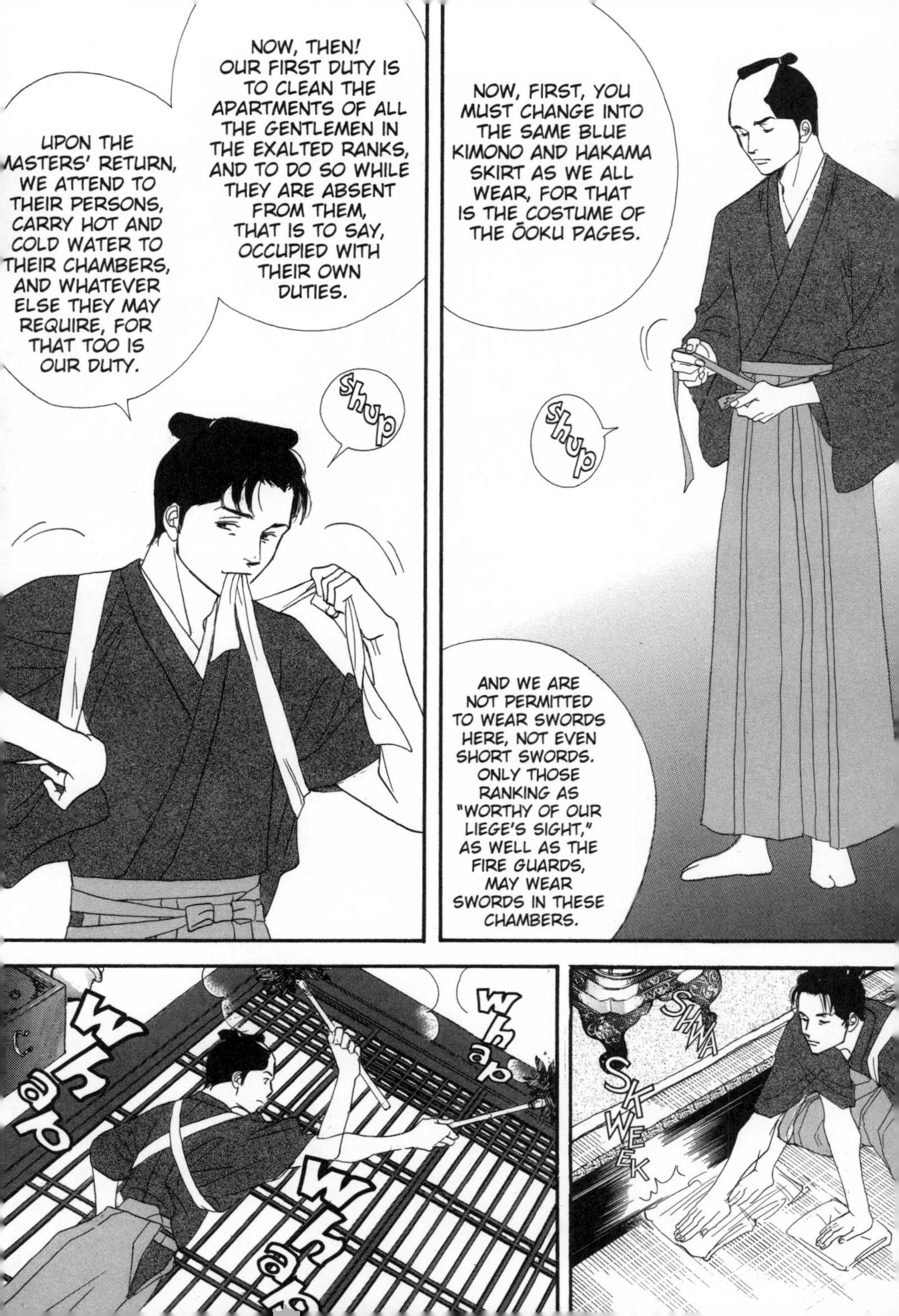
NOW, FIRST, YOU MUST CHANGE INTO THE SAME BLUE KIMONO AND HAKAMA SKIRT AS WE ALL WEAR, FOR THAT IS THE COSTUME OF THE ŌOKU PAGES.
Shup
AND WE ARE NOT PERMITTED TO WEAR SWORDS HERE, NOT EVEN SHORT SWORDS. ONLY THOSE RANKING AS "WORTHY OF OUR LIEGE'S SIGHT," AS WELL AS THE FIRE GUARDS, MAY WEAR SWORDS IN THESE CHAMBERS.
NOW, THEN! OUR FIRST DUTY IS TO CLEAN THE APARTMENTS OF ALL THE GENTLEMEN IN THE EXALTED RANKS, AND TO DO SO WHILE THEY ARE ABSENT FROM THEM, THAT IS TO SAY, OCCUPIED WITH THEIR OWN DUTIES.
UPON THE MASTERS' RETURN, WE ATTEND TO THEIR PERSONS, CARRY HOT AND COLD WATER TO THEIR CHAMBERS, AND WHATEVER ELSE THEY MAY REQUIRE, FOR THAT TOO IS OUR DUTY.
Shup
SHWA
SKWEEK
whap
whap
whap

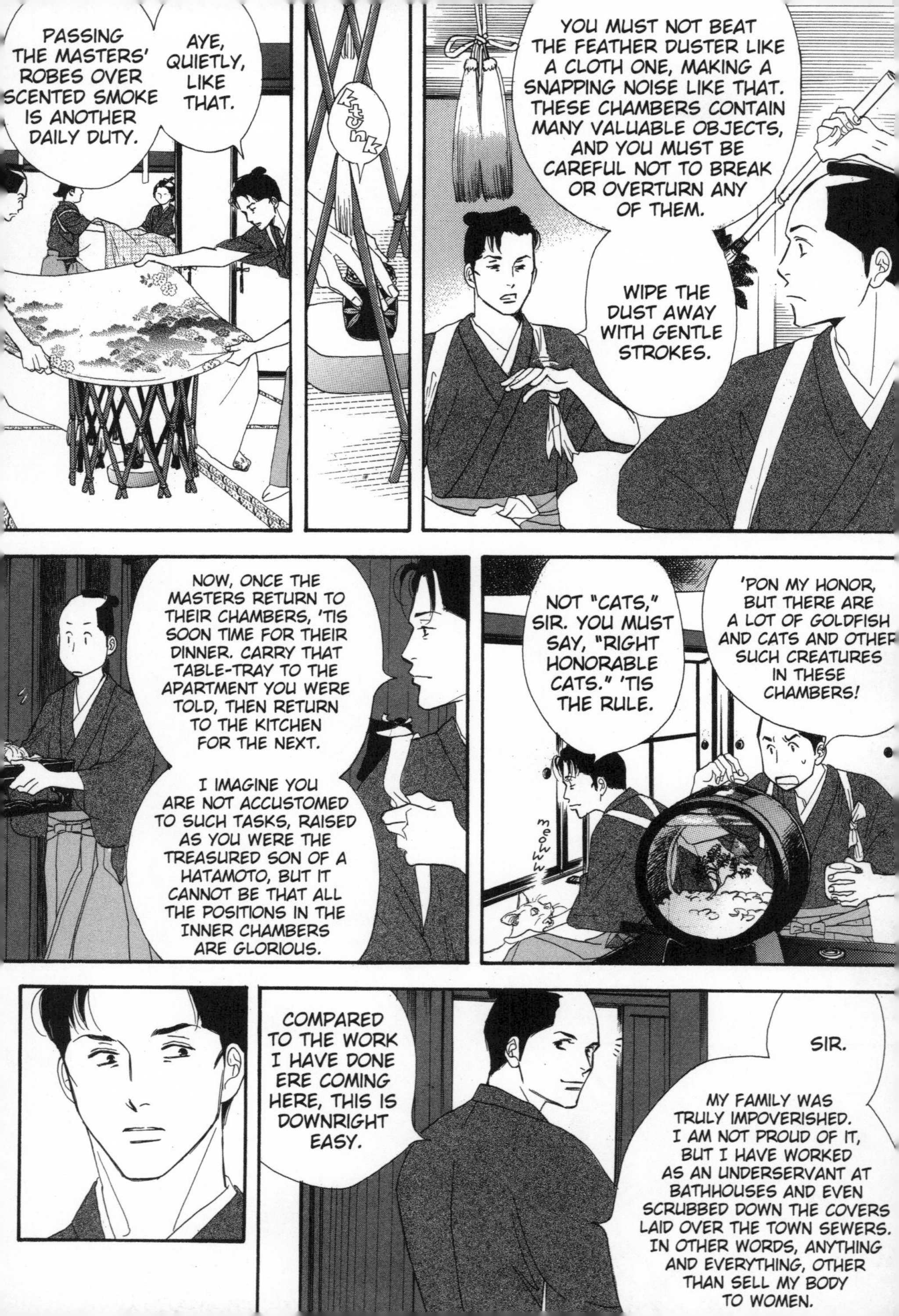
YOU MUST NOT BEAT THE FEATHER DUSTER LIKE A CLOTH ONE, MAKING A SNAPPING NOISE LIKE THAT. THESE CHAMBERS CONTAIN MANY VALUABLE OBJECTS, AND YOU MUST BE CAREFUL NOT TO BREAK OR OVERTURN ANY OF THEM.
WIPE THE DUST AWAY WITH GENTLE STROKES.
ktunk
AYE, QUIETLY, LIKE THAT.
PASSING THE MASTERS' ROBES OVER SCENTED SMOKE IS ANOTHER DAILY DUTY.
'PON MY HONOR, BUT THERE ARE A LOT OF GOLDFISH AND CATS AND OTHER SUCH CREATURES IN THESE CHAMBERS!
NOT "CATS," SIR. YOU MUST SAY, "RIGHT HONORABLE CATS." 'TIS THE RULE.
meowww
NOW, ONCE THE MASTERS RETURN TO THEIR CHAMBERS, 'TIS SOON TIME FOR THEIR DINNER. CARRY THAT TABLE-TRAY TO THE APARTMENT YOU WERE TOLD, THEN RETURN TO THE KITCHEN FOR THE NEXT.
I IMAGINE YOU ARE NOT ACCUSTOMED TO SUCH TASKS, RAISED AS YOU WERE THE TREASURED SON OF A HATAMOTO, BUT IT CANNOT BE THAT ALL THE POSITIONS IN THE INNER CHAMBERS ARE GLORIOUS.
SIR.
MY FAMILY WAS TRULY IMPOVERISHED. I AM NOT PROUD OF IT, BUT I HAVE WORKED AS AN UNDERSERVANT AT BATHHOUSES AND EVEN SCRUBBED DOWN THE COVERS LAID OVER THE TOWN SEWERS. IN OTHER WORDS, ANYTHING AND EVERYTHING, OTHER THAN SELL MY BODY TO WOMEN.
COMPARED TO THE WORK I HAVE DONE ERE COMING HERE, THIS IS DOWNRIGHT EASY.

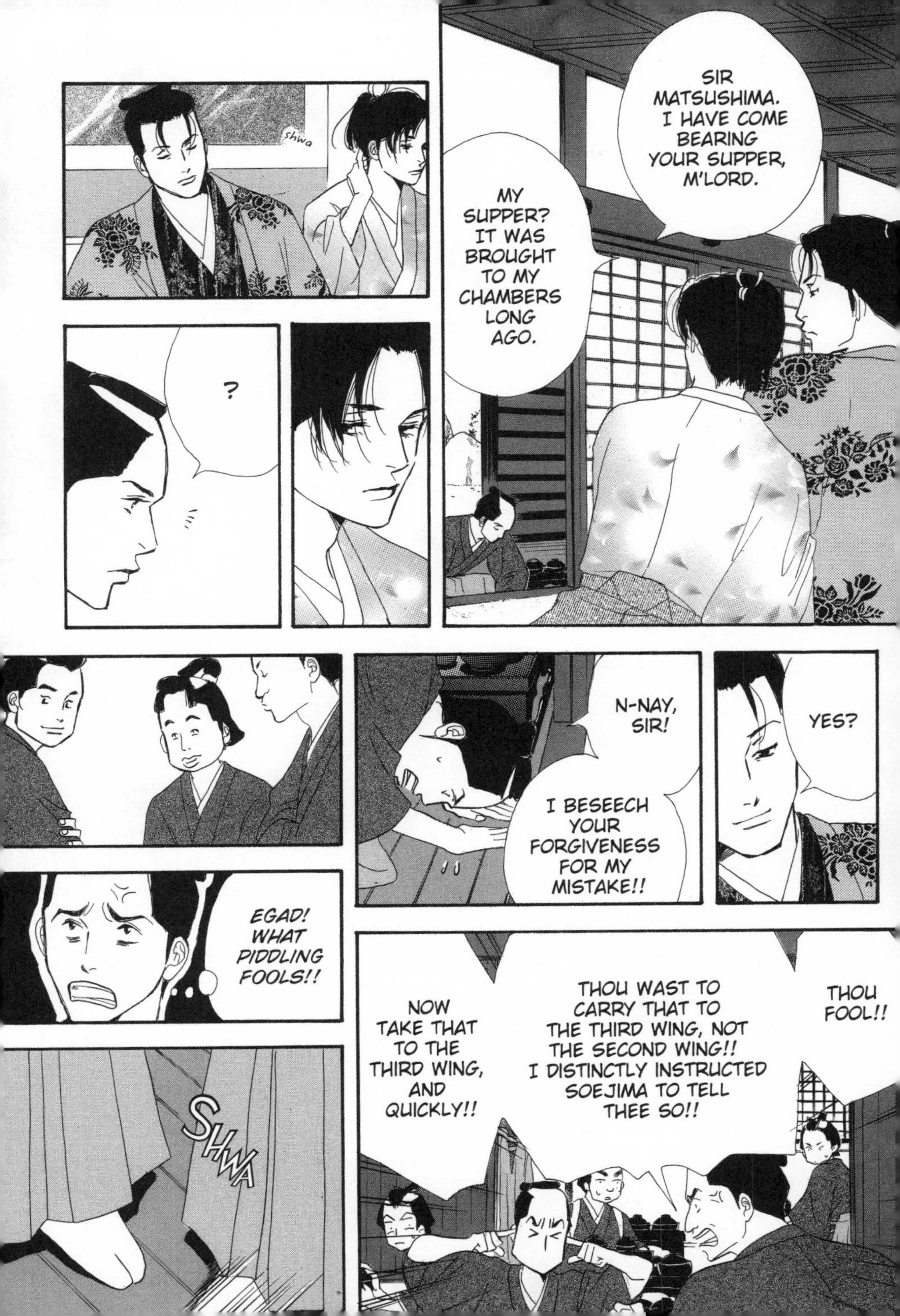
SIR MATSUSHIMA. I HAVE COME BEARING YOUR SUPPER, M'LORD.
MY SUPPER? IT WAS BROUGHT TO MY CHAMBERS LONG AGO.
shwa
?
YES?
N-NAY, SIR!
I BESEECH YOUR FORGIVENESS FOR MY MISTAKE!!
THOU FOOL!!
THOU WAST TO CARRY THAT TO THE THIRD WING, NOT THE SECOND WING!! I DISTINCTLY INSTRUCTED SOEJIMA TO TELL THEE SO!!
NOW TAKE THAT TO THE THIRD WING, AND QUICKLY!!
EGAD! WHAT PIDDLING FOOLS!!
SHWA

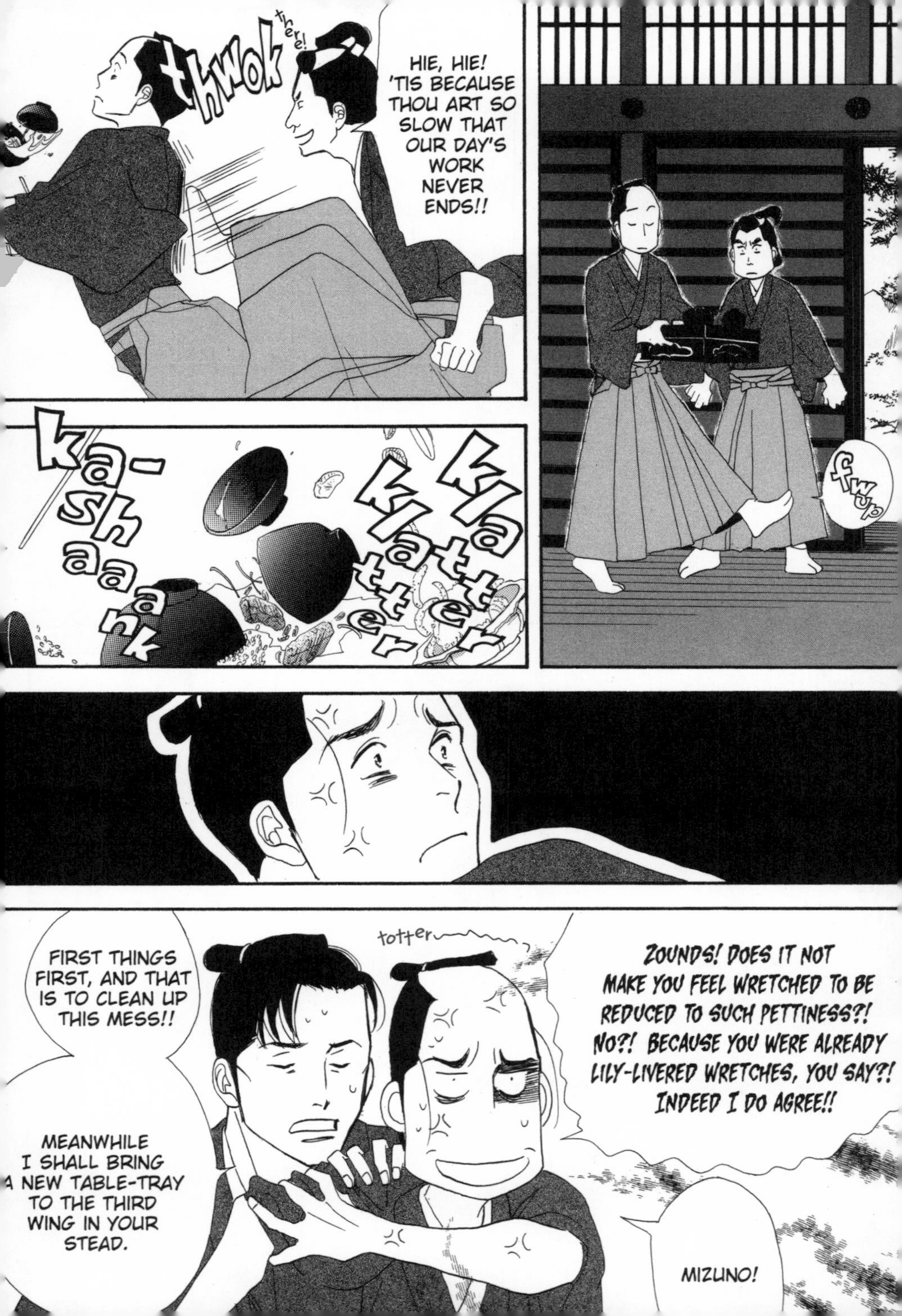

fwup
there!
thwok
HIE, HIE! 'TIS BECAUSE THOU ART SO SLOW THAT OUR DAY'S WORK NEVER ENDS!!
klatter
klatter
ka-shaaaank
ZOUNDS! DOES IT NOT MAKE YOU FEEL WRETCHED TO BE REDUCED TO SUCH PETTINESS?! NO?! BECAUSE YOU WERE ALREADY LILY-LIVERED WRETCHES, YOU SAY?! INDEED I DO AGREE!!
totter
FIRST THINGS FIRST, AND THAT IS TO CLEAN UP THIS MESS!!
MIZUNO!
MEANWHILE I SHALL BRING A NEW TABLE-TRAY TO THE THIRD WING IN YOUR STEAD.

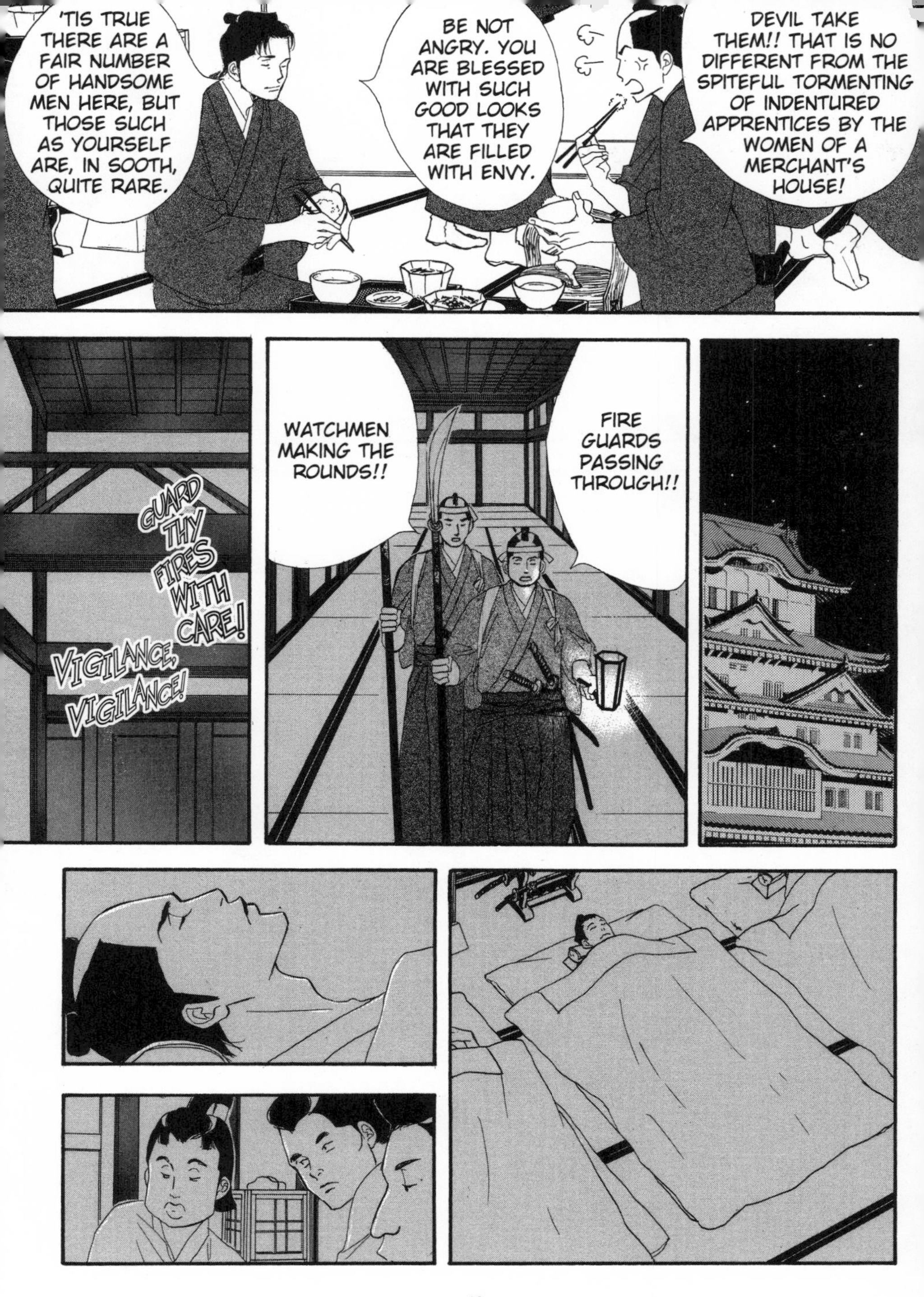
DEVIL TAKE THEM!! THAT IS NO DIFFERENT FROM THE SPITEFUL TORMENTING OF INDENTURED APPRENTICES BY THE WOMEN OF A MERCHANT'S HOUSE!
BE NOT ANGRY. YOU ARE BLESSED WITH SUCH GOOD LOOKS THAT THEY ARE FILLED WITH ENVY.
'TIS TRUE THERE ARE A FAIR NUMBER OF HANDSOME MEN HERE, BUT THOSE SUCH AS YOURSELF ARE, IN SOOTH, QUITE RARE.
FIRE GUARDS PASSING THROUGH!!
WATCHMEN MAKING THE ROUNDS!!
GUARD THY FIRES WITH CARE!
VIGILANCE, VIGILANCE!

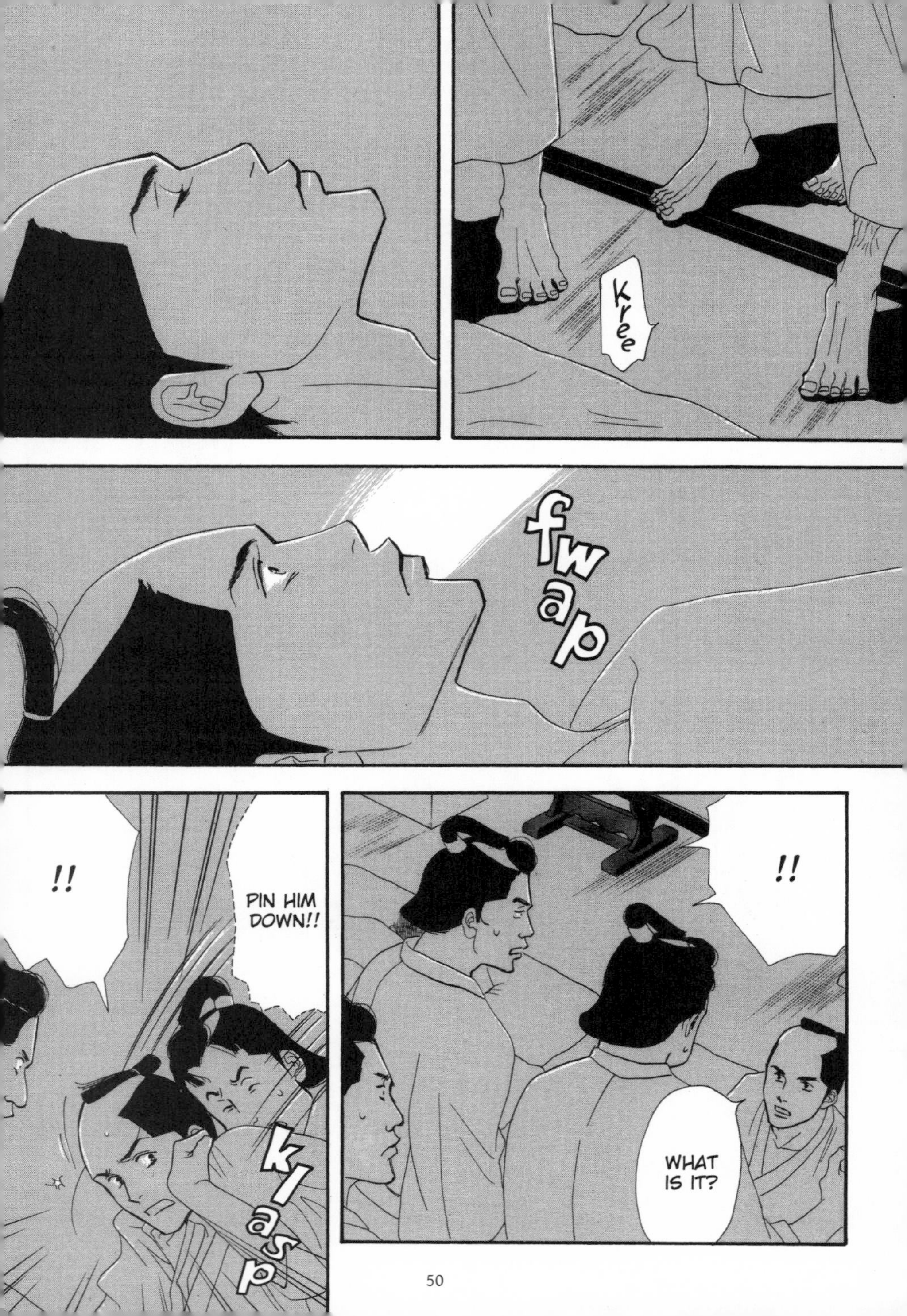
Kree
fwap
!!
WHAT IS IT?
PIN HIM DOWN!!
!!
klasp

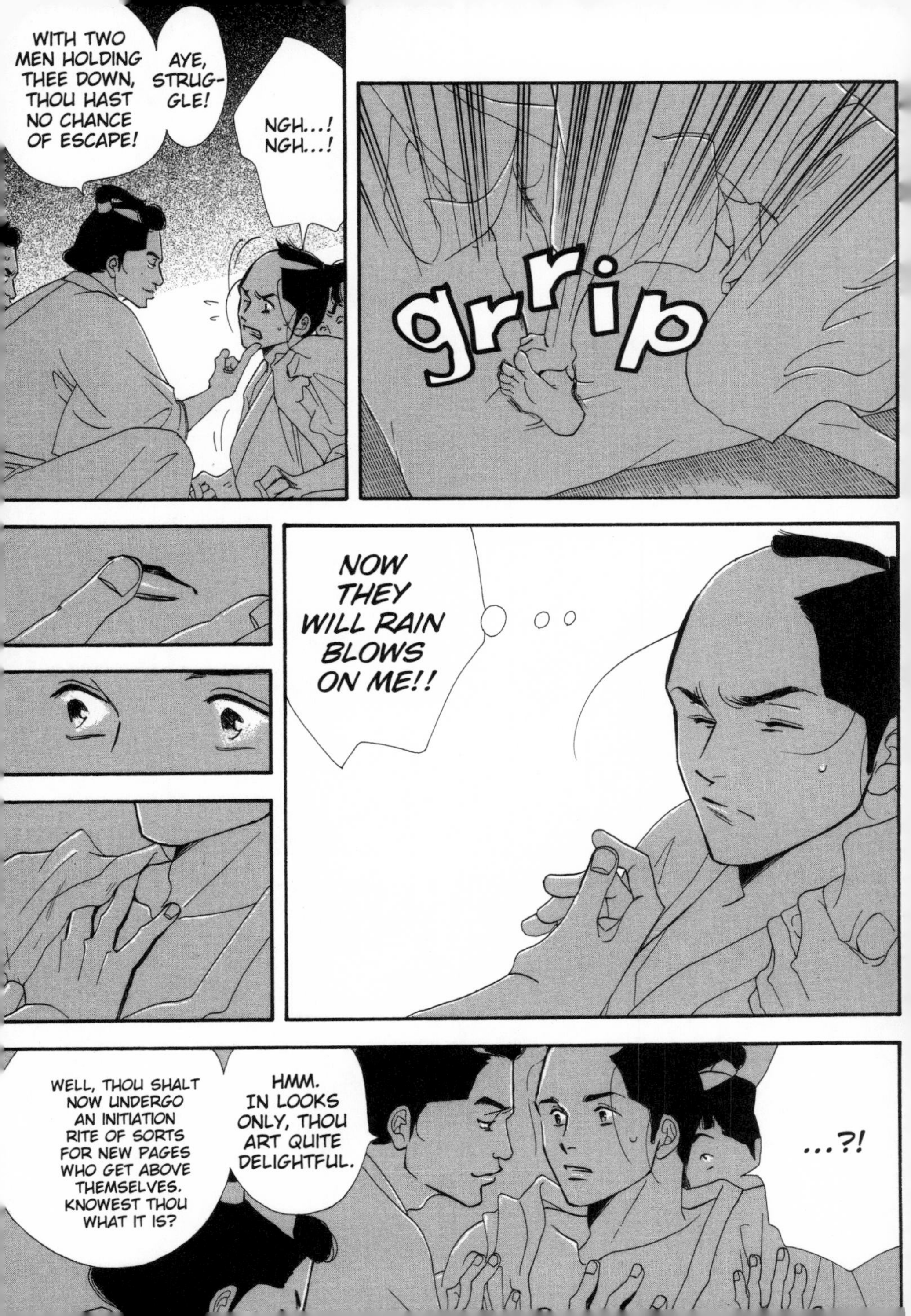
grrip
NGH...! NGH...!
AYE, STRUG-GLE!
WITH TWO MEN HOLDING THEE DOWN, THOU HAST NO CHANCE OF ESCAPE!
NOW THEY WILL RAIN BLOWS ON ME!!
...?!
HMM. IN LOOKS ONLY, THOU ART QUITE DELIGHTFUL.
WELL, THOU SHALT NOW UNDERGO AN INITIATION RITE OF SORTS FOR NEW PAGES WHO GET ABOVE THEMSELVES. KNOWEST THOU WHAT IT IS?

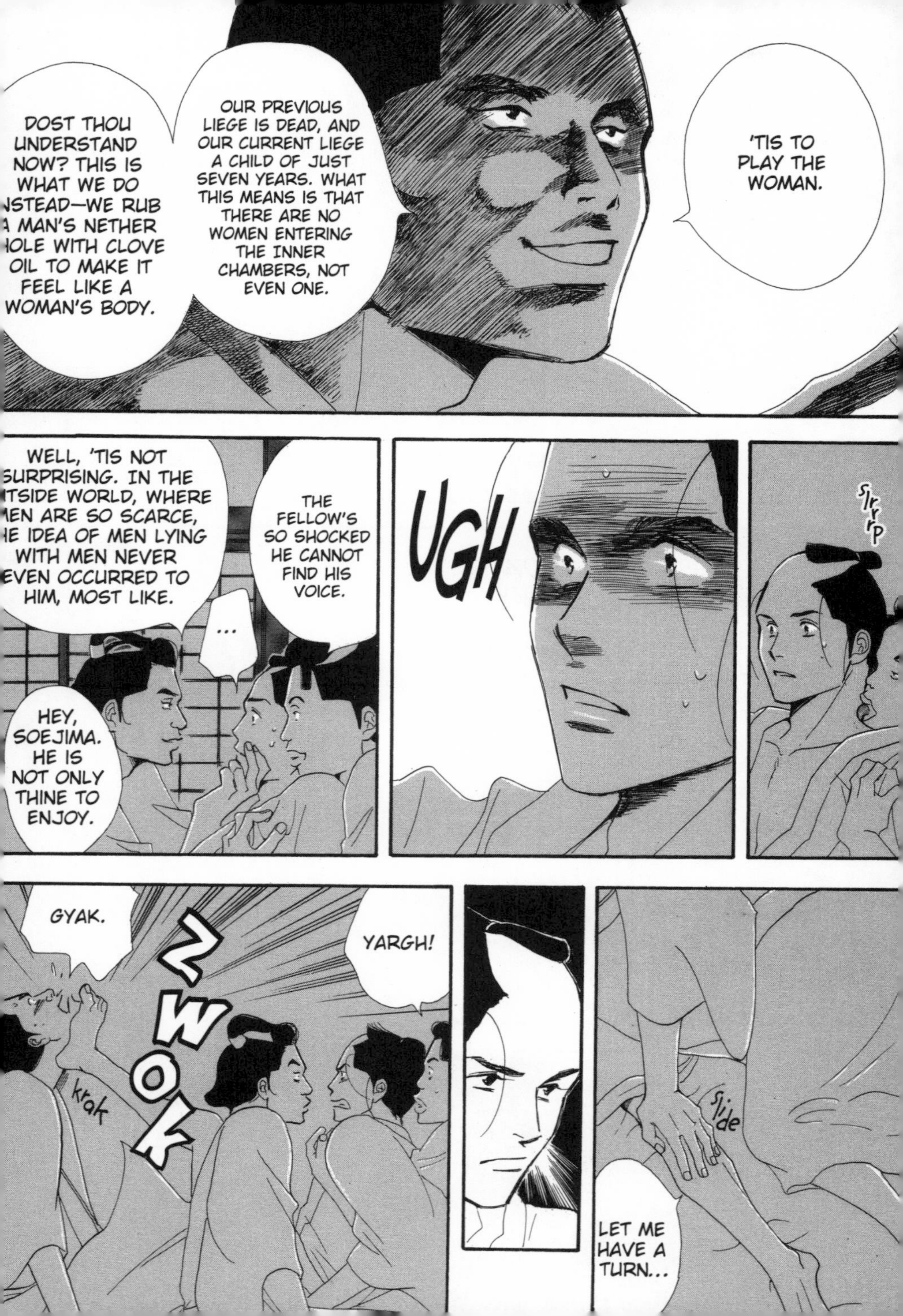
'TIS TO PLAY THE WOMAN.
OUR PREVIOUS LIEGE IS DEAD, AND OUR CURRENT LIEGE A CHILD OF JUST SEVEN YEARS. WHAT THIS MEANS IS THAT THERE ARE NO WOMEN ENTERING THE INNER CHAMBERS, NOT EVEN ONE.
DOST THOU UNDERSTAND NOW? THIS IS WHAT WE DO NSTEAD—WE RUB A MAN'S NETHER HOLE WITH CLOVE OIL TO MAKE IT FEEL LIKE A WOMAN'S BODY.
slrrp
UGH
THE FELLOW'S SO SHOCKED HE CANNOT FIND HIS VOICE.
WELL, 'TIS NOT SURPRISING. IN THE TSIDE WORLD, WHERE MEN ARE SO SCARCE, HE IDEA OF MEN LYING WITH MEN NEVER EVEN OCCURRED TO HIM, MOST LIKE.
...
HEY, SOEJIMA. HE IS NOT ONLY THINE TO ENJOY.
slide
LET ME HAVE A TURN...
YARGH!
ZWOK
GYAK.
krak

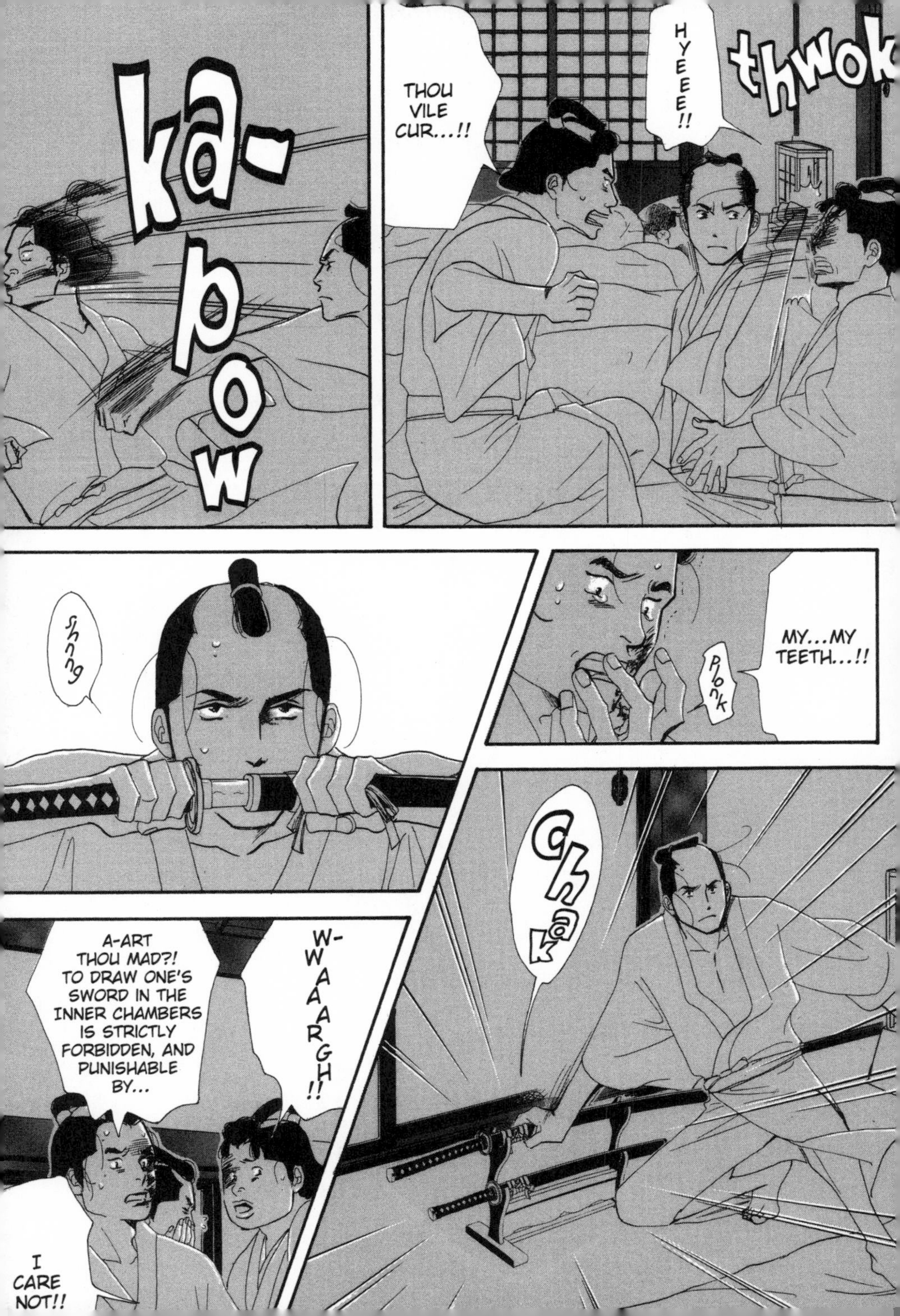
thwok
HYEEE!!
THOU VILE CUR...!!
ka-pow
MY...MY TEETH...!!
Plonk
shnng
chak
W-WAAAARGH!!
A-ART THOU MAD?! TO DRAW ONE'S SWORD IN THE INNER CHAMBERS IS STRICTLY FORBIDDEN, AND PUNISHABLE BY...
I CARE NOT!!

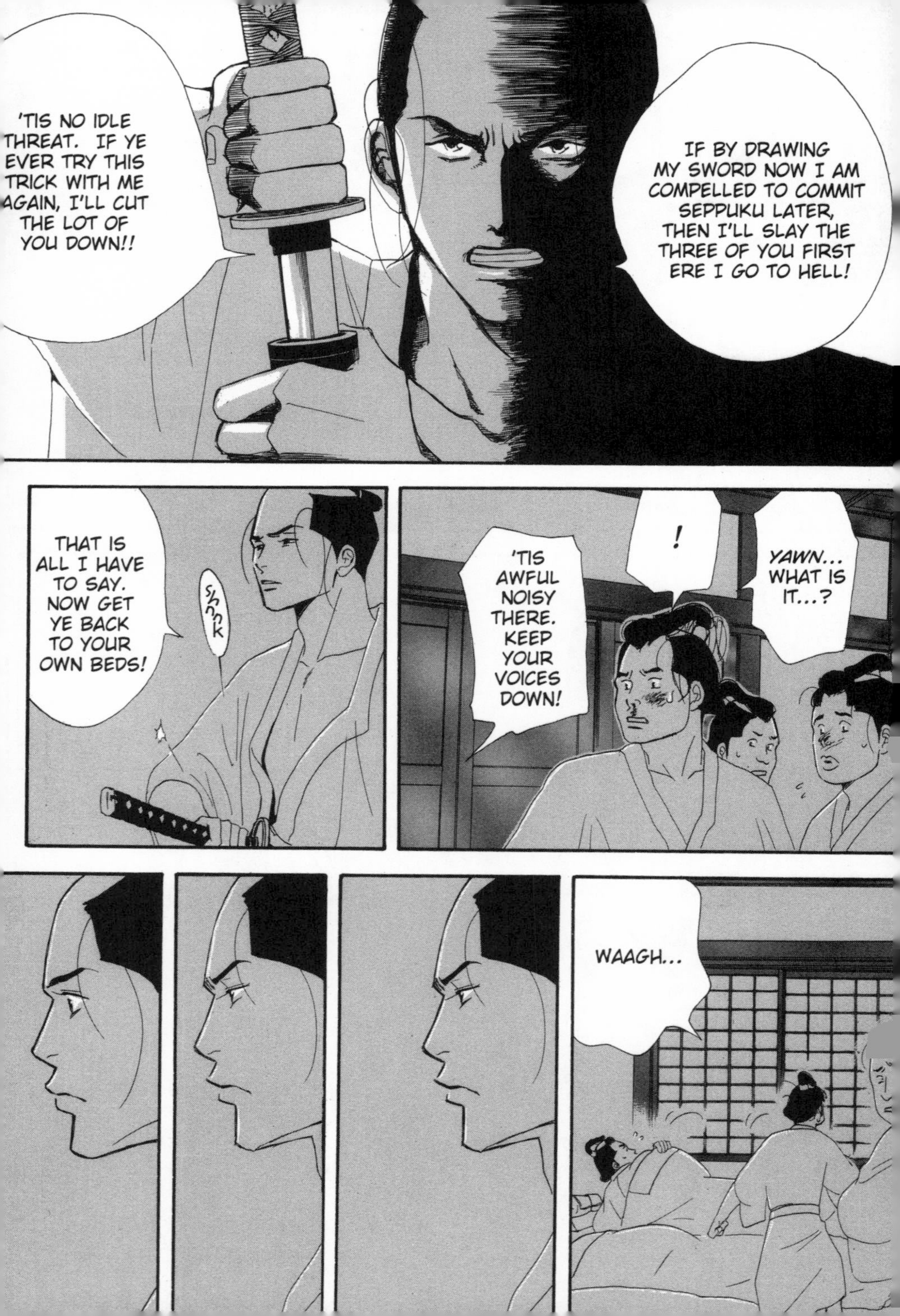
IF BY DRAWING MY SWORD NOW I AM COMPELLED TO COMMIT SEPPUKU LATER, THEN I'LL SLAY THE THREE OF YOU FIRST ERE I GO TO HELL!
'TIS NO IDLE THREAT. IF YE EVER TRY THIS TRICK WITH ME AGAIN, I'LL CUT THE LOT OF YOU DOWN!!
YAWN... WHAT IS IT...?
!
'TIS AWFUL NOISY THERE. KEEP YOUR VOICES DOWN!
THAT IS ALL I HAVE TO SAY. NOW GET YE BACK TO YOUR OWN BEDS!
shnk
WAAGH...

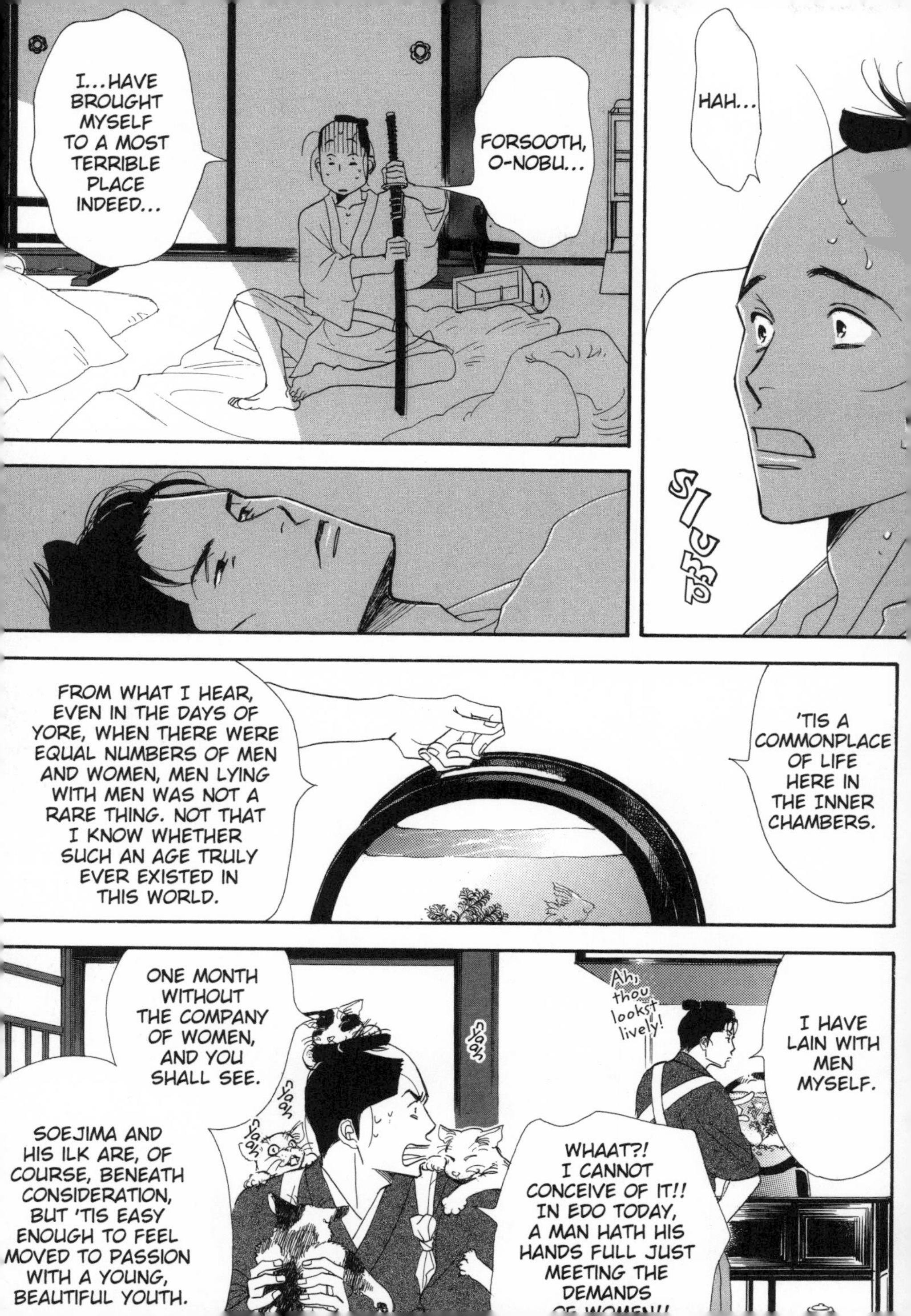
HAH...
SLUMP
FORSOOTH, O-NOBU...
I...HAVE BROUGHT MYSELF TO A MOST TERRIBLE PLACE INDEED...
'TIS A COMMONPLACE OF LIFE HERE IN THE INNER CHAMBERS.
FROM WHAT I HEAR, EVEN IN THE DAYS OF YORE, WHEN THERE WERE EQUAL NUMBERS OF MEN AND WOMEN, MEN LYING WITH MEN WAS NOT A RARE THING. NOT THAT I KNOW WHETHER SUCH AN AGE TRULY EVER EXISTED IN THIS WORLD.
I HAVE LAIN WITH MEN MYSELF.
Ah, thou lookst lively!
WHAAT?! I CANNOT CONCEIVE OF IT!! IN EDO TODAY, A MAN HATH HIS HANDS FULL JUST MEETING THE DEMANDS OF WOMEN!!
nyah
ONE MONTH WITHOUT THE COMPANY OF WOMEN, AND YOU SHALL SEE.
SOEJIMA AND HIS ILK ARE, OF COURSE, BENEATH CONSIDERATION, BUT 'TIS EASY ENOUGH TO FEEL MOVED TO PASSION WITH A YOUNG, BEAUTIFUL YOUTH.
nyah
nyah

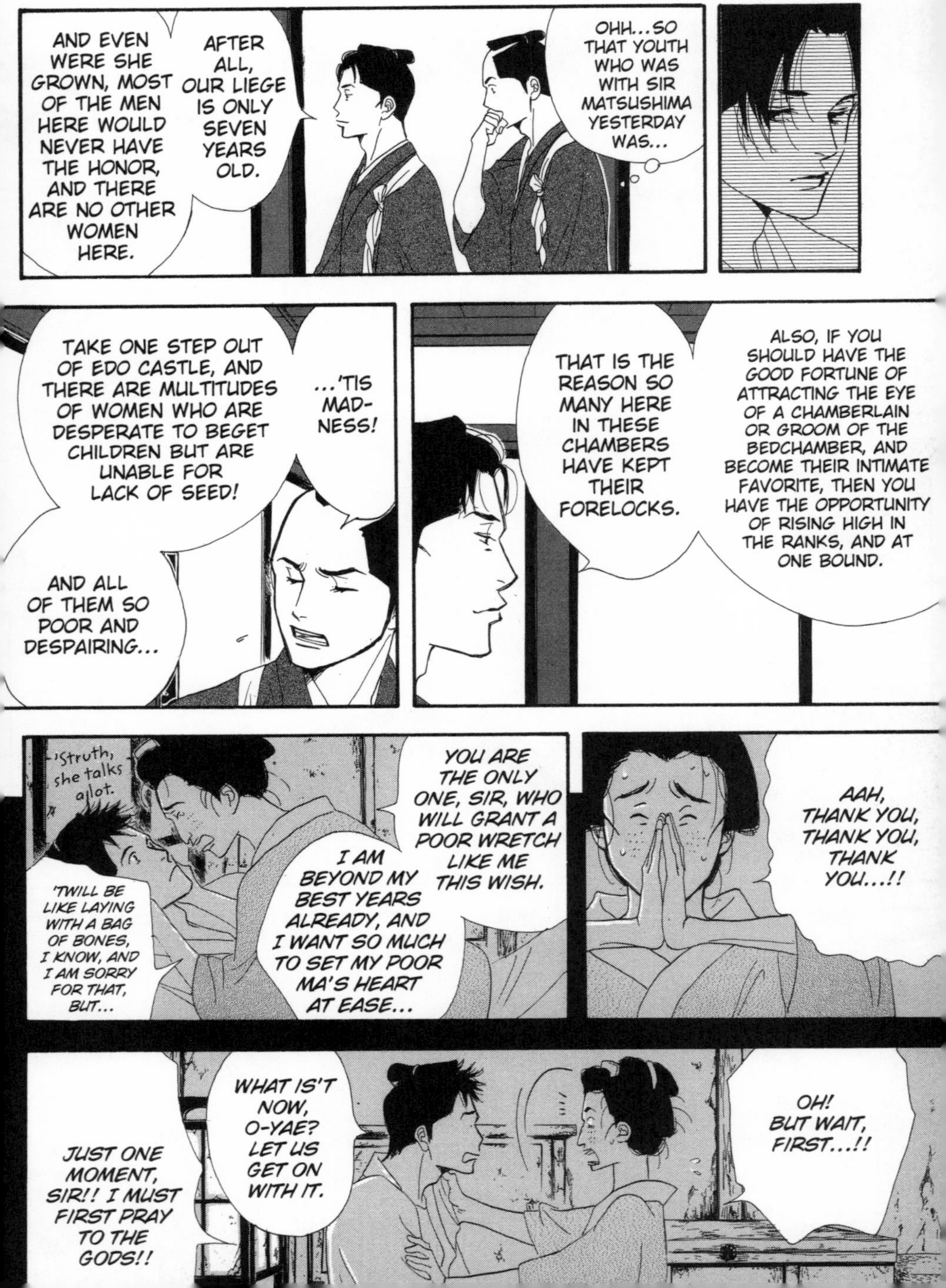
OHH...SO THAT YOUTH WHO WAS WITH SIR MATSUSHIMA YESTERDAY WAS...
AFTER ALL, OUR LIEGE IS ONLY SEVEN YEARS OLD.
AND EVEN WERE SHE GROWN, MOST OF THE MEN HERE WOULD NEVER HAVE THE HONOR, AND THERE ARE NO OTHER WOMEN HERE.
ALSO, IF YOU SHOULD HAVE THE GOOD FORTUNE OF ATTRACTING THE EYE OF A CHAMBERLAIN OR GROOM OF THE BEDCHAMBER, AND BECOME THEIR INTIMATE FAVORITE, THEN YOU HAVE THE OPPORTUNITY OF RISING HIGH IN THE RANKS, AND AT ONE BOUND.
THAT IS THE REASON SO MANY HERE IN THESE CHAMBERS HAVE KEPT THEIR FORELOCKS.
...'TIS MADNESS!
TAKE ONE STEP OUT OF EDO CASTLE, AND THERE ARE MULTITUDES OF WOMEN WHO ARE DESPERATE TO BEGET CHILDREN BUT ARE UNABLE FOR LACK OF SEED!
AND ALL OF THEM SO POOR AND DESPAIRING...
AAH, THANK YOU, THANK YOU, THANK YOU...!!
YOU ARE THE ONLY ONE, SIR, WHO WILL GRANT A POOR WRETCH LIKE ME THIS WISH.
'Struth, she talks a lot.
I AM BEYOND MY BEST YEARS ALREADY, AND I WANT SO MUCH TO SET MY POOR MA'S HEART AT EASE...
'TWILL BE LIKE LAYING WITH A BAG OF BONES, I KNOW, AND I AM SORRY FOR THAT, BUT...
OH! BUT WAIT, FIRST...!!
WHAT IS'T NOW, O-YAE? LET US GET ON WITH IT.
JUST ONE MOMENT, SIR!! I MUST FIRST PRAY TO THE GODS!!

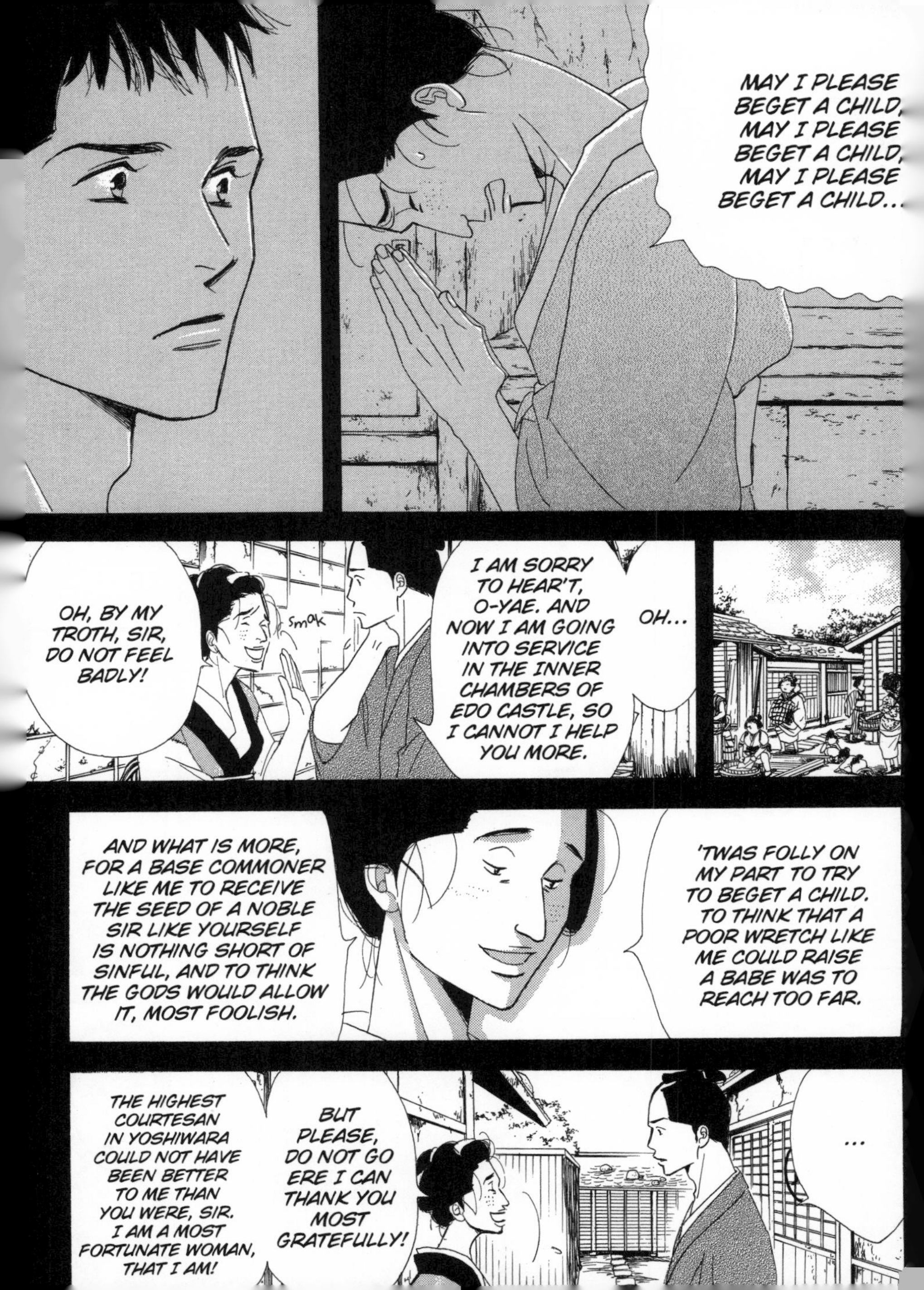
MAY I PLEASE BEGET A CHILD, MAY I PLEASE BEGET A CHILD, MAY I PLEASE BEGET A CHILD...
OH...
I AM SORRY TO HEAR'T, O-YAE. AND NOW I AM GOING INTO SERVICE IN THE INNER CHAMBERS OF EDO CASTLE, SO I CANNOT I HELP YOU MORE.
smak
OH, BY MY TROTH, SIR, DO NOT FEEL BADLY!
'TWAS FOLLY ON MY PART TO TRY TO BEGET A CHILD. TO THINK THAT A POOR WRETCH LIKE ME COULD RAISE A BABE WAS TO REACH TOO FAR.
AND WHAT IS MORE, FOR A BASE COMMONER LIKE ME TO RECEIVE THE SEED OF A NOBLE SIR LIKE YOURSELF IS NOTHING SHORT OF SINFUL, AND TO THINK THE GODS WOULD ALLOW IT, MOST FOOLISH.
...
BUT PLEASE, DO NOT GO ERE I CAN THANK YOU MOST GRATEFULLY!
THE HIGHEST COURTESAN IN YOSHIWARA COULD NOT HAVE BEEN BETTER TO ME THAN YOU WERE, SIR. I AM A MOST FORTUNATE WOMAN, THAT I AM!

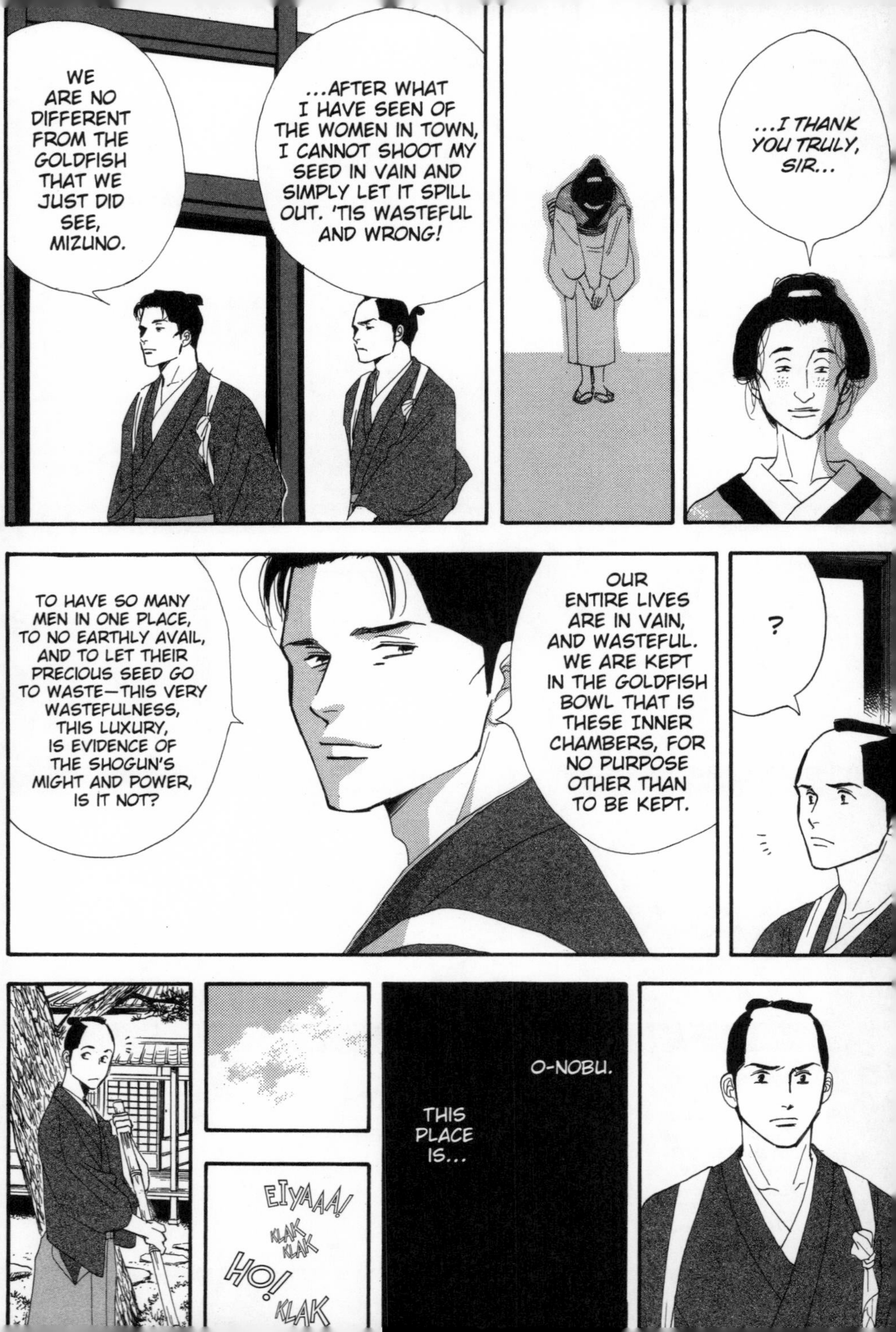
...I THANK YOU TRULY, SIR...
...AFTER WHAT I HAVE SEEN OF THE WOMEN IN TOWN, I CANNOT SHOOT MY SEED IN VAIN AND SIMPLY LET IT SPILL OUT. 'TIS WASTEFUL AND WRONG!
WE ARE NO DIFFERENT FROM THE GOLDFISH THAT WE JUST DID SEE, MIZUNO.
?
OUR ENTIRE LIVES ARE IN VAIN, AND WASTEFUL. WE ARE KEPT IN THE GOLDFISH BOWL THAT IS THESE INNER CHAMBERS, FOR NO PURPOSE OTHER THAN TO BE KEPT.
TO HAVE SO MANY MEN IN ONE PLACE, TO NO EARTHLY AVAIL, AND TO LET THEIR PRECIOUS SEED GO TO WASTE—THIS VERY WASTEFULNESS, THIS LUXURY, IS EVIDENCE OF THE SHOGUN'S MIGHT AND POWER, IS IT NOT?
O-NOBU.
THIS PLACE IS...
EIYAAA!
KLAK KLAK
HO!
KLAK

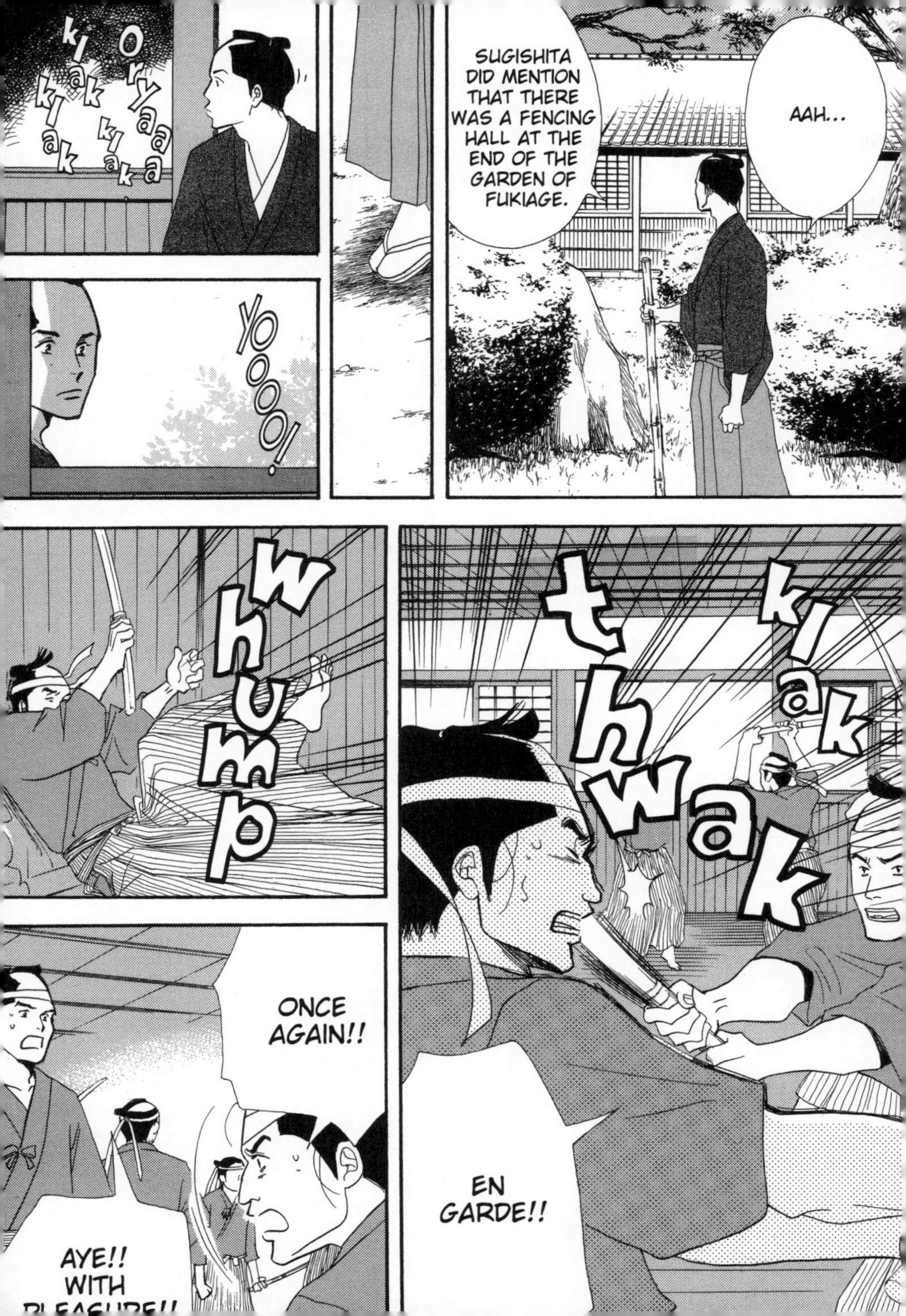

AAH...
SUGISHITA DID MENTION THAT THERE WAS A FENCING HALL AT THE END OF THE GARDEN OF FUKIAGE.
Oryaaa
kiak kiak
kiak
YOOOO!
kiak
thwak
EN GARDE!!
whump
ONCE AGAIN!!
AYE!! WITH

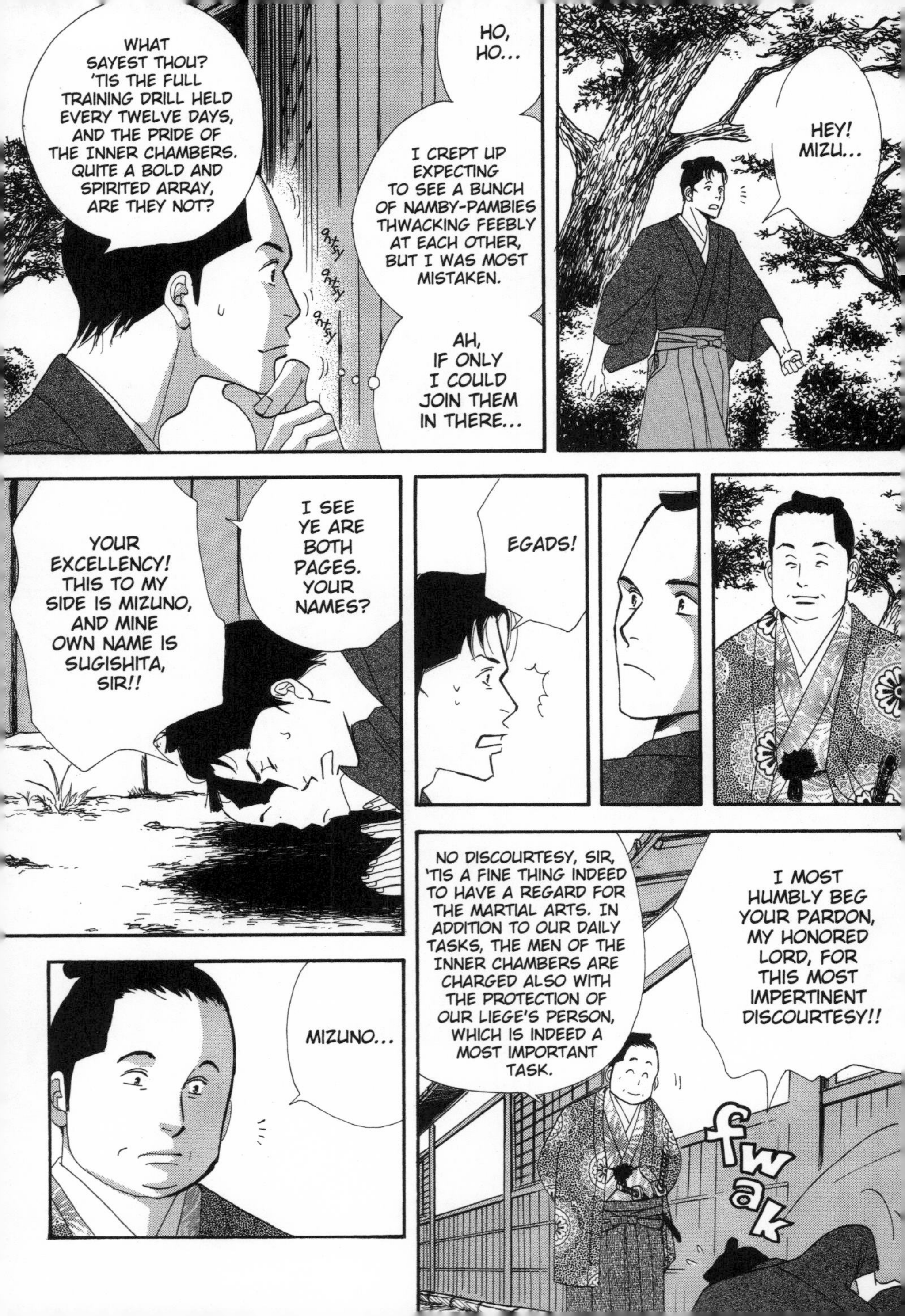
HEY! MIZU...
HO, HO...
I CREPT UP EXPECTING TO SEE A BUNCH OF NAMBY-PAMBIES THWACKING FEEBLY AT EACH OTHER, BUT I WAS MOST MISTAKEN.
AH, IF ONLY I COULD JOIN THEM IN THERE...
antsy antsy antsy
WHAT SAYEST THOU? 'TIS THE FULL TRAINING DRILL HELD EVERY TWELVE DAYS, AND THE PRIDE OF THE INNER CHAMBERS. QUITE A BOLD AND SPIRITED ARRAY, ARE THEY NOT?
EGADS!
I SEE YE ARE BOTH PAGES. YOUR NAMES?
YOUR EXCELLENCY! THIS TO MY SIDE IS MIZUNO, AND MINE OWN NAME IS SUGISHITA, SIR!!
I MOST HUMBLY BEG YOUR PARDON, MY HONORED LORD, FOR THIS MOST IMPERTINENT DISCOURTESY!!
NO DISCOURTESY, SIR, 'TIS A FINE THING INDEED TO HAVE A REGARD FOR THE MARTIAL ARTS. IN ADDITION TO OUR DAILY TASKS, THE MEN OF THE INNER CHAMBERS ARE CHARGED ALSO WITH THE PROTECTION OF OUR LIEGE'S PERSON, WHICH IS INDEED A MOST IMPORTANT TASK.
fwak
MIZUNO...

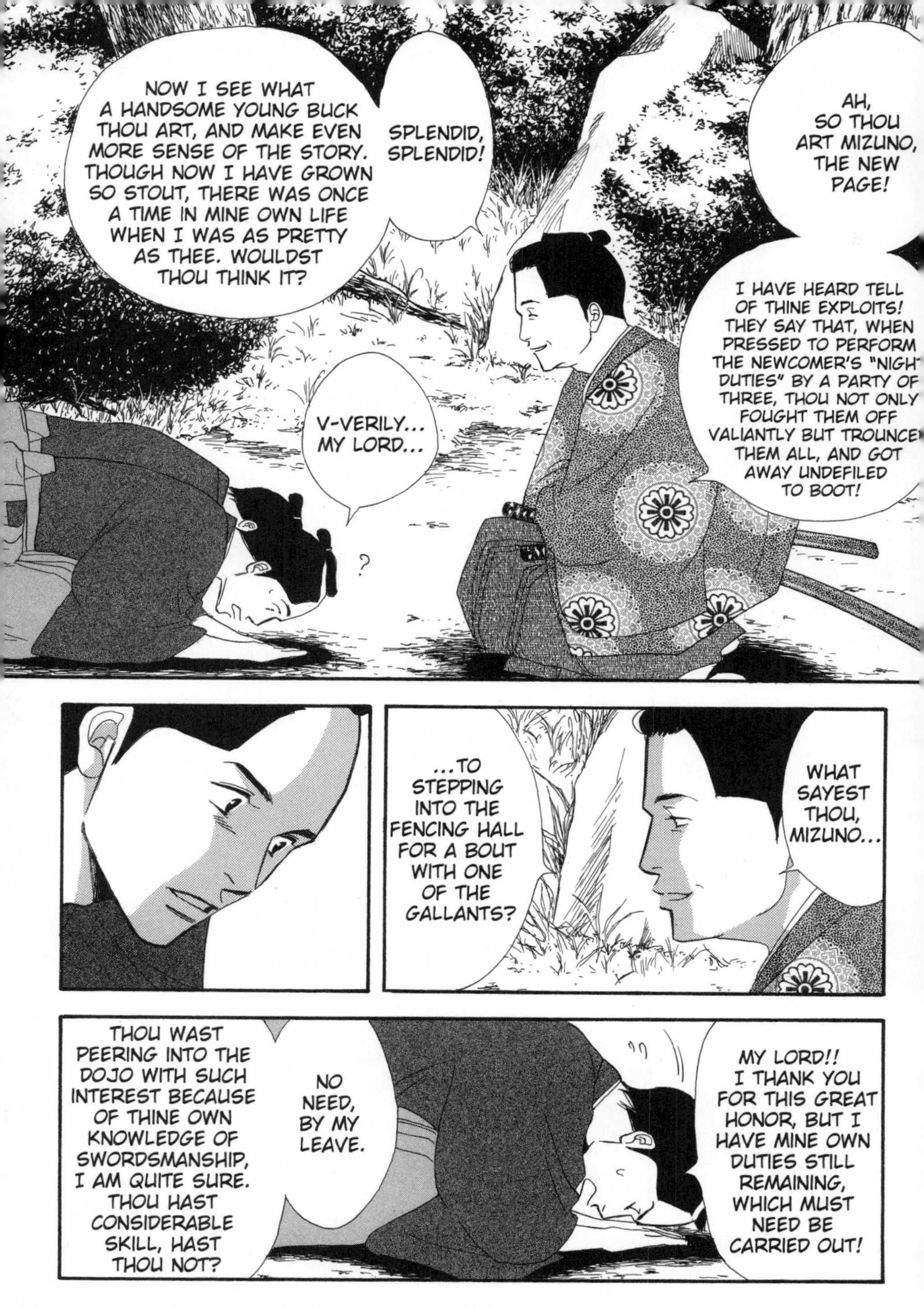
AH, SO THOU ART MIZUNO, THE NEW PAGE!
I HAVE HEARD TELL OF THINE EXPLOITS! THEY SAY THAT, WHEN PRESSED TO PERFORM THE NEWCOMER'S "NIGH DUTIES" BY A PARTY OF THREE, THOU NOT ONLY FOUGHT THEM OFF VALIANTLY BUT TROUNCE THEM ALL, AND GOT AWAY UNDEFILED TO BOOT!
SPLENDID, SPLENDID!
NOW I SEE WHAT A HANDSOME YOUNG BUCK THOU ART, AND MAKE EVEN MORE SENSE OF THE STORY. THOUGH NOW I HAVE GROWN SO STOUT, THERE WAS ONCE A TIME IN MINE OWN LIFE WHEN I WAS AS PRETTY AS THEE. WOULDST THOU THINK IT?
V-VERILY... MY LORD...
?
WHAT SAYEST THOU, MIZUNO...
...TO STEPPING INTO THE FENCING HALL FOR A BOUT WITH ONE OF THE GALLANTS?
MY LORD!! I THANK YOU FOR THIS GREAT HONOR, BUT I HAVE MINE OWN DUTIES STILL REMAINING, WHICH MUST NEED BE CARRIED OUT!
NO NEED, BY MY LEAVE.
THOU WAST PEERING INTO THE DOJO WITH SUCH INTEREST BECAUSE OF THINE OWN KNOWLEDGE OF SWORDSMANSHIP, I AM QUITE SURE. THOU HAST CONSIDERABLE SKILL, HAST THOU NOT?

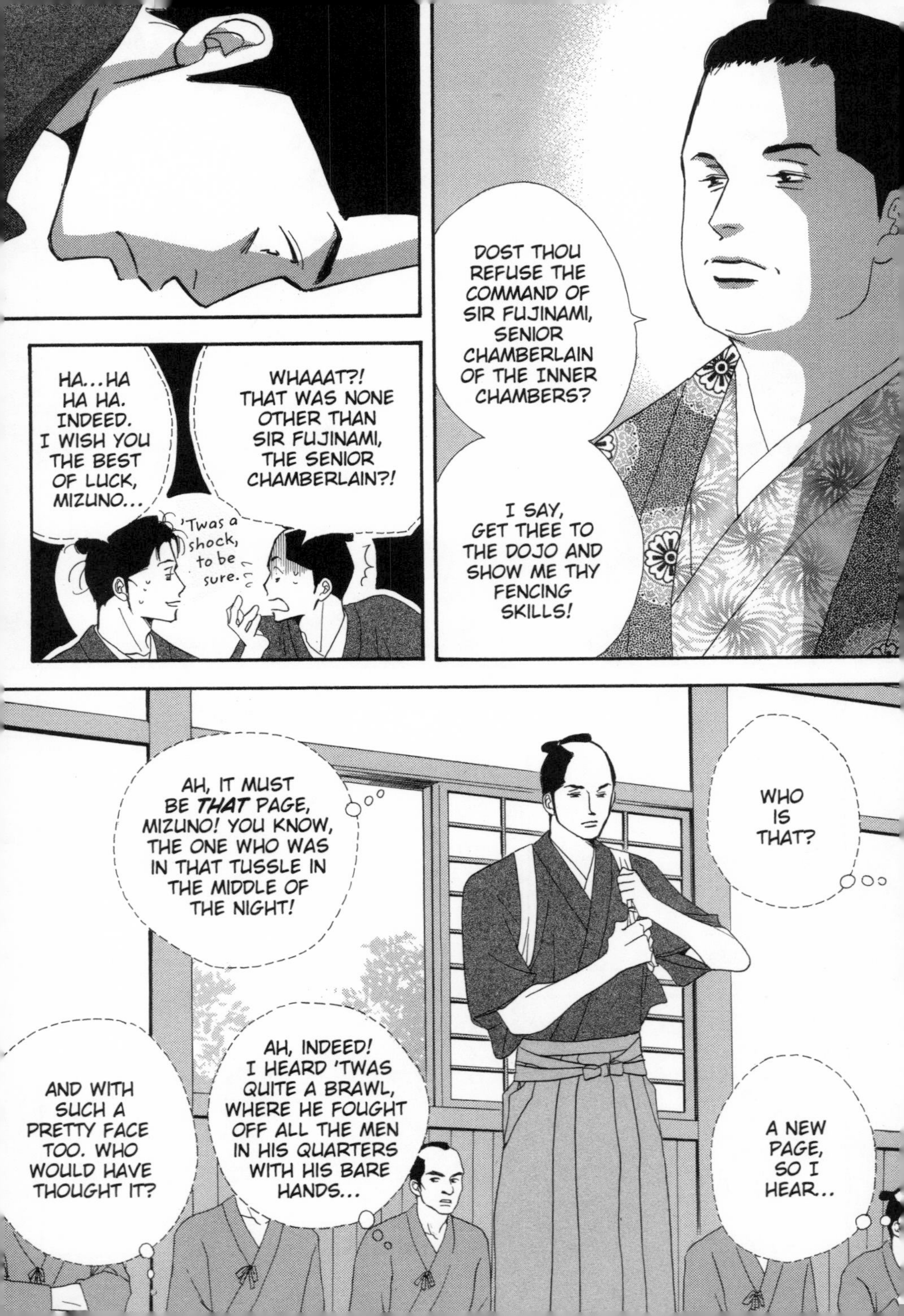
DOST THOU REFUSE THE COMMAND OF SIR FUJINAMI, SENIOR CHAMBERLAIN OF THE INNER CHAMBERS?
I SAY, GET THEE TO THE DOJO AND SHOW ME THY FENCING SKILLS!
WHAAAT?! THAT WAS NONE OTHER THAN SIR FUJINAMI, THE SENIOR CHAMBERLAIN?!
'Twas a shock, to be sure.
HA...HA HA HA. INDEED. I WISH YOU THE BEST OF LUCK, MIZUNO...
WHO IS THAT?
AH, IT MUST BE *THAT* PAGE, MIZUNO! YOU KNOW, THE ONE WHO WAS IN THAT TUSSLE IN THE MIDDLE OF THE NIGHT!
A NEW PAGE, SO I HEAR...
AH, INDEED! I HEARD 'TWAS QUITE A BRAWL, WHERE HE FOUGHT OFF ALL THE MEN IN HIS QUARTERS WITH HIS BARE HANDS...
AND WITH SUCH A PRETTY FACE TOO. WHO WOULD HAVE THOUGHT IT?

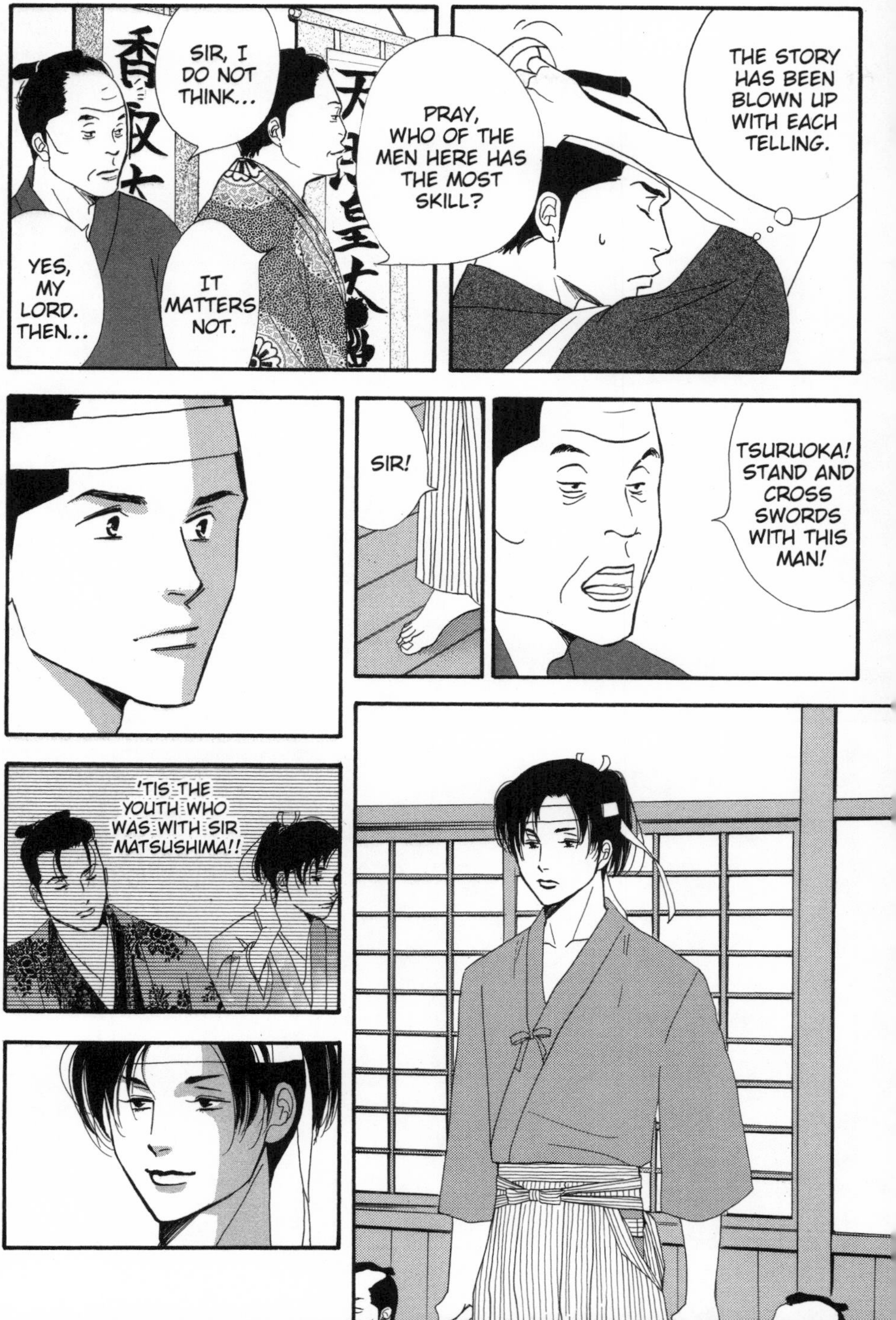
THE STORY HAS BEEN BLOWN UP WITH EACH TELLING.
PRAY, WHO OF THE MEN HERE HAS THE MOST SKILL?
SIR, I DO NOT THINK...
IT MATTERS NOT.
YES, MY LORD. THEN...
TSURUOKA! STAND AND CROSS SWORDS WITH THIS MAN!
SIR!
'TIS THE YOUTH WHO WAS WITH SIR MATSUSHIMA!!

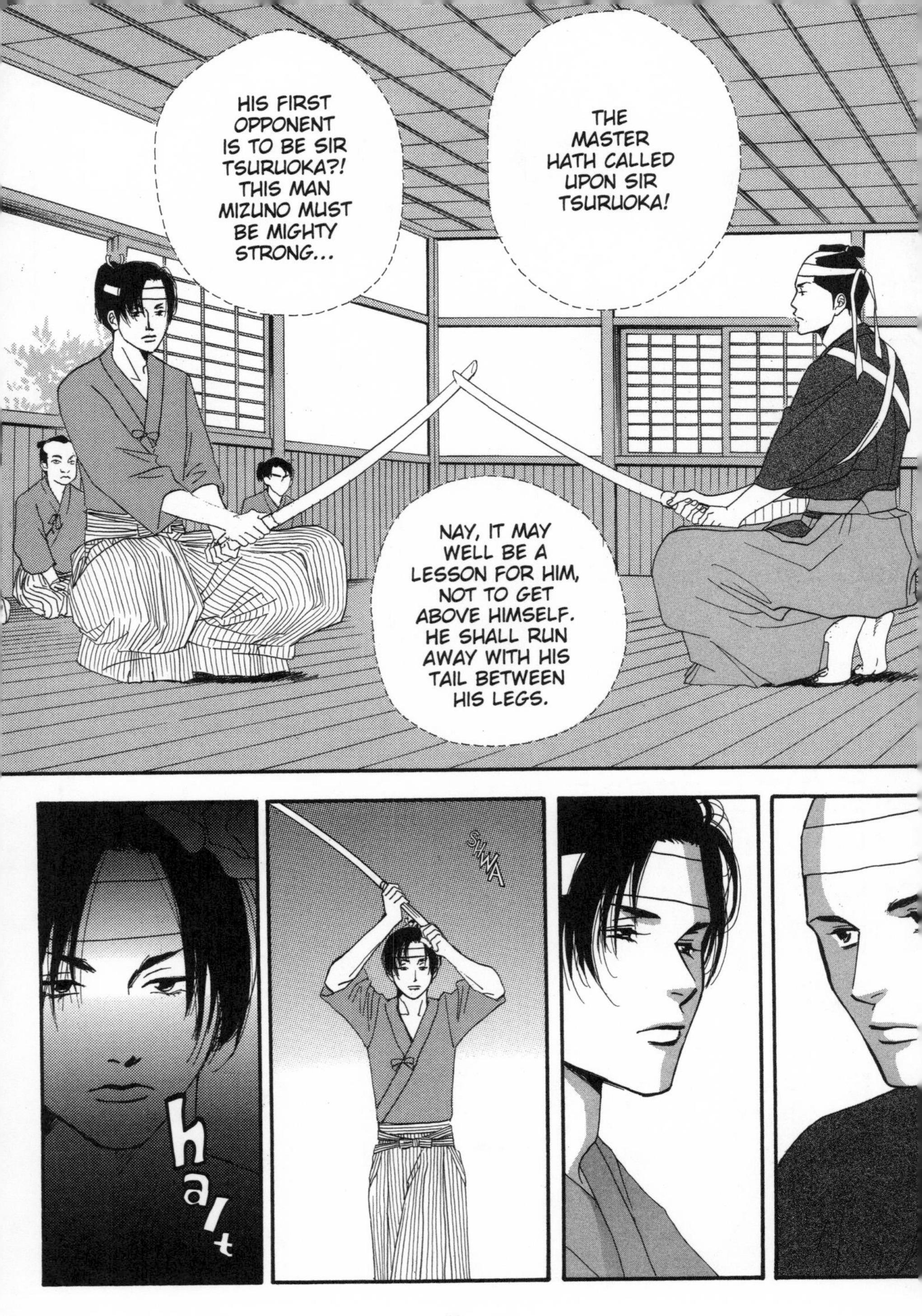
THE MASTER HATH CALLED UPON SIR TSURUOKA!
HIS FIRST OPPONENT IS TO BE SIR TSURUOKA?! THIS MAN MIZUNO MUST BE MIGHTY STRONG...
NAY, IT MAY WELL BE A LESSON FOR HIM, NOT TO GET ABOVE HIMSELF. HE SHALL RUN AWAY WITH HIS TAIL BETWEEN HIS LEGS.
SHWA
halt

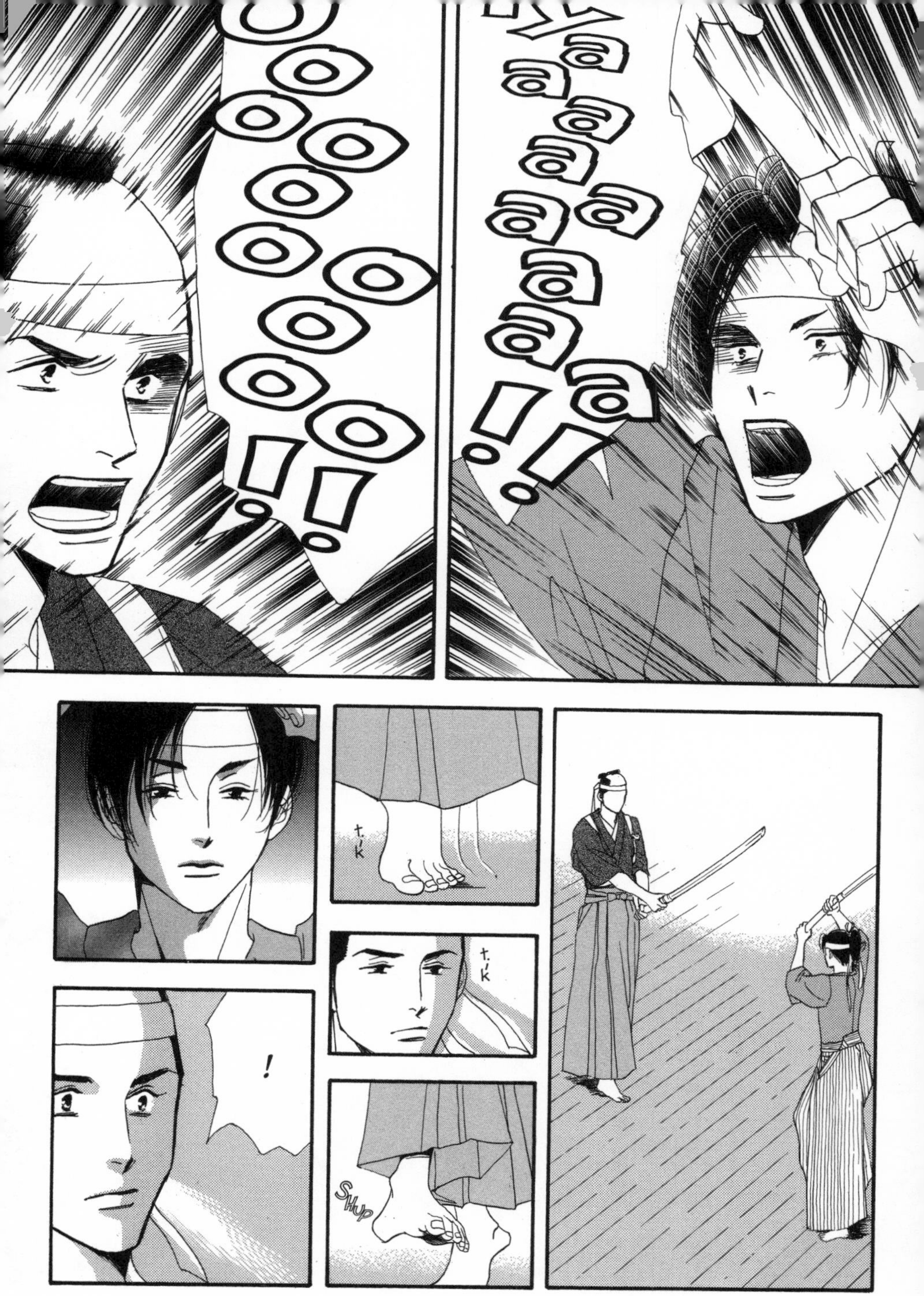
Yaaaaaaaaaaaaa!!
Oooooooooooooooooo!!
t'k
t'k
SHUP
!

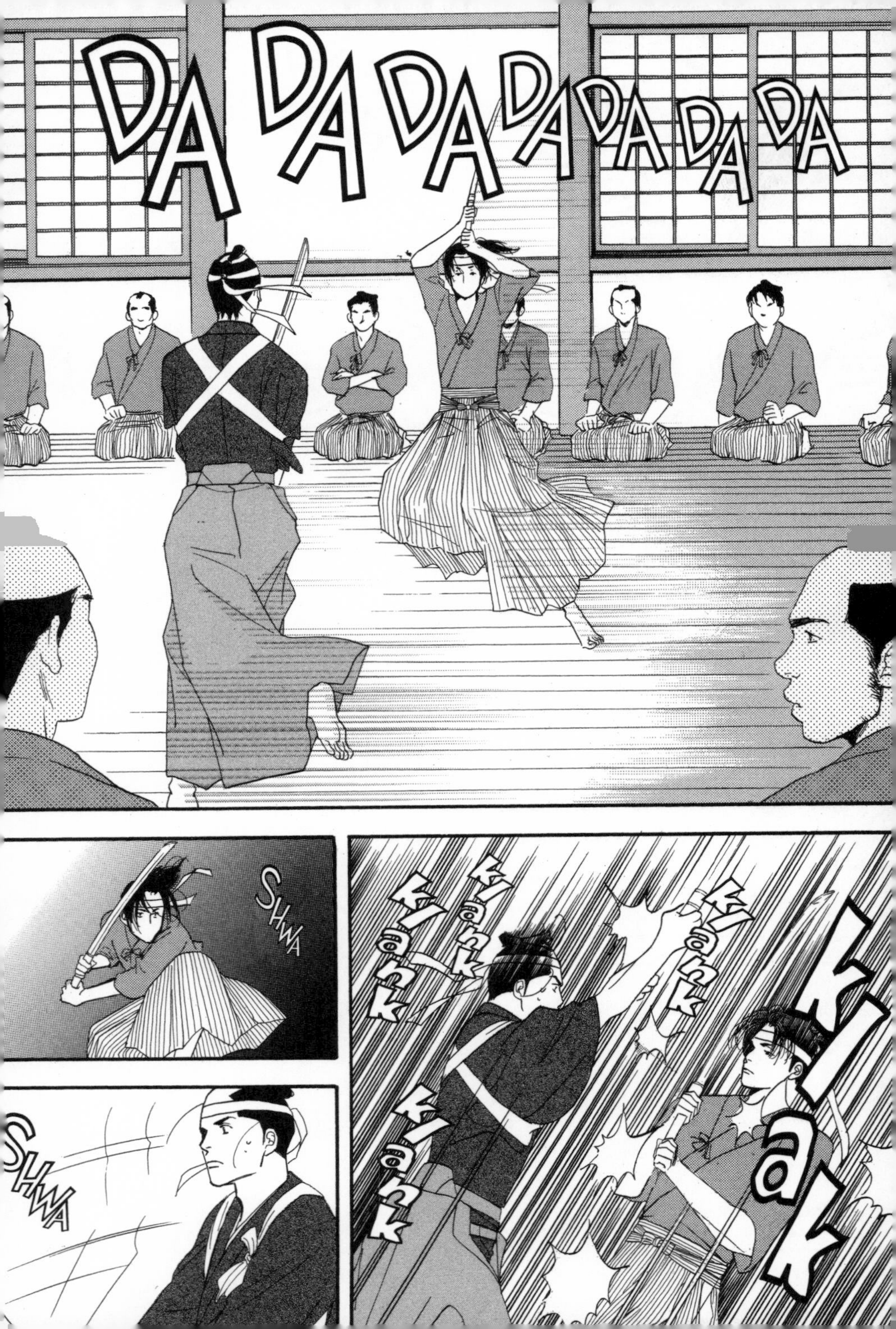
DA DA DA DA DA DA DA
klak
klank
klank
klank
klank
SHWA
SHWA

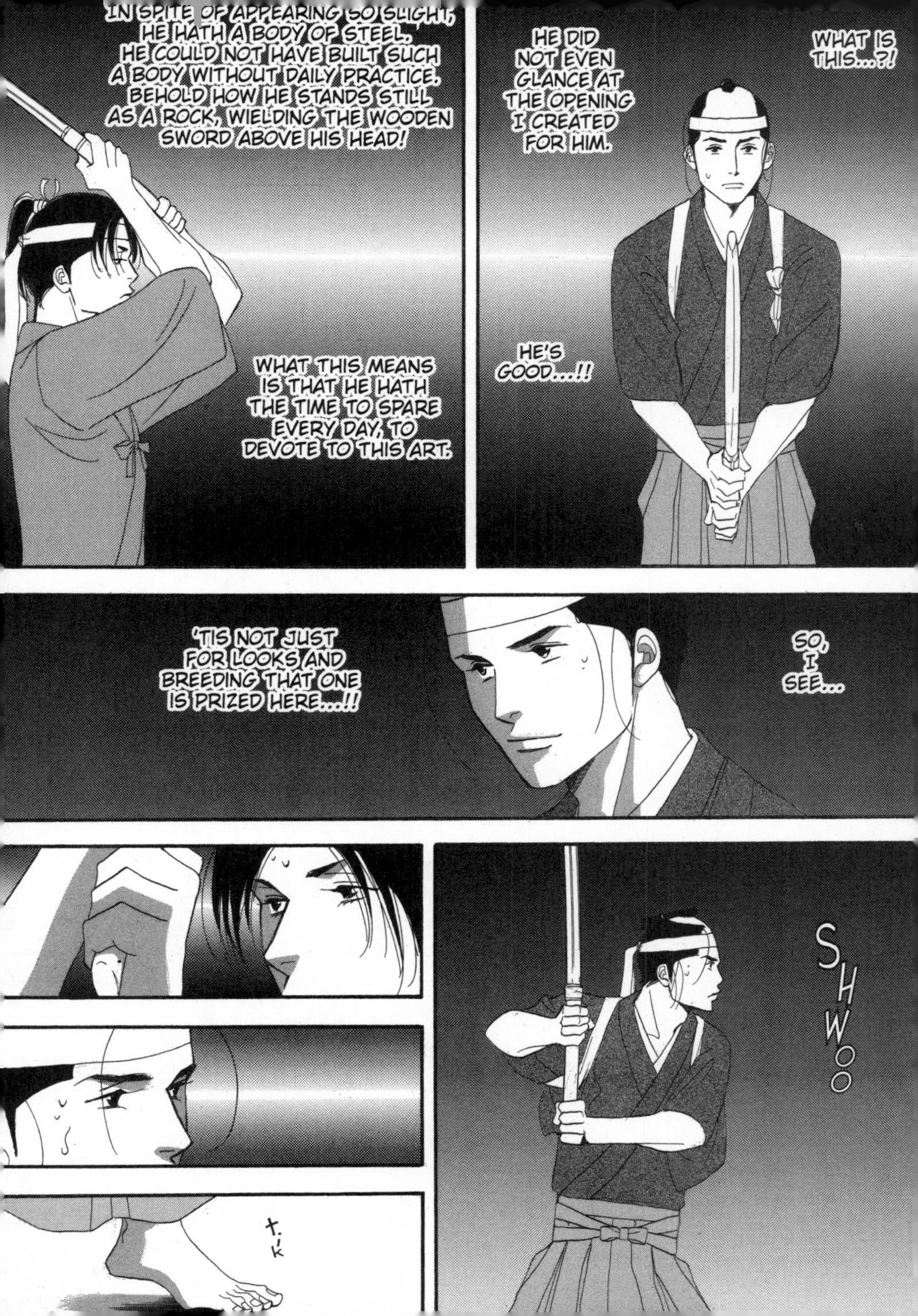
WHAT IS THIS...?!
HE DID NOT EVEN GLANCE AT THE OPENING I CREATED FOR HIM.
HE'S GOOD...!!
IN SPITE OF APPEARING SO SLIGHT, HE HATH A BODY OF STEEL. HE COULD NOT HAVE BUILT SUCH A BODY WITHOUT DAILY PRACTICE. BEHOLD HOW HE STANDS STILL AS A ROCK, WIELDING THE WOODEN SWORD ABOVE HIS HEAD!
WHAT THIS MEANS IS THAT HE HATH THE TIME TO SPARE EVERY DAY, TO DEVOTE TO THIS ART.
SO, I SEE...
'TIS NOT JUST FOR LOOKS AND BREEDING THAT ONE IS PRIZED HERE...!!
SHWOO
tik

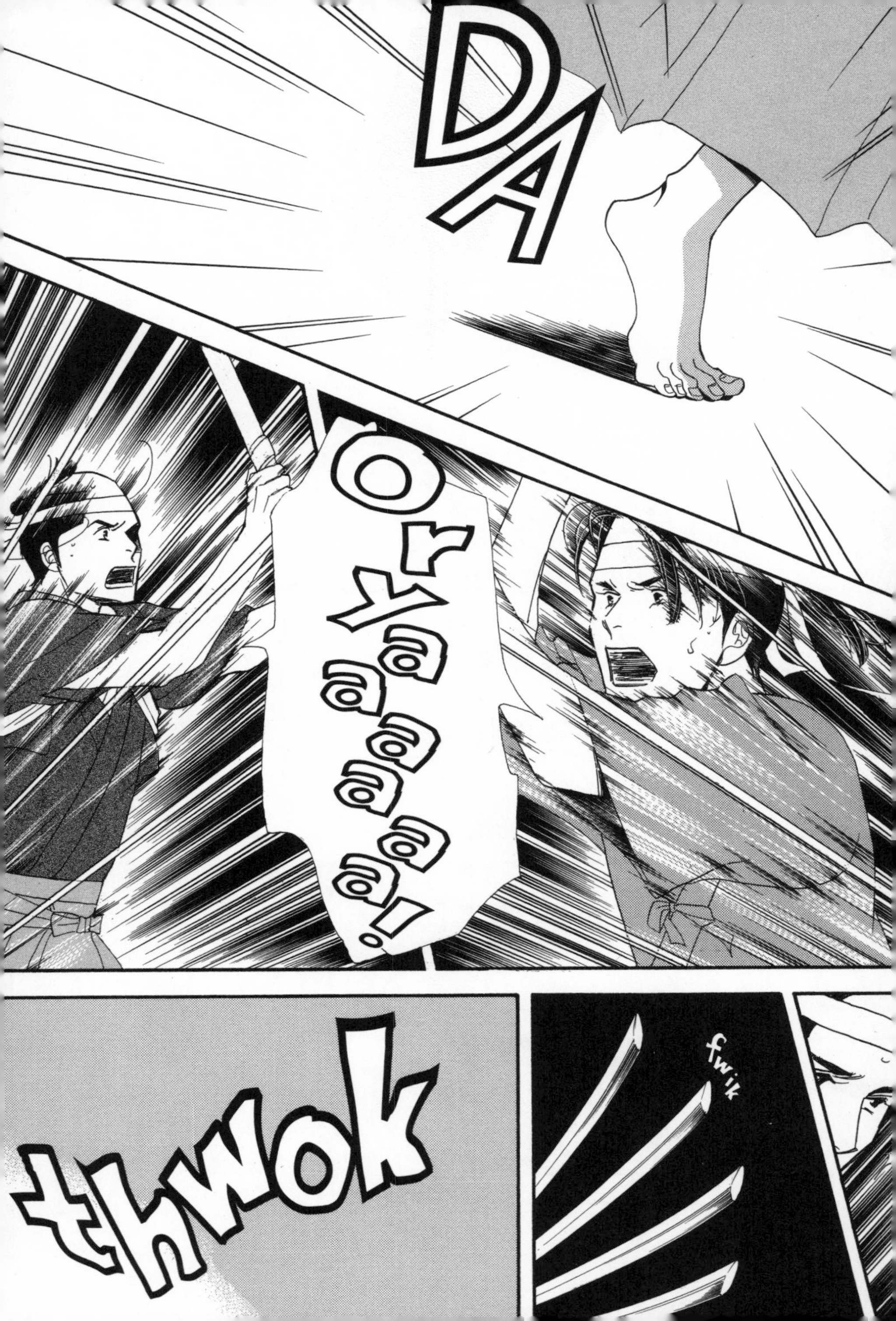
DA
Oryaaaaaaa!
fwik
thwok

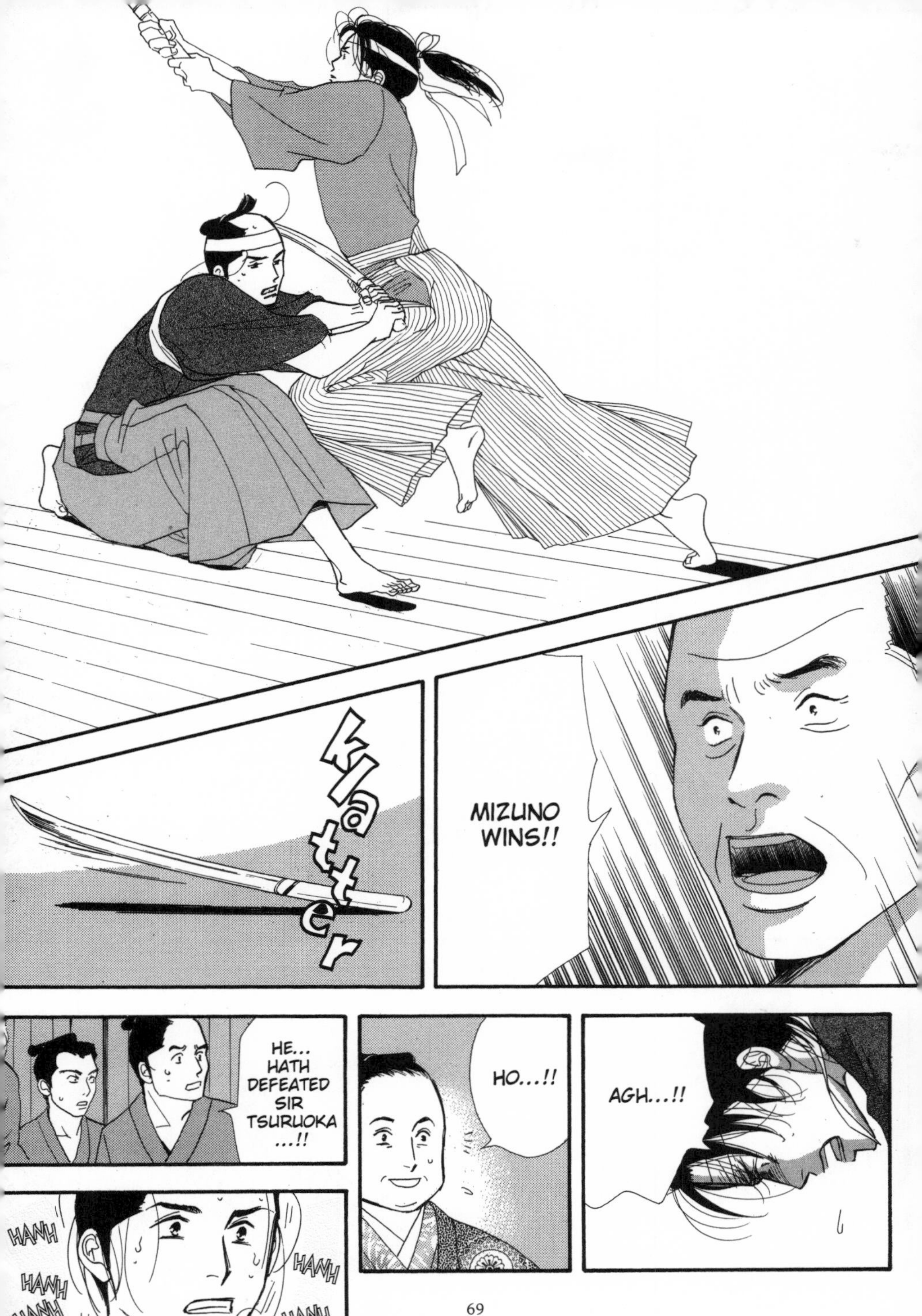
MIZUNO WINS!!
klatter
AGH...!!
HO...!!
HE... HATH DEFEATED SIR TSURUOKA ...!!
HANH HANH HANH HANH HANH HANH

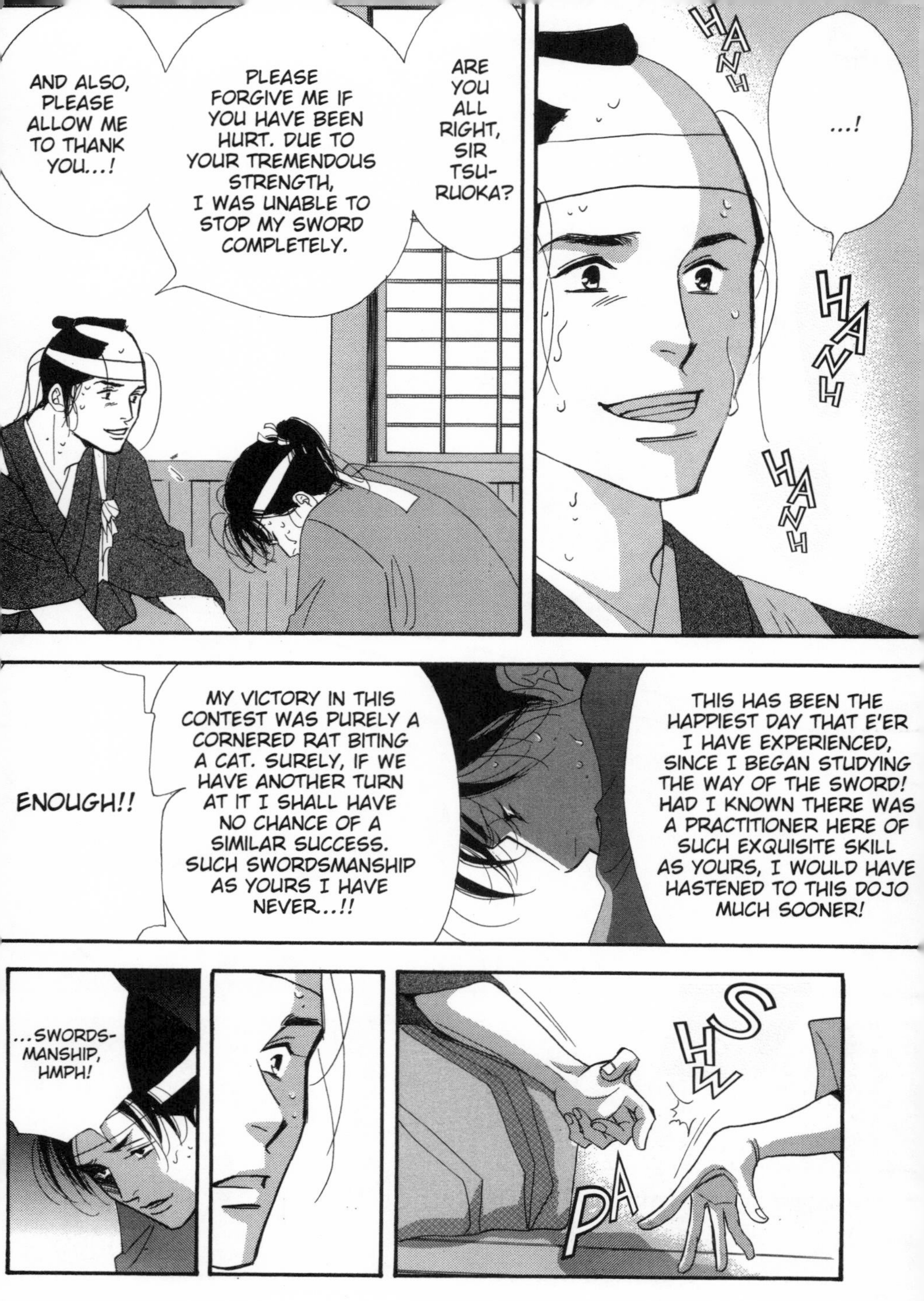
HANH
...!
HANH
HANH
ARE YOU ALL RIGHT, SIR TSU-RUOKA?
PLEASE FORGIVE ME IF YOU HAVE BEEN HURT. DUE TO YOUR TREMENDOUS STRENGTH, I WAS UNABLE TO STOP MY SWORD COMPLETELY.
AND ALSO, PLEASE ALLOW ME TO THANK YOU...!
THIS HAS BEEN THE HAPPIEST DAY THAT E'ER I HAVE EXPERIENCED, SINCE I BEGAN STUDYING THE WAY OF THE SWORD! HAD I KNOWN THERE WAS A PRACTITIONER HERE OF SUCH EXQUISITE SKILL AS YOURS, I WOULD HAVE HASTENED TO THIS DOJO MUCH SOONER!
MY VICTORY IN THIS CONTEST WAS PURELY A CORNERED RAT BITING A CAT. SURELY, IF WE HAVE ANOTHER TURN AT IT I SHALL HAVE NO CHANCE OF A SIMILAR SUCCESS. SUCH SWORDSMANSHIP AS YOURS I HAVE NEVER...!!
ENOUGH!!
SHW
PA
...SWORDS-MANSHIP, HMPH!

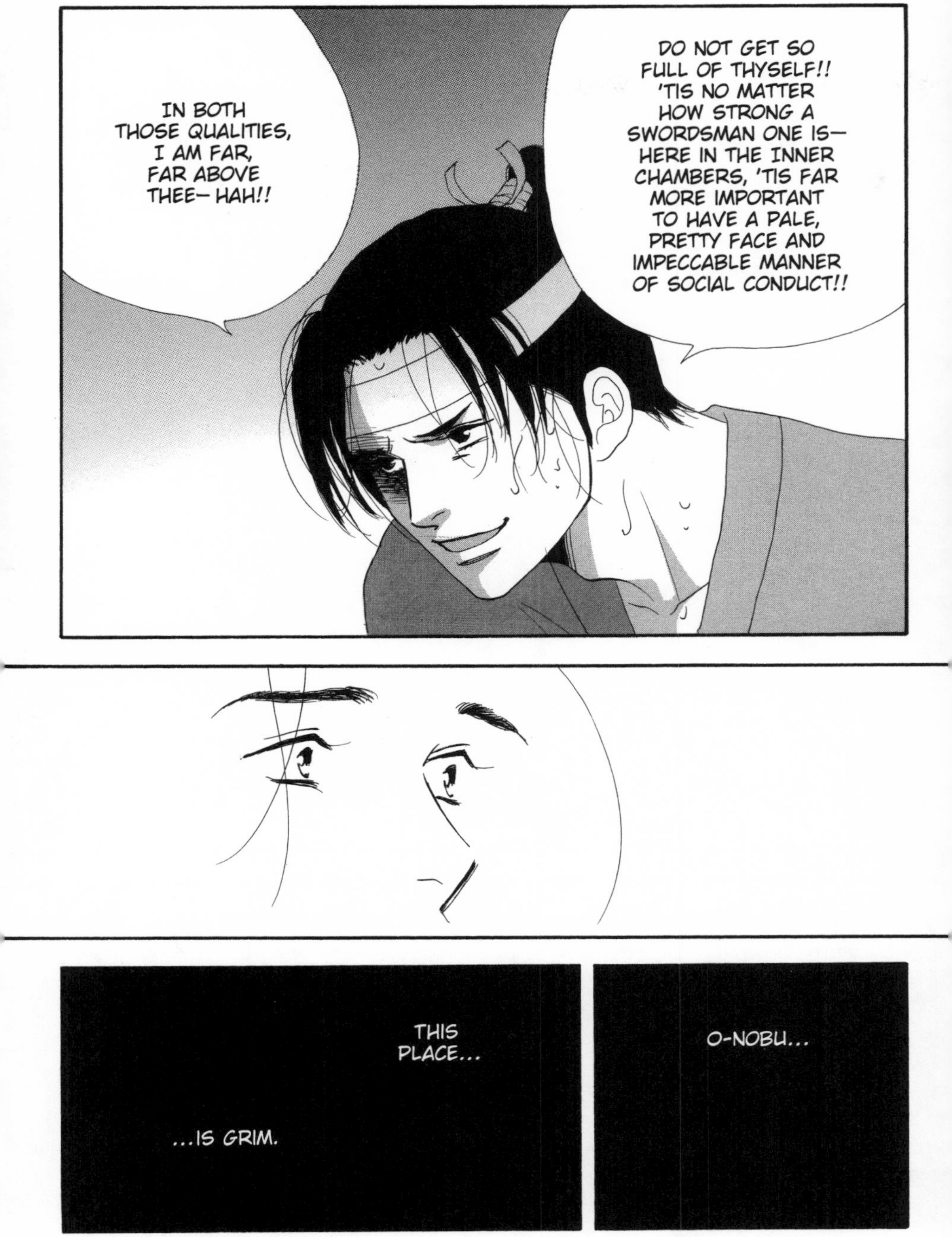
DO NOT GET SO FULL OF THYSELF!! 'TIS NO MATTER HOW STRONG A SWORDSMAN ONE IS— HERE IN THE INNER CHAMBERS, 'TIS FAR MORE IMPORTANT TO HAVE A PALE, PRETTY FACE AND IMPECCABLE MANNER OF SOCIAL CONDUCT!!
IN BOTH THOSE QUALITIES, I AM FAR, FAR ABOVE THEE— HAH!!
O-NOBU...
THIS PLACE...
...IS GRIM.

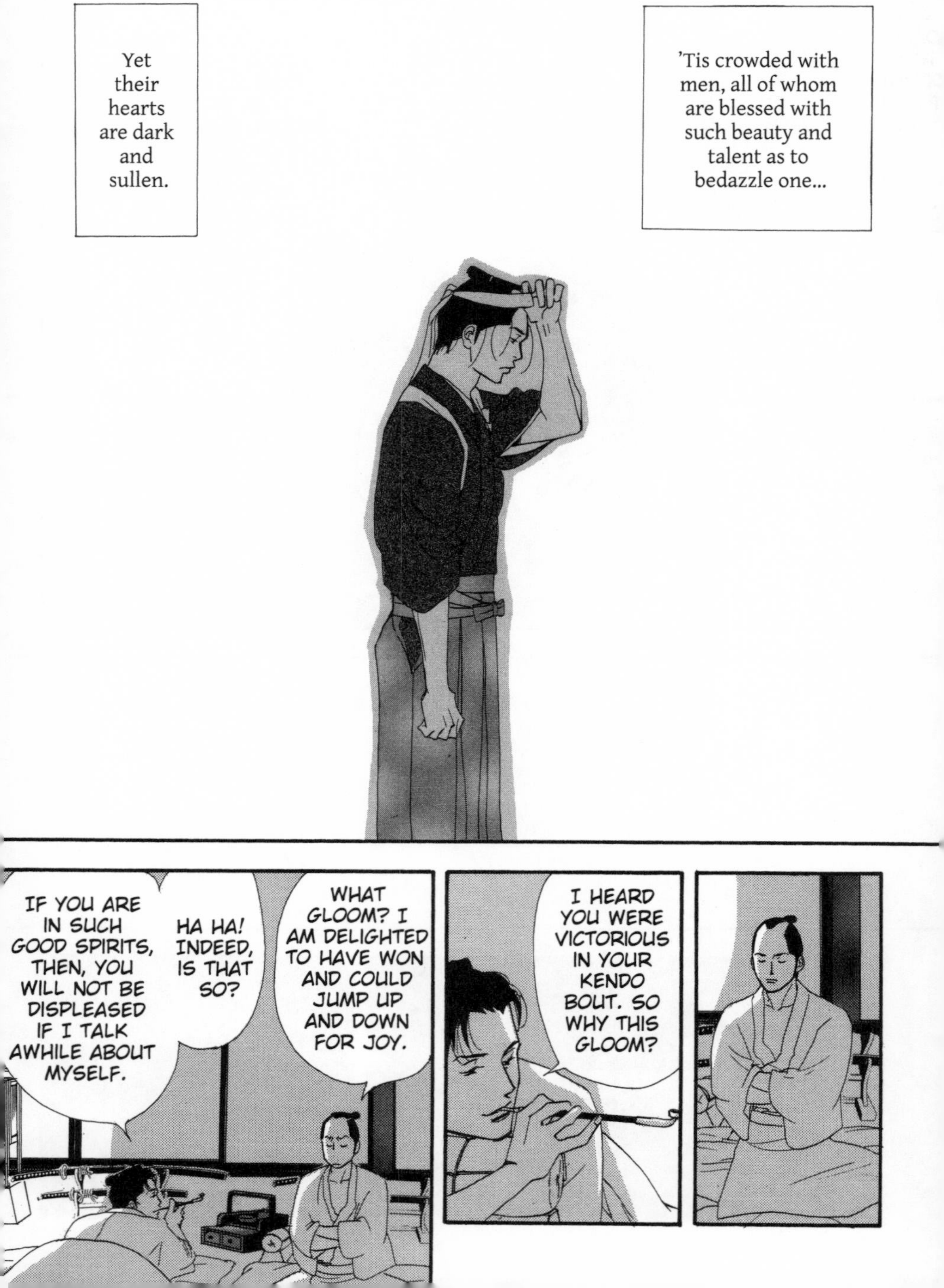
'Tis crowded with men, all of whom are blessed with such beauty and talent as to bedazzle one...
Yet their hearts are dark and sullen.
I HEARD YOU WERE VICTORIOUS IN YOUR KENDO BOUT. SO WHY THIS GLOOM?
WHAT GLOOM? I AM DELIGHTED TO HAVE WON AND COULD JUMP UP AND DOWN FOR JOY.
HA HA! INDEED, IS THAT SO?
IF YOU ARE IN SUCH GOOD SPIRITS, THEN, YOU WILL NOT BE DISPLEASED IF I TALK AWHILE ABOUT MYSELF.

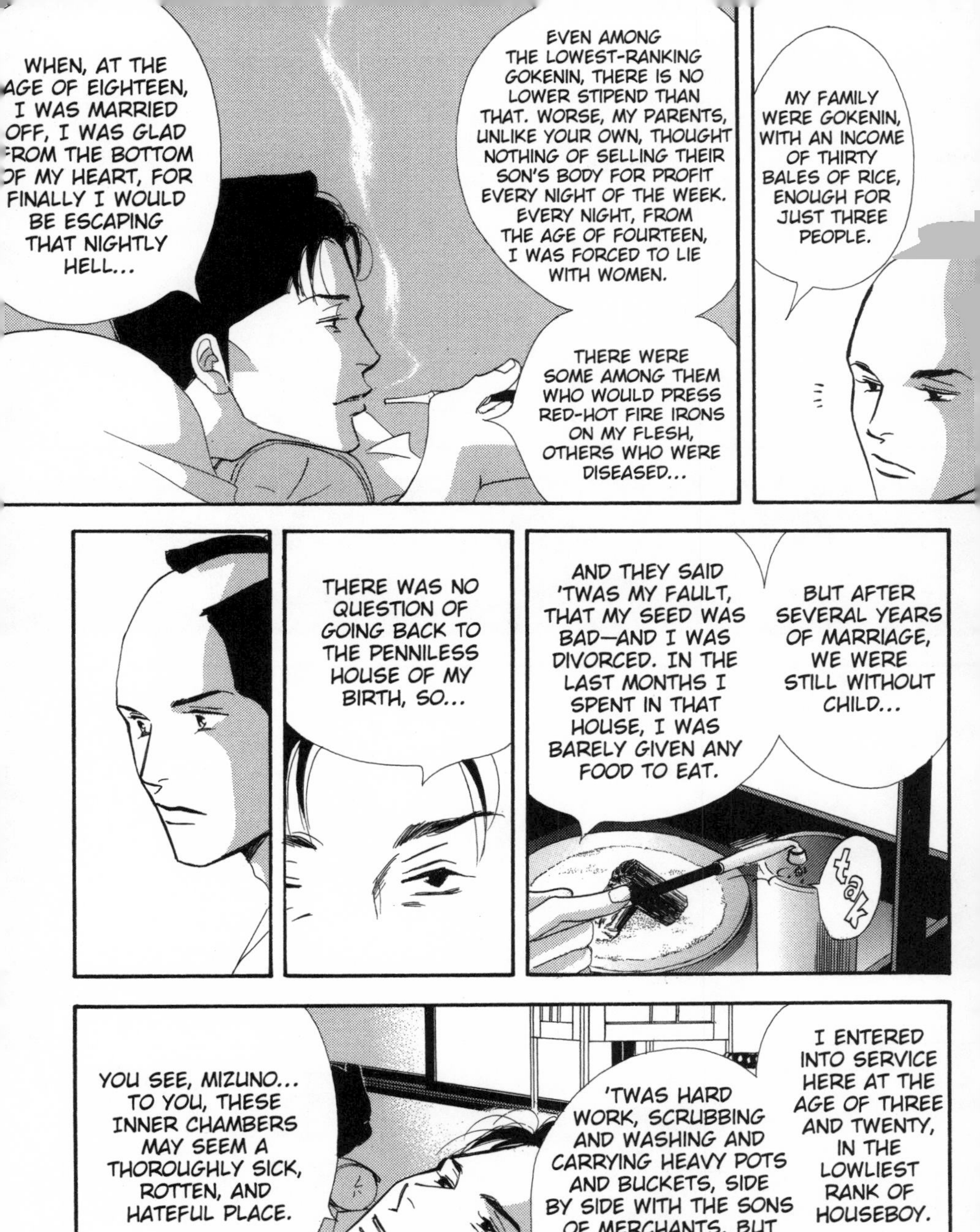
MY FAMILY WERE GOKENIN, WITH AN INCOME OF THIRTY BALES OF RICE, ENOUGH FOR JUST THREE PEOPLE.
EVEN AMONG THE LOWEST-RANKING GOKENIN, THERE IS NO LOWER STIPEND THAN THAT. WORSE, MY PARENTS, UNLIKE YOUR OWN, THOUGHT NOTHING OF SELLING THEIR SON'S BODY FOR PROFIT EVERY NIGHT OF THE WEEK. EVERY NIGHT, FROM THE AGE OF FOURTEEN, I WAS FORCED TO LIE WITH WOMEN.
THERE WERE SOME AMONG THEM WHO WOULD PRESS RED-HOT FIRE IRONS ON MY FLESH, OTHERS WHO WERE DISEASED...
WHEN, AT THE AGE OF EIGHTEEN, I WAS MARRIED OFF, I WAS GLAD FROM THE BOTTOM OF MY HEART, FOR FINALLY I WOULD BE ESCAPING THAT NIGHTLY HELL...
BUT AFTER SEVERAL YEARS OF MARRIAGE, WE WERE STILL WITHOUT CHILD...
AND THEY SAID 'TWAS MY FAULT, THAT MY SEED WAS BAD—AND I WAS DIVORCED. IN THE LAST MONTHS I SPENT IN THAT HOUSE, I WAS BARELY GIVEN ANY FOOD TO EAT.
tak
THERE WAS NO QUESTION OF GOING BACK TO THE PENNILESS HOUSE OF MY BIRTH, SO...
I ENTERED INTO SERVICE HERE AT THE AGE OF THREE AND TWENTY, IN THE LOWLIEST RANK OF HOUSEBOY.
'TWAS HARD WORK, SCRUBBING AND WASHING AND CARRYING HEAVY POTS AND BUCKETS, SIDE BY SIDE WITH THE SONS OF MERCHANTS. BUT NEITHER THAT, NOR BEING VIOLATED BY THOSE ABOVE ME, DID PAIN ME MUCH ANY LONGER.
YOU SEE, MIZUNO... TO YOU, THESE INNER CHAMBERS MAY SEEM A THOROUGHLY SICK, ROTTEN, AND HATEFUL PLACE.

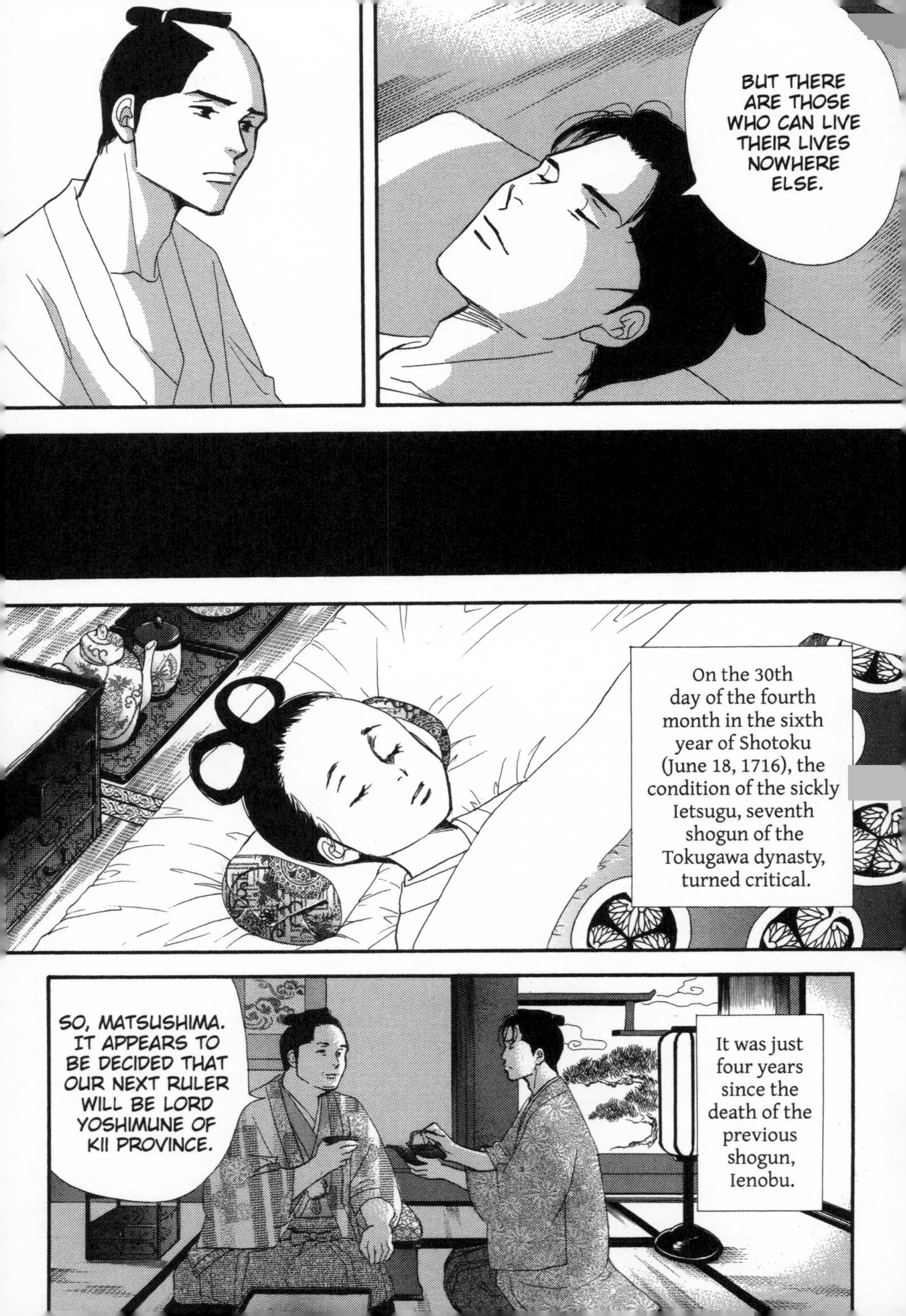
BUT THERE ARE THOSE WHO CAN LIVE THEIR LIVES NOWHERE ELSE.
On the 30th day of the fourth month in the sixth year of Shotoku (June 18, 1716), the condition of the sickly Ietsugu, seventh shogun of the Tokugawa dynasty, turned critical.
It was just four years since the death of the previous shogun, Ienobu.
SO, MATSUSHIMA. IT APPEARS TO BE DECIDED THAT OUR NEXT RULER WILL BE LORD YOSHIMUNE OF KII PROVINCE.

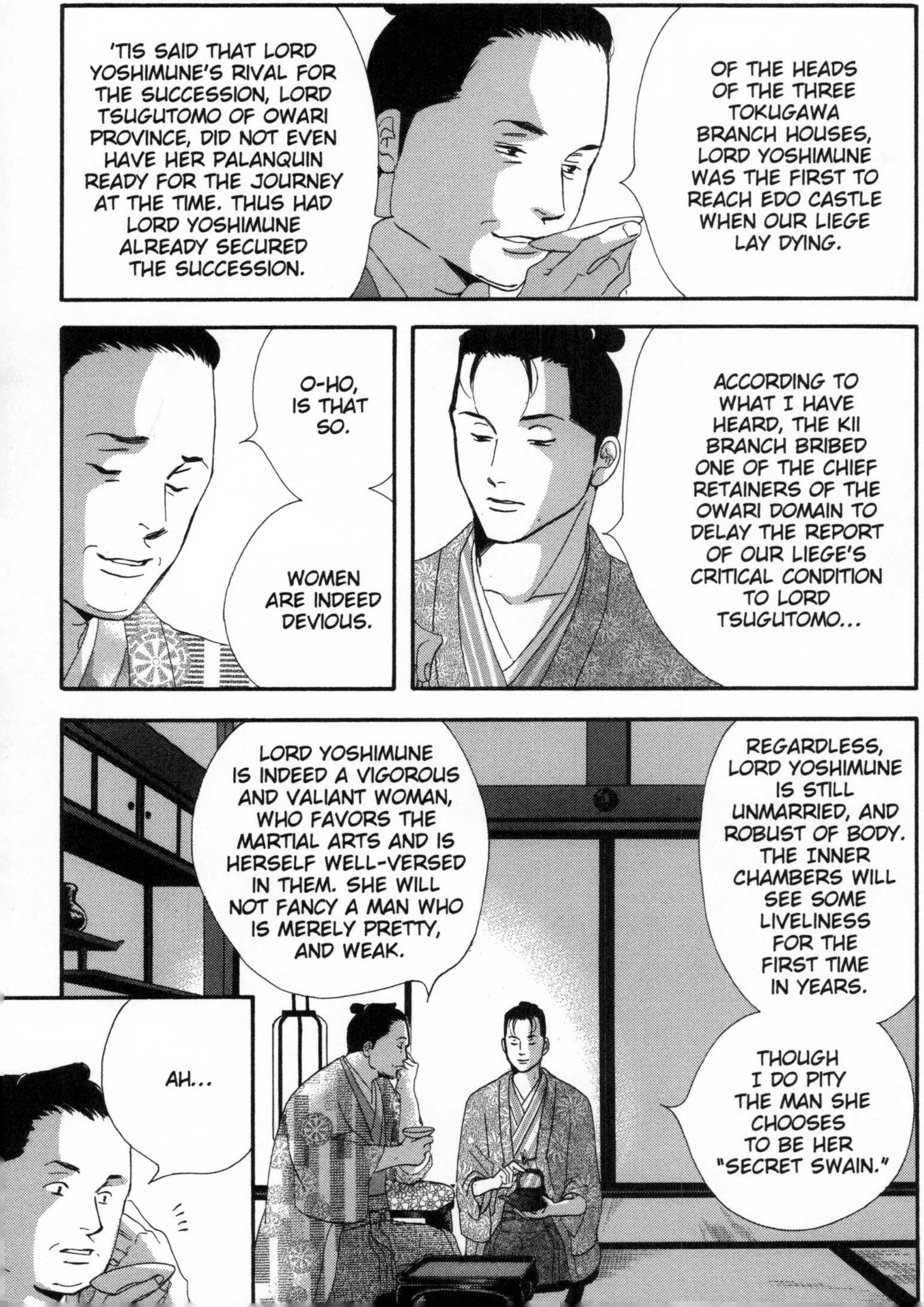
OF THE HEADS OF THE THREE TOKUGAWA BRANCH HOUSES, LORD YOSHIMUNE WAS THE FIRST TO REACH EDO CASTLE WHEN OUR LIEGE LAY DYING.
'TIS SAID THAT LORD YOSHIMUNE'S RIVAL FOR THE SUCCESSION, LORD TSUGUTOMO OF OWARI PROVINCE, DID NOT EVEN HAVE HER PALANQUIN READY FOR THE JOURNEY AT THE TIME. THUS HAD LORD YOSHIMUNE ALREADY SECURED THE SUCCESSION.
ACCORDING TO WHAT I HAVE HEARD, THE KII BRANCH BRIBED ONE OF THE CHIEF RETAINERS OF THE OWARI DOMAIN TO DELAY THE REPORT OF OUR LIEGE'S CRITICAL CONDITION TO LORD TSUGUTOMO...
O-HO, IS THAT SO.
WOMEN ARE INDEED DEVIOUS.
REGARDLESS, LORD YOSHIMUNE IS STILL UNMARRIED, AND ROBUST OF BODY. THE INNER CHAMBERS WILL SEE SOME LIVELINESS FOR THE FIRST TIME IN YEARS.
THOUGH I DO PITY THE MAN SHE CHOOSES TO BE HER "SECRET SWAIN."
LORD YOSHIMUNE IS INDEED A VIGOROUS AND VALIANT WOMAN, WHO FAVORS THE MARTIAL ARTS AND IS HERSELF WELL-VERSED IN THEM. SHE WILL NOT FANCY A MAN WHO IS MERELY PRETTY, AND WEAK.
AH...

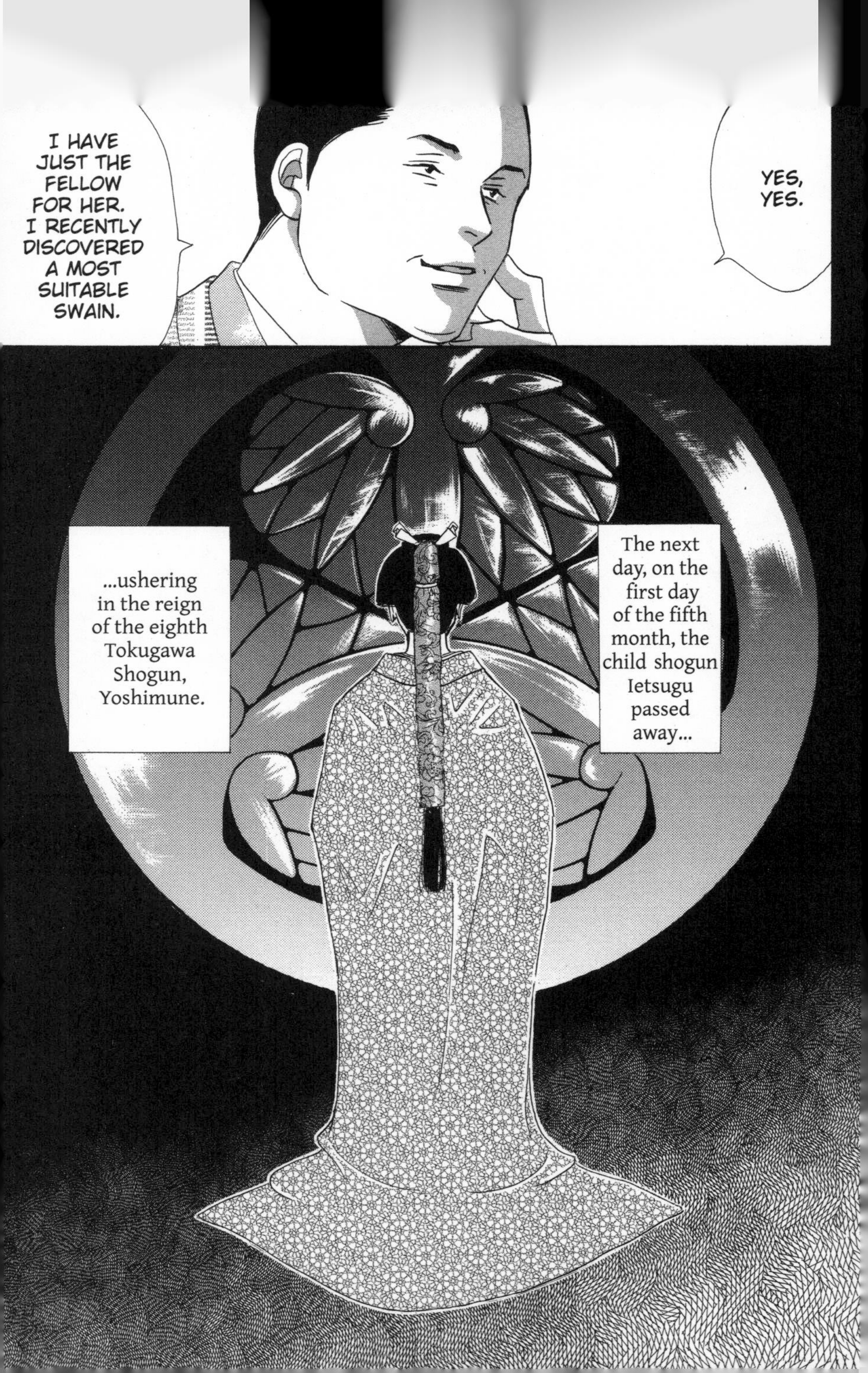
YES, YES.
I HAVE JUST THE FELLOW FOR HER. I RECENTLY DISCOVERED A MOST SUITABLE SWAIN.
The next day, on the first day of the fifth month, the child shogun Ietsugu passed away...
...ushering in the reign of the eighth Tokugawa Shogun, Yoshimune.

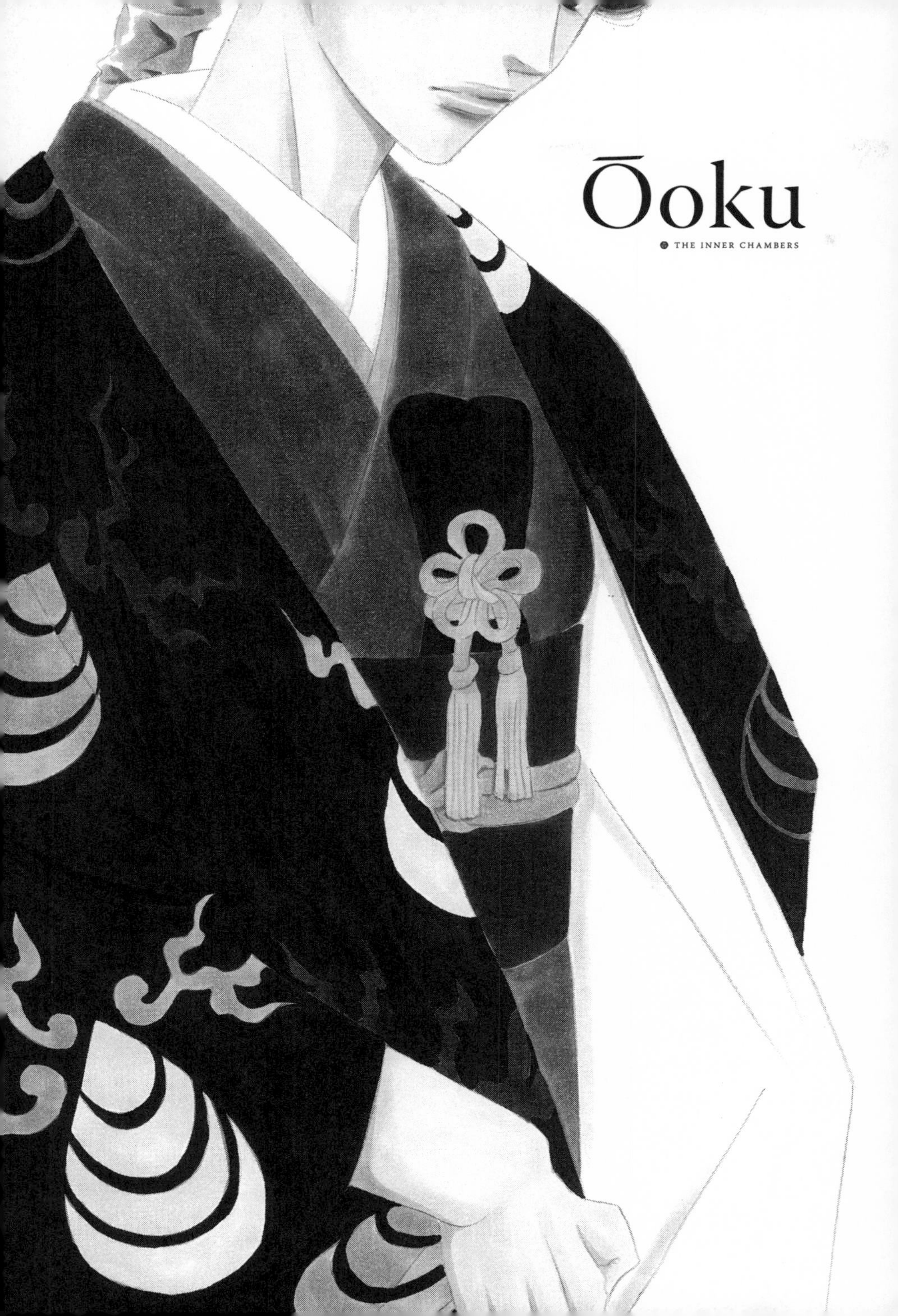
Ōoku
THE INNER CHAMBERS

Ōoku

THE INNER CHAMBERS

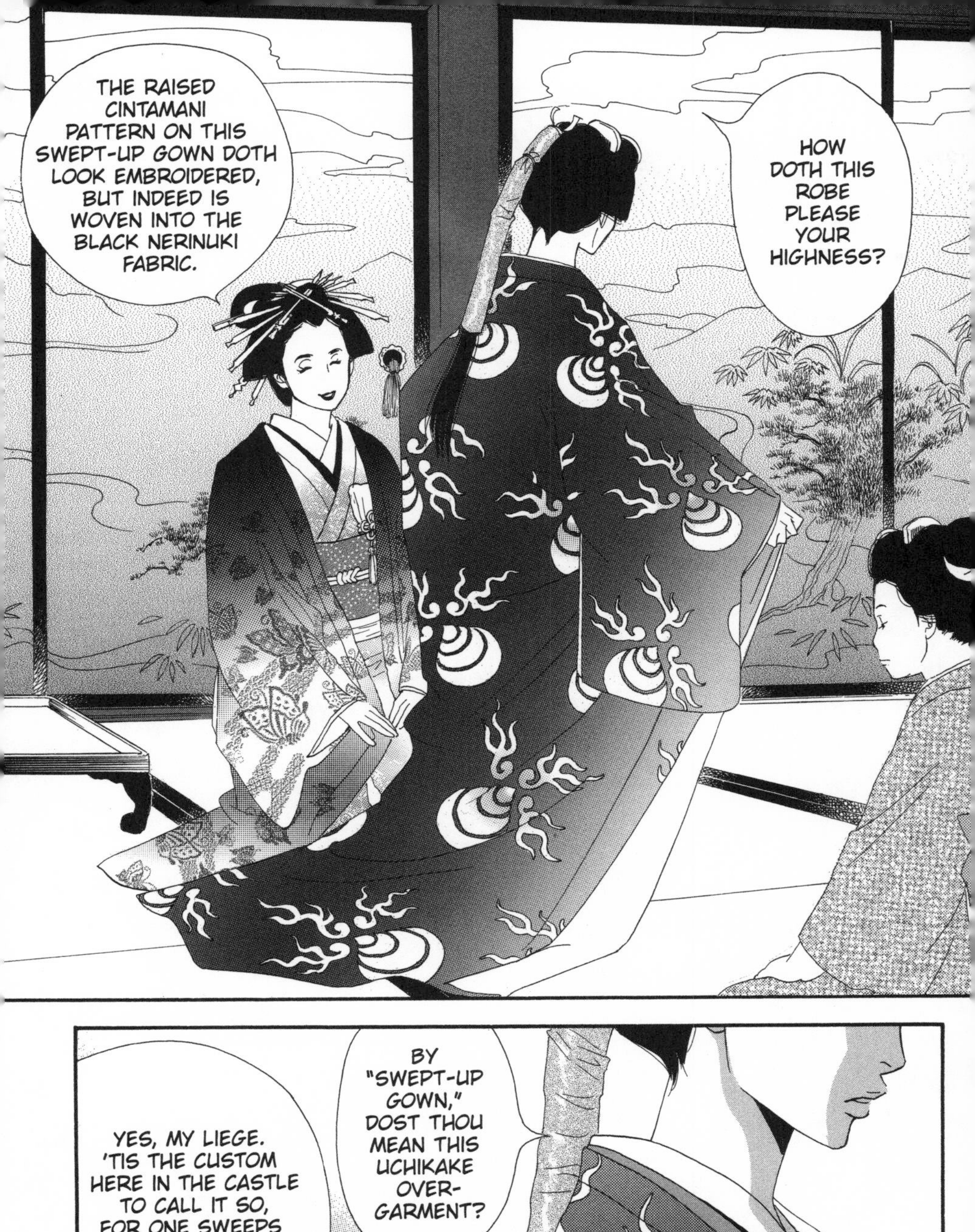
HOW DOTH THIS ROBE PLEASE YOUR HIGHNESS?
THE RAISED CINTAMANI PATTERN ON THIS SWEPT-UP GOWN DOTH LOOK EMBROIDERED, BUT INDEED IS WOVEN INTO THE BLACK NERINUKI FABRIC.
BY "SWEPT-UP GOWN," DOST THOU MEAN THIS UCHIKAKE OVER-GARMENT?
YES, MY LIEGE. 'TIS THE CUSTOM HERE IN THE CASTLE TO CALL IT SO, FOR ONE SWEEPS UP THE HEM OF IT WITH ONE'S HANDS WHEN WALKING.

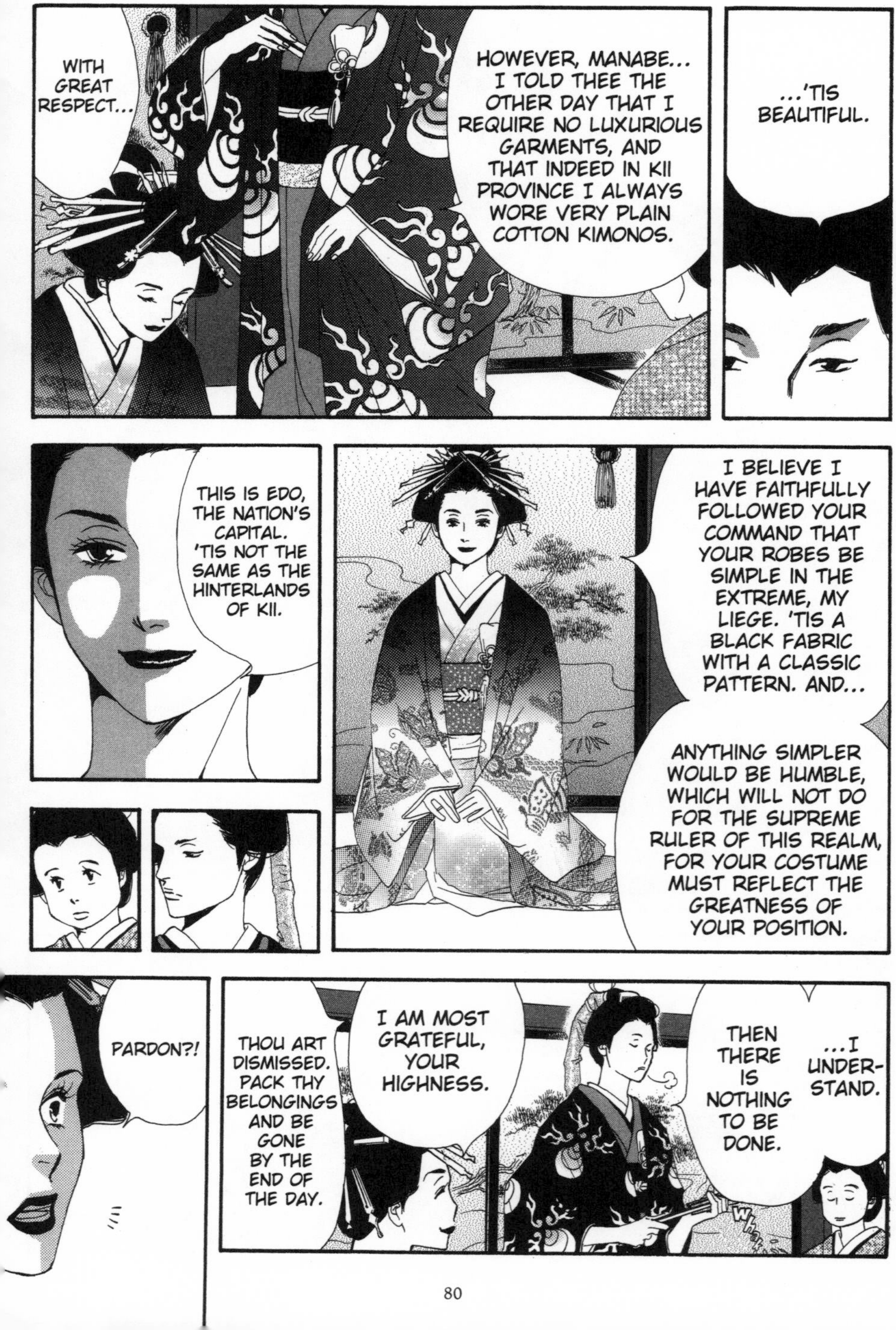
...'TIS BEAUTIFUL.
HOWEVER, MANABE... I TOLD THEE THE OTHER DAY THAT I REQUIRE NO LUXURIOUS GARMENTS, AND THAT INDEED IN KII PROVINCE I ALWAYS WORE VERY PLAIN COTTON KIMONOS.
WITH GREAT RESPECT...
I BELIEVE I HAVE FAITHFULLY FOLLOWED YOUR COMMAND THAT YOUR ROBES BE SIMPLE IN THE EXTREME, MY LIEGE. 'TIS A BLACK FABRIC WITH A CLASSIC PATTERN. AND...
ANYTHING SIMPLER WOULD BE HUMBLE, WHICH WILL NOT DO FOR THE SUPREME RULER OF THIS REALM, FOR YOUR COSTUME MUST REFLECT THE GREATNESS OF YOUR POSITION.
THIS IS EDO, THE NATION'S CAPITAL. 'TIS NOT THE SAME AS THE HINTERLANDS OF KII.
...I UNDERSTAND.
THEN THERE IS NOTHING TO BE DONE.
I AM MOST GRATEFUL, YOUR HIGHNESS.
THOU ART DISMISSED. PACK THY BELONGINGS AND BE GONE BY THE END OF THE DAY.
PARDON?!

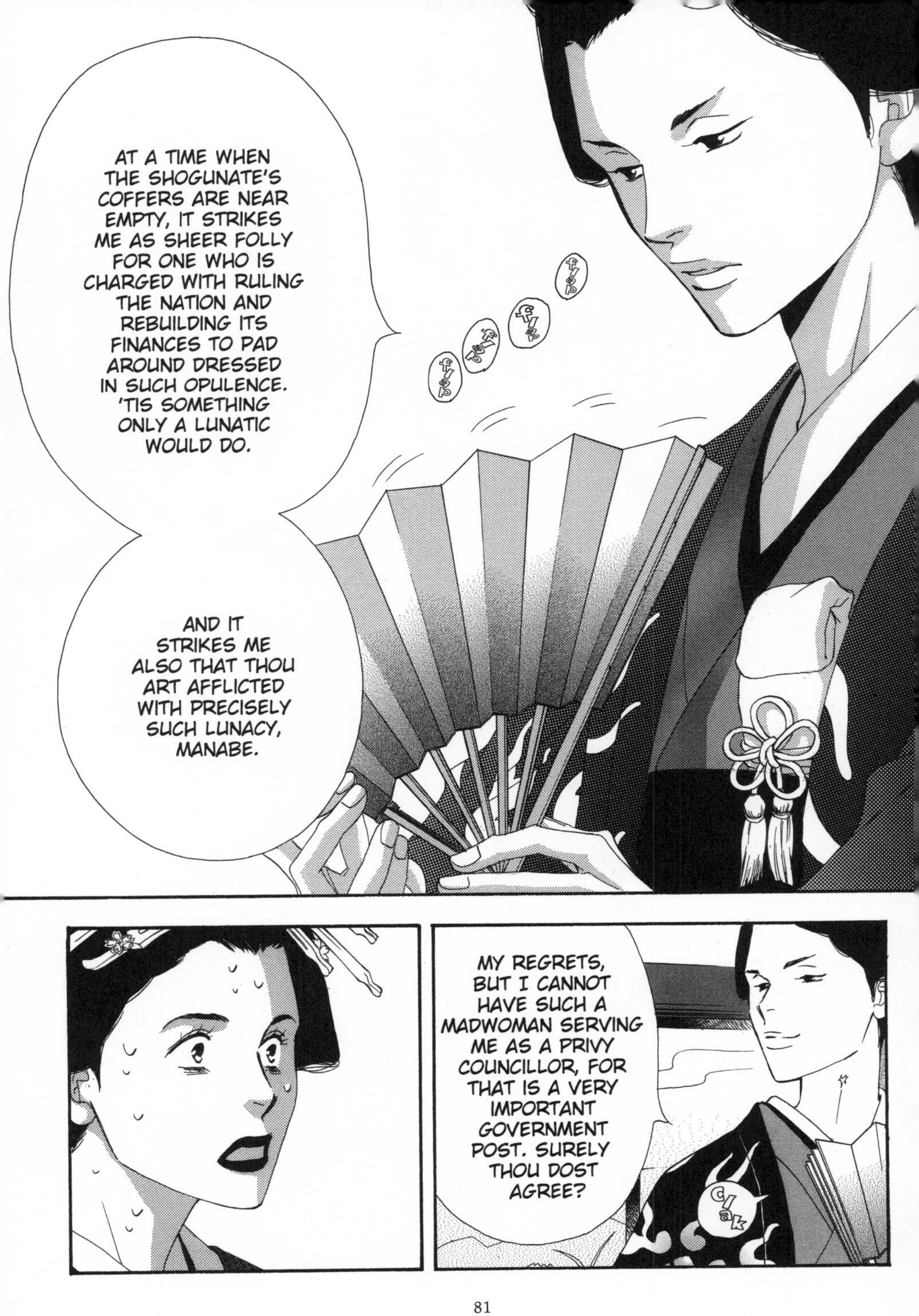
AT A TIME WHEN THE SHOGUNATE'S COFFERS ARE NEAR EMPTY, IT STRIKES ME AS SHEER FOLLY FOR ONE WHO IS CHARGED WITH RULING THE NATION AND REBUILDING ITS FINANCES TO PAD AROUND DRESSED IN SUCH OPULENCE. 'TIS SOMETHING ONLY A LUNATIC WOULD DO.
flap flap flap flap
AND IT STRIKES ME ALSO THAT THOU ART AFFLICTED WITH PRECISELY SUCH LUNACY, MANABE.
MY REGRETS, BUT I CANNOT HAVE SUCH A MADWOMAN SERVING ME AS A PRIVY COUNCILLOR, FOR THAT IS A VERY IMPORTANT GOVERNMENT POST. SURELY THOU DOST AGREE?
clak

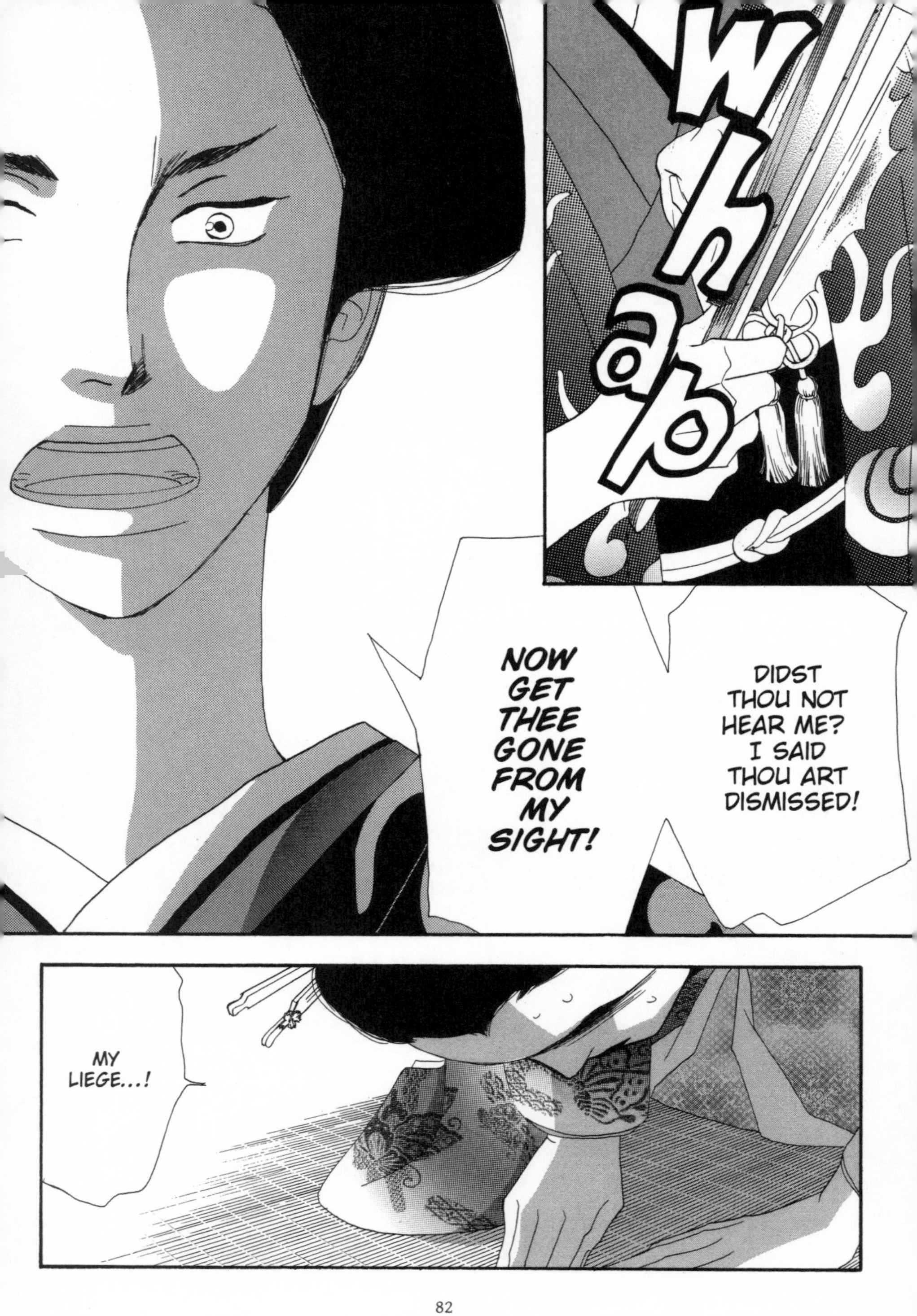
WHAP
DIDST THOU NOT HEAR ME? I SAID THOU ART DISMISSED!
NOW GET THEE GONE FROM MY SIGHT!
MY LIEGE...!

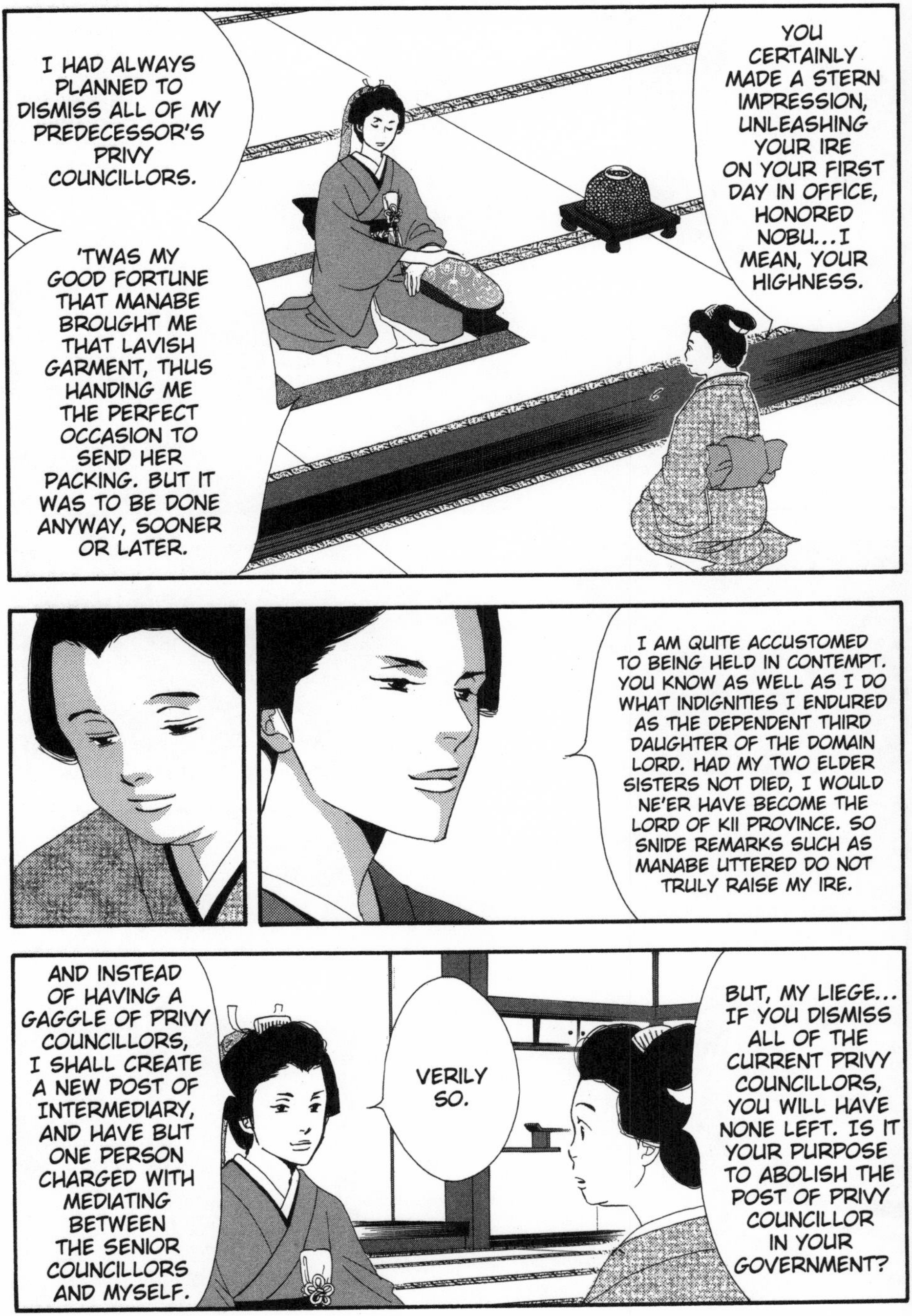
YOU CERTAINLY MADE A STERN IMPRESSION, UNLEASHING YOUR IRE ON YOUR FIRST DAY IN OFFICE, HONORED NOBU...I MEAN, YOUR HIGHNESS.
I HAD ALWAYS PLANNED TO DISMISS ALL OF MY PREDECESSOR'S PRIVY COUNCILLORS.
'TWAS MY GOOD FORTUNE THAT MANABE BROUGHT ME THAT LAVISH GARMENT, THUS HANDING ME THE PERFECT OCCASION TO SEND HER PACKING. BUT IT WAS TO BE DONE ANYWAY, SOONER OR LATER.
I AM QUITE ACCUSTOMED TO BEING HELD IN CONTEMPT. YOU KNOW AS WELL AS I DO WHAT INDIGNITIES I ENDURED AS THE DEPENDENT THIRD DAUGHTER OF THE DOMAIN LORD. HAD MY TWO ELDER SISTERS NOT DIED, I WOULD NE'ER HAVE BECOME THE LORD OF KII PROVINCE. SO SNIDE REMARKS SUCH AS MANABE UTTERED DO NOT TRULY RAISE MY IRE.
BUT, MY LIEGE... IF YOU DISMISS ALL OF THE CURRENT PRIVY COUNCILLORS, YOU WILL HAVE NONE LEFT. IS IT YOUR PURPOSE TO ABOLISH THE POST OF PRIVY COUNCILLOR IN YOUR GOVERNMENT?
VERILY SO.
AND INSTEAD OF HAVING A GAGGLE OF PRIVY COUNCILLORS, I SHALL CREATE A NEW POST OF INTERMEDIARY, AND HAVE BUT ONE PERSON CHARGED WITH MEDIATING BETWEEN THE SENIOR COUNCILLORS AND MYSELF.

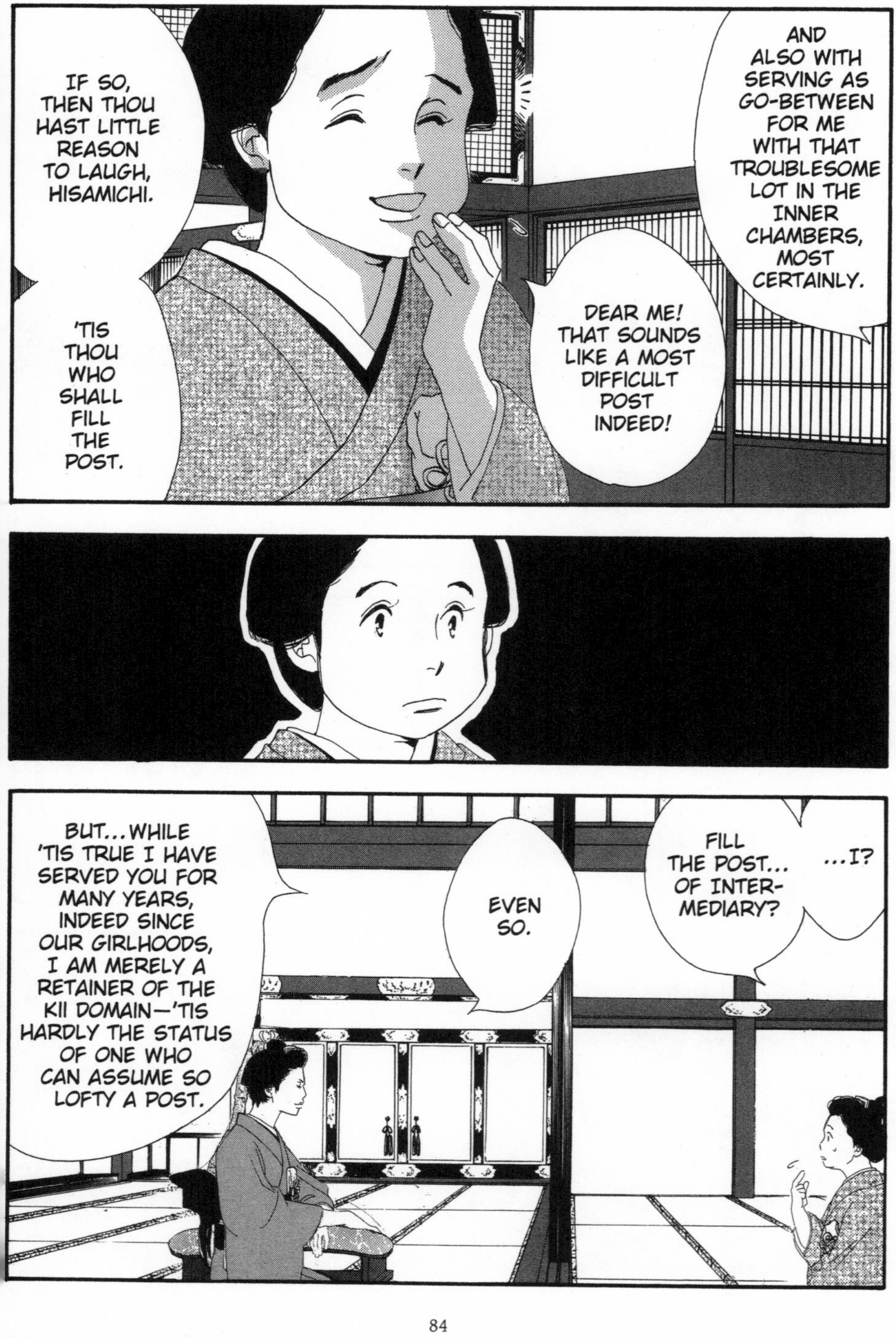
AND ALSO WITH SERVING AS GO-BETWEEN FOR ME WITH THAT TROUBLESOME LOT IN THE INNER CHAMBERS, MOST CERTAINLY.
DEAR ME! THAT SOUNDS LIKE A MOST DIFFICULT POST INDEED!
IF SO, THEN THOU HAST LITTLE REASON TO LAUGH, HISAMICHI.
'TIS THOU WHO SHALL FILL THE POST.
...I?
FILL THE POST... OF INTER-MEDIARY?
EVEN SO.
BUT...WHILE 'TIS TRUE I HAVE SERVED YOU FOR MANY YEARS, INDEED SINCE OUR GIRLHOODS, I AM MERELY A RETAINER OF THE KII DOMAIN—'TIS HARDLY THE STATUS OF ONE WHO CAN ASSUME SO LOFTY A POST.

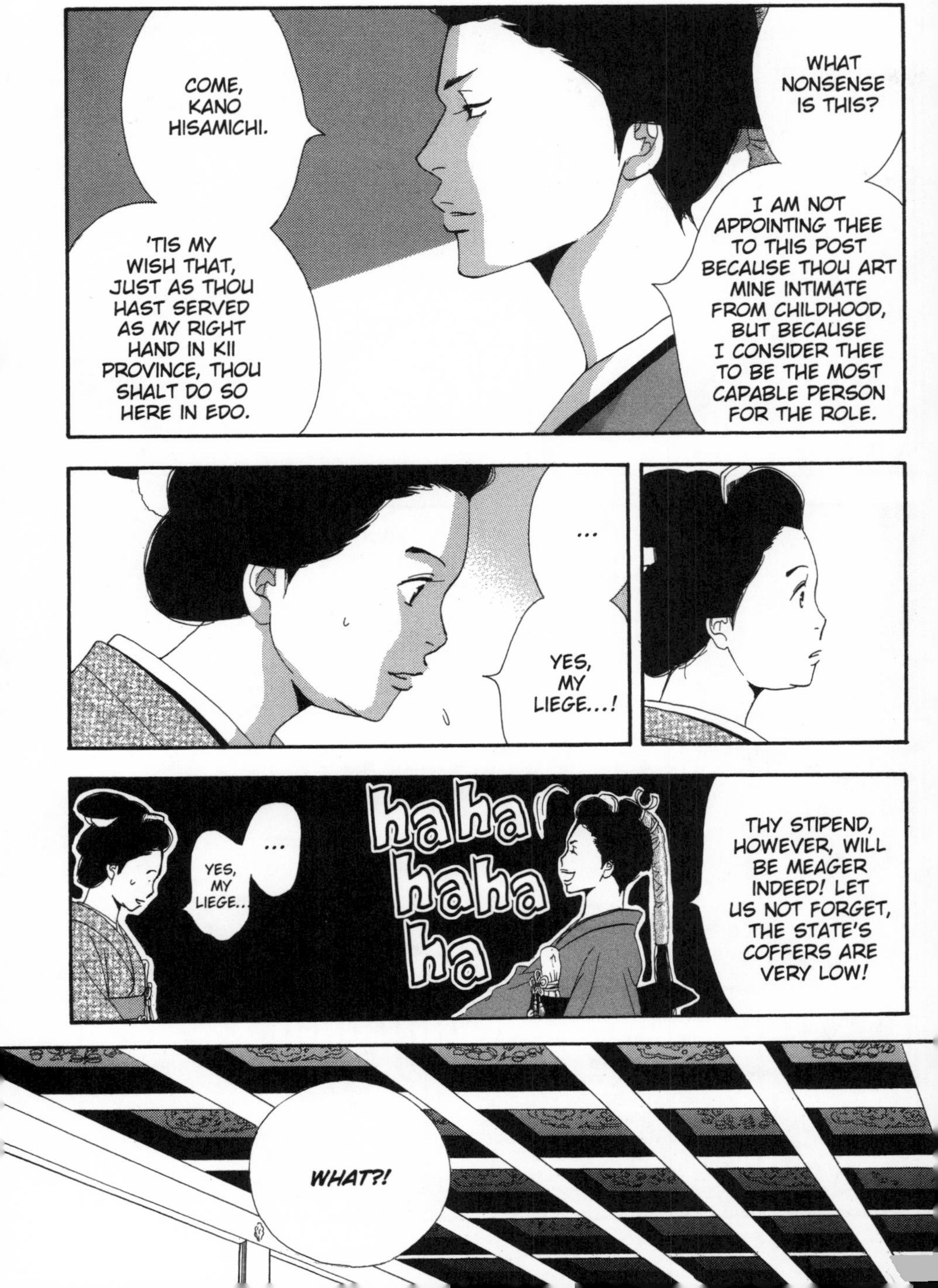
WHAT NONSENSE IS THIS?
I AM NOT APPOINTING THEE TO THIS POST BECAUSE THOU ART MINE INTIMATE FROM CHILDHOOD, BUT BECAUSE I CONSIDER THEE TO BE THE MOST CAPABLE PERSON FOR THE ROLE.
COME, KANO HISAMICHI.
'TIS MY WISH THAT, JUST AS THOU HAST SERVED AS MY RIGHT HAND IN KII PROVINCE, THOU SHALT DO SO HERE IN EDO.
...
YES, MY LIEGE...!
THY STIPEND, HOWEVER, WILL BE MEAGER INDEED! LET US NOT FORGET, THE STATE'S COFFERS ARE VERY LOW!
haha haha ha
...
YES, MY LIEGE...
WHAT?!

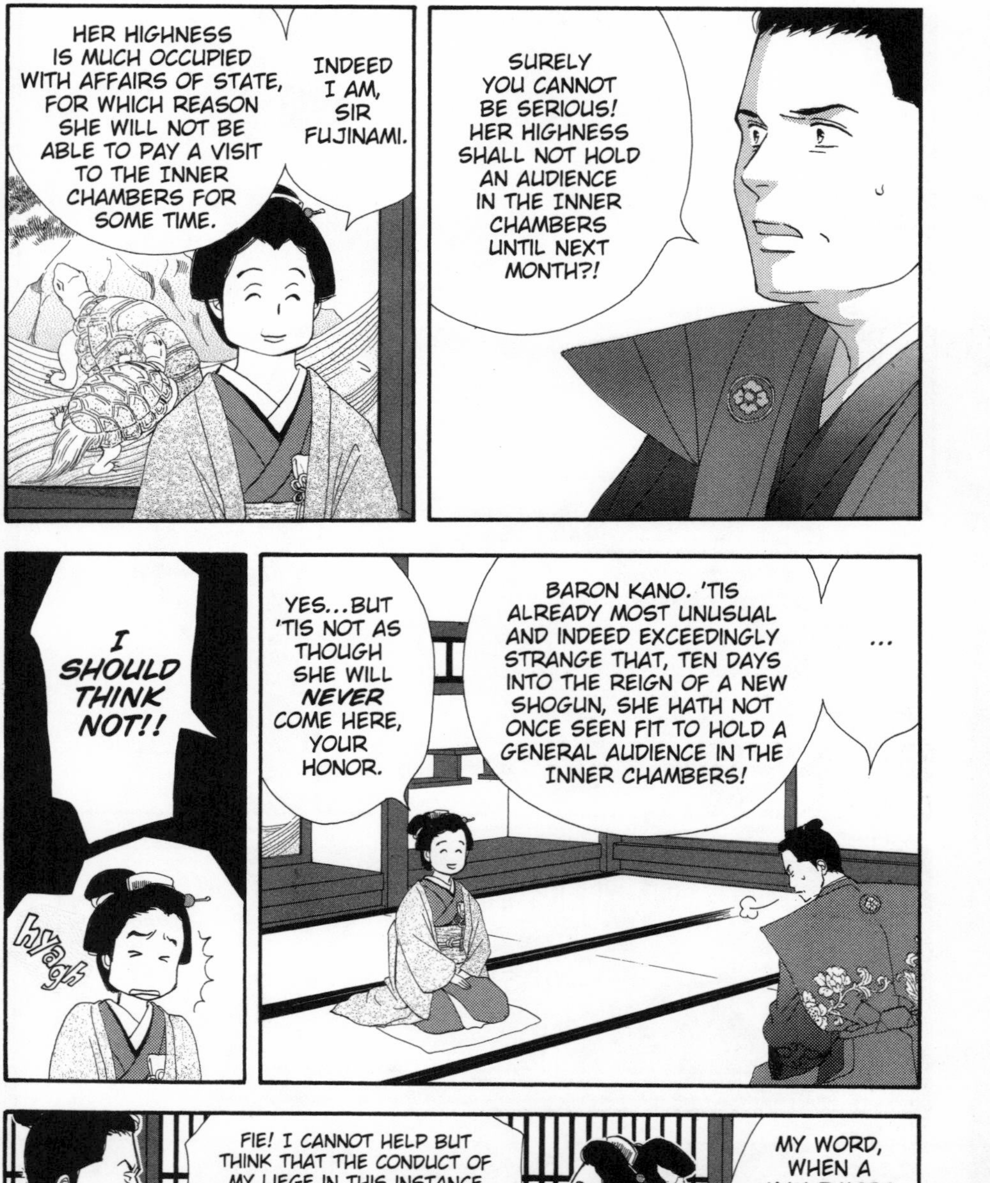
SURELY YOU CANNOT BE SERIOUS! HER HIGHNESS SHALL NOT HOLD AN AUDIENCE IN THE INNER CHAMBERS UNTIL NEXT MONTH?!
INDEED I AM, SIR FUJINAMI.
HER HIGHNESS IS MUCH OCCUPIED WITH AFFAIRS OF STATE, FOR WHICH REASON SHE WILL NOT BE ABLE TO PAY A VISIT TO THE INNER CHAMBERS FOR SOME TIME.
...
BARON KANO. 'TIS ALREADY MOST UNUSUAL AND INDEED EXCEEDINGLY STRANGE THAT, TEN DAYS INTO THE REIGN OF A NEW SHOGUN, SHE HATH NOT ONCE SEEN FIT TO HOLD A GENERAL AUDIENCE IN THE INNER CHAMBERS!
YES...BUT 'TIS NOT AS THOUGH SHE WILL NEVER COME HERE, YOUR HONOR.
I SHOULD THINK NOT!!
hyagh
MY WORD, WHEN A MAN RAISES HIS VOICE, 'TIS SO LOUD AND DEEP AS TO BE QUITE FRIGHTENING.
FIE! I CANNOT HELP BUT THINK THAT THE CONDUCT OF MY LIEGE IN THIS INSTANCE BETRAYS SCORN FOR THE INNER CHAMBERS! FOR ONE THING, I AM OF HIGH ENOUGH RANK TO BE ALLOWED A PERSONAL INTERVIEW, NOT DEAL WITH AN INTERMEDIARY!

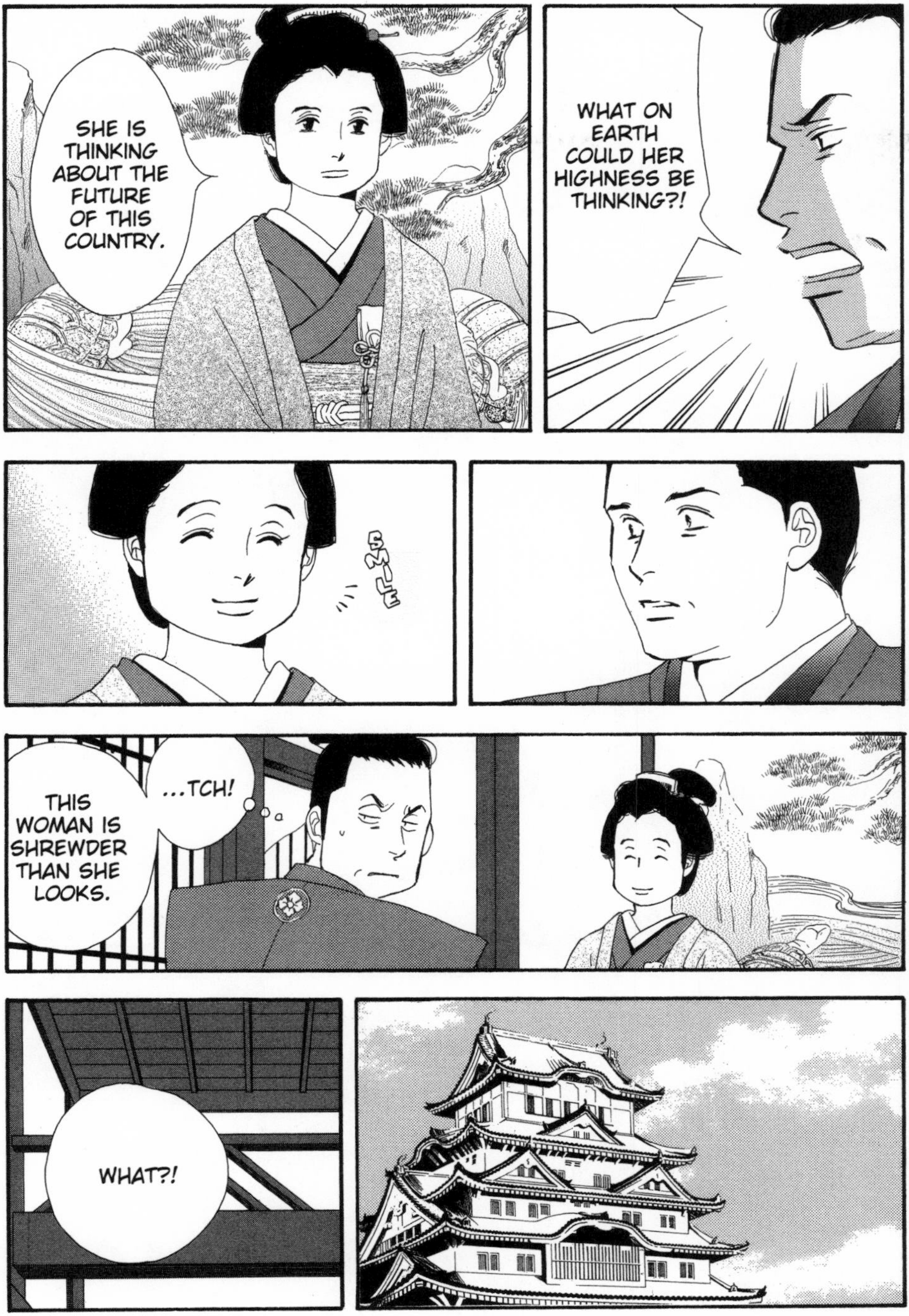
WHAT ON EARTH COULD HER HIGHNESS BE THINKING?!
SHE IS THINKING ABOUT THE FUTURE OF THIS COUNTRY.
SMILE
...TCH!
THIS WOMAN IS SHREWDER THAN SHE LOOKS.
WHAT?!

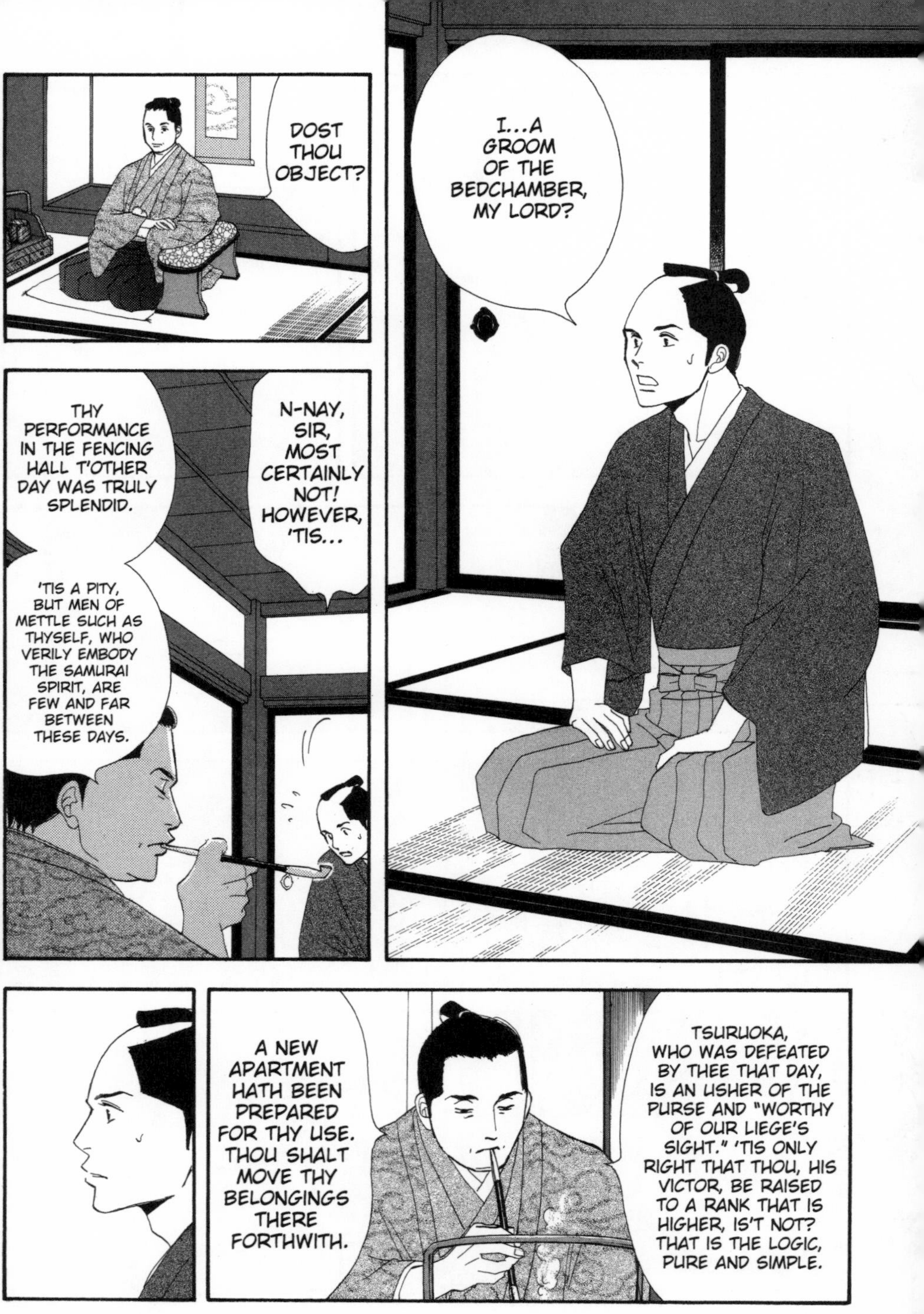
I...A GROOM OF THE BEDCHAMBER, MY LORD?
DOST THOU OBJECT?
N-NAY, SIR, MOST CERTAINLY NOT! HOWEVER, 'TIS...
THY PERFORMANCE IN THE FENCING HALL T'OTHER DAY WAS TRULY SPLENDID.
'TIS A PITY, BUT MEN OF METTLE SUCH AS THYSELF, WHO VERILY EMBODY THE SAMURAI SPIRIT, ARE FEW AND FAR BETWEEN THESE DAYS.
TSURUOKA, WHO WAS DEFEATED BY THEE THAT DAY, IS AN USHER OF THE PURSE AND "WORTHY OF OUR LIEGE'S SIGHT." 'TIS ONLY RIGHT THAT THOU, HIS VICTOR, BE RAISED TO A RANK THAT IS HIGHER, IS'T NOT? THAT IS THE LOGIC, PURE AND SIMPLE.
A NEW APARTMENT HATH BEEN PREPARED FOR THY USE. THOU SHALT MOVE THY BELONGINGS THERE FORTHWITH.

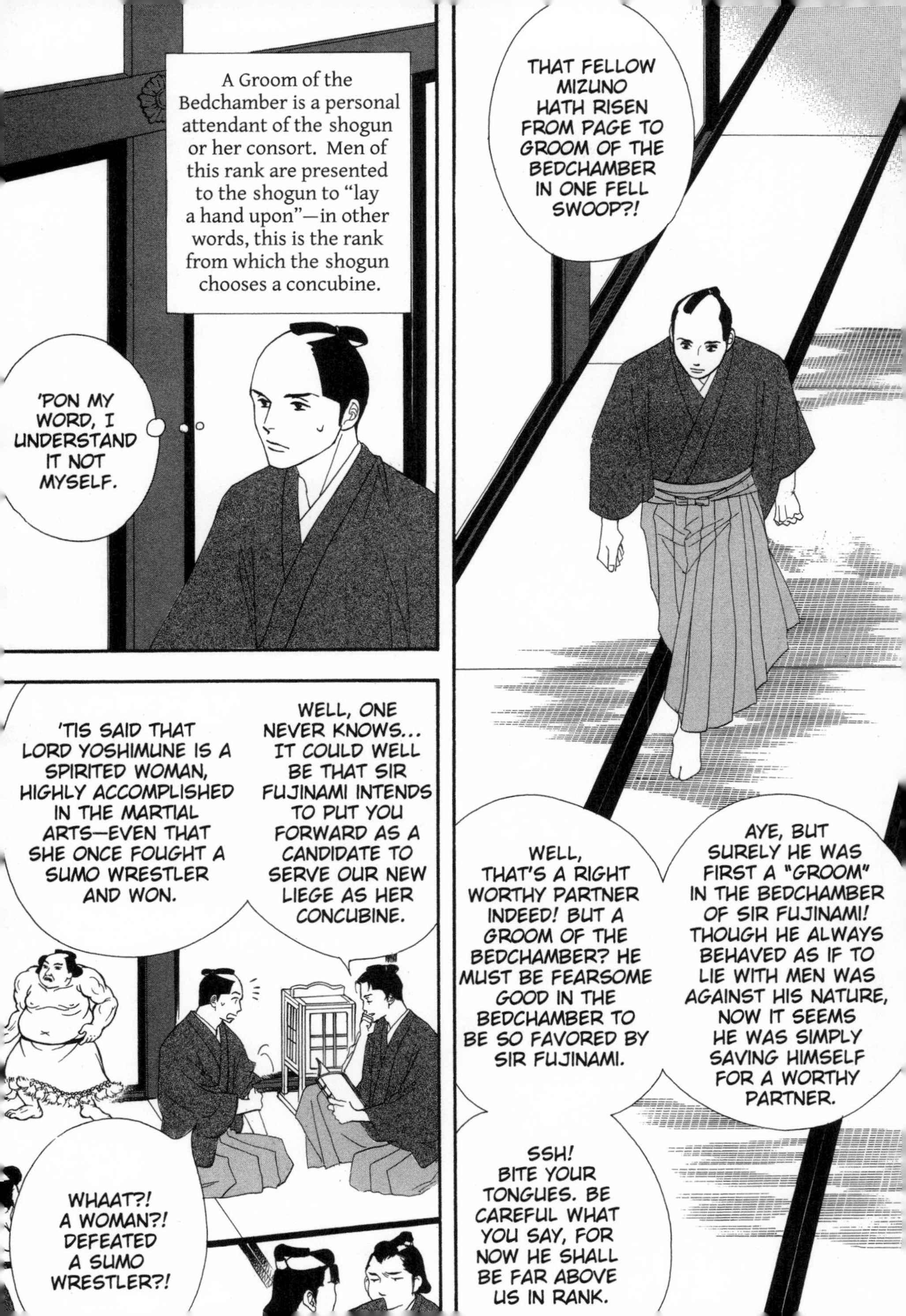
THAT FELLOW MIZUNO HATH RISEN FROM PAGE TO GROOM OF THE BEDCHAMBER IN ONE FELL SWOOP?!
AYE, BUT SURELY HE WAS FIRST A "GROOM" IN THE BEDCHAMBER OF SIR FUJINAMI! THOUGH HE ALWAYS BEHAVED AS IF TO LIE WITH MEN WAS AGAINST HIS NATURE, NOW IT SEEMS HE WAS SIMPLY SAVING HIMSELF FOR A WORTHY PARTNER.
WELL, THAT'S A RIGHT WORTHY PARTNER INDEED! BUT A GROOM OF THE BEDCHAMBER? HE MUST BE FEARSOME GOOD IN THE BEDCHAMBER TO BE SO FAVORED BY SIR FUJINAMI.
SSH! BITE YOUR TONGUES. BE CAREFUL WHAT YOU SAY, FOR NOW HE SHALL BE FAR ABOVE US IN RANK.
A Groom of the Bedchamber is a personal attendant of the shogun or her consort. Men of this rank are presented to the shogun to "lay a hand upon"—in other words, this is the rank from which the shogun chooses a concubine.
'PON MY WORD, I UNDERSTAND IT NOT MYSELF.
WELL, ONE NEVER KNOWS... IT COULD WELL BE THAT SIR FUJINAMI INTENDS TO PUT YOU FORWARD AS A CANDIDATE TO SERVE OUR NEW LIEGE AS HER CONCUBINE.
'TIS SAID THAT LORD YOSHIMUNE IS A SPIRITED WOMAN, HIGHLY ACCOMPLISHED IN THE MARTIAL ARTS—EVEN THAT SHE ONCE FOUGHT A SUMO WRESTLER AND WON.
WHAAT?! A WOMAN?! DEFEATED A SUMO WRESTLER?!

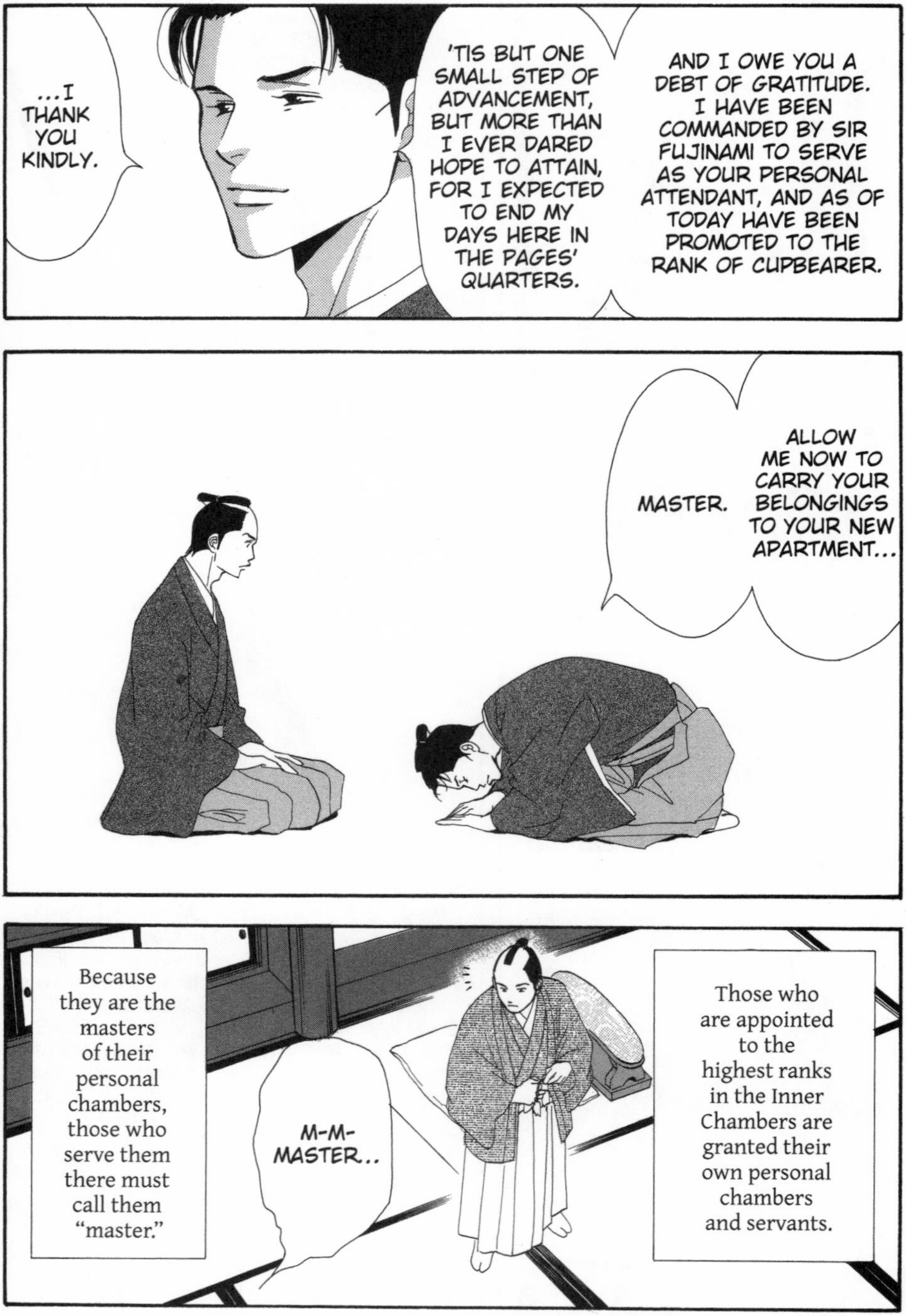
AND I OWE YOU A DEBT OF GRATITUDE. I HAVE BEEN COMMANDED BY SIR FUJINAMI TO SERVE AS YOUR PERSONAL ATTENDANT, AND AS OF TODAY HAVE BEEN PROMOTED TO THE RANK OF CUPBEARER.
'TIS BUT ONE SMALL STEP OF ADVANCEMENT, BUT MORE THAN I EVER DARED HOPE TO ATTAIN, FOR I EXPECTED TO END MY DAYS HERE IN THE PAGES' QUARTERS.
...I THANK YOU KINDLY.
ALLOW ME NOW TO CARRY YOUR BELONGINGS TO YOUR NEW APARTMENT...
MASTER.
Those who are appointed to the highest ranks in the Inner Chambers are granted their own personal chambers and servants.
Because they are the masters of their personal chambers, those who serve them there must call them "master."
M-M-MASTER...

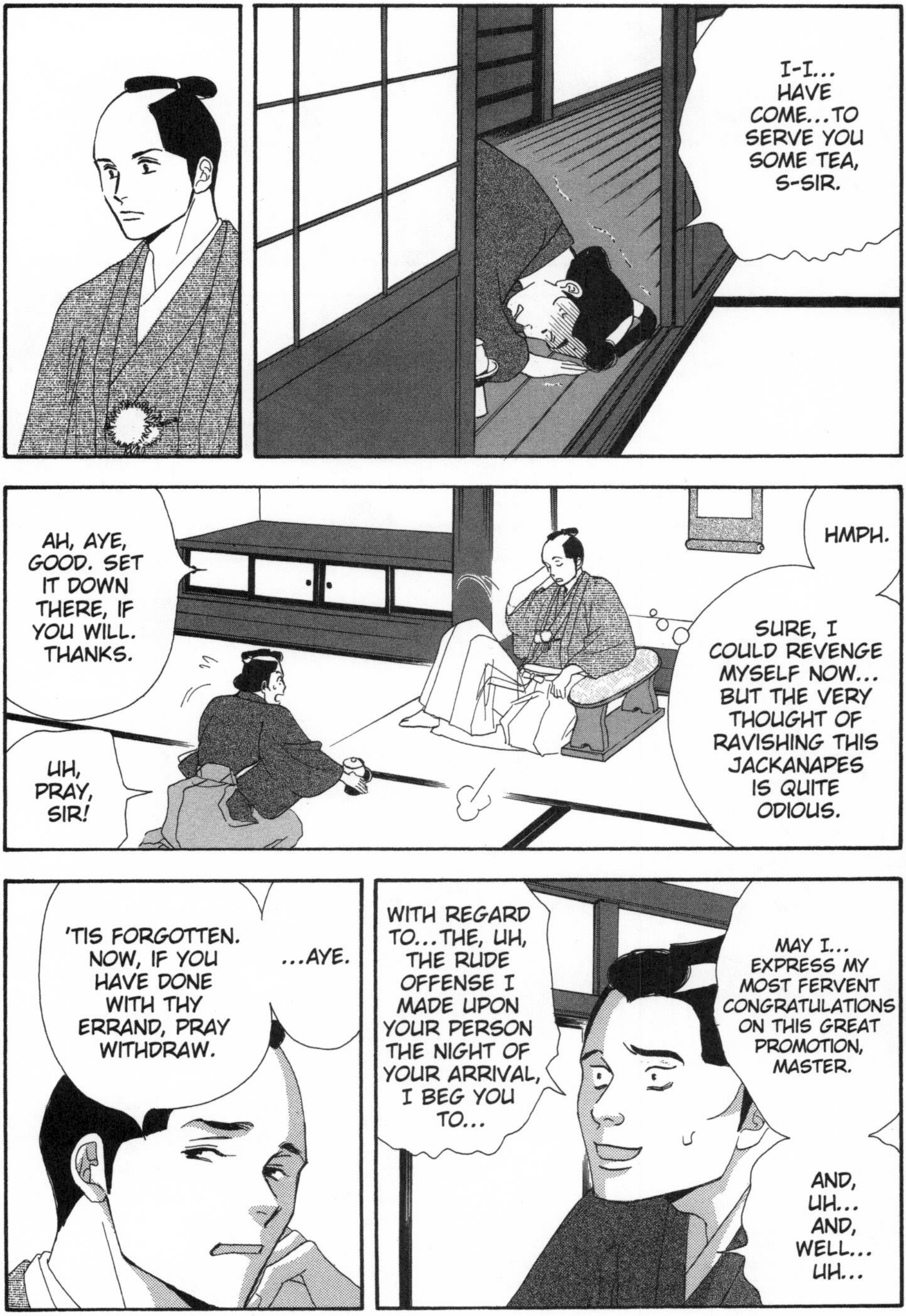
I-I... HAVE COME...TO SERVE YOU SOME TEA, S-SIR.
HMPH.
AH, AYE, GOOD. SET IT DOWN THERE, IF YOU WILL. THANKS.
SURE, I COULD REVENGE MYSELF NOW... BUT THE VERY THOUGHT OF RAVISHING THIS JACKANAPES IS QUITE ODIOUS.
UH, PRAY, SIR!
MAY I... EXPRESS MY MOST FERVENT CONGRATULATIONS ON THIS GREAT PROMOTION, MASTER.
AND, UH... AND, WELL... UH...
WITH REGARD TO...THE, UH, THE RUDE OFFENSE I MADE UPON YOUR PERSON THE NIGHT OF YOUR ARRIVAL, I BEG YOU TO...
...AYE.
'TIS FORGOTTEN. NOW, IF YOU HAVE DONE WITH THY ERRAND, PRAY WITHDRAW.

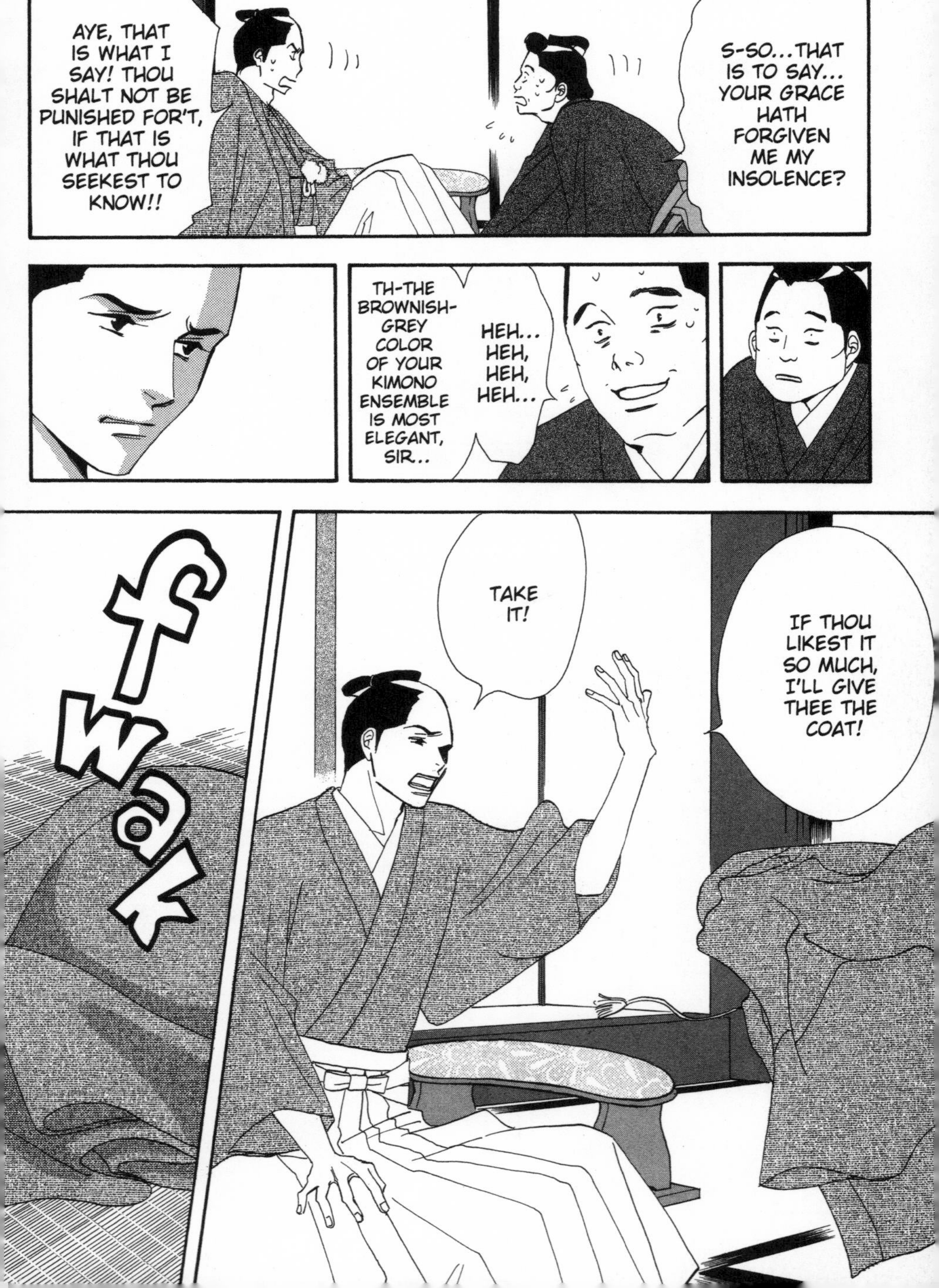
S-SO...THAT IS TO SAY... YOUR GRACE HATH FORGIVEN ME MY INSOLENCE?
AYE, THAT IS WHAT I SAY! THOU SHALT NOT BE PUNISHED FOR'T, IF THAT IS WHAT THOU SEEKEST TO KNOW!!
HEH... HEH, HEH, HEH...
TH-THE BROWNISH-GREY COLOR OF YOUR KIMONO ENSEMBLE IS MOST ELEGANT, SIR..
IF THOU LIKEST IT SO MUCH, I'LL GIVE THEE THE COAT!
TAKE IT!
fwak

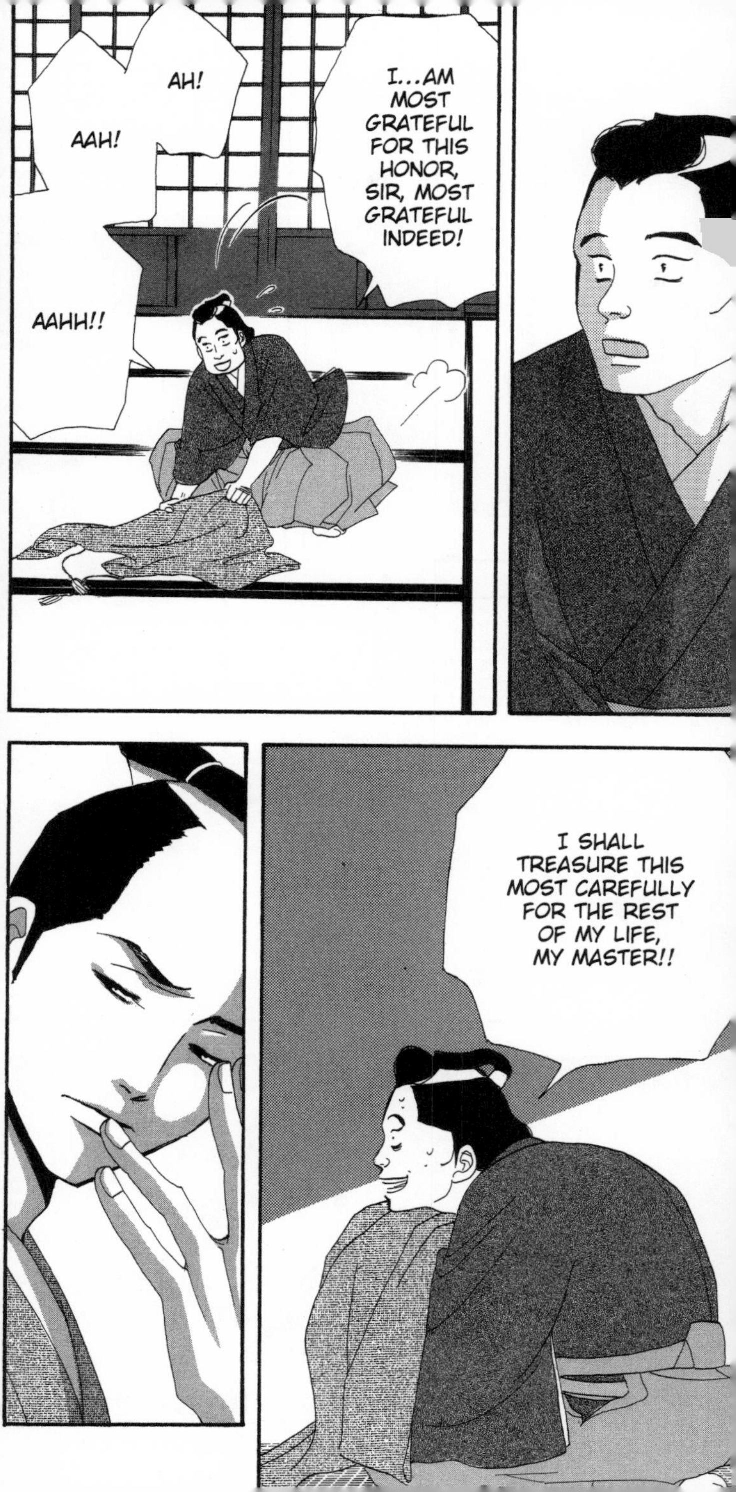
I...AM MOST GRATEFUL FOR THIS HONOR, SIR, MOST GRATEFUL INDEED!
AH!
AAH!
AAHH!!
I SHALL TREASURE THIS MOST CAREFULLY FOR THE REST OF MY LIFE, MY MASTER!!

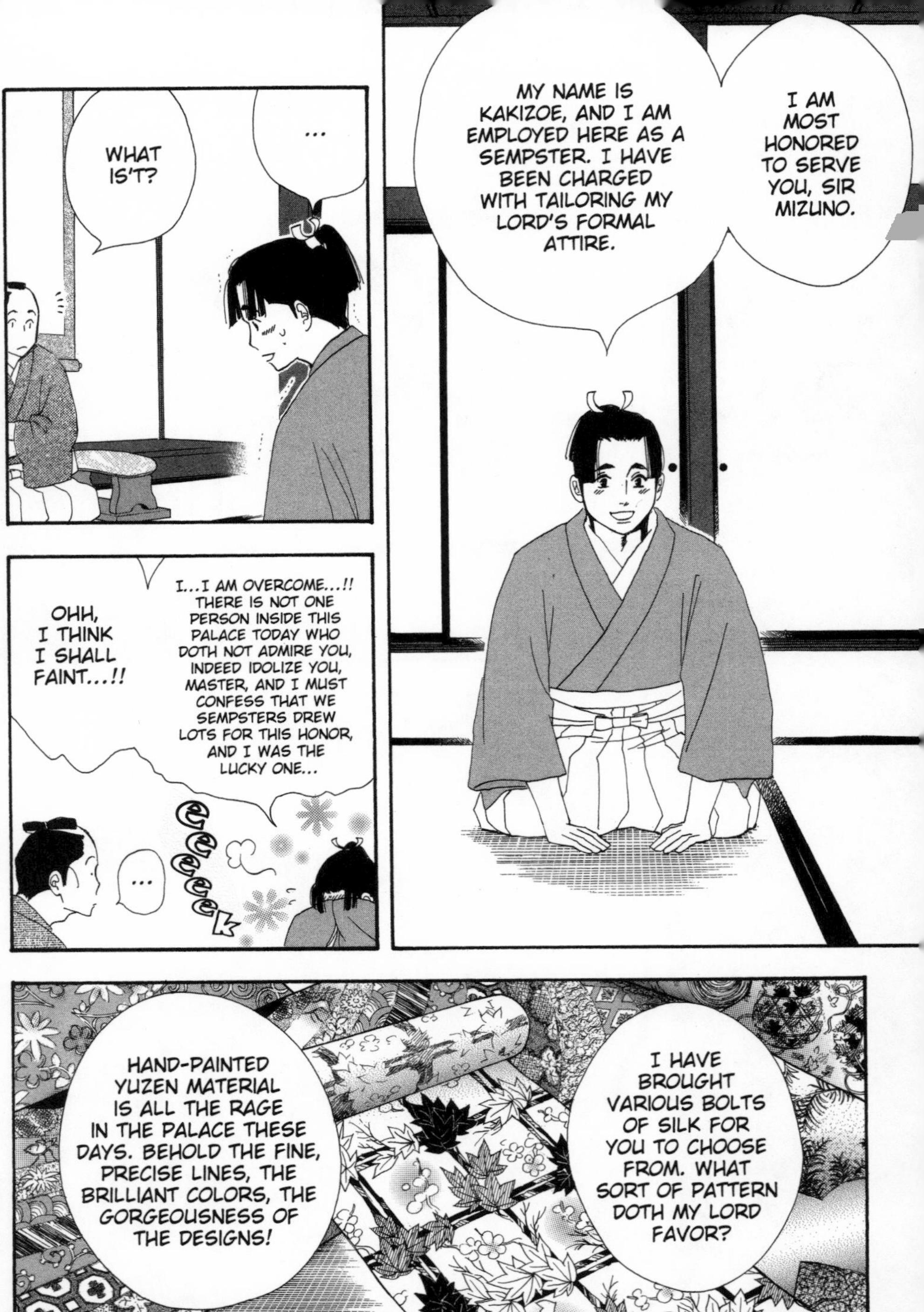
I AM MOST HONORED TO SERVE YOU, SIR MIZUNO.
MY NAME IS KAKIZOE, AND I AM EMPLOYED HERE AS A SEMPSTER. I HAVE BEEN CHARGED WITH TAILORING MY LORD'S FORMAL ATTIRE.
...
WHAT IS'T?
I...I AM OVERCOME...!! THERE IS NOT ONE PERSON INSIDE THIS PALACE TODAY WHO DOTH NOT ADMIRE YOU, INDEED IDOLIZE YOU, MASTER, AND I MUST CONFESS THAT WE SEMPSTERS DREW LOTS FOR THIS HONOR, AND I WAS THE LUCKY ONE...
OHH, I THINK I SHALL FAINT...!!
EEEEEEK
...
I HAVE BROUGHT VARIOUS BOLTS OF SILK FOR YOU TO CHOOSE FROM. WHAT SORT OF PATTERN DOTH MY LORD FAVOR?
HAND-PAINTED YUZEN MATERIAL IS ALL THE RAGE IN THE PALACE THESE DAYS. BEHOLD THE FINE, PRECISE LINES, THE BRILLIANT COLORS, THE GORGEOUSNESS OF THE DESIGNS!

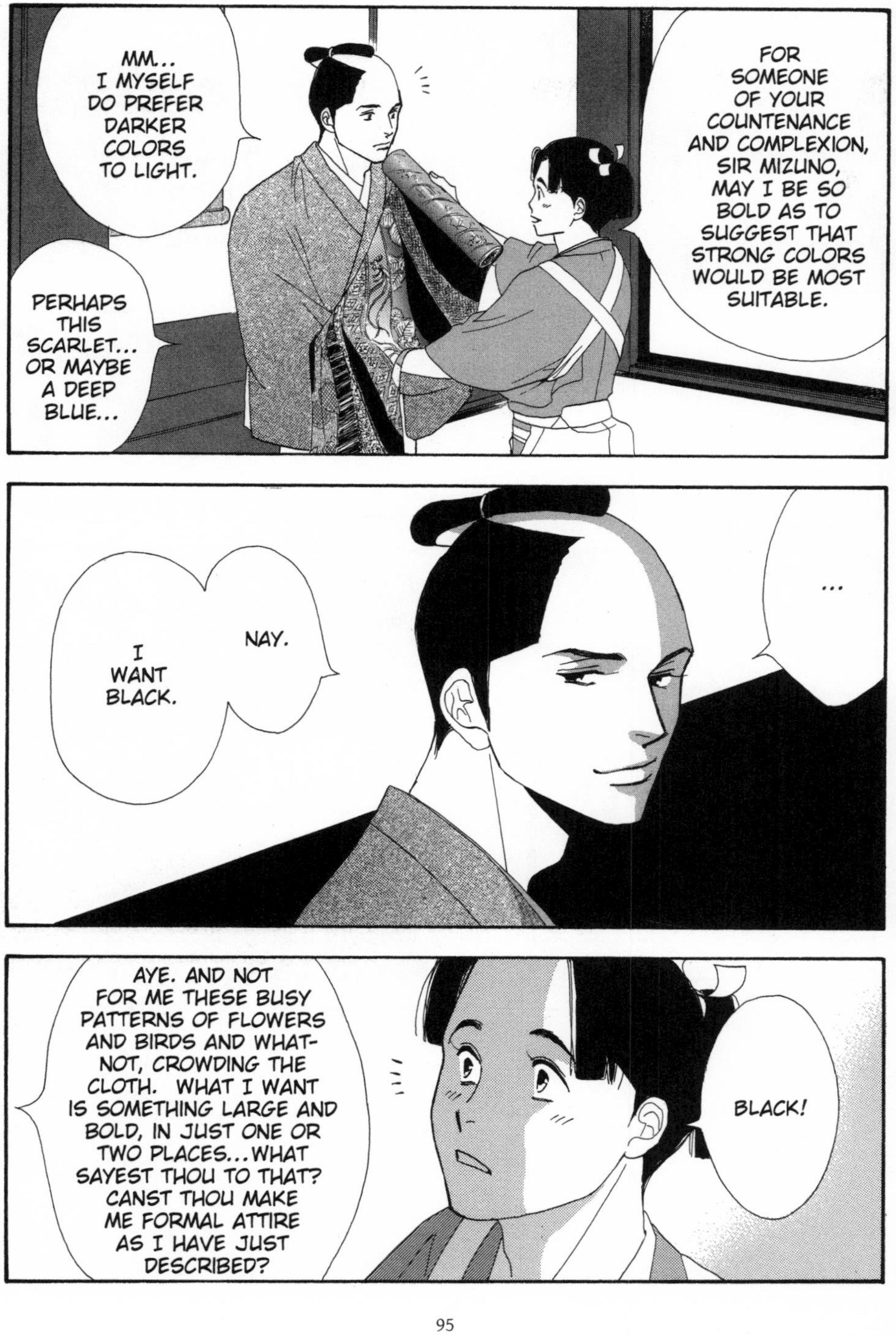
FOR SOMEONE OF YOUR COUNTENANCE AND COMPLEXION, SIR MIZUNO, MAY I BE SO BOLD AS TO SUGGEST THAT STRONG COLORS WOULD BE MOST SUITABLE.
MM... I MYSELF DO PREFER DARKER COLORS TO LIGHT.
PERHAPS THIS SCARLET... OR MAYBE A DEEP BLUE...
...
NAY.
I WANT BLACK.
BLACK!
AYE. AND NOT FOR ME THESE BUSY PATTERNS OF FLOWERS AND BIRDS AND WHAT-NOT, CROWDING THE CLOTH. WHAT I WANT IS SOMETHING LARGE AND BOLD, IN JUST ONE OR TWO PLACES...WHAT SAYEST THOU TO THAT? CANST THOU MAKE ME FORMAL ATTIRE AS I HAVE JUST DESCRIBED?

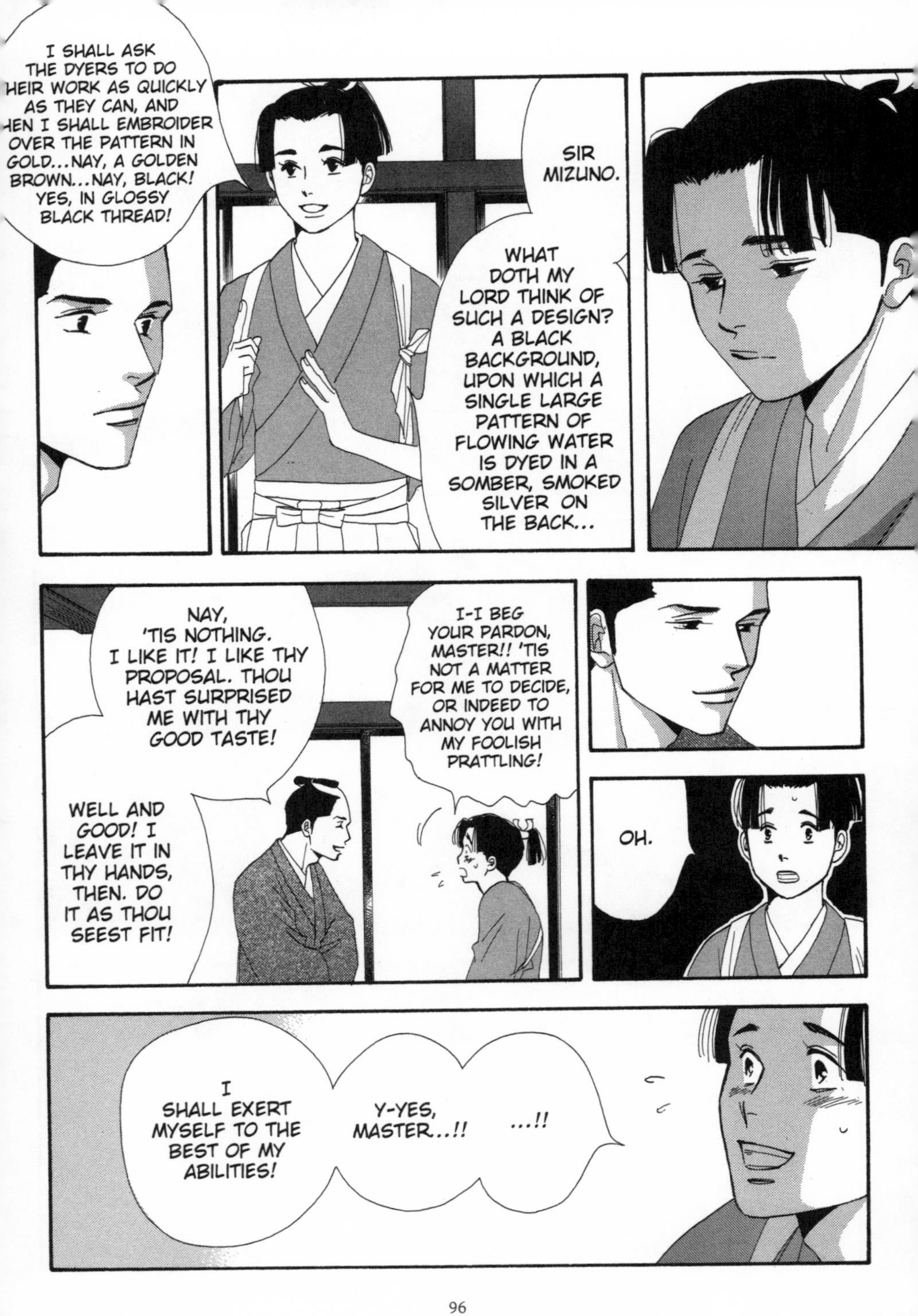
SIR MIZUNO.
WHAT DOTH MY LORD THINK OF SUCH A DESIGN? A BLACK BACKGROUND, UPON WHICH A SINGLE LARGE PATTERN OF FLOWING WATER IS DYED IN A SOMBER, SMOKED SILVER ON THE BACK...
I SHALL ASK THE DYERS TO DO HEIR WORK AS QUICKLY AS THEY CAN, AND HEN I SHALL EMBROIDER OVER THE PATTERN IN GOLD...NAY, A GOLDEN BROWN...NAY, BLACK! YES, IN GLOSSY BLACK THREAD!
OH.
I-I BEG YOUR PARDON, MASTER!! 'TIS NOT A MATTER FOR ME TO DECIDE, OR INDEED TO ANNOY YOU WITH MY FOOLISH PRATTLING!
NAY, 'TIS NOTHING. I LIKE IT! I LIKE THY PROPOSAL. THOU HAST SURPRISED ME WITH THY GOOD TASTE!
WELL AND GOOD! I LEAVE IT IN THY HANDS, THEN. DO IT AS THOU SEEST FIT!
...!!
Y-YES, MASTER...!!
I SHALL EXERT MYSELF TO THE BEST OF MY ABILITIES!

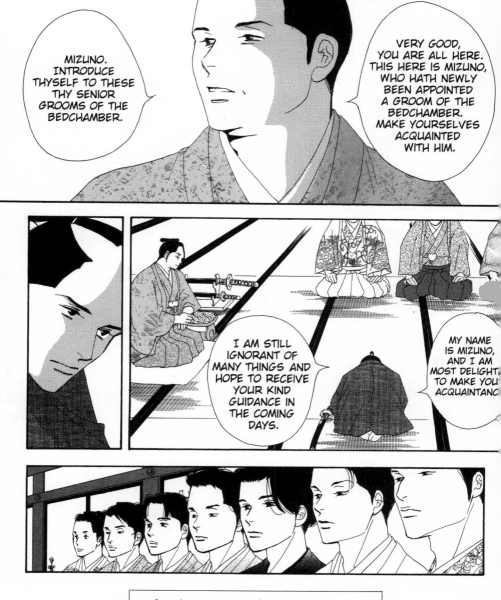

VERY GOOD, YOU ARE ALL HERE. THIS HERE IS MIZUNO, WHO HATH NEWLY BEEN APPOINTED A GROOM OF THE BEDCHAMBER. MAKE YOURSELVES ACQUAINTED WITH HIM.
MIZUNO. INTRODUCE THYSELF TO THESE THY SENIOR GROOMS OF THE BEDCHAMBER.
MY NAME IS MIZUNO, AND I AM MOST DELIGHT TO MAKE YOU ACQUAINTANC
I AM STILL IGNORANT OF MANY THINGS AND HOPE TO RECEIVE YOUR KIND GUIDANCE IN THE COMING DAYS.

Before the promotion of Mizuno to their ranks, the Grooms of the Bedchamber had been seven in number, and they were Hanabusa, Matsushima, Kashiwagi, Suzumoto, Shiragawa, Shingyoji, and Segawa. While there were no restrictions concerning their age, all of them were young, handsome, and accomplished men from good families.

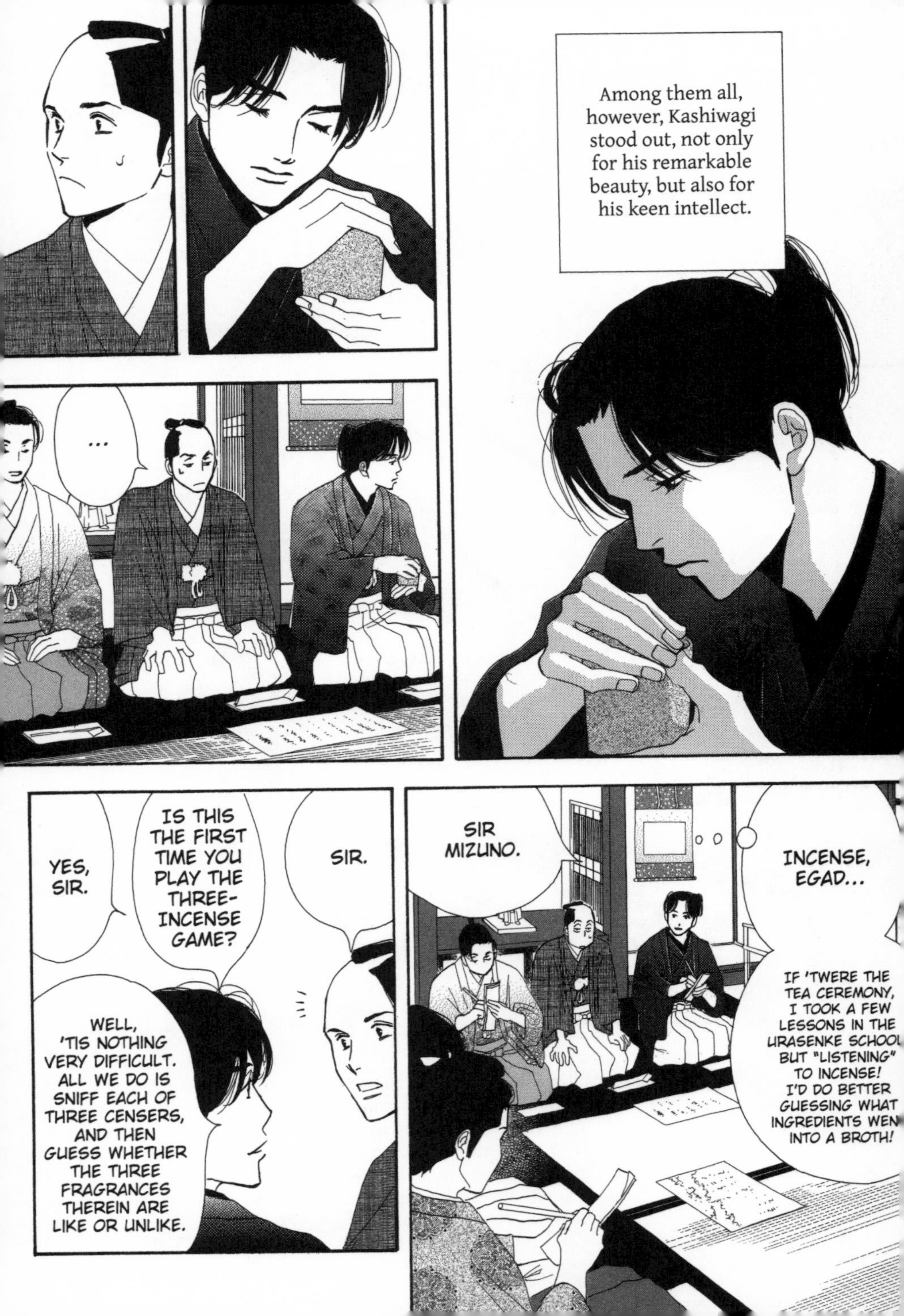
Among them all, however, Kashiwagi stood out, not only for his remarkable beauty, but also for his keen intellect.
...
INCENSE, EGAD...
SIR MIZUNO.
IF 'TWERE THE TEA CEREMONY, I TOOK A FEW LESSONS IN THE URASENKE SCHOOL BUT "LISTENING" TO INCENSE! I'D DO BETTER GUESSING WHAT INGREDIENTS WEN INTO A BROTH!
SIR.
IS THIS THE FIRST TIME YOU PLAY THE THREE-INCENSE GAME?
YES, SIR.
WELL, 'TIS NOTHING VERY DIFFICULT. ALL WE DO IS SNIFF EACH OF THREE CENSERS, AND THEN GUESS WHETHER THE THREE FRAGRANCES THEREIN ARE LIKE OR UNLIKE.

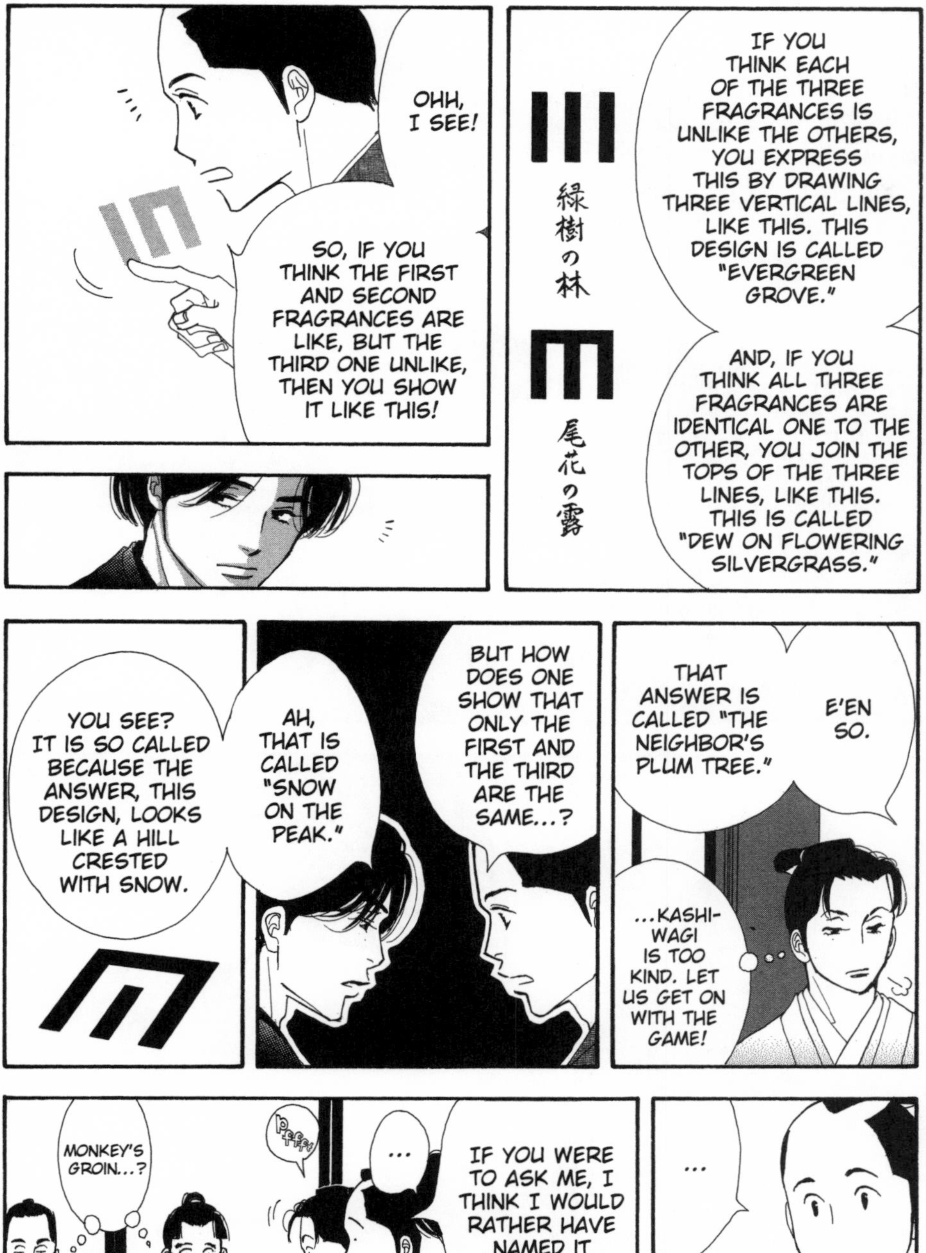
IF YOU THINK EACH OF THE THREE FRAGRANCES IS UNLIKE THE OTHERS, YOU EXPRESS THIS BY DRAWING THREE VERTICAL LINES, LIKE THIS. THIS DESIGN IS CALLED "EVERGREEN GROVE."
緑樹の林
AND, IF YOU THINK ALL THREE FRAGRANCES ARE IDENTICAL ONE TO THE OTHER, YOU JOIN THE TOPS OF THE THREE LINES, LIKE THIS. THIS IS CALLED "DEW ON FLOWERING SILVERGRASS."
尾花の露
OHH, I SEE!
SO, IF YOU THINK THE FIRST AND SECOND FRAGRANCES ARE LIKE, BUT THE THIRD ONE UNLIKE, THEN YOU SHOW IT LIKE THIS!
THAT ANSWER IS CALLED "THE NEIGHBOR'S PLUM TREE."
E'EN SO.
...KASHI-WAGI IS TOO KIND. LET US GET ON WITH THE GAME!
BUT HOW DOES ONE SHOW THAT ONLY THE FIRST AND THE THIRD ARE THE SAME...?
AH, THAT IS CALLED "SNOW ON THE PEAK."
YOU SEE? IT IS SO CALLED BECAUSE THE ANSWER, THIS DESIGN, LOOKS LIKE A HILL CRESTED WITH SNOW.
...
IF YOU WERE TO ASK ME, I THINK I WOULD RATHER HAVE NAMED IT "MONKEY'S GROIN"...
...
pffft
MONKEY'S GROIN...?

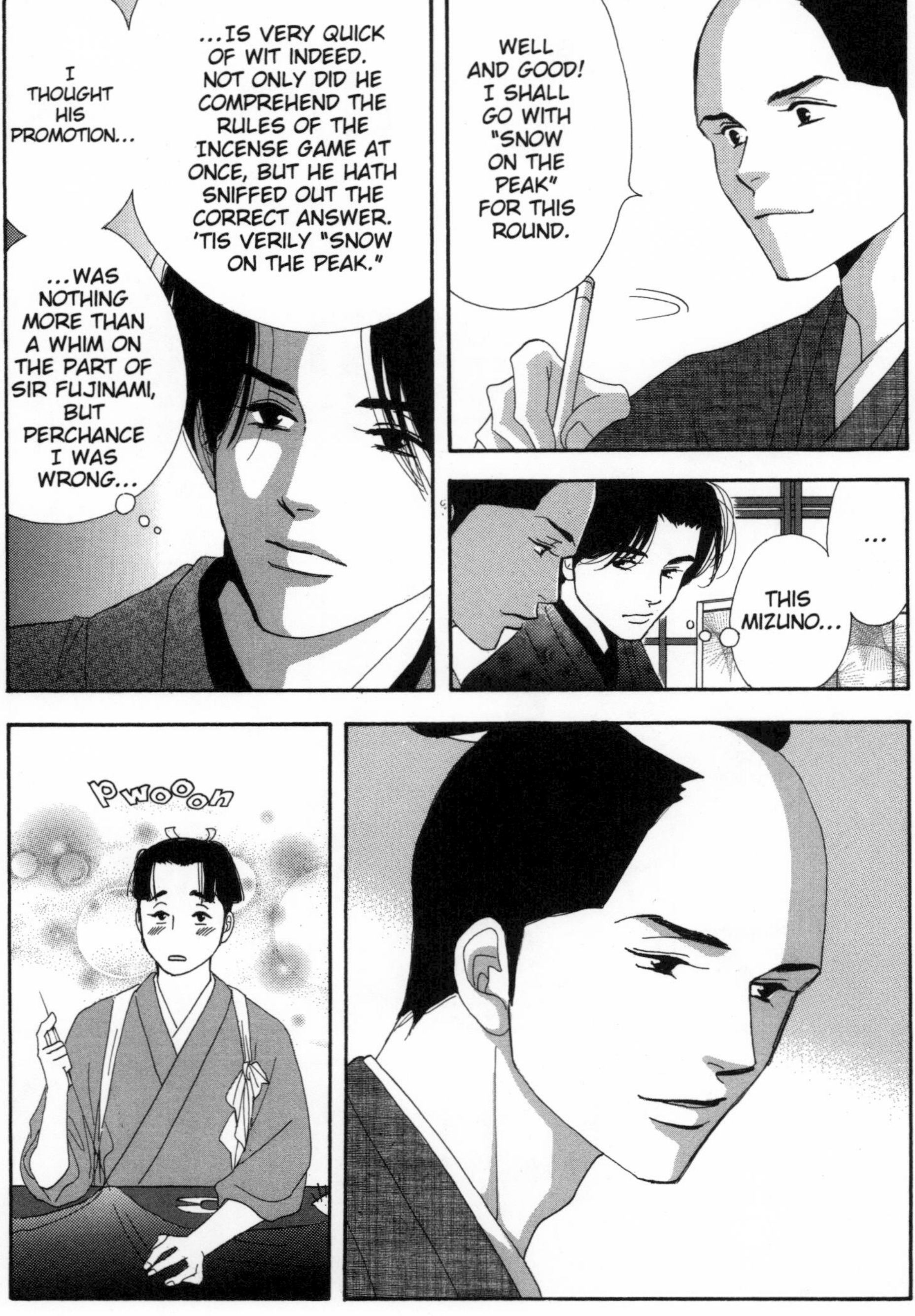
WELL AND GOOD! I SHALL GO WITH "SNOW ON THE PEAK" FOR THIS ROUND.
...
THIS MIZUNO...
...IS VERY QUICK OF WIT INDEED. NOT ONLY DID HE COMPREHEND THE RULES OF THE INCENSE GAME AT ONCE, BUT HE HATH SNIFFED OUT THE CORRECT ANSWER. 'TIS VERILY "SNOW ON THE PEAK."
I THOUGHT HIS PROMOTION...
...WAS NOTHING MORE THAN A WHIM ON THE PART OF SIR FUJINAMI, BUT PERCHANCE I WAS WRONG...
pwoooh

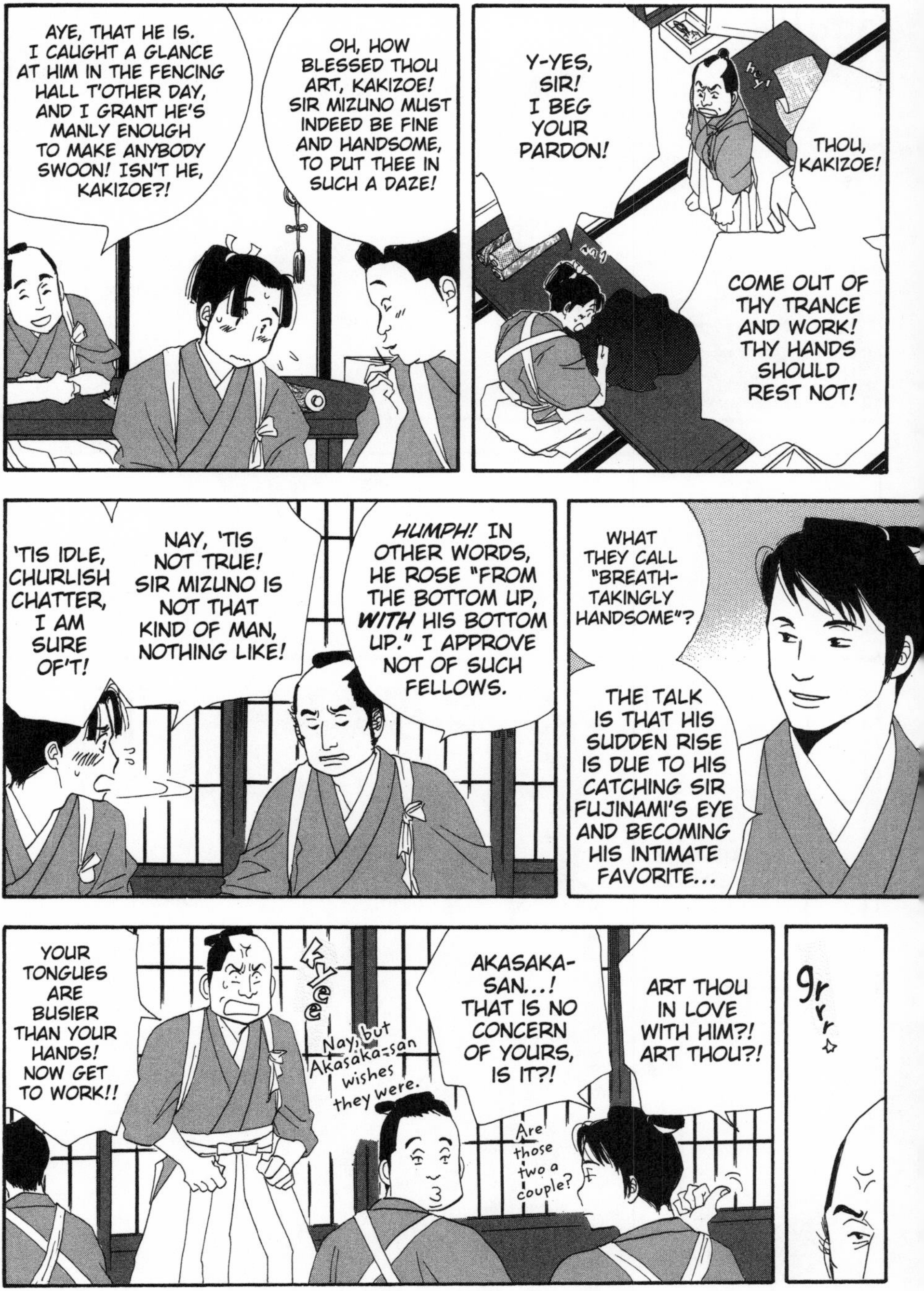
hey!
THOU, KAKIZOE!
Y-YES, SIR! I BEG YOUR PARDON!
COME OUT OF THY TRANCE AND WORK! THY HANDS SHOULD REST NOT!
OH, HOW BLESSED THOU ART, KAKIZOE! SIR MIZUNO MUST INDEED BE FINE AND HANDSOME, TO PUT THEE IN SUCH A DAZE!
AYE, THAT HE IS. I CAUGHT A GLANCE AT HIM IN THE FENCING HALL T'OTHER DAY, AND I GRANT HE'S MANLY ENOUGH TO MAKE ANYBODY SWOON! ISN'T HE, KAKIZOE?!
WHAT THEY CALL "BREATH-TAKINGLY HANDSOME"?
THE TALK IS THAT HIS SUDDEN RISE IS DUE TO HIS CATCHING SIR FUJINAMI'S EYE AND BECOMING HIS INTIMATE FAVORITE...
HUMPH! IN OTHER WORDS, HE ROSE "FROM THE BOTTOM UP, ***WITH*** HIS BOTTOM UP." I APPROVE NOT OF SUCH FELLOWS.
NAY, 'TIS NOT TRUE! SIR MIZUNO IS NOT THAT KIND OF MAN, NOTHING LIKE!
'TIS IDLE, CHURLISH CHATTER, I AM SURE OF'T!
grrr
ART THOU IN LOVE WITH HIM?! ART THOU?!
AKASAKA-SAN...! THAT IS NO CONCERN OF YOURS, IS IT?!
kyee
YOUR TONGUES ARE BUSIER THAN YOUR HANDS! NOW GET TO WORK!!
Nay, but Akasaka-san wishes they were.
Are those two a couple?

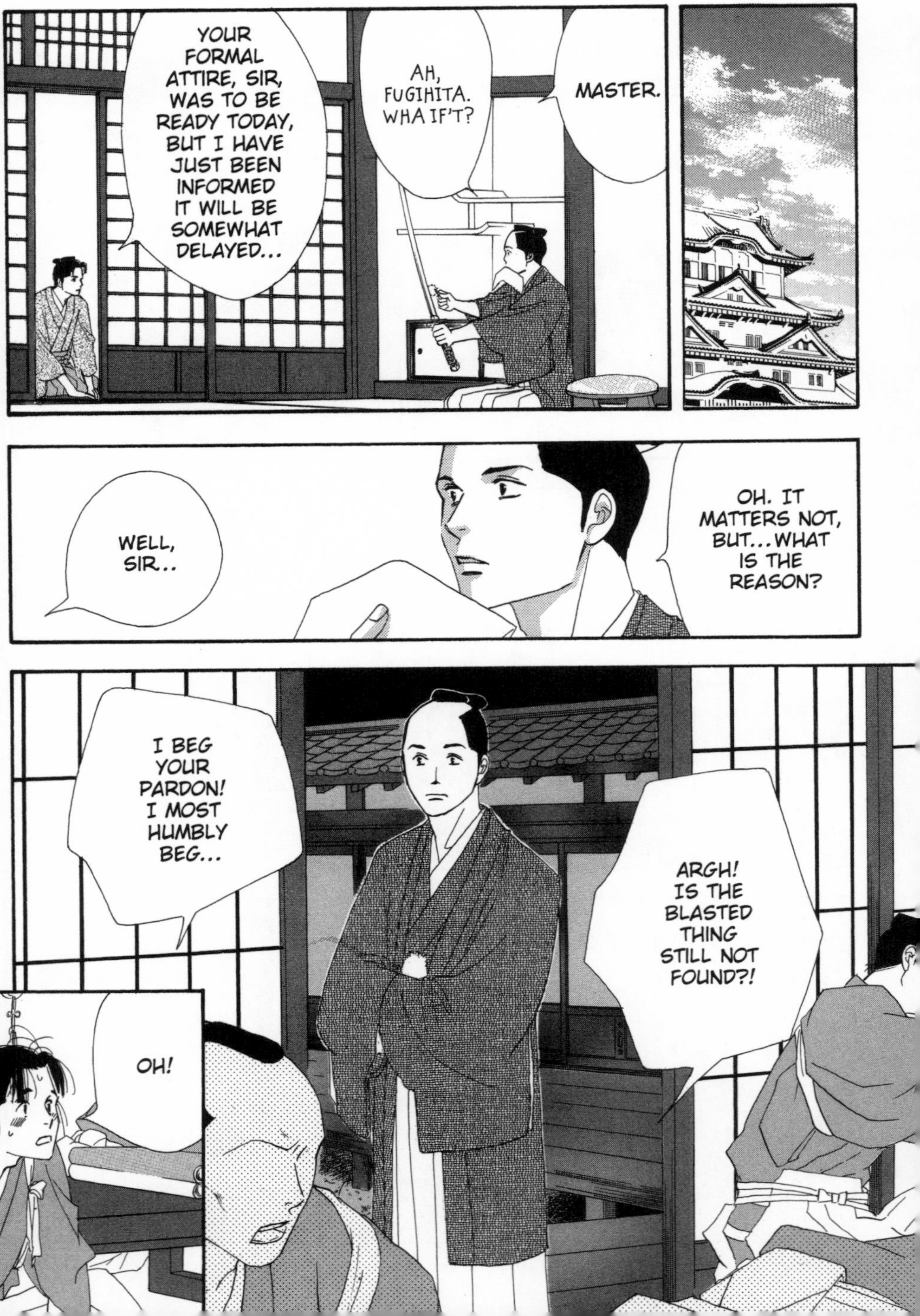
MASTER.
AH, FUGIHITA. WHA IF'T?
YOUR FORMAL ATTIRE, SIR, WAS TO BE READY TODAY, BUT I HAVE JUST BEEN INFORMED IT WILL BE SOMEWHAT DELAYED...
OH. IT MATTERS NOT, BUT...WHAT IS THE REASON?
WELL, SIR..
ARGH! IS THE BLASTED THING STILL NOT FOUND?!
I BEG YOUR PARDON! I MOST HUMBLY BEG...
OH!

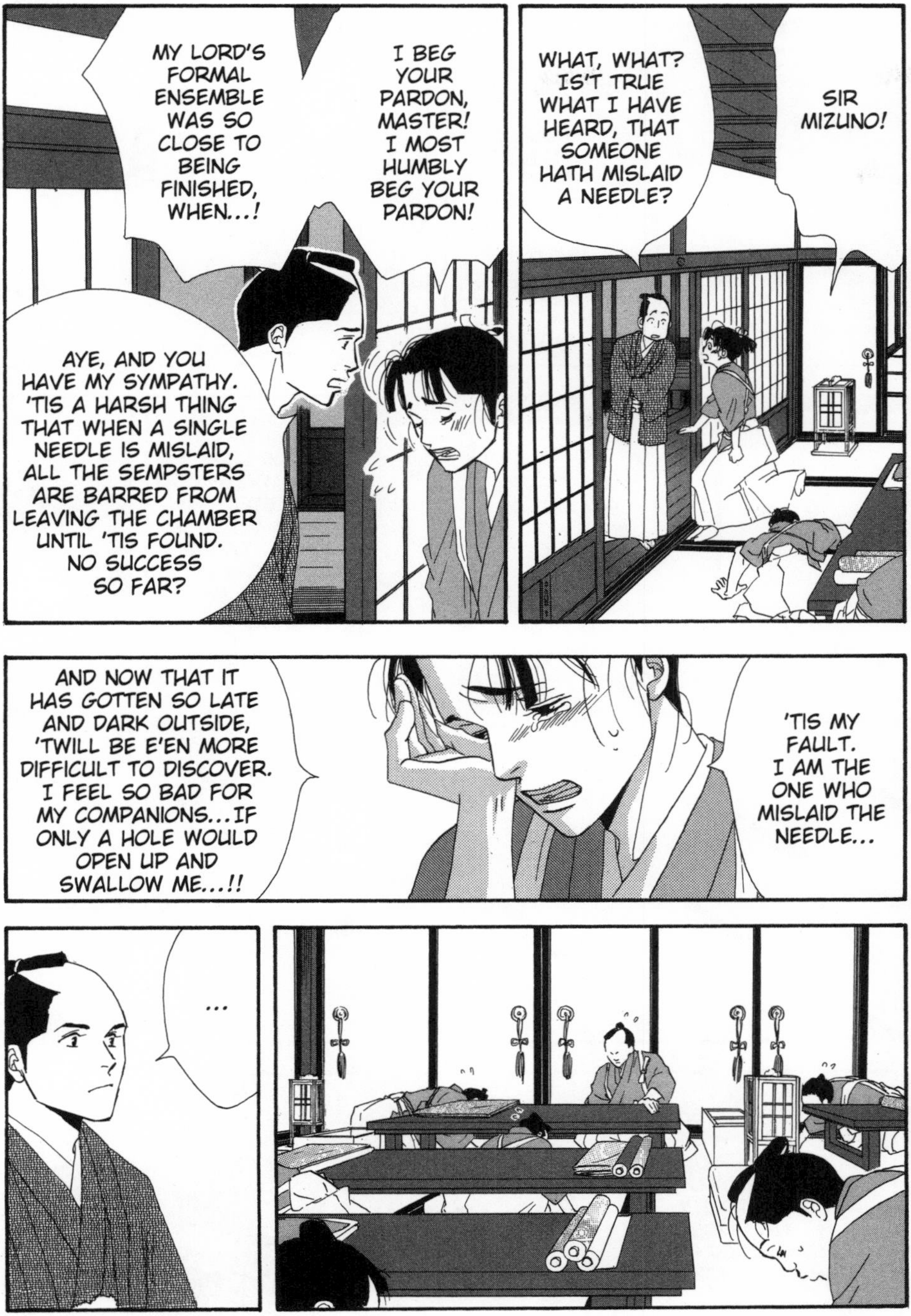
SIR MIZUNO!
WHAT, WHAT? IS'T TRUE WHAT I HAVE HEARD, THAT SOMEONE HATH MISLAID A NEEDLE?
I BEG YOUR PARDON, MASTER! I MOST HUMBLY BEG YOUR PARDON!
MY LORD'S FORMAL ENSEMBLE WAS SO CLOSE TO BEING FINISHED, WHEN...!
AYE, AND YOU HAVE MY SYMPATHY. 'TIS A HARSH THING THAT WHEN A SINGLE NEEDLE IS MISLAID, ALL THE SEMPSTERS ARE BARRED FROM LEAVING THE CHAMBER UNTIL 'TIS FOUND. NO SUCCESS SO FAR?
'TIS MY FAULT. I AM THE ONE WHO MISLAID THE NEEDLE...
AND NOW THAT IT HAS GOTTEN SO LATE AND DARK OUTSIDE, 'TWILL BE E'EN MORE DIFFICULT TO DISCOVER. I FEEL SO BAD FOR MY COMPANIONS...IF ONLY A HOLE WOULD OPEN UP AND SWALLOW ME...!!
...

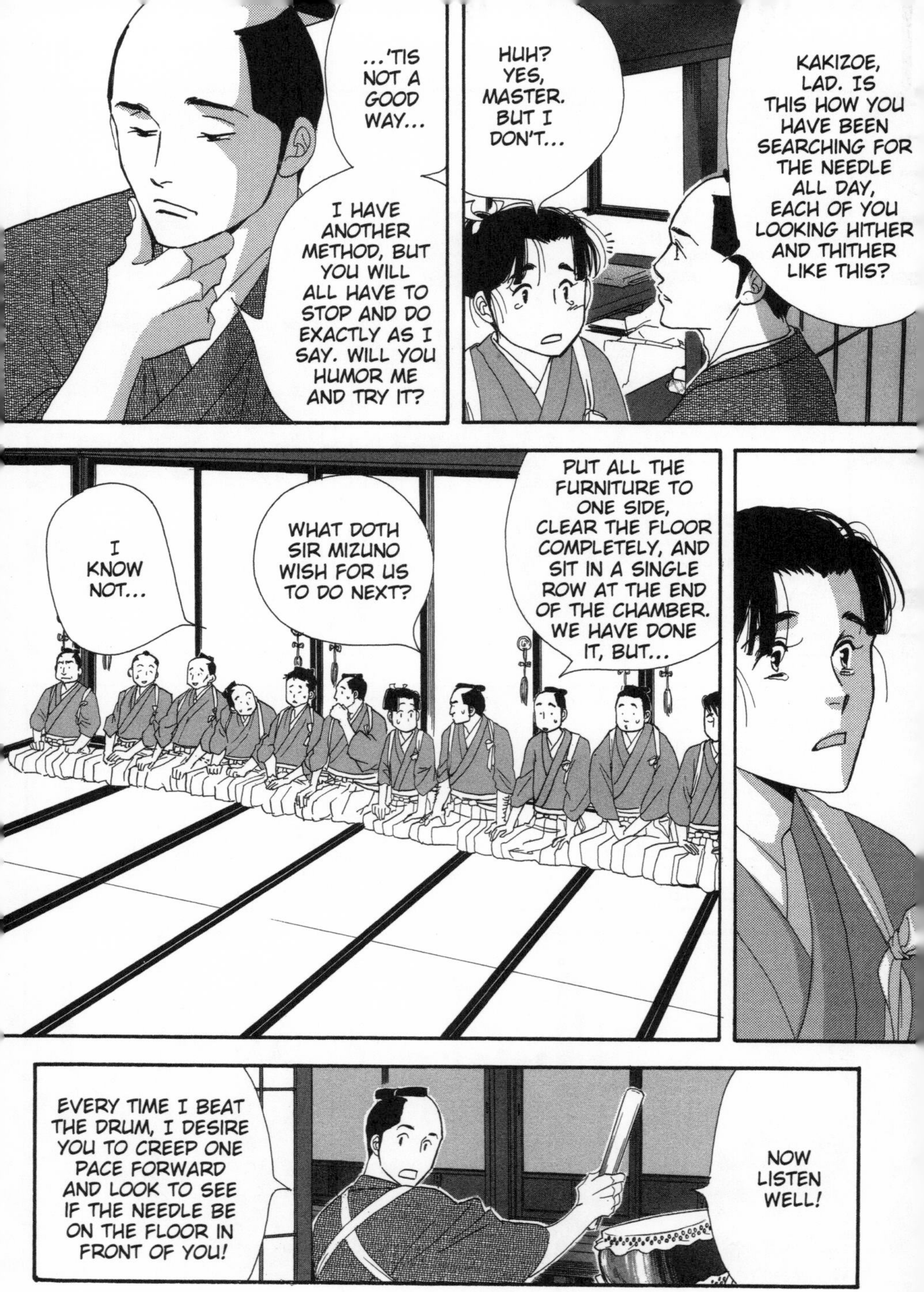
KAKIZOE, LAD. IS THIS HOW YOU HAVE BEEN SEARCHING FOR THE NEEDLE ALL DAY, EACH OF YOU LOOKING HITHER AND THITHER LIKE THIS?
HUH? YES, MASTER. BUT I DON'T...
...'TIS NOT A GOOD WAY...
I HAVE ANOTHER METHOD, BUT YOU WILL ALL HAVE TO STOP AND DO EXACTLY AS I SAY. WILL YOU HUMOR ME AND TRY IT?
PUT ALL THE FURNITURE TO ONE SIDE, CLEAR THE FLOOR COMPLETELY, AND SIT IN A SINGLE ROW AT THE END OF THE CHAMBER. WE HAVE DONE IT, BUT...
WHAT DOTH SIR MIZUNO WISH FOR US TO DO NEXT?
I KNOW NOT...
NOW LISTEN WELL!
EVERY TIME I BEAT THE DRUM, I DESIRE YOU TO CREEP ONE PACE FORWARD AND LOOK TO SEE IF THE NEEDLE BE ON THE FLOOR IN FRONT OF YOU!

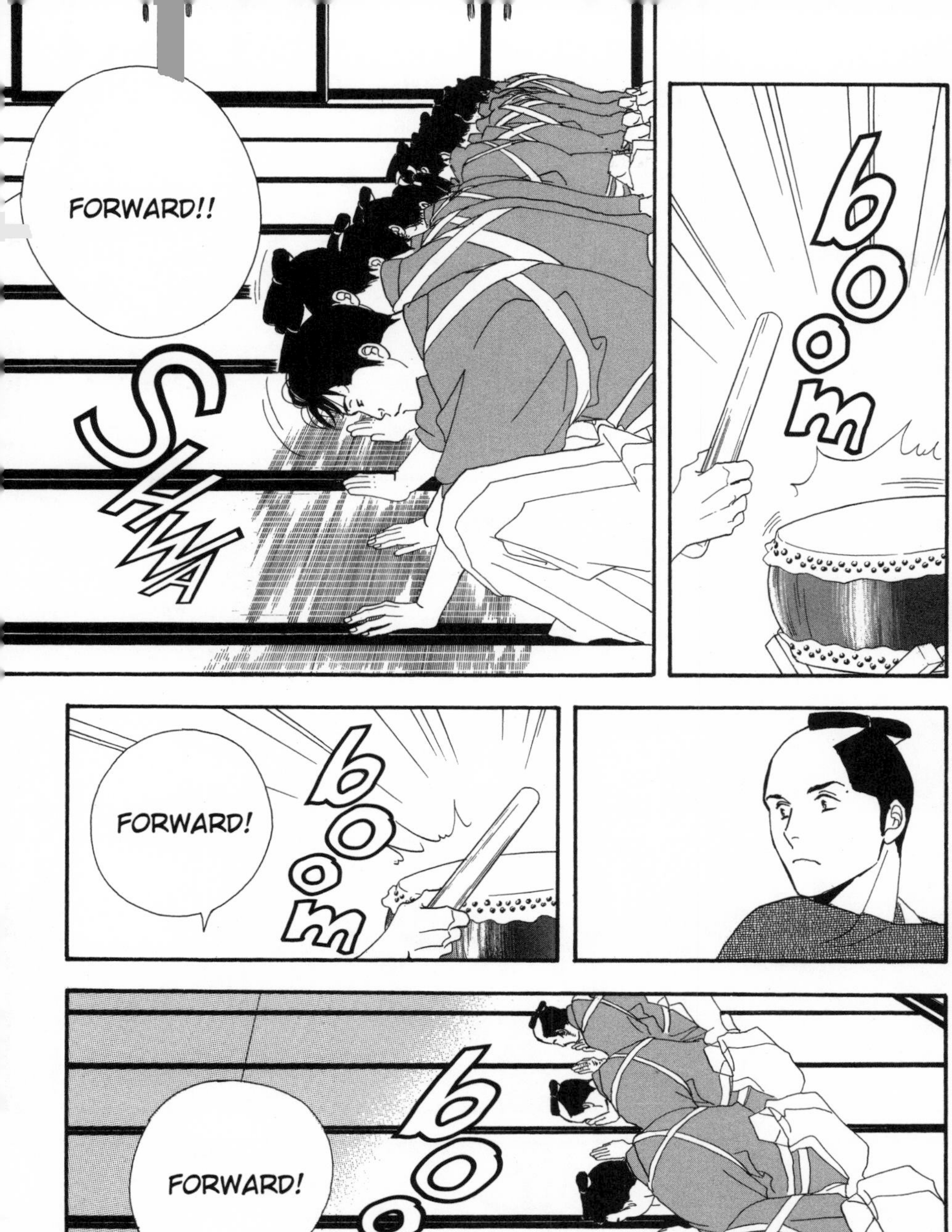
boom
FORWARD!!
SHWA
boom
FORWARD!
boom
FORWARD!

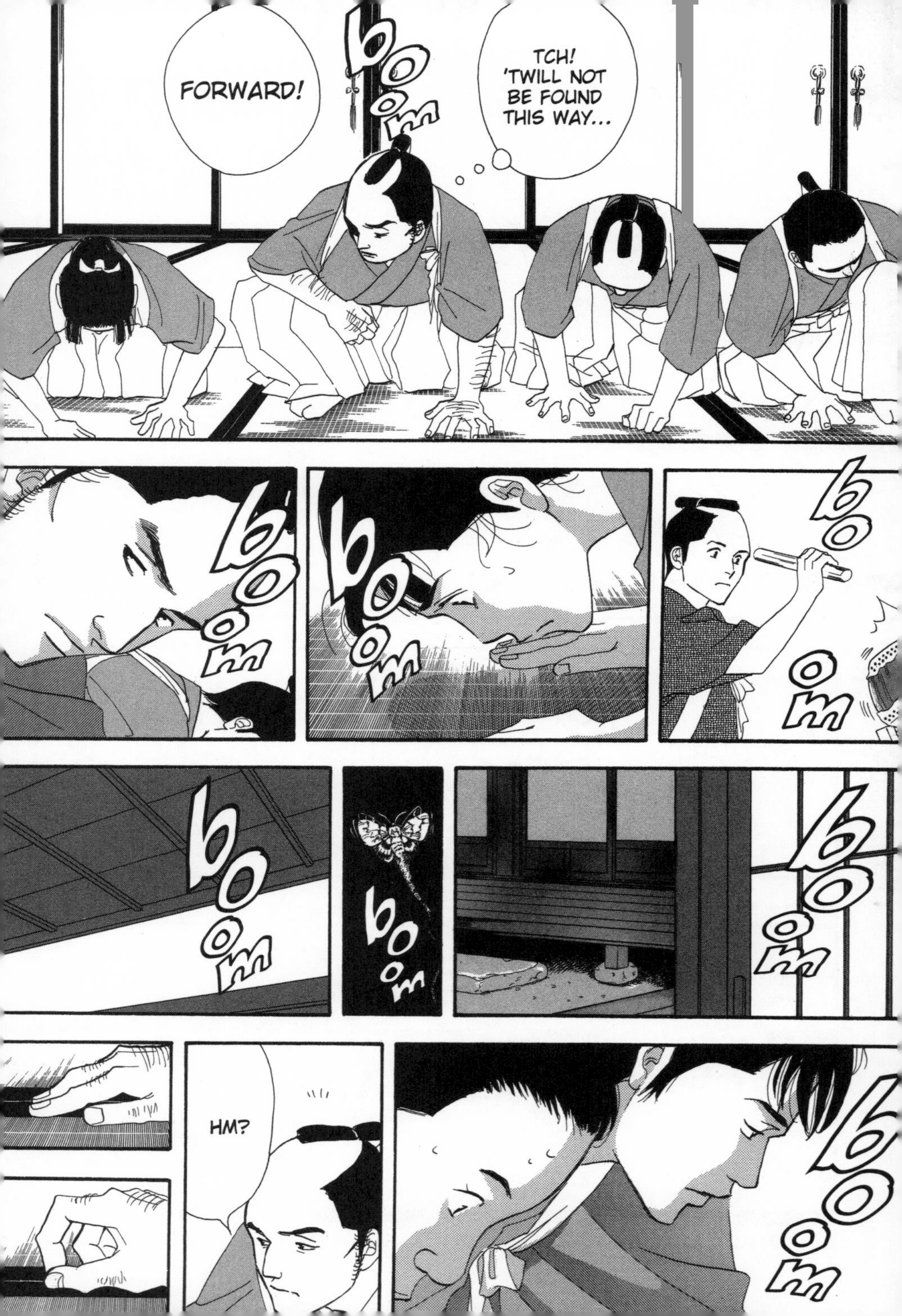
TCH! 'TWILL NOT BE FOUND THIS WAY...
boom
FORWARD!
boom
boom
boom
boom
boom
boom
boom
HM?

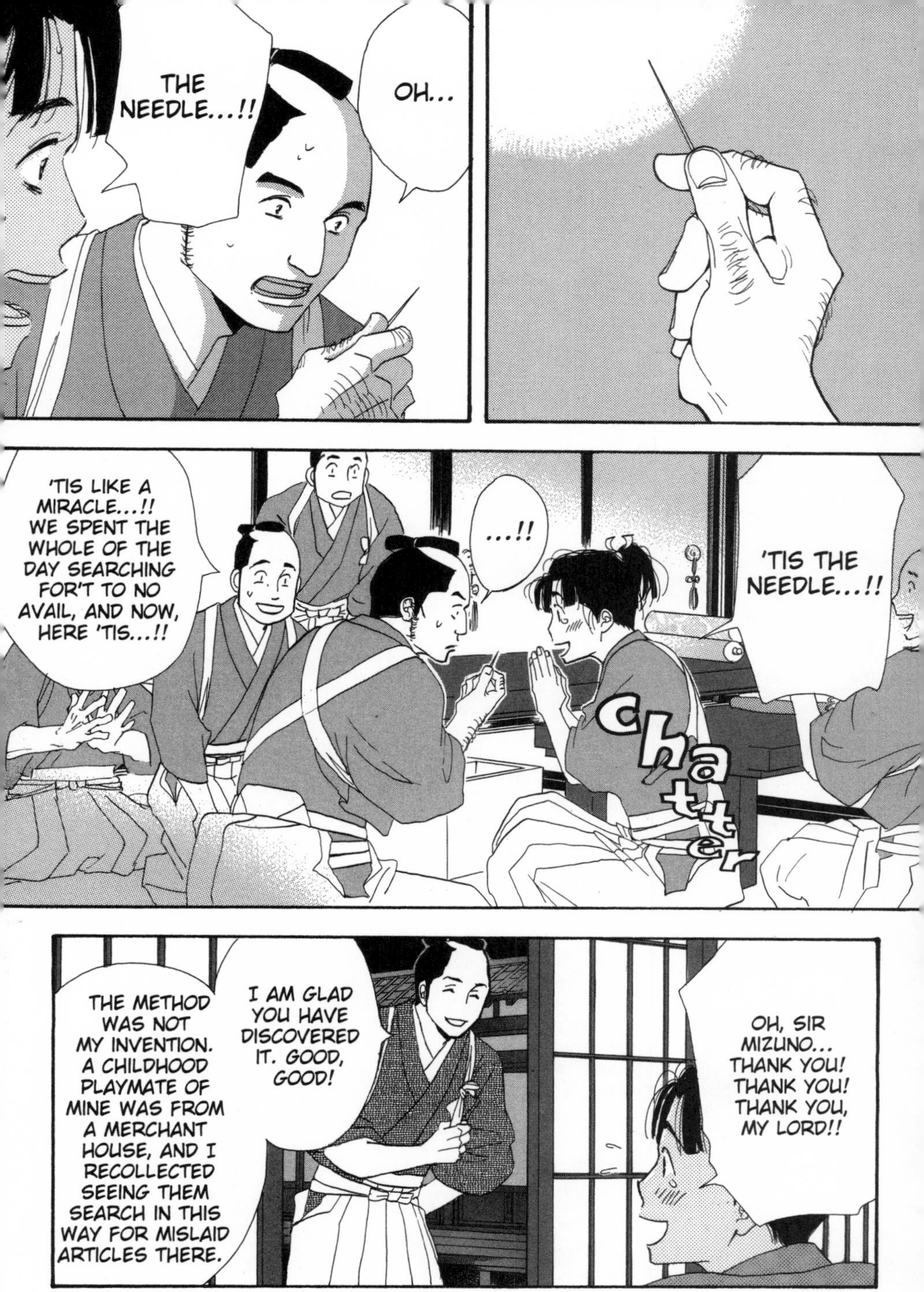
OH…
THE NEEDLE…!!
'TIS THE NEEDLE…!!
…!!
'TIS LIKE A MIRACLE…!! WE SPENT THE WHOLE OF THE DAY SEARCHING FOR'T TO NO AVAIL, AND NOW, HERE 'TIS…!!
Chatter
OH, SIR MIZUNO… THANK YOU! THANK YOU! THANK YOU, MY LORD!!
I AM GLAD YOU HAVE DISCOVERED IT. GOOD, GOOD!
THE METHOD WAS NOT MY INVENTION. A CHILDHOOD PLAYMATE OF MINE WAS FROM A MERCHANT HOUSE, AND I RECOLLECTED SEEING THEM SEARCH IN THIS WAY FOR MISLAID ARTICLES THERE.

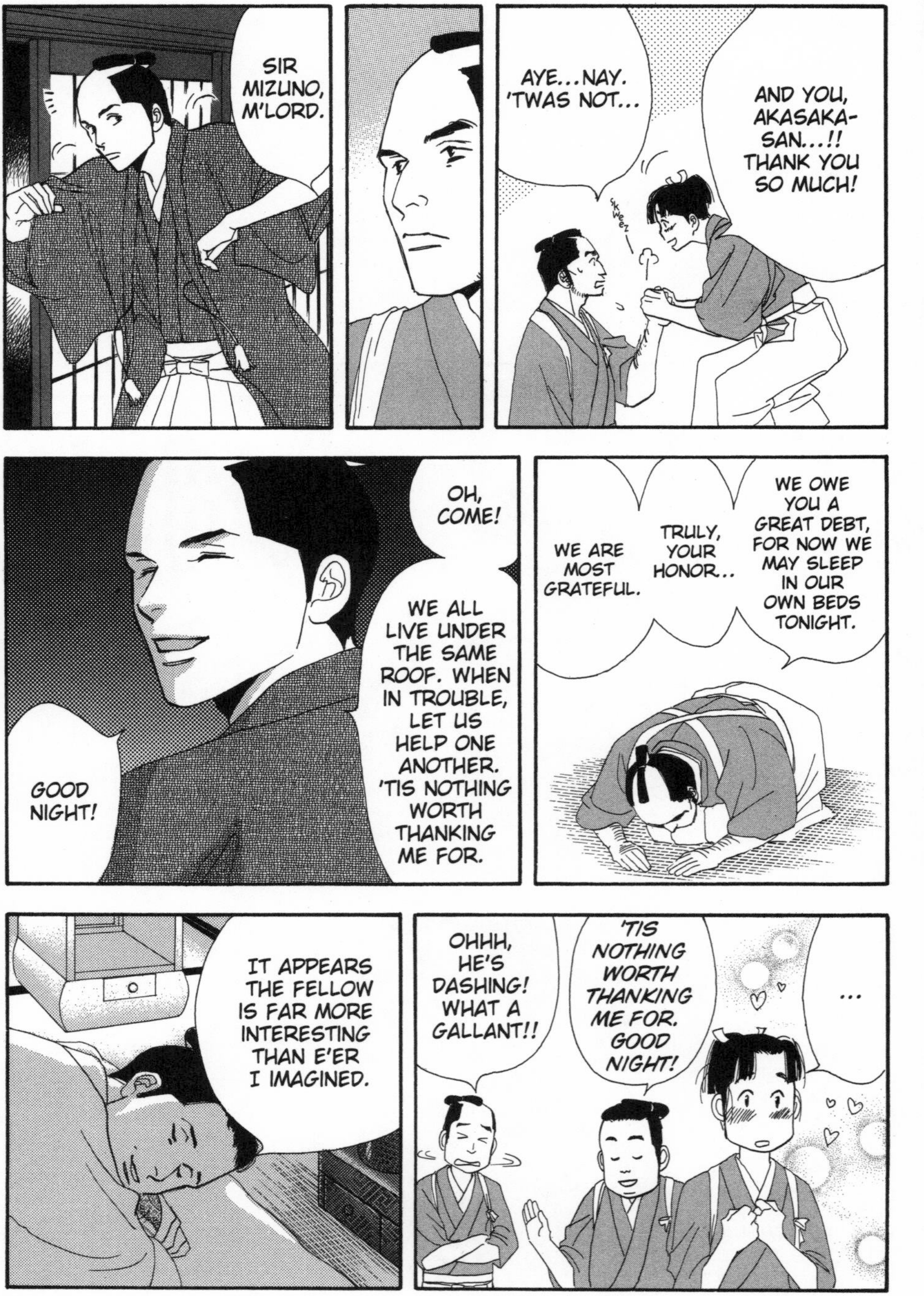
AND YOU, AKASAKA-SAN...!! THANK YOU SO MUCH!
AYE...NAY. 'TWAS NOT...
SKWEEZ
SIR MIZUNO, M'LORD.
WE OWE YOU A GREAT DEBT, FOR NOW WE MAY SLEEP IN OUR OWN BEDS TONIGHT.
TRULY, YOUR HONOR...
WE ARE MOST GRATEFUL.
OH, COME!
WE ALL LIVE UNDER THE SAME ROOF. WHEN IN TROUBLE, LET US HELP ONE ANOTHER. 'TIS NOTHING WORTH THANKING ME FOR.
GOOD NIGHT!
...
'TIS NOTHING WORTH THANKING ME FOR. GOOD NIGHT!
OHHH, HE'S DASHING! WHAT A GALLANT!!
IT APPEARS THE FELLOW IS FAR MORE INTERESTING THAN E'ER I IMAGINED.

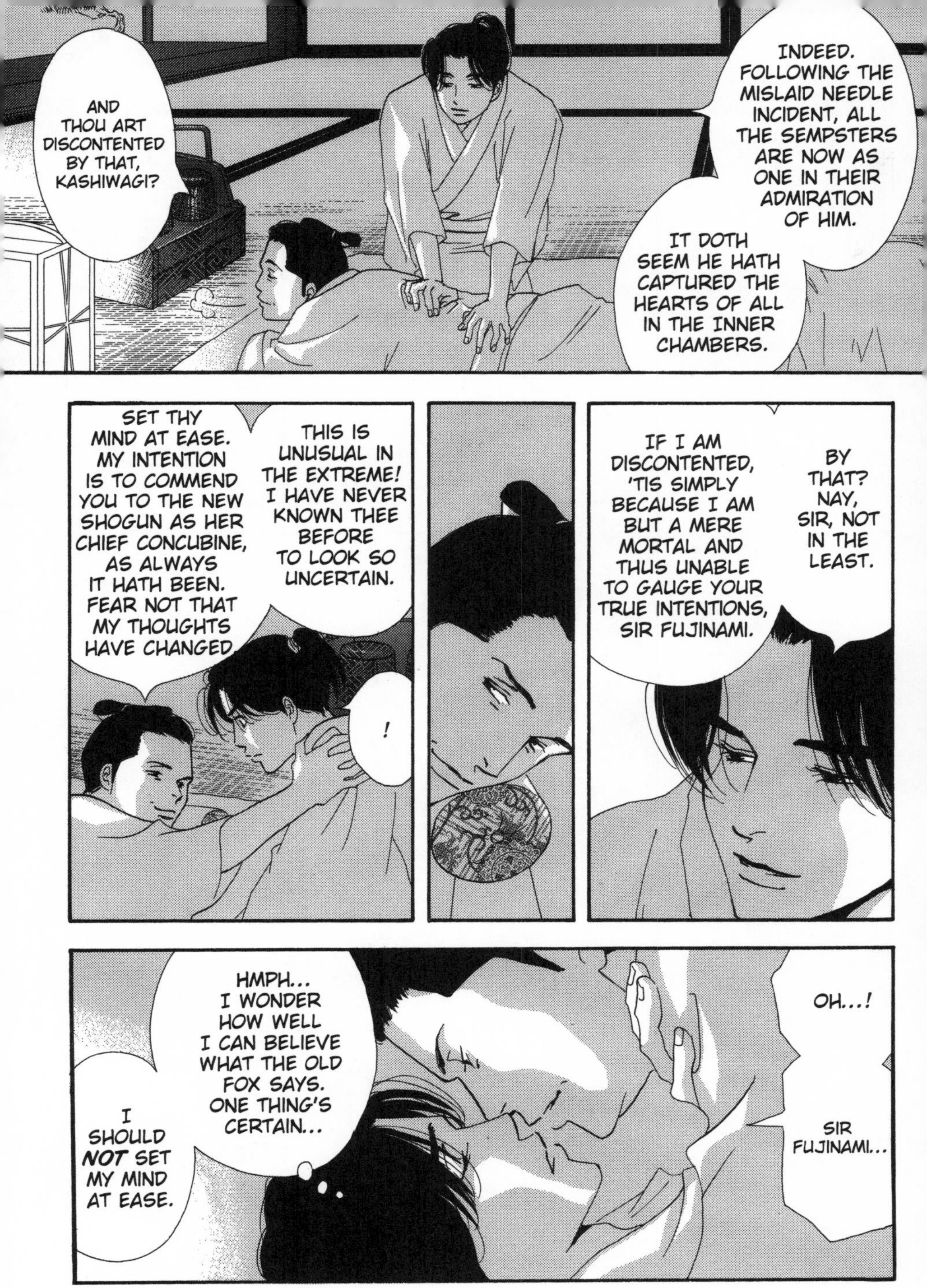
INDEED. FOLLOWING THE MISLAID NEEDLE INCIDENT, ALL THE SEMPSTERS ARE NOW AS ONE IN THEIR ADMIRATION OF HIM.
IT DOTH SEEM HE HATH CAPTURED THE HEARTS OF ALL IN THE INNER CHAMBERS.
AND THOU ART DISCONTENTED BY THAT, KASHIWAGI?
BY THAT? NAY, SIR, NOT IN THE LEAST.
IF I AM DISCONTENTED, 'TIS SIMPLY BECAUSE I AM BUT A MERE MORTAL AND THUS UNABLE TO GAUGE YOUR TRUE INTENTIONS, SIR FUJINAMI.
THIS IS UNUSUAL IN THE EXTREME! I HAVE NEVER KNOWN THEE BEFORE TO LOOK SO UNCERTAIN.
SET THY MIND AT EASE. MY INTENTION IS TO COMMEND YOU TO THE NEW SHOGUN AS HER CHIEF CONCUBINE, AS ALWAYS IT HATH BEEN. FEAR NOT THAT MY THOUGHTS HAVE CHANGED
!
OH...!
SIR FUJINAMI...
HMPH... I WONDER HOW WELL I CAN BELIEVE WHAT THE OLD FOX SAYS. ONE THING'S CERTAIN...
I SHOULD ***NOT*** SET MY MIND AT EASE.

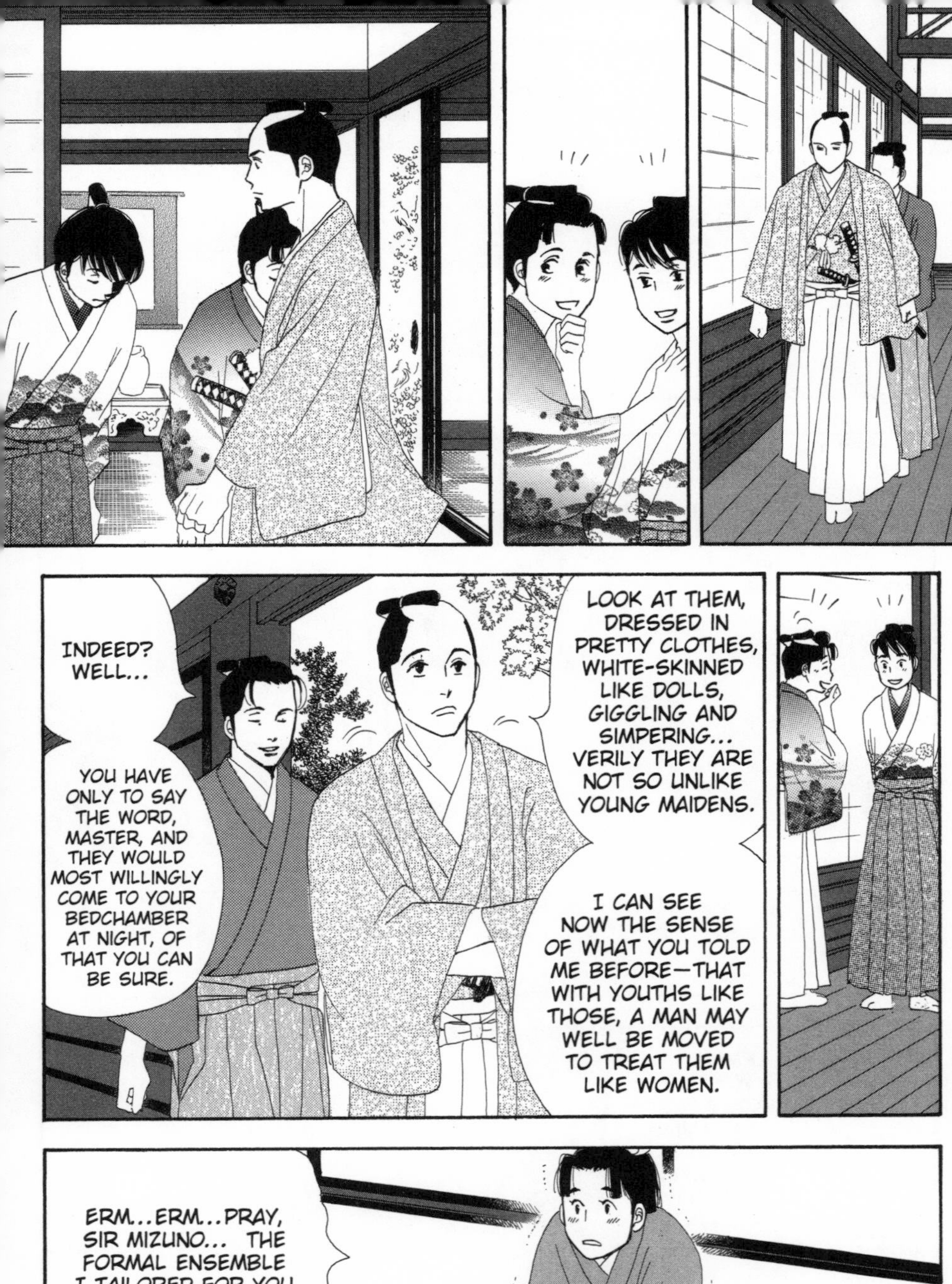
LOOK AT THEM, DRESSED IN PRETTY CLOTHES, WHITE-SKINNED LIKE DOLLS, GIGGLING AND SIMPERING... VERILY THEY ARE NOT SO UNLIKE YOUNG MAIDENS.
I CAN SEE NOW THE SENSE OF WHAT YOU TOLD ME BEFORE—THAT WITH YOUTHS LIKE THOSE, A MAN MAY WELL BE MOVED TO TREAT THEM LIKE WOMEN.
INDEED? WELL...
YOU HAVE ONLY TO SAY THE WORD, MASTER, AND THEY WOULD MOST WILLINGLY COME TO YOUR BEDCHAMBER AT NIGHT, OF THAT YOU CAN BE SURE.
ERM...ERM...PRAY, SIR MIZUNO... THE FORMAL ENSEMBLE I TAILORED FOR YOU DID NOT MEET WITH YOUR APPROVAL...?

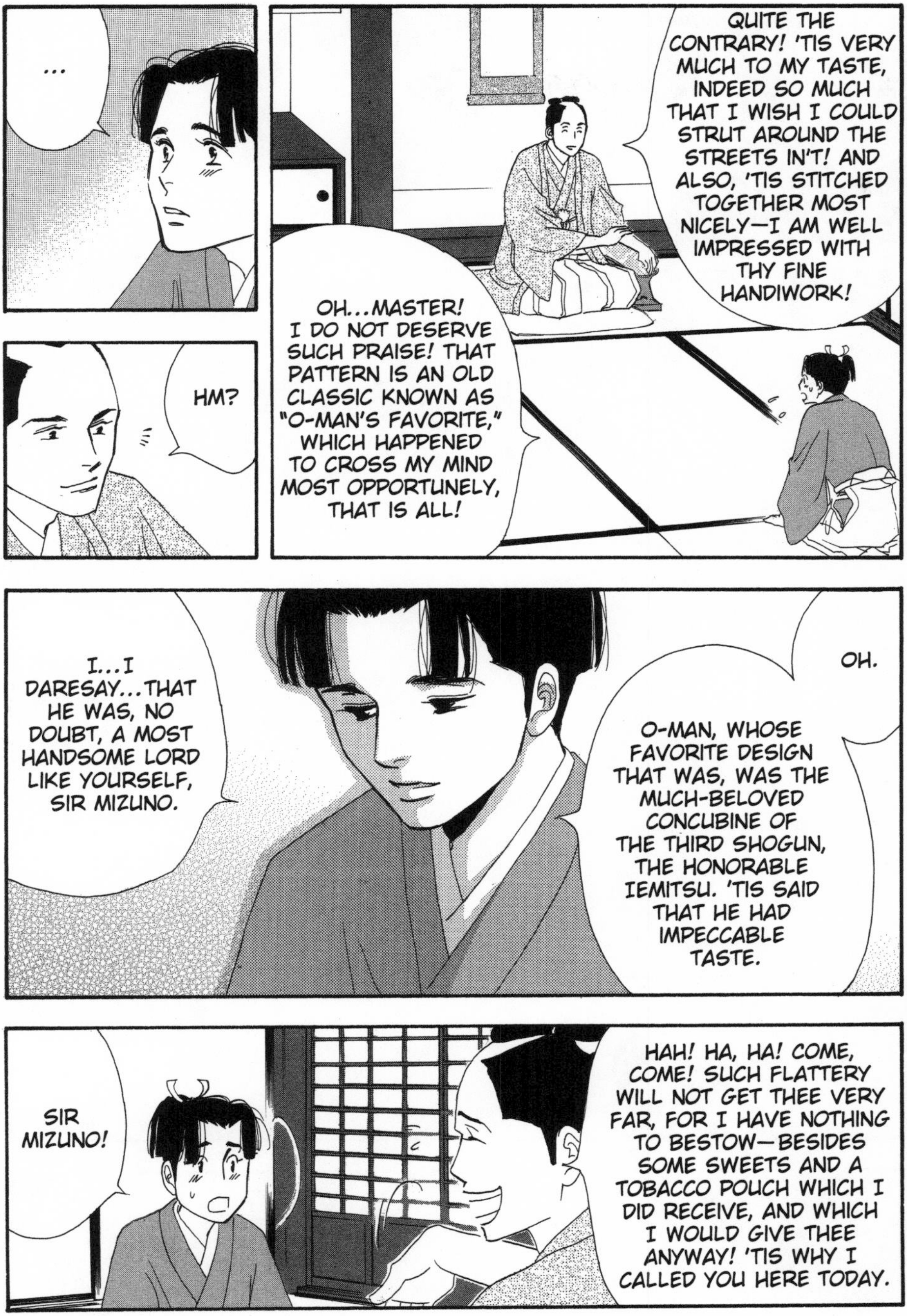
QUITE THE CONTRARY! 'TIS VERY MUCH TO MY TASTE, INDEED SO MUCH THAT I WISH I COULD STRUT AROUND THE STREETS IN'T! AND ALSO, 'TIS STITCHED TOGETHER MOST NICELY—I AM WELL IMPRESSED WITH THY FINE HANDIWORK!
OH...MASTER! I DO NOT DESERVE SUCH PRAISE! THAT PATTERN IS AN OLD CLASSIC KNOWN AS "O-MAN'S FAVORITE," WHICH HAPPENED TO CROSS MY MIND MOST OPPORTUNELY, THAT IS ALL!
...
HM?
OH.
O-MAN, WHOSE FAVORITE DESIGN THAT WAS, WAS THE MUCH-BELOVED CONCUBINE OF THE THIRD SHOGUN, THE HONORABLE IEMITSU. 'TIS SAID THAT HE HAD IMPECCABLE TASTE.
I...I DARESAY...THAT HE WAS, NO DOUBT, A MOST HANDSOME LORD LIKE YOURSELF, SIR MIZUNO.
HAH! HA, HA! COME, COME! SUCH FLATTERY WILL NOT GET THEE VERY FAR, FOR I HAVE NOTHING TO BESTOW—BESIDES SOME SWEETS AND A TOBACCO POUCH WHICH I DID RECEIVE, AND WHICH I WOULD GIVE THEE ANYWAY! 'TIS WHY I CALLED YOU HERE TODAY.
SIR MIZUNO!

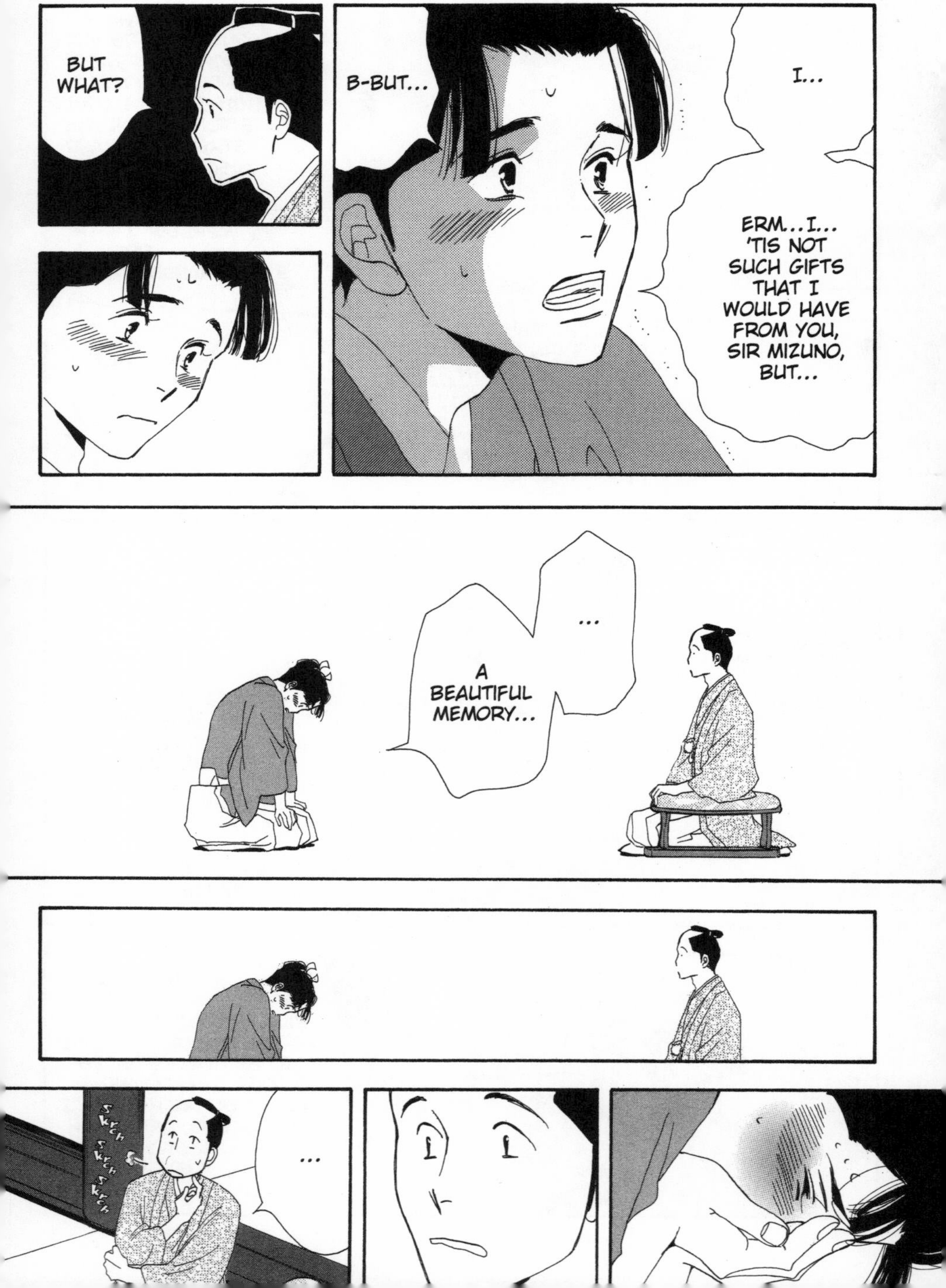

I...
B-BUT...
ERM...I... 'TIS NOT SUCH GIFTS THAT I WOULD HAVE FROM YOU, SIR MIZUNO, BUT...
BUT WHAT?
...
A BEAUTIFUL MEMORY...
...
Skrch Skrch Skrch

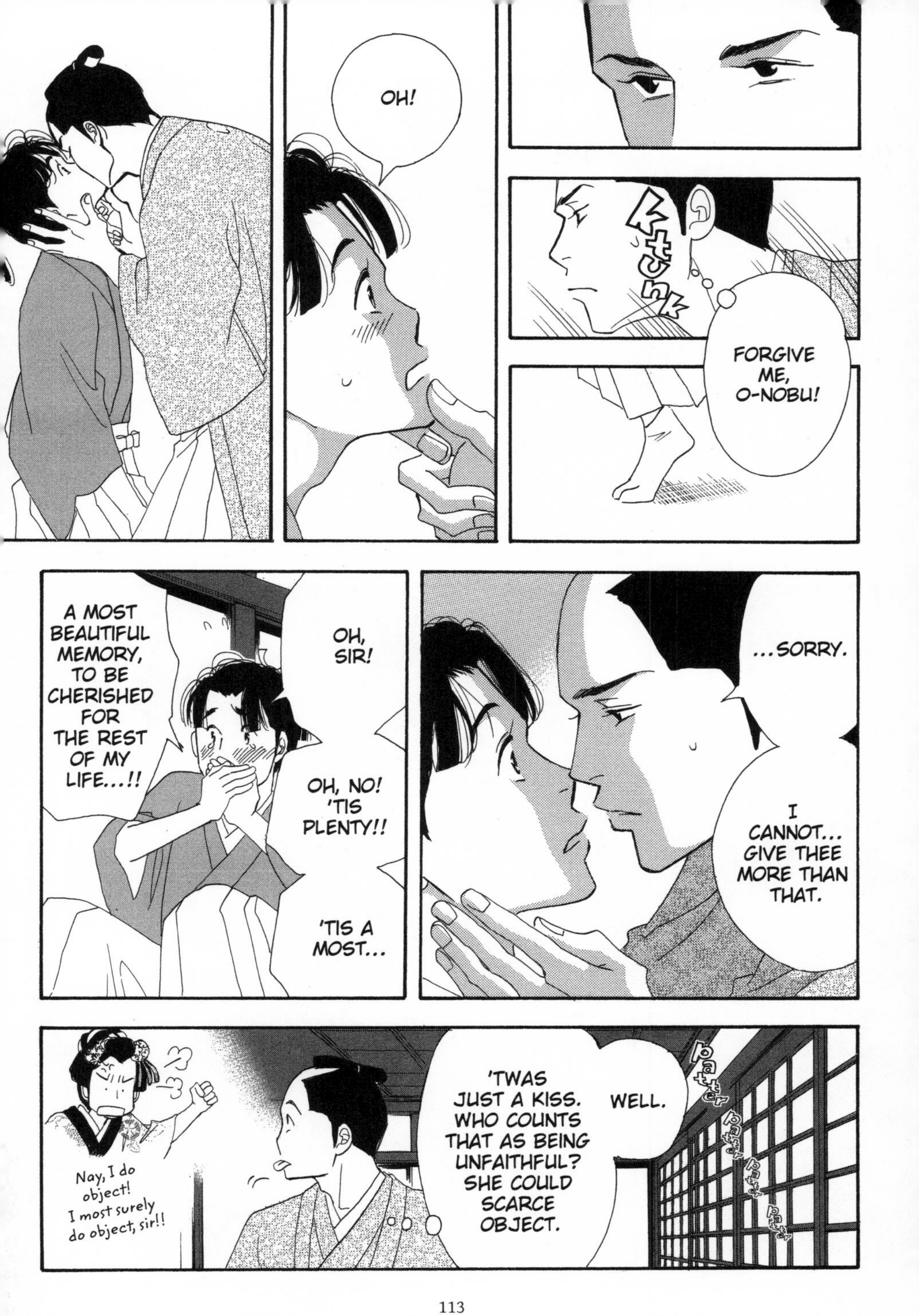
ktunk
FORGIVE ME, O-NOBU!
OH!
...SORRY.
I CANNOT... GIVE THEE MORE THAN THAT.
OH, SIR!
OH, NO! 'TIS PLENTY!!
'TIS A MOST...
A MOST BEAUTIFUL MEMORY, TO BE CHERISHED FOR THE REST OF MY LIFE...!!
patter patter patter patter
WELL.
'TWAS JUST A KISS. WHO COUNTS THAT AS BEING UNFAITHFUL? SHE COULD SCARCE OBJECT.
Nay, I do object! I most surely do object, sir!!

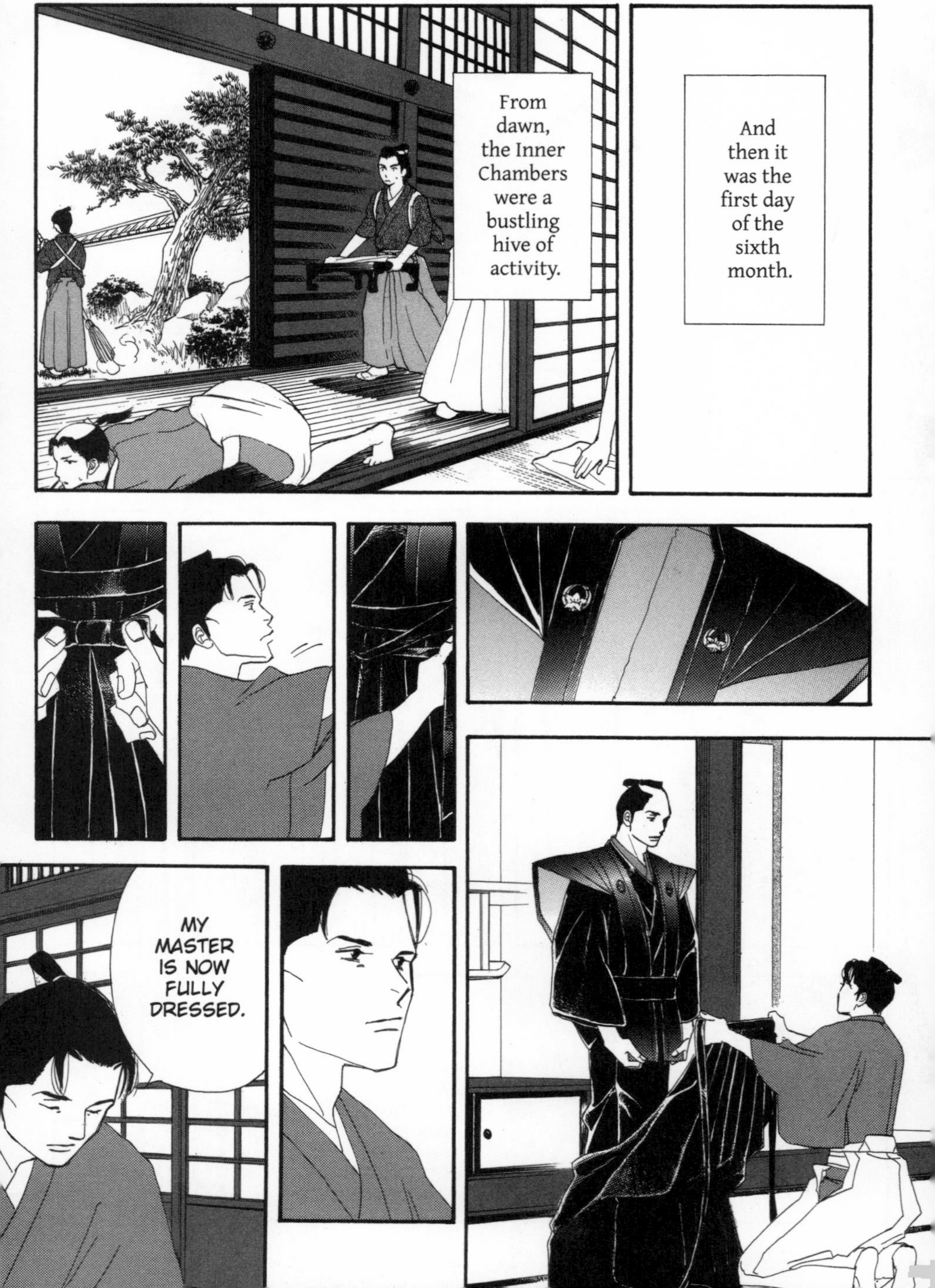
And then it was the first day of the sixth month.
From dawn, the Inner Chambers were a bustling hive of activity.
MY MASTER IS NOW FULLY DRESSED.

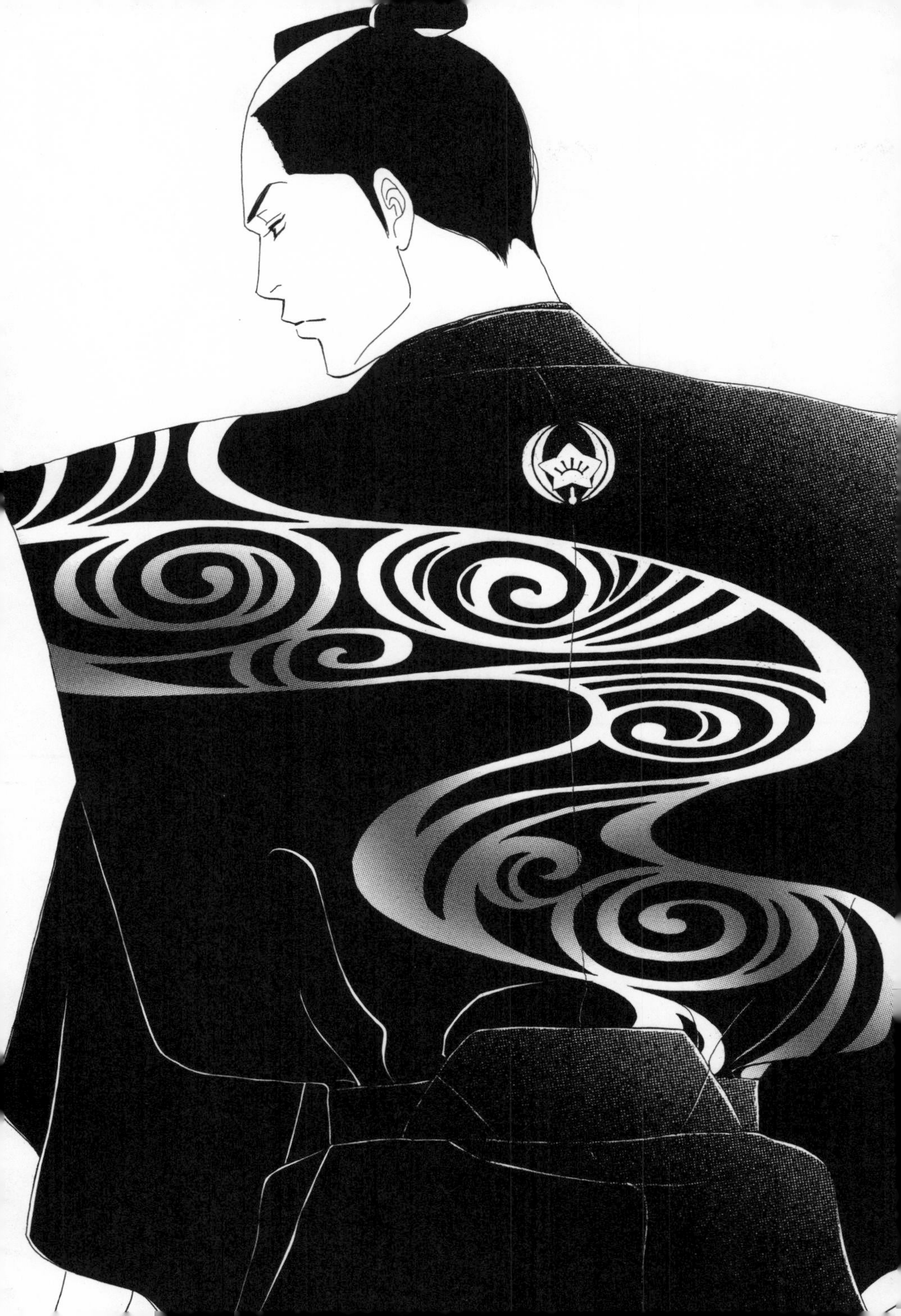

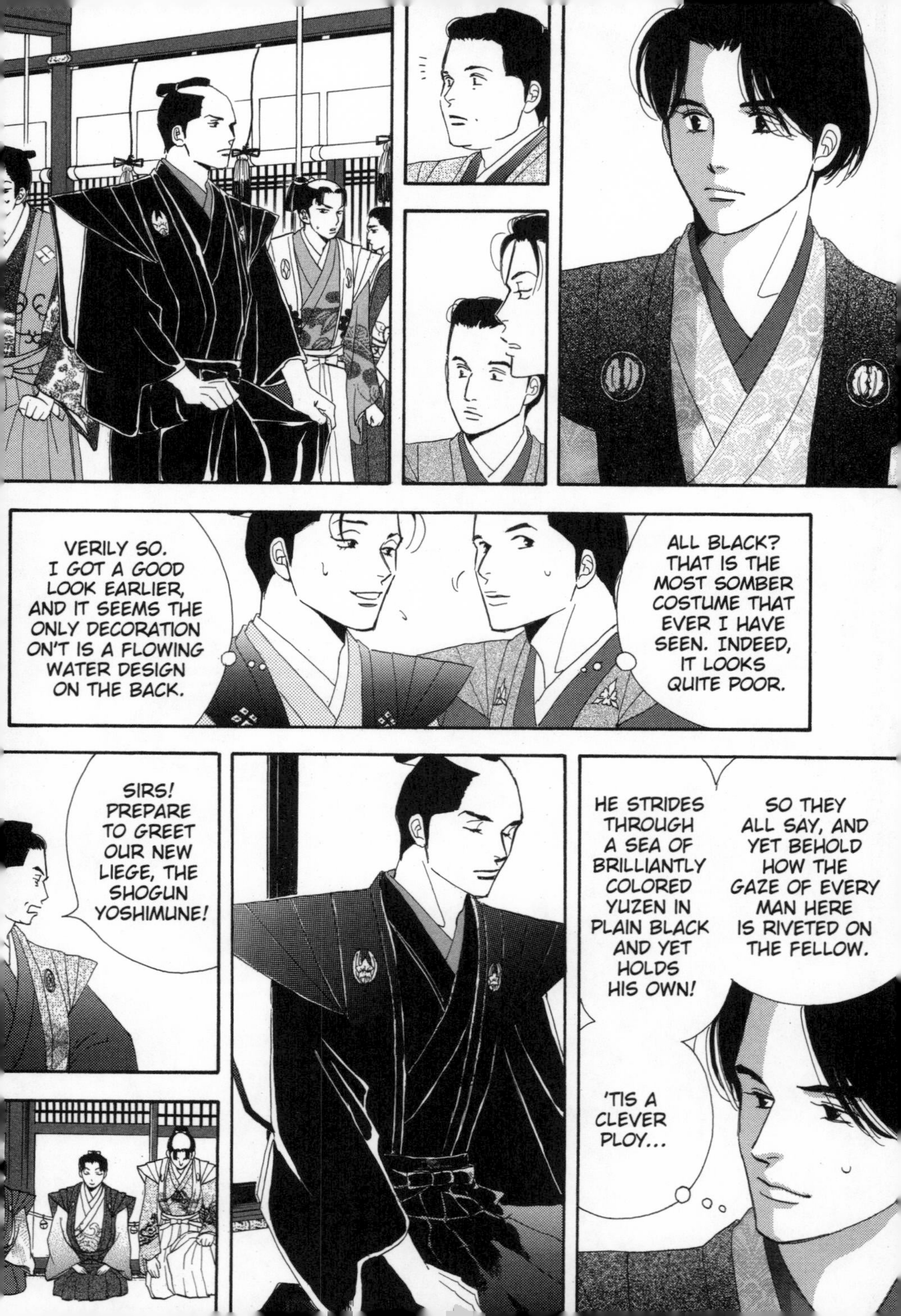
ALL BLACK? THAT IS THE MOST SOMBER COSTUME THAT EVER I HAVE SEEN. INDEED, IT LOOKS QUITE POOR.
VERILY SO. I GOT A GOOD LOOK EARLIER, AND IT SEEMS THE ONLY DECORATION ON'T IS A FLOWING WATER DESIGN ON THE BACK.
SO THEY ALL SAY, AND YET BEHOLD HOW THE GAZE OF EVERY MAN HERE IS RIVETED ON THE FELLOW.
HE STRIDES THROUGH A SEA OF BRILLIANTLY COLORED YUZEN IN PLAIN BLACK AND YET HOLDS HIS OWN!
'TIS A CLEVER PLOY...
SIRS! PREPARE TO GREET OUR NEW LIEGE, THE SHOGUN YOSHIMUNE!

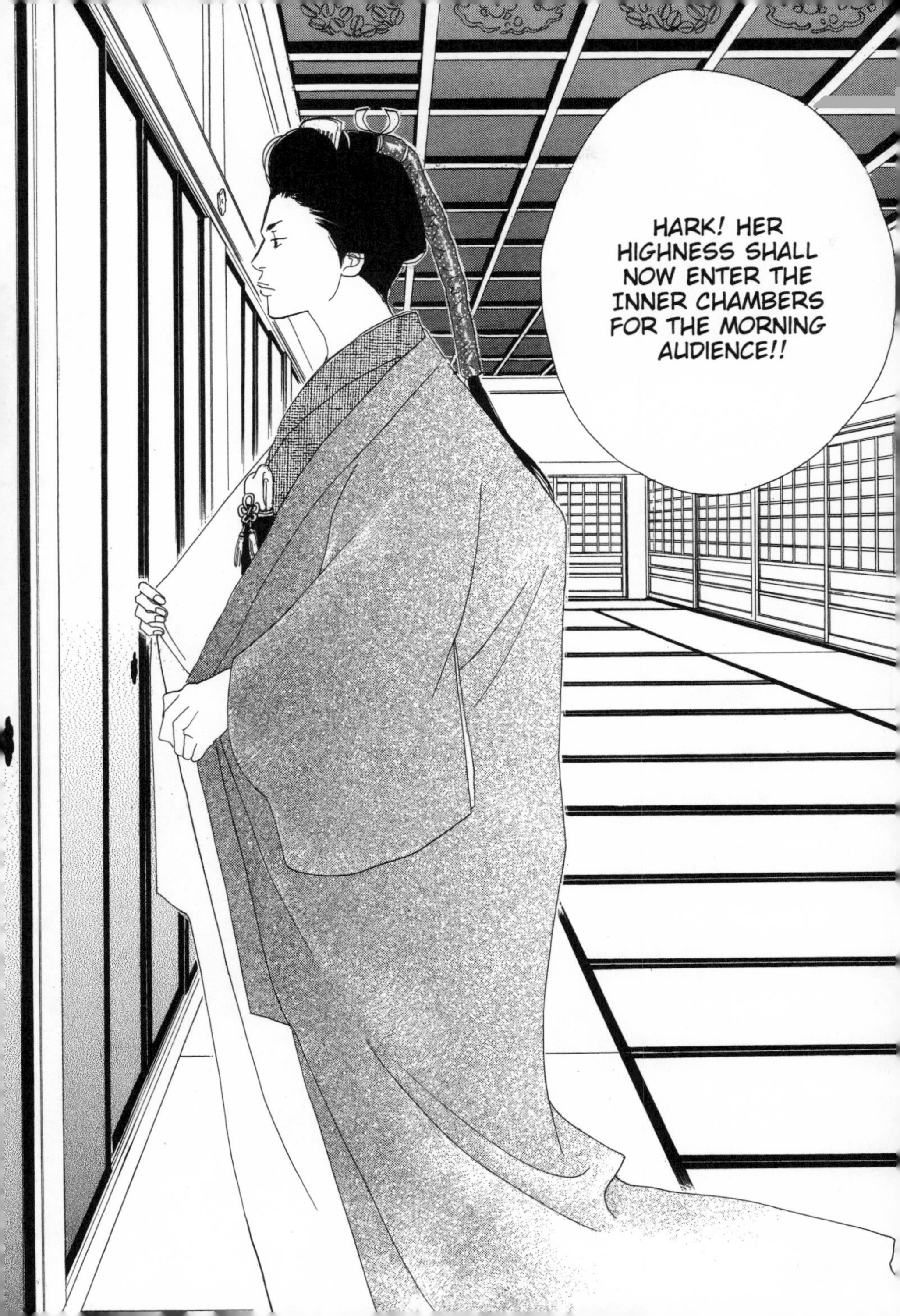
HARK! HER HIGHNESS SHALL NOW ENTER THE INNER CHAMBERS FOR THE MORNING AUDIENCE!!

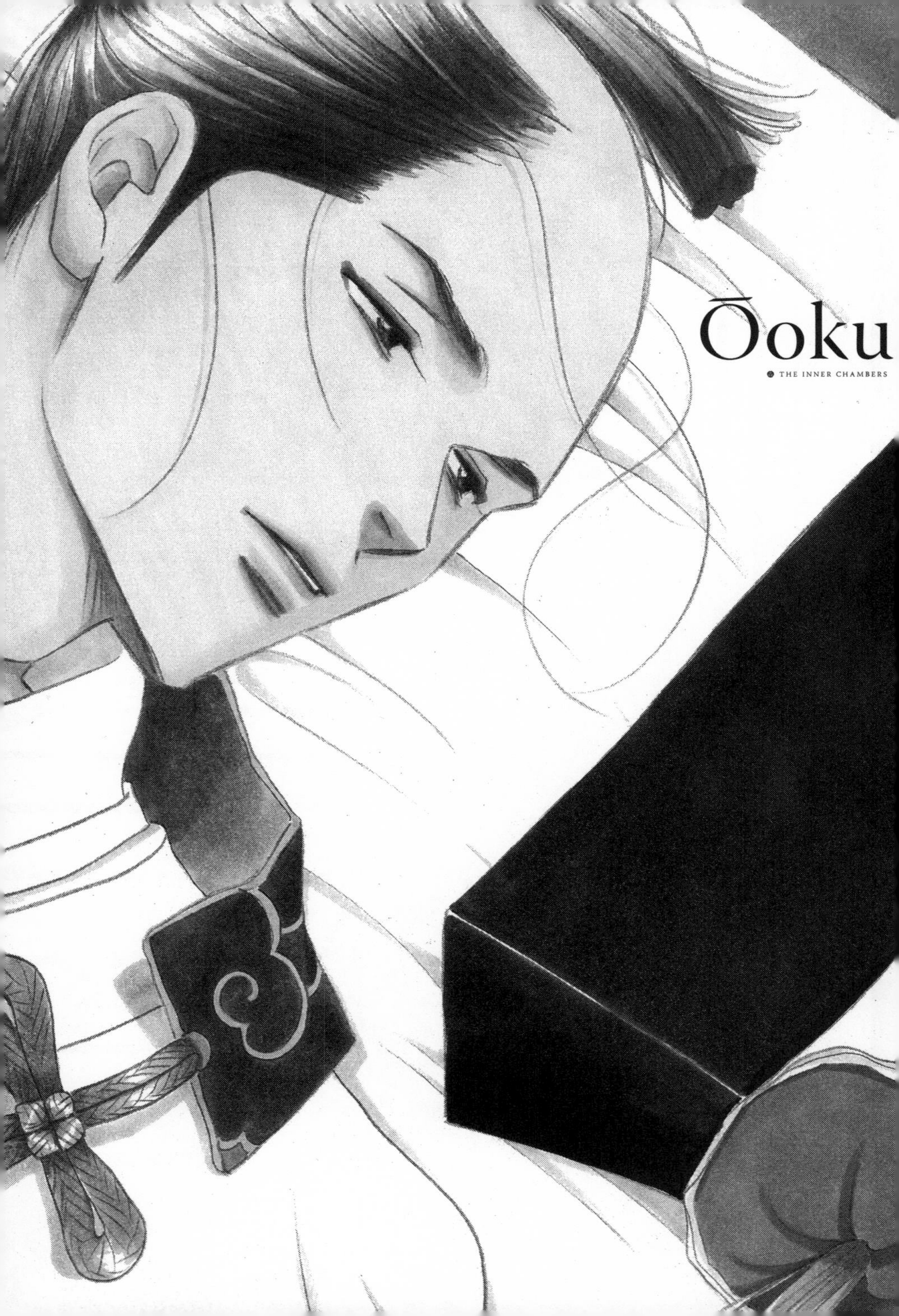
Ōoku
THE INNER CHAMBERS

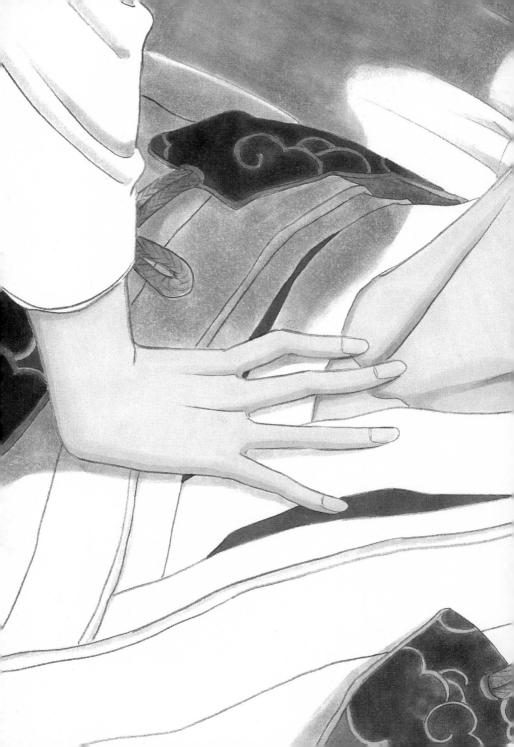

Ōoku

THE INNER CHAMBERS

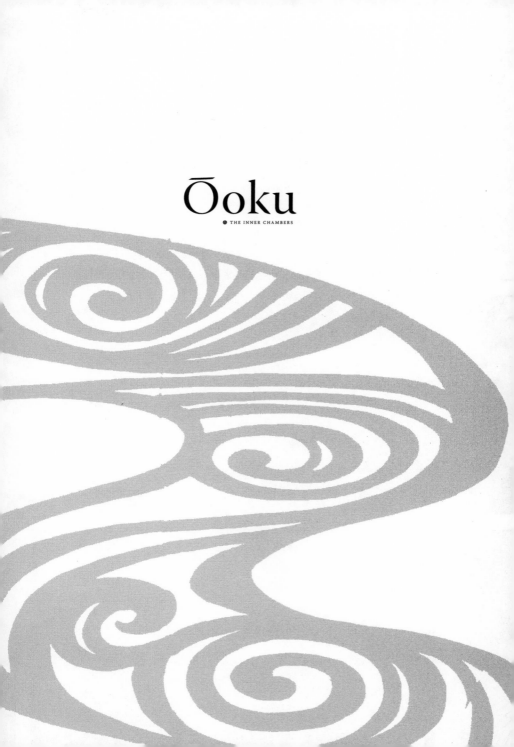

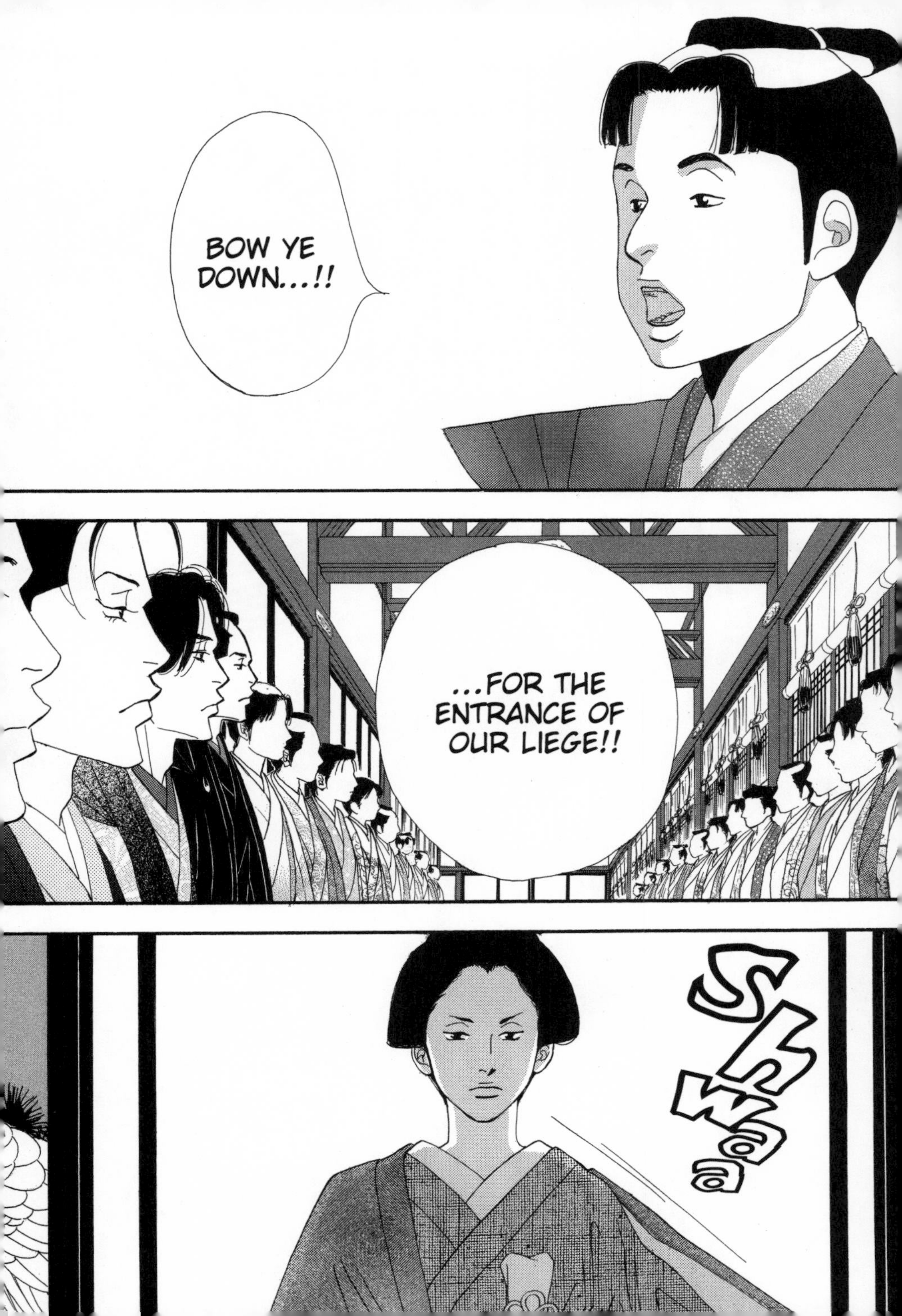
BOW YE DOWN...!!
...FOR THE ENTRANCE OF OUR LIEGE!!
Shwaa

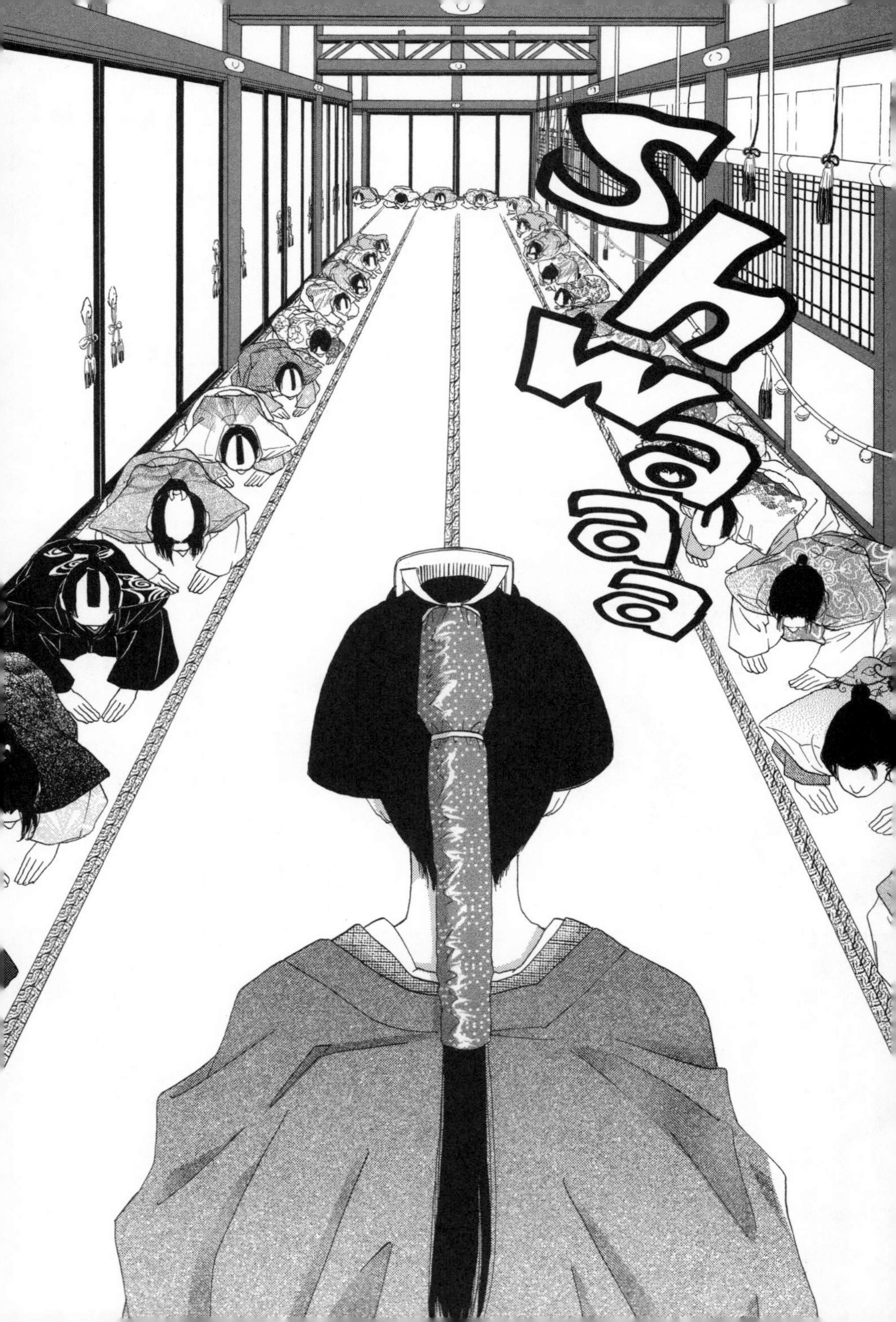
Shwaaa

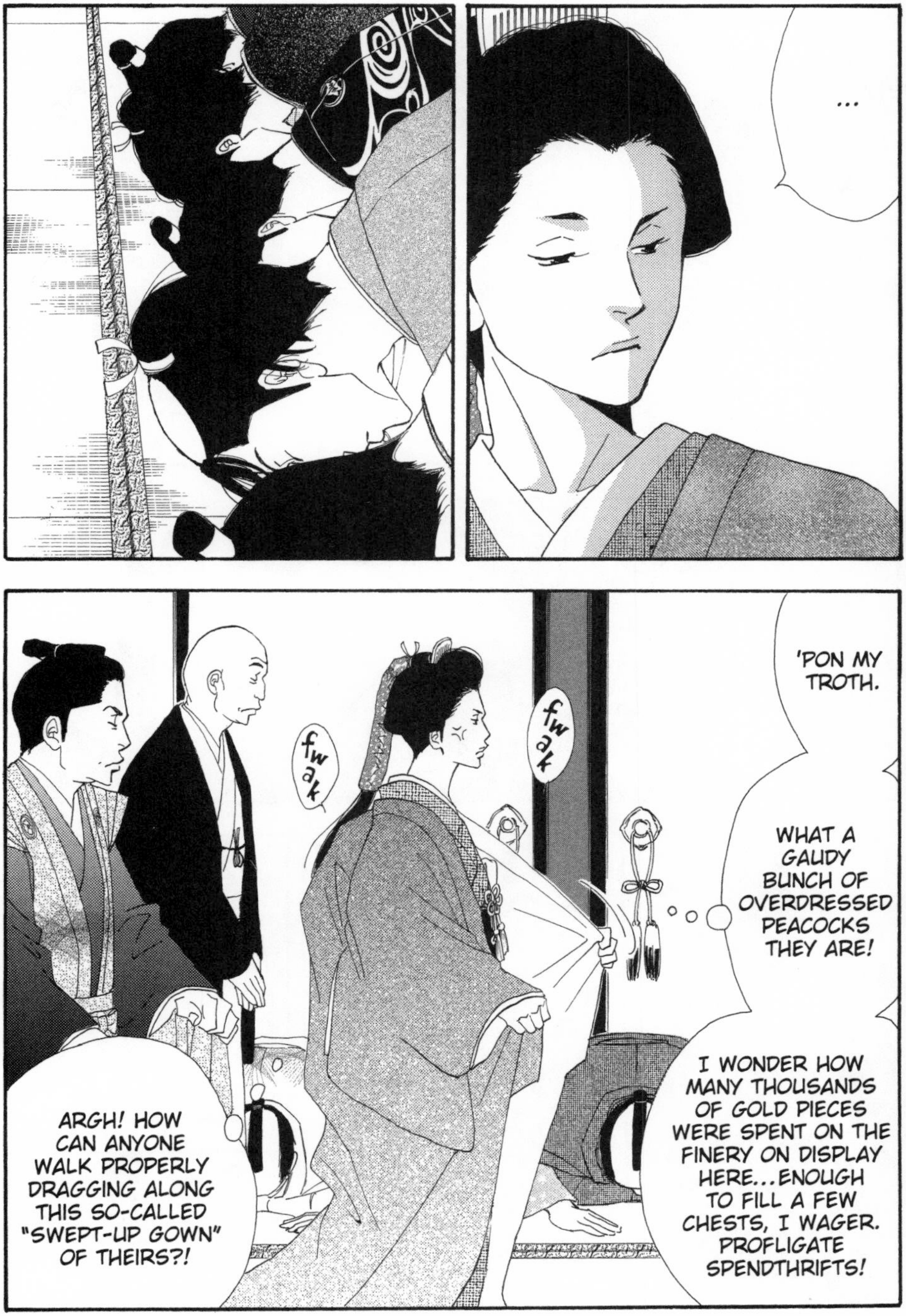
...
'PON MY TROTH.
fwak
WHAT A GAUDY BUNCH OF OVERDRESSED PEACOCKS THEY ARE!
fwak
I WONDER HOW MANY THOUSANDS OF GOLD PIECES WERE SPENT ON THE FINERY ON DISPLAY HERE...ENOUGH TO FILL A FEW CHESTS, I WAGER. PROFLIGATE SPENDTHRIFTS!
ARGH! HOW CAN ANYONE WALK PROPERLY DRAGGING ALONG THIS SO-CALLED "SWEPT-UP GOWN" OF THEIRS?!

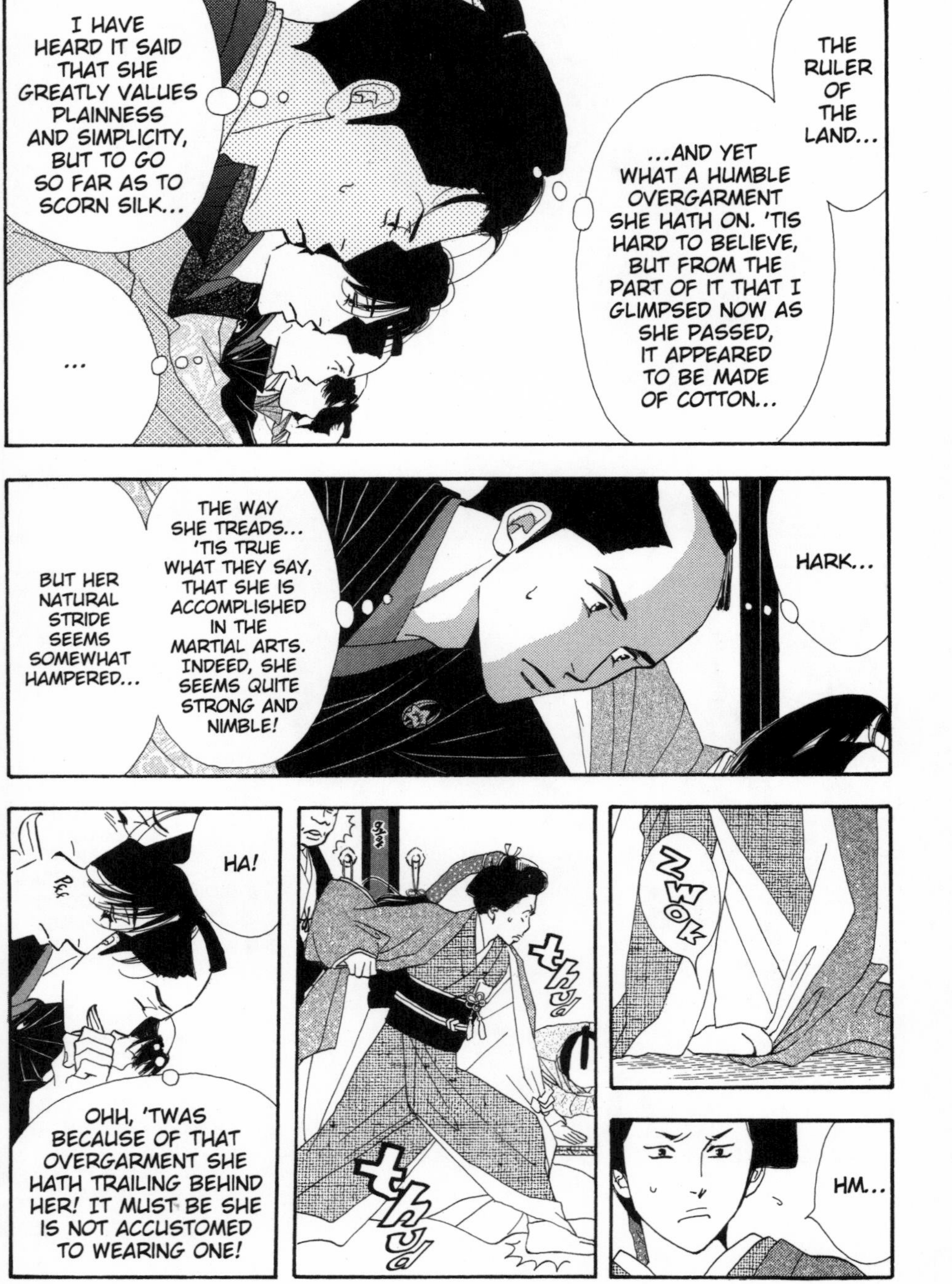
THE RULER OF THE LAND...
...AND YET WHAT A HUMBLE OVERGARMENT SHE HATH ON. 'TIS HARD TO BELIEVE, BUT FROM THE PART OF IT THAT I GLIMPSED NOW AS SHE PASSED, IT APPEARED TO BE MADE OF COTTON...
I HAVE HEARD IT SAID THAT SHE GREATLY VALUES PLAINNESS AND SIMPLICITY, BUT TO GO SO FAR AS TO SCORN SILK...
...
HARK...
THE WAY SHE TREADS... 'TIS TRUE WHAT THEY SAY, THAT SHE IS ACCOMPLISHED IN THE MARTIAL ARTS. INDEED, SHE SEEMS QUITE STRONG AND NIMBLE!
BUT HER NATURAL STRIDE SEEMS SOMEWHAT HAMPERED...
ZWOK
HM...
HA!
OHH, 'TWAS BECAUSE OF THAT OVERGARMENT SHE HATH TRAILING BEHIND HER! IT MUST BE SHE IS NOT ACCUSTOMED TO WEARING ONE!

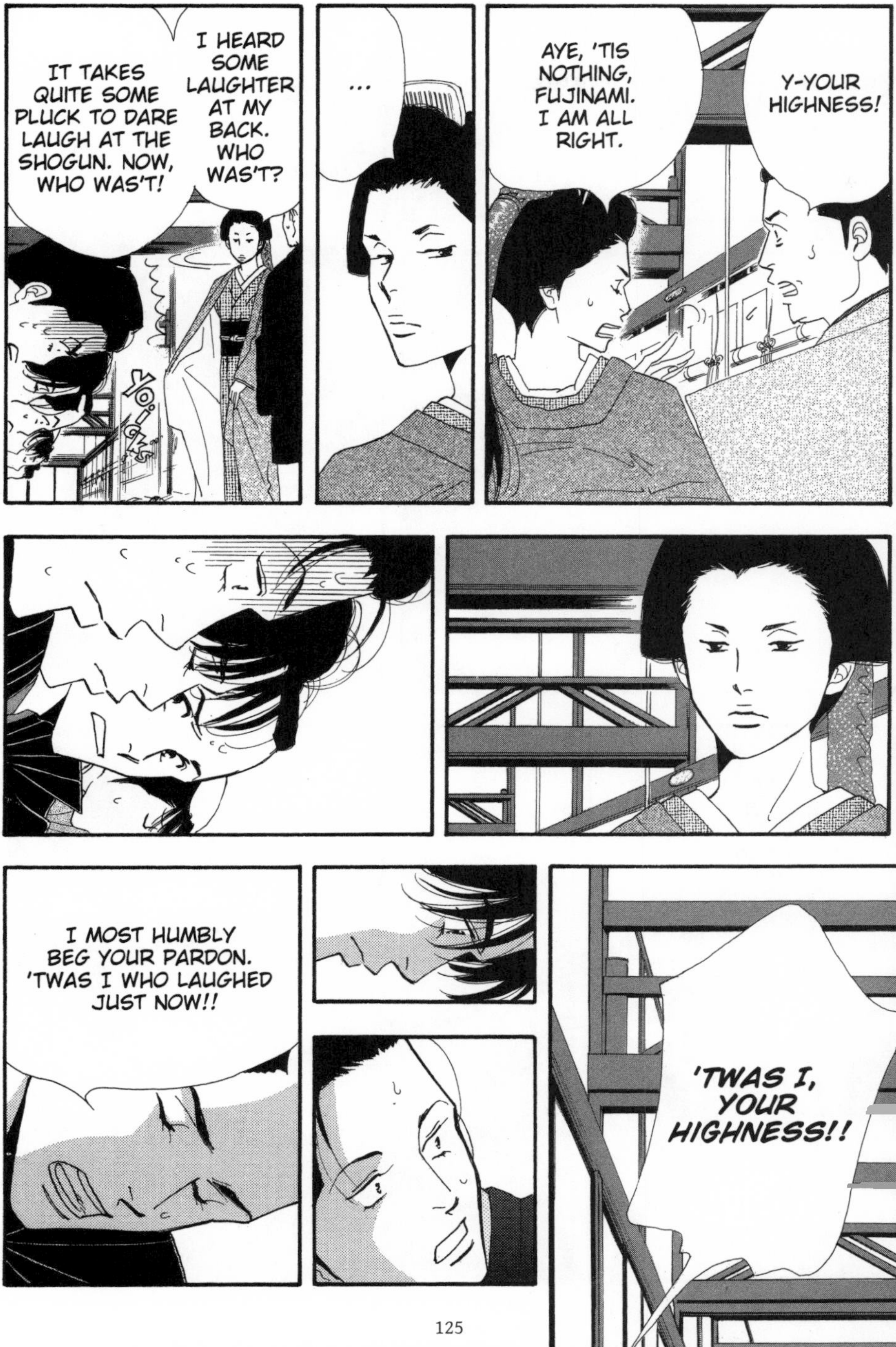
Y-YOUR HIGHNESS!
AYE, 'TIS NOTHING, FUJINAMI. I AM ALL RIGHT.
...
I HEARD SOME LAUGHTER AT MY BACK. WHO WAS'T?
IT TAKES QUITE SOME PLUCK TO DARE LAUGH AT THE SHOGUN. NOW, WHO WAS'T!
YOICKS
'TWAS I, YOUR HIGHNESS!!
I MOST HUMBLY BEG YOUR PARDON. 'TWAS I WHO LAUGHED JUST NOW!!

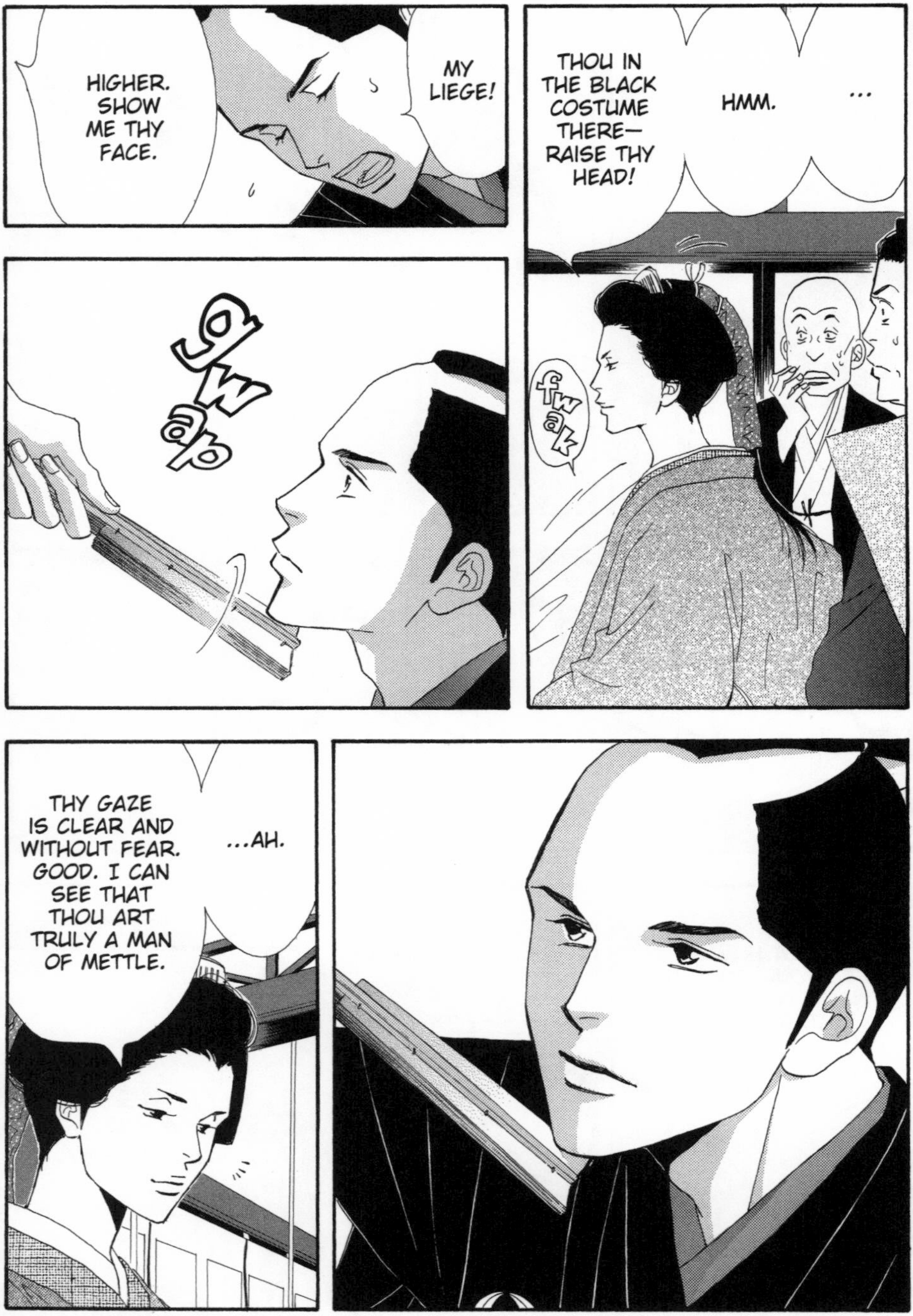
...
HMM.
THOU IN THE BLACK COSTUME THERE— RAISE THY HEAD!
fwak
MY LIEGE!
HIGHER. SHOW ME THY FACE.
gwap
...AH.
THY GAZE IS CLEAR AND WITHOUT FEAR. GOOD. I CAN SEE THAT THOU ART TRULY A MAN OF METTLE.

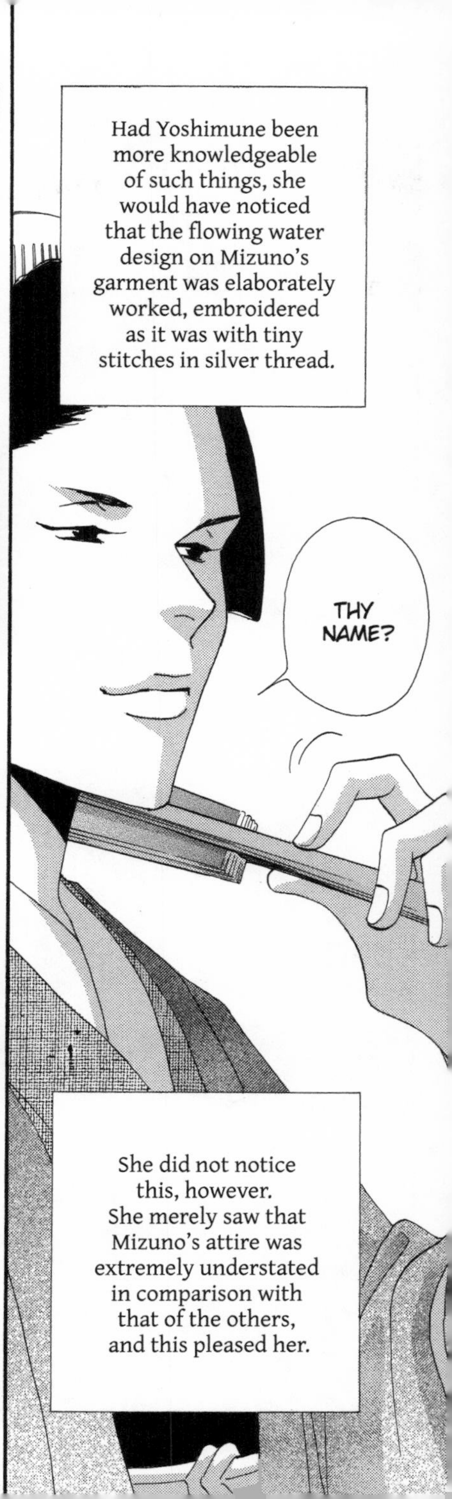
Had Yoshimune been more knowledgeable of such things, she would have noticed that the flowing water design on Mizuno's garment was elaborately worked, embroidered as it was with tiny stitches in silver thread.
THY NAME?
She did not notice this, however. She merely saw that Mizuno's attire was extremely understated in comparison with that of the others, and this pleased her.

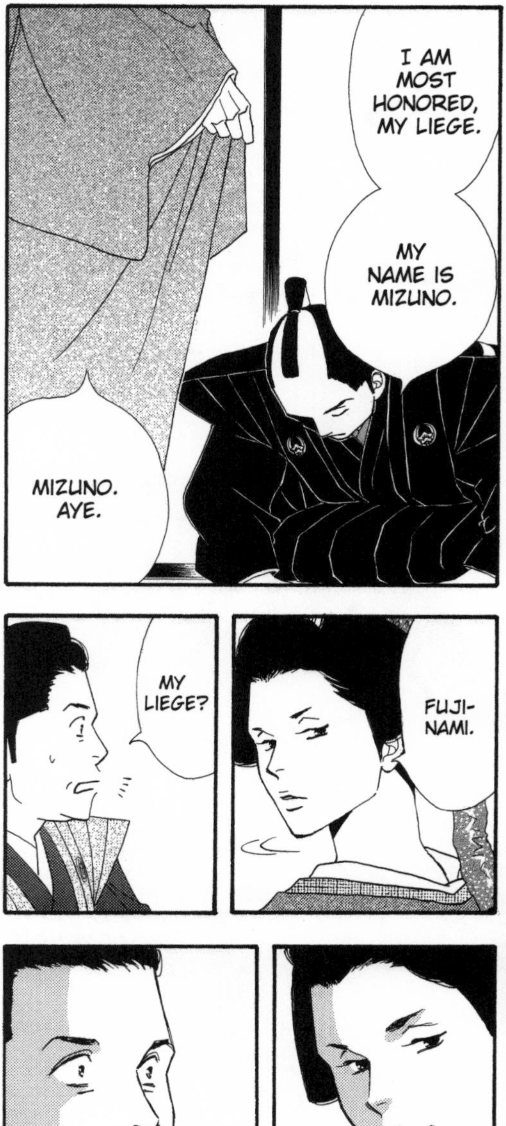
I AM MOST HONORED, MY LIEGE.
MY NAME IS MIZUNO.
MIZUNO. AYE.
FUJI-NAMI.
MY LIEGE?
flik

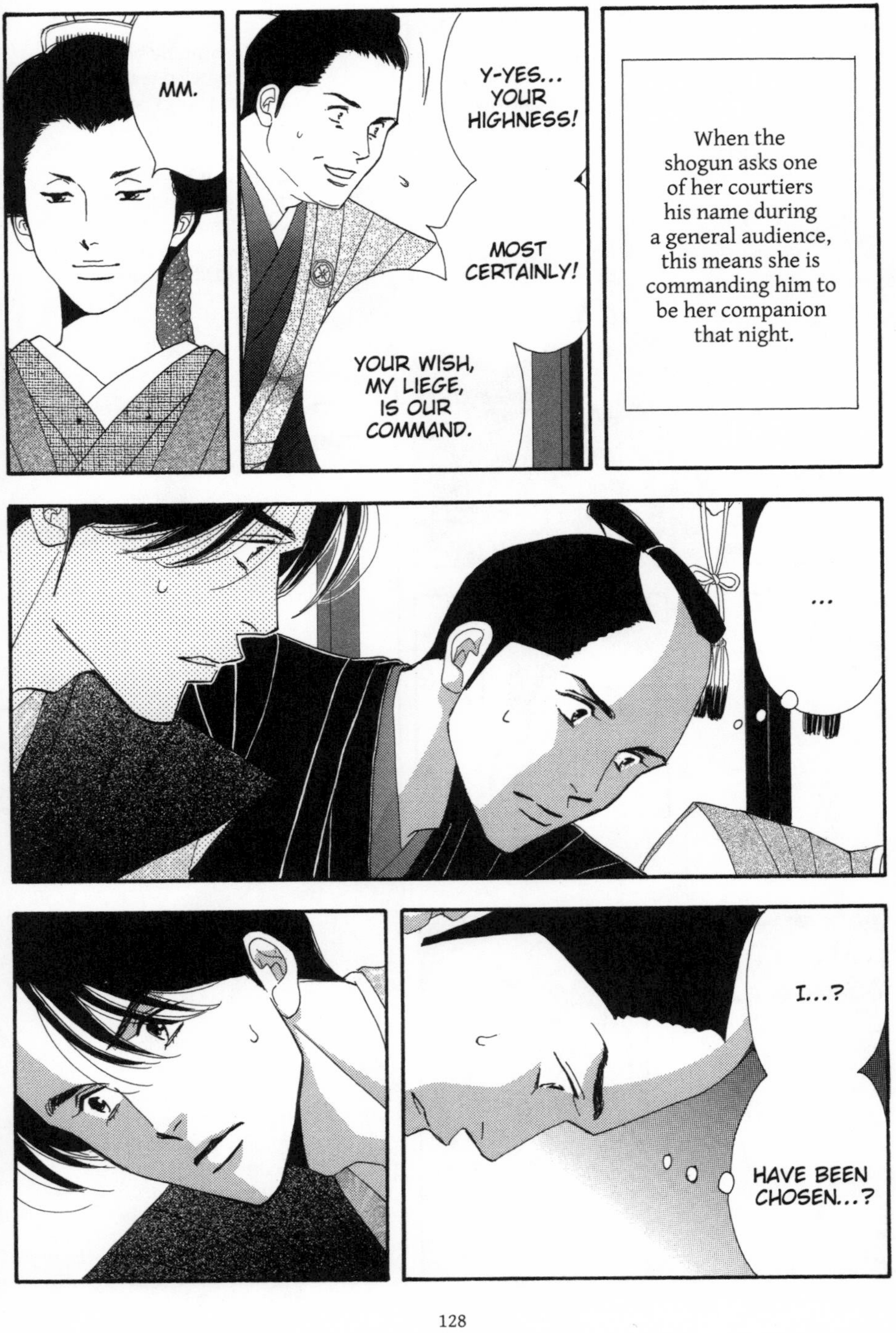
When the shogun asks one of her courtiers his name during a general audience, this means she is commanding him to be her companion that night.
Y-YES... YOUR HIGHNESS!
MOST CERTAINLY!
YOUR WISH, MY LIEGE, IS OUR COMMAND.
MM.
...
I...?
HAVE BEEN CHOSEN...?

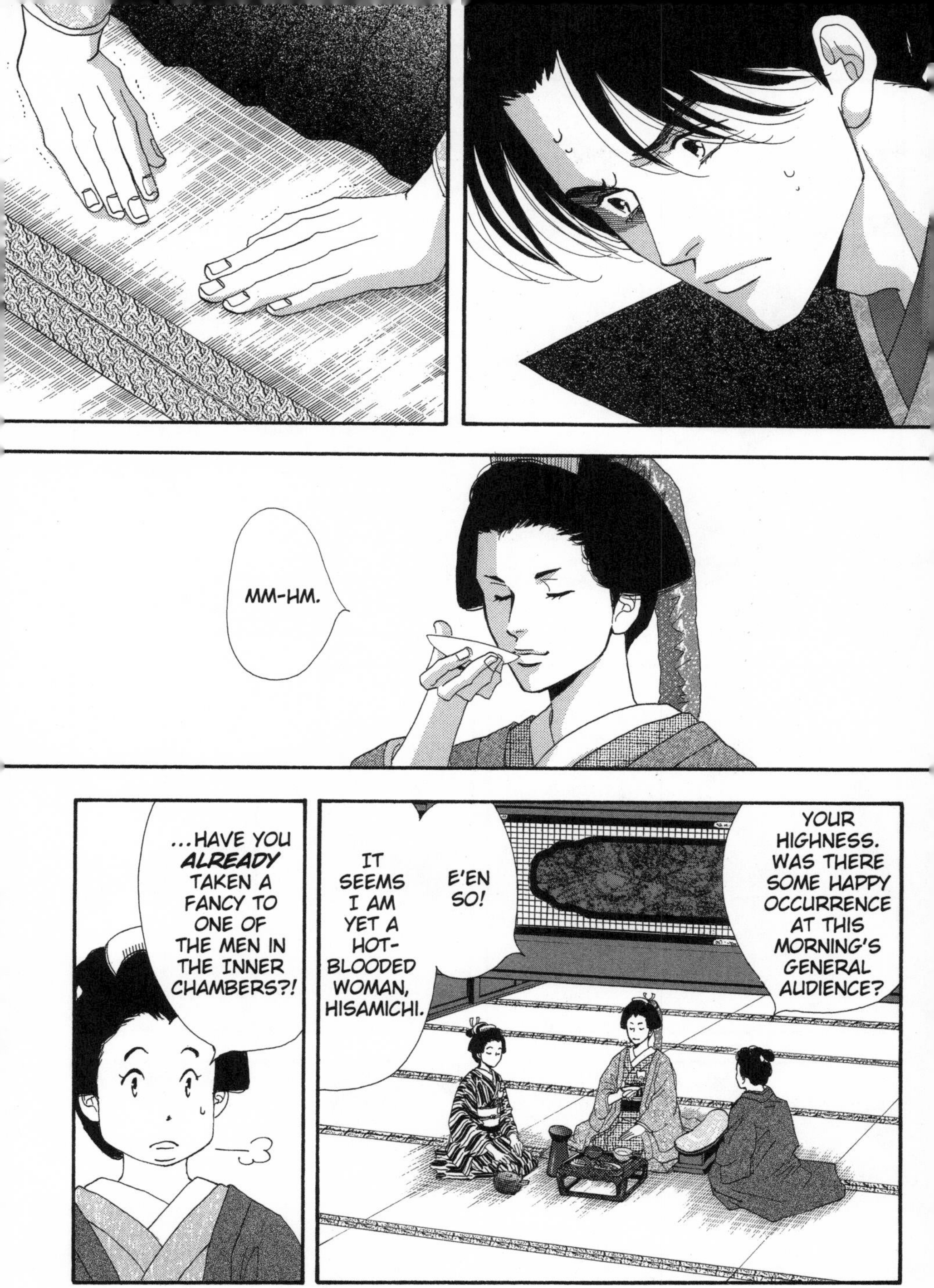
MM-HM.
YOUR HIGHNESS. WAS THERE SOME HAPPY OCCURRENCE AT THIS MORNING'S GENERAL AUDIENCE?
E'EN SO!
IT SEEMS I AM YET A HOT-BLOODED WOMAN, HISAMICHI.
...HAVE YOU ALREADY TAKEN A FANCY TO ONE OF THE MEN IN THE INNER CHAMBERS?!

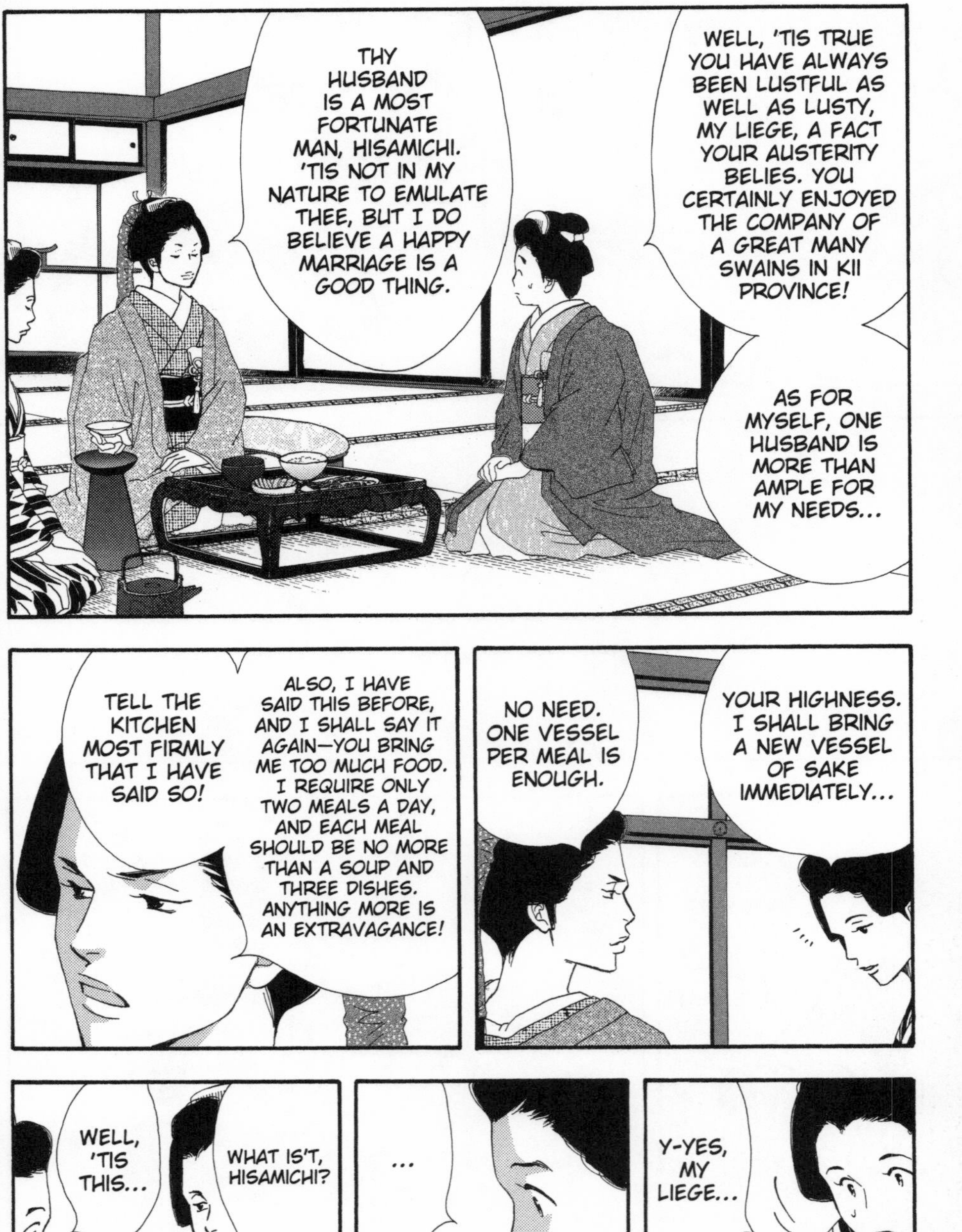
THY HUSBAND IS A MOST FORTUNATE MAN, HISAMICHI. 'TIS NOT IN MY NATURE TO EMULATE THEE, BUT I DO BELIEVE A HAPPY MARRIAGE IS A GOOD THING.
WELL, 'TIS TRUE YOU HAVE ALWAYS BEEN LUSTFUL AS WELL AS LUSTY, MY LIEGE, A FACT YOUR AUSTERITY BELIES. YOU CERTAINLY ENJOYED THE COMPANY OF A GREAT MANY SWAINS IN KII PROVINCE!
AS FOR MYSELF, ONE HUSBAND IS MORE THAN AMPLE FOR MY NEEDS...
YOUR HIGHNESS. I SHALL BRING A NEW VESSEL OF SAKE IMMEDIATELY...
NO NEED. ONE VESSEL PER MEAL IS ENOUGH.
ALSO, I HAVE SAID THIS BEFORE, AND I SHALL SAY IT AGAIN—YOU BRING ME TOO MUCH FOOD. I REQUIRE ONLY TWO MEALS A DAY, AND EACH MEAL SHOULD BE NO MORE THAN A SOUP AND THREE DISHES. ANYTHING MORE IS AN EXTRAVAGANCE!
TELL THE KITCHEN MOST FIRMLY THAT I HAVE SAID SO!
Y-YES, MY LIEGE...
...
WHAT IS'T, HISAMICHI?
WELL, 'TIS THIS...

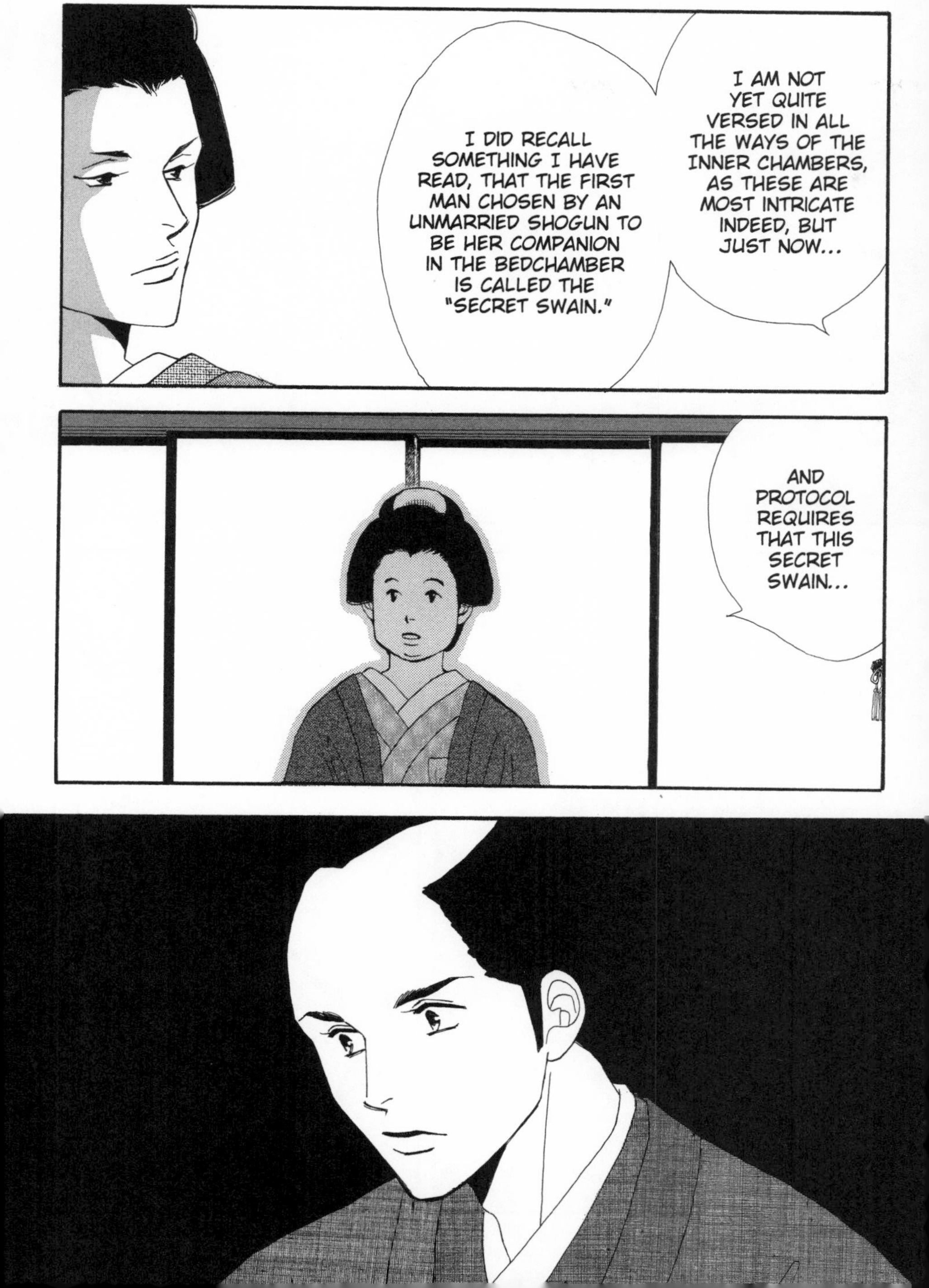
I AM NOT YET QUITE VERSED IN ALL THE WAYS OF THE INNER CHAMBERS, AS THESE ARE MOST INTRICATE INDEED, BUT JUST NOW...
I DID RECALL SOMETHING I HAVE READ, THAT THE FIRST MAN CHOSEN BY AN UNMARRIED SHOGUN TO BE HER COMPANION IN THE BEDCHAMBER IS CALLED THE "SECRET SWAIN."
AND PROTOCOL REQUIRES THAT THIS SECRET SWAIN...

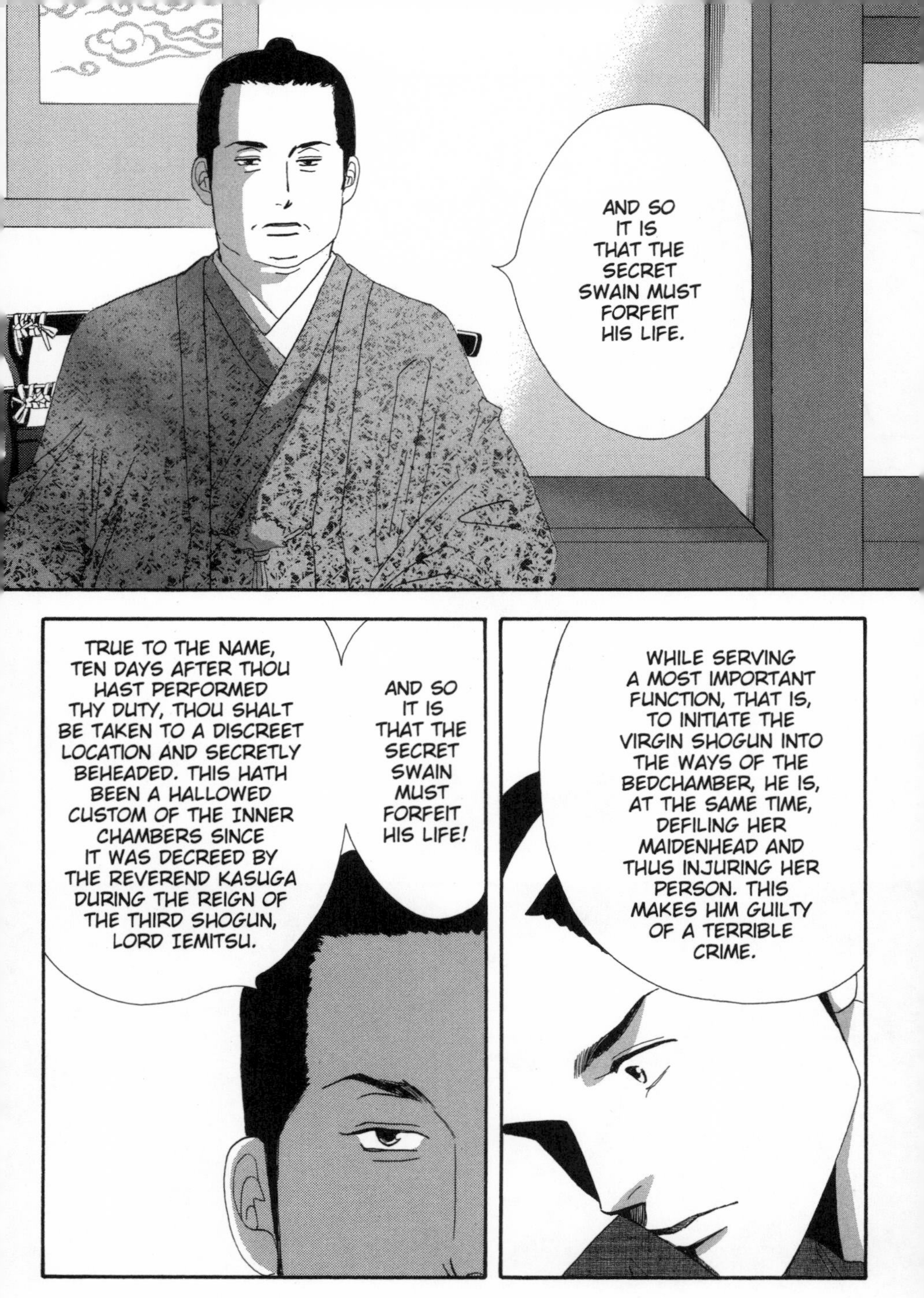
AND SO IT IS THAT THE SECRET SWAIN MUST FORFEIT HIS LIFE.
WHILE SERVING A MOST IMPORTANT FUNCTION, THAT IS, TO INITIATE THE VIRGIN SHOGUN INTO THE WAYS OF THE BEDCHAMBER, HE IS, AT THE SAME TIME, DEFILING HER MAIDENHEAD AND THUS INJURING HER PERSON. THIS MAKES HIM GUILTY OF A TERRIBLE CRIME.
AND SO IT IS THAT THE SECRET SWAIN MUST FORFEIT HIS LIFE!
TRUE TO THE NAME, TEN DAYS AFTER THOU HAST PERFORMED THY DUTY, THOU SHALT BE TAKEN TO A DISCREET LOCATION AND SECRETLY BEHEADED. THIS HATH BEEN A HALLOWED CUSTOM OF THE INNER CHAMBERS SINCE IT WAS DECREED BY THE REVEREND KASUGA DURING THE REIGN OF THE THIRD SHOGUN, LORD IEMITSU.

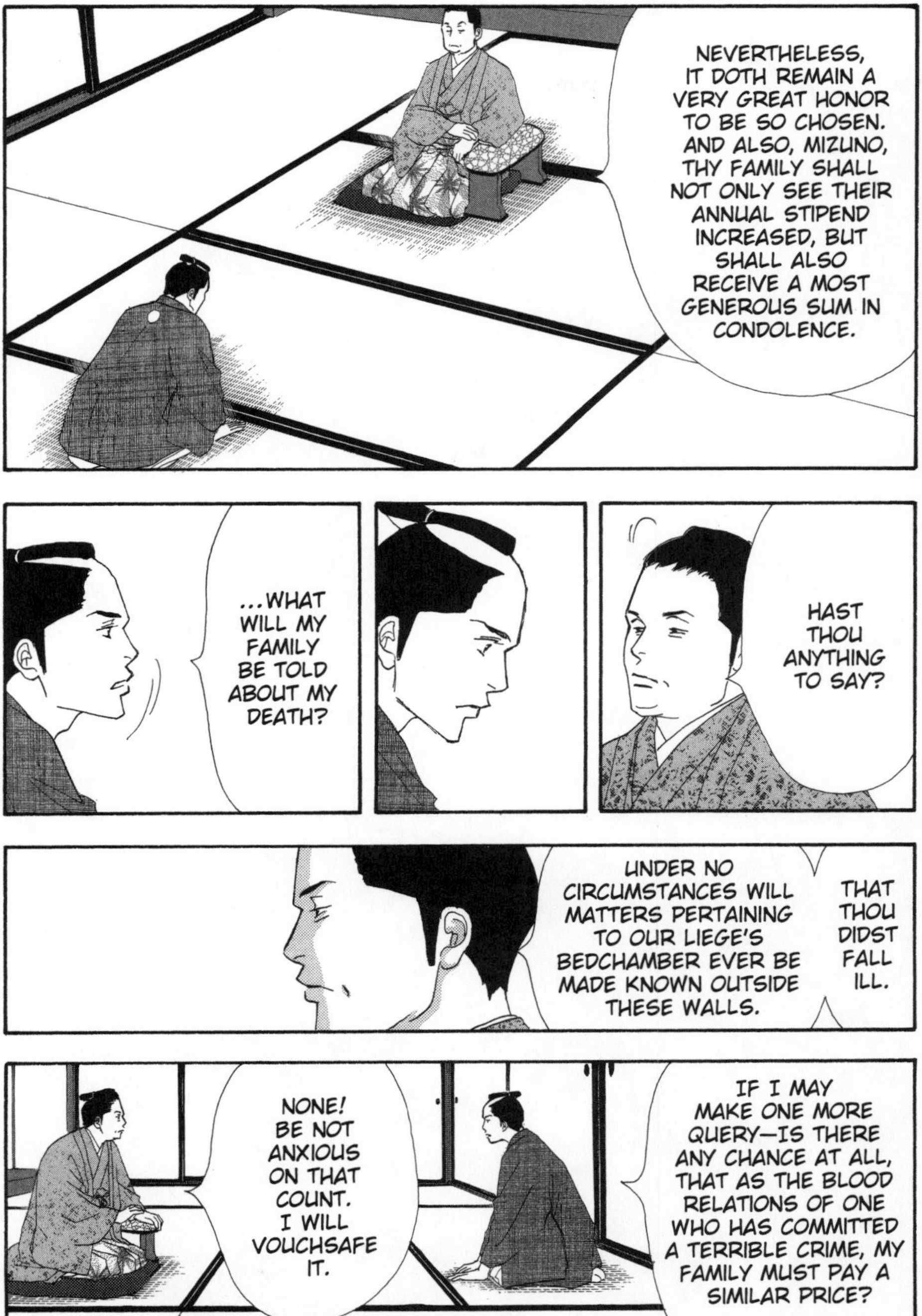
NEVERTHELESS, IT DOTH REMAIN A VERY GREAT HONOR TO BE SO CHOSEN. AND ALSO, MIZUNO, THY FAMILY SHALL NOT ONLY SEE THEIR ANNUAL STIPEND INCREASED, BUT SHALL ALSO RECEIVE A MOST GENEROUS SUM IN CONDOLENCE.
HAST THOU ANYTHING TO SAY?
...WHAT WILL MY FAMILY BE TOLD ABOUT MY DEATH?
THAT THOU DIDST FALL ILL.
UNDER NO CIRCUMSTANCES WILL MATTERS PERTAINING TO OUR LIEGE'S BEDCHAMBER EVER BE MADE KNOWN OUTSIDE THESE WALLS.
IF I MAY MAKE ONE MORE QUERY—IS THERE ANY CHANCE AT ALL, THAT AS THE BLOOD RELATIONS OF ONE WHO HAS COMMITTED A TERRIBLE CRIME, MY FAMILY MUST PAY A SIMILAR PRICE?
NONE! BE NOT ANXIOUS ON THAT COUNT. I WILL VOUCHSAFE IT.

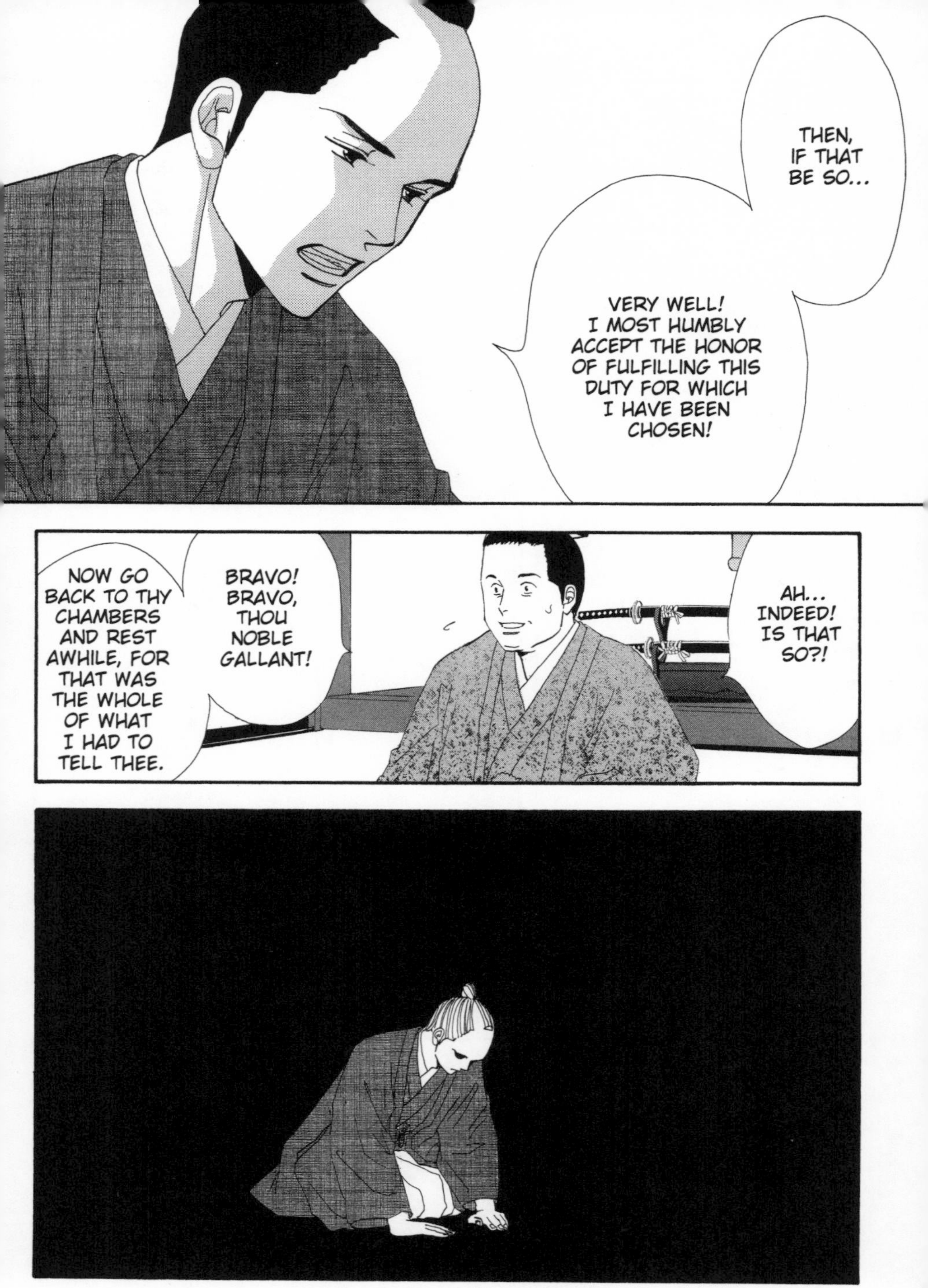
THEN, IF THAT BE SO...
VERY WELL! I MOST HUMBLY ACCEPT THE HONOR OF FULFILLING THIS DUTY FOR WHICH I HAVE BEEN CHOSEN!
AH... INDEED! IS THAT SO?!
BRAVO! BRAVO, THOU NOBLE GALLANT!
NOW GO BACK TO THY CHAMBERS AND REST AWHILE, FOR THAT WAS THE WHOLE OF WHAT I HAD TO TELL THEE.

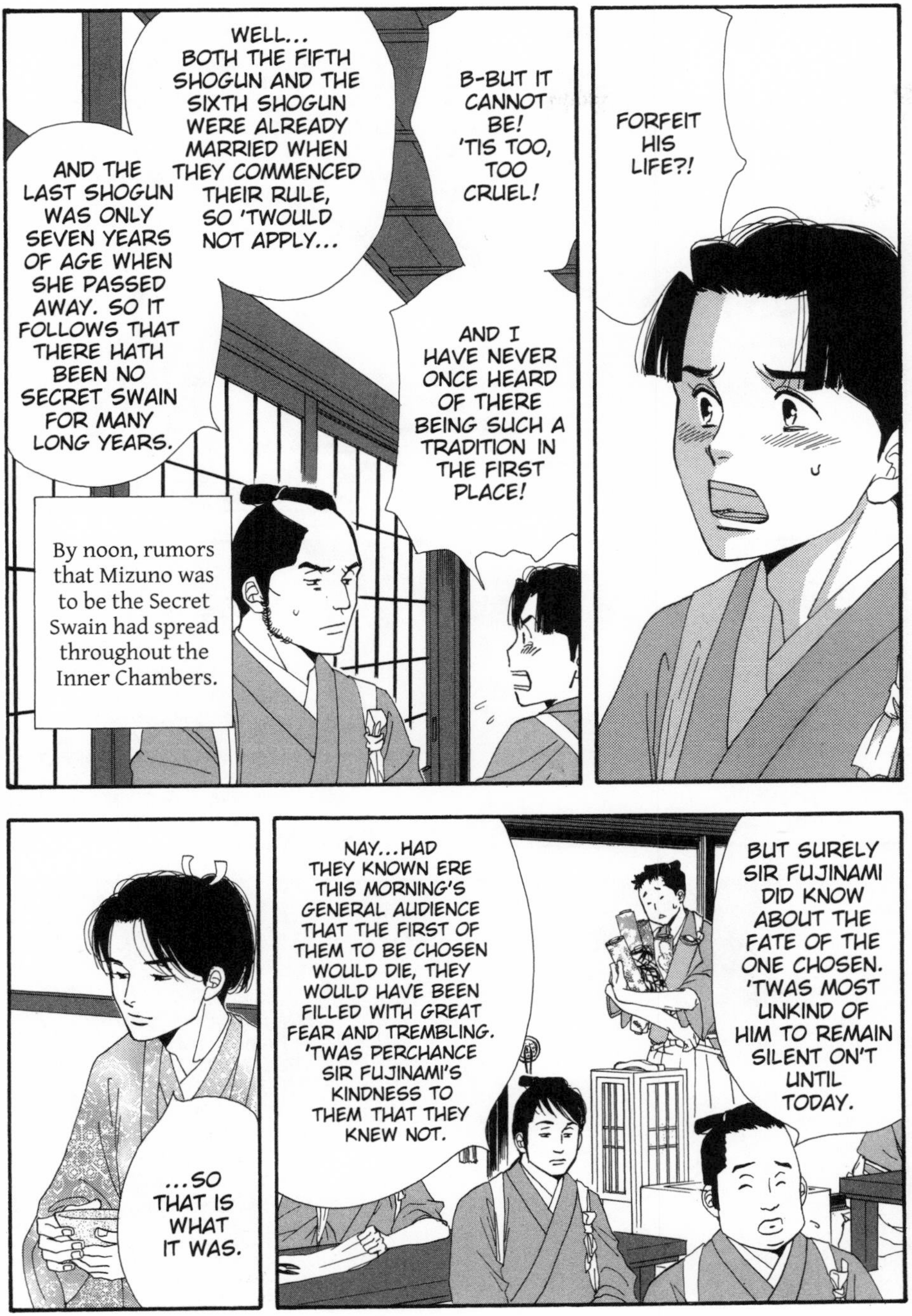
FORFEIT HIS LIFE?!
B-BUT IT CANNOT BE! 'TIS TOO, TOO CRUEL!
WELL... BOTH THE FIFTH SHOGUN AND THE SIXTH SHOGUN WERE ALREADY MARRIED WHEN THEY COMMENCED THEIR RULE, SO 'TWOULD NOT APPLY...
AND THE LAST SHOGUN WAS ONLY SEVEN YEARS OF AGE WHEN SHE PASSED AWAY. SO IT FOLLOWS THAT THERE HATH BEEN NO SECRET SWAIN FOR MANY LONG YEARS.
AND I HAVE NEVER ONCE HEARD OF THERE BEING SUCH A TRADITION IN THE FIRST PLACE!
By noon, rumors that Mizuno was to be the Secret Swain had spread throughout the Inner Chambers.
BUT SURELY SIR FUJINAMI DID KNOW ABOUT THE FATE OF THE ONE CHOSEN. 'TWAS MOST UNKIND OF HIM TO REMAIN SILENT ON'T UNTIL TODAY.
NAY...HAD THEY KNOWN ERE THIS MORNING'S GENERAL AUDIENCE THAT THE FIRST OF THEM TO BE CHOSEN WOULD DIE, THEY WOULD HAVE BEEN FILLED WITH GREAT FEAR AND TREMBLING. 'TWAS PERCHANCE SIR FUJINAMI'S KINDNESS TO THEM THAT THEY KNEW NOT.
...SO THAT IS WHAT IT WAS.

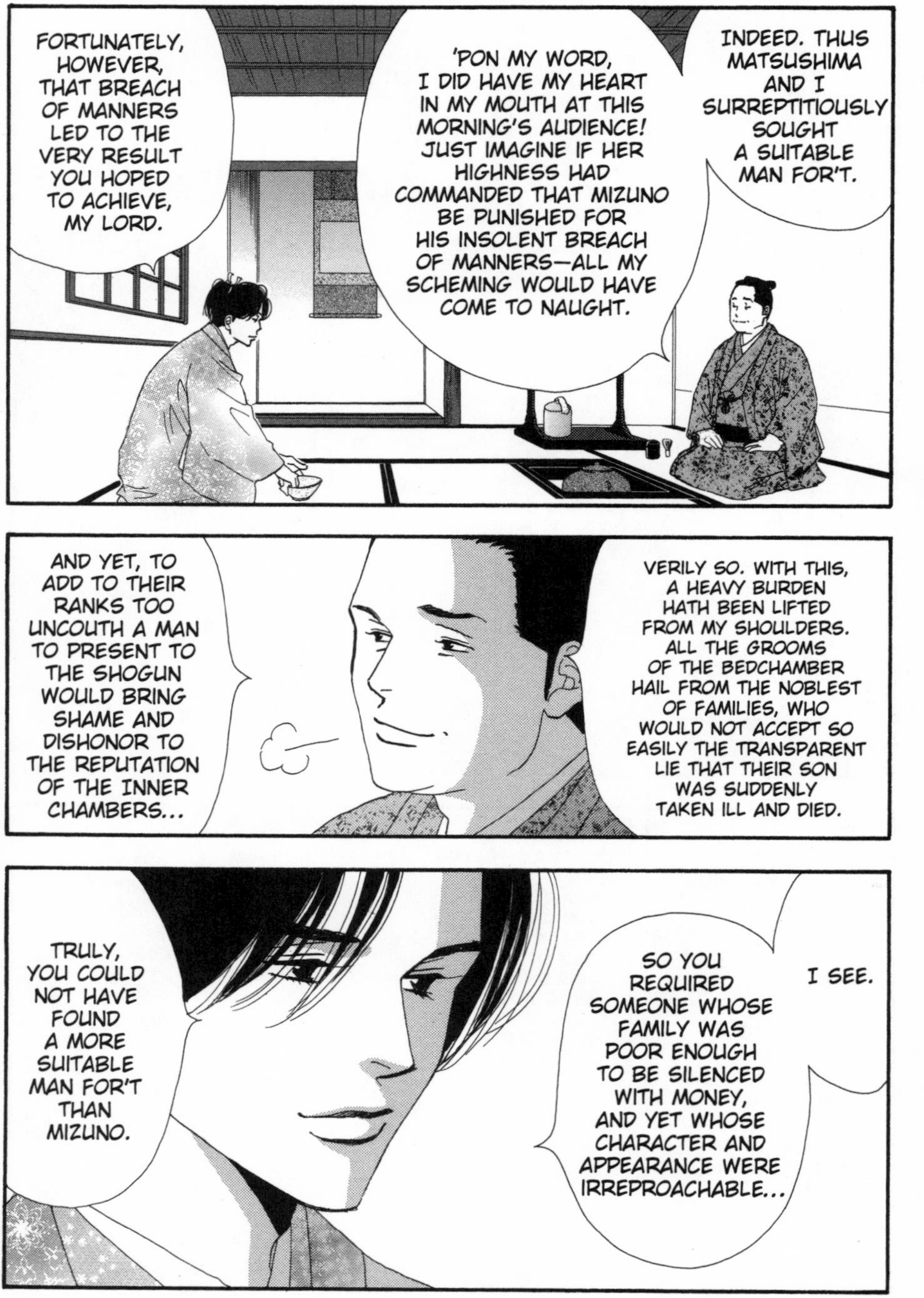
INDEED. THUS MATSUSHIMA AND I SURREPTITIOUSLY SOUGHT A SUITABLE MAN FOR'T.
'PON MY WORD, I DID HAVE MY HEART IN MY MOUTH AT THIS MORNING'S AUDIENCE! JUST IMAGINE IF HER HIGHNESS HAD COMMANDED THAT MIZUNO BE PUNISHED FOR HIS INSOLENT BREACH OF MANNERS—ALL MY SCHEMING WOULD HAVE COME TO NAUGHT.
FORTUNATELY, HOWEVER, THAT BREACH OF MANNERS LED TO THE VERY RESULT YOU HOPED TO ACHIEVE, MY LORD.
VERILY SO. WITH THIS, A HEAVY BURDEN HATH BEEN LIFTED FROM MY SHOULDERS. ALL THE GROOMS OF THE BEDCHAMBER HAIL FROM THE NOBLEST OF FAMILIES, WHO WOULD NOT ACCEPT SO EASILY THE TRANSPARENT LIE THAT THEIR SON WAS SUDDENLY TAKEN ILL AND DIED.
AND YET, TO ADD TO THEIR RANKS TOO UNCOUTH A MAN TO PRESENT TO THE SHOGUN WOULD BRING SHAME AND DISHONOR TO THE REPUTATION OF THE INNER CHAMBERS...
I SEE.
SO YOU REQUIRED SOMEONE WHOSE FAMILY WAS POOR ENOUGH TO BE SILENCED WITH MONEY, AND YET WHOSE CHARACTER AND APPEARANCE WERE IRREPROACHABLE...
TRULY, YOU COULD NOT HAVE FOUND A MORE SUITABLE MAN FOR'T THAN MIZUNO.

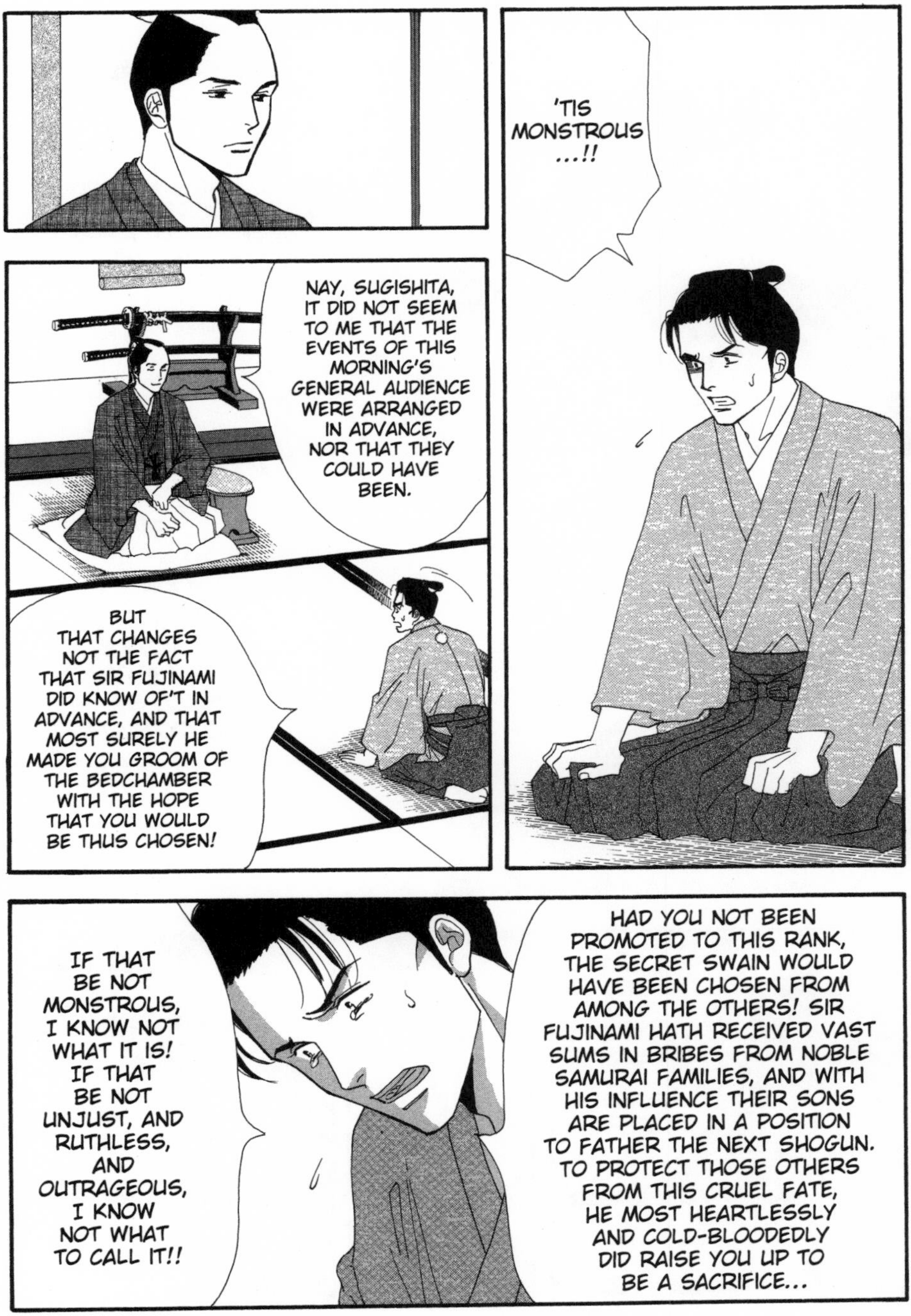
'TIS MONSTROUS ...!!
NAY, SUGISHITA, IT DID NOT SEEM TO ME THAT THE EVENTS OF THIS MORNING'S GENERAL AUDIENCE WERE ARRANGED IN ADVANCE, NOR THAT THEY COULD HAVE BEEN.
BUT THAT CHANGES NOT THE FACT THAT SIR FUJINAMI DID KNOW OF'T IN ADVANCE, AND THAT MOST SURELY HE MADE YOU GROOM OF THE BEDCHAMBER WITH THE HOPE THAT YOU WOULD BE THUS CHOSEN!
HAD YOU NOT BEEN PROMOTED TO THIS RANK, THE SECRET SWAIN WOULD HAVE BEEN CHOSEN FROM AMONG THE OTHERS! SIR FUJINAMI HATH RECEIVED VAST SUMS IN BRIBES FROM NOBLE SAMURAI FAMILIES, AND WITH HIS INFLUENCE THEIR SONS ARE PLACED IN A POSITION TO FATHER THE NEXT SHOGUN. TO PROTECT THOSE OTHERS FROM THIS CRUEL FATE, HE MOST HEARTLESSLY AND COLD-BLOODEDLY DID RAISE YOU UP TO BE A SACRIFICE...
IF THAT BE NOT MONSTROUS, I KNOW NOT WHAT IT IS! IF THAT BE NOT UNJUST, AND RUTHLESS, AND OUTRAGEOUS, I KNOW NOT WHAT TO CALL IT!!

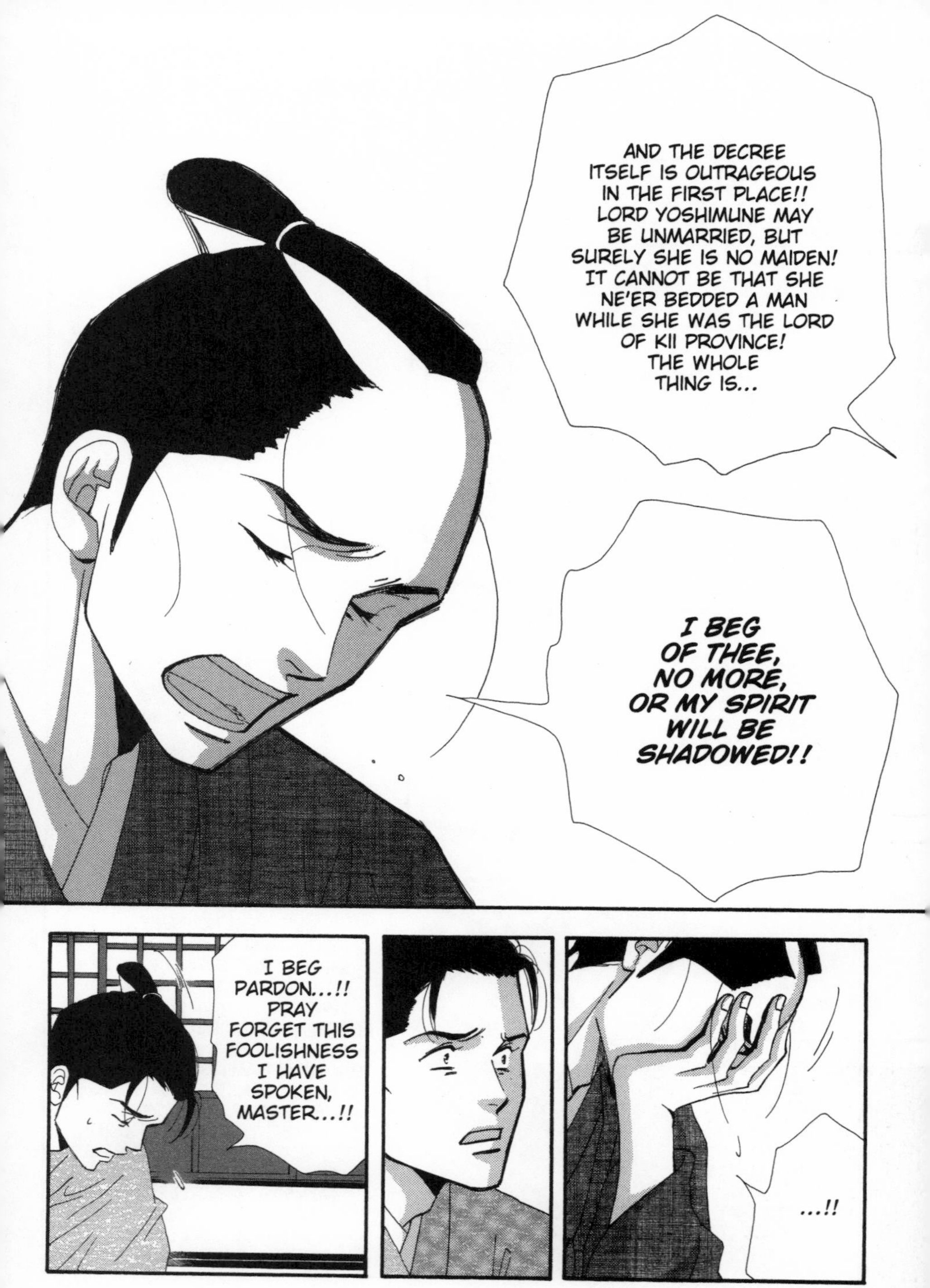
AND THE DECREE ITSELF IS OUTRAGEOUS IN THE FIRST PLACE!! LORD YOSHIMUNE MAY BE UNMARRIED, BUT SURELY SHE IS NO MAIDEN! IT CANNOT BE THAT SHE NE'ER BEDDED A MAN WHILE SHE WAS THE LORD OF KII PROVINCE! THE WHOLE THING IS...
I BEG OF THEE, NO MORE, OR MY SPIRIT WILL BE SHADOWED!!
...!!
I BEG PARDON...!! PRAY FORGET THIS FOOLISHNESS I HAVE SPOKEN, MASTER...!!

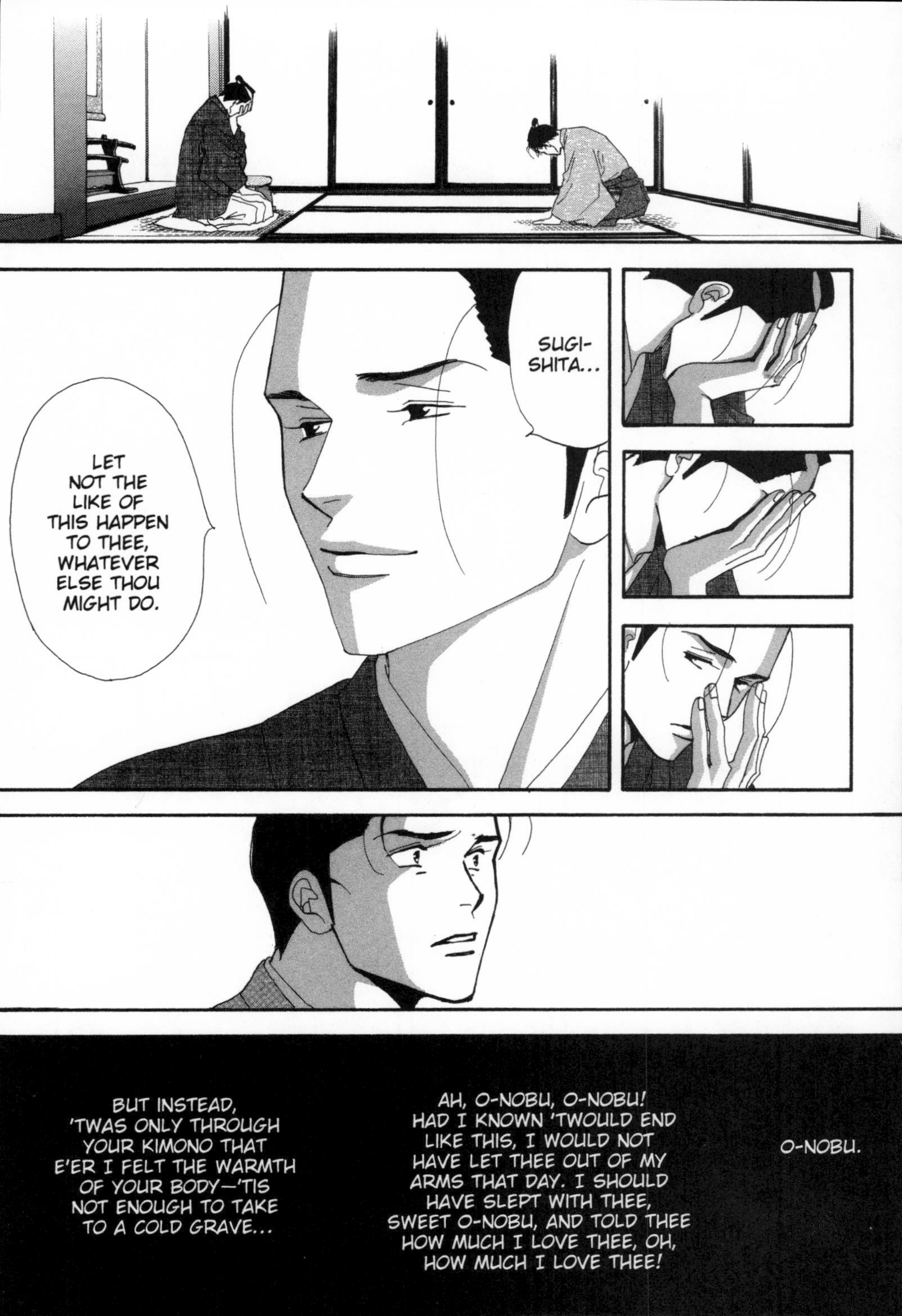
SUGI-SHITA...
LET NOT THE LIKE OF THIS HAPPEN TO THEE, WHATEVER ELSE THOU MIGHT DO.
O-NOBU.
AH, O-NOBU, O-NOBU! HAD I KNOWN 'TWOULD END LIKE THIS, I WOULD NOT HAVE LET THEE OUT OF MY ARMS THAT DAY. I SHOULD HAVE SLEPT WITH THEE, SWEET O-NOBU, AND TOLD THEE HOW MUCH I LOVE THEE, OH, HOW MUCH I LOVE THEE!
BUT INSTEAD, 'TWAS ONLY THROUGH YOUR KIMONO THAT E'ER I FELT THE WARMTH OF YOUR BODY—'TIS NOT ENOUGH TO TAKE TO A COLD GRAVE...

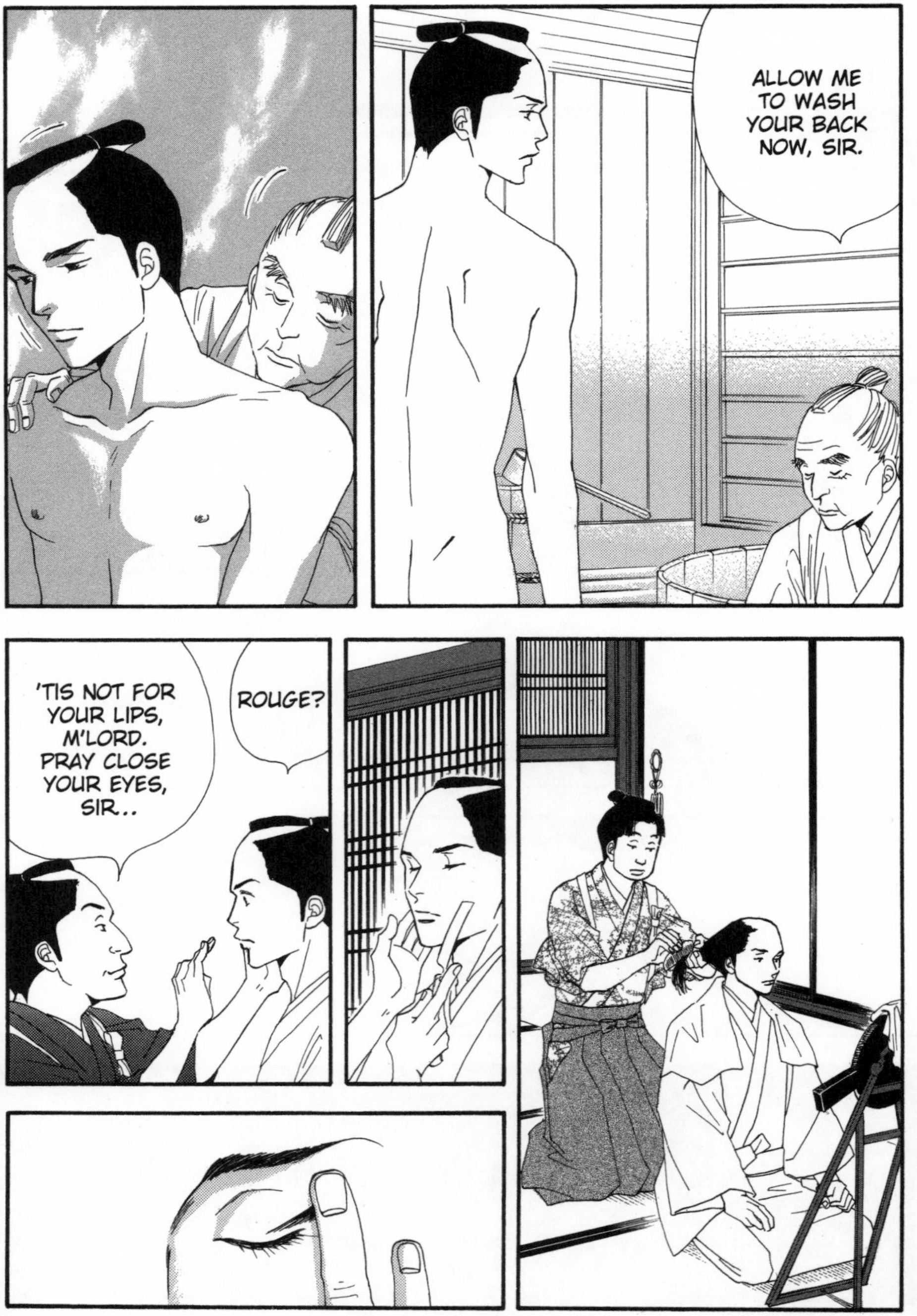
ALLOW ME TO WASH YOUR BACK NOW, SIR.
ROUGE?
'TIS NOT FOR YOUR LIPS, M'LORD. PRAY CLOSE YOUR EYES, SIR...

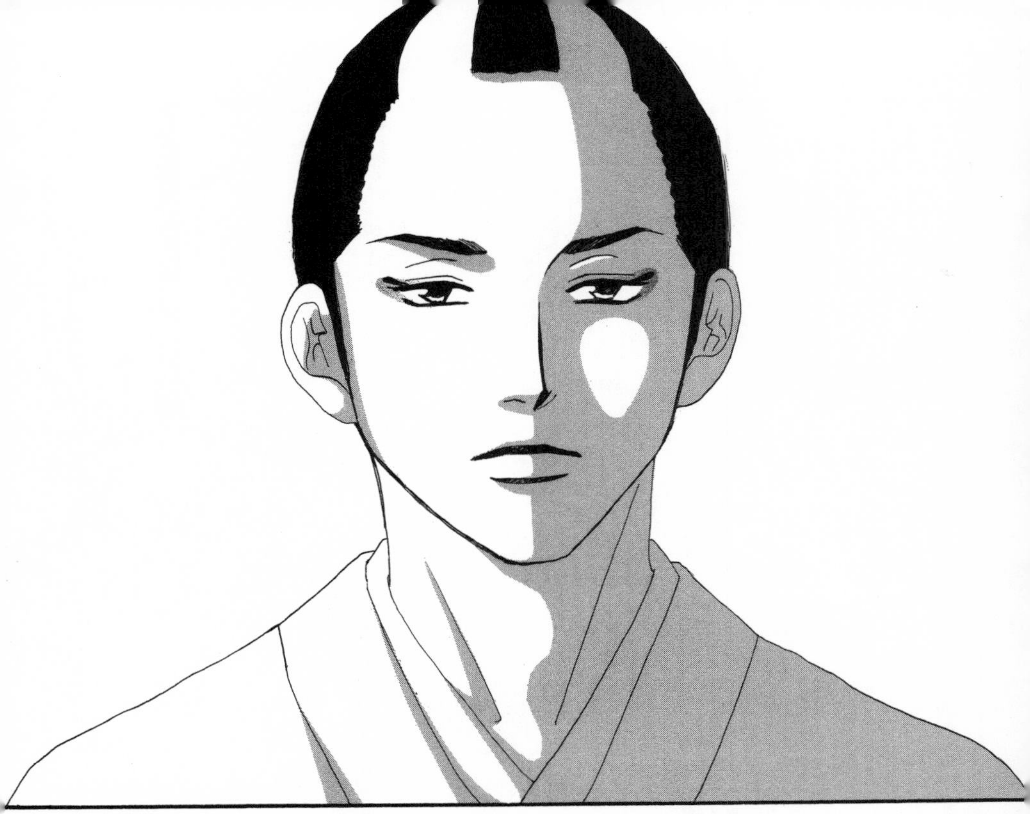

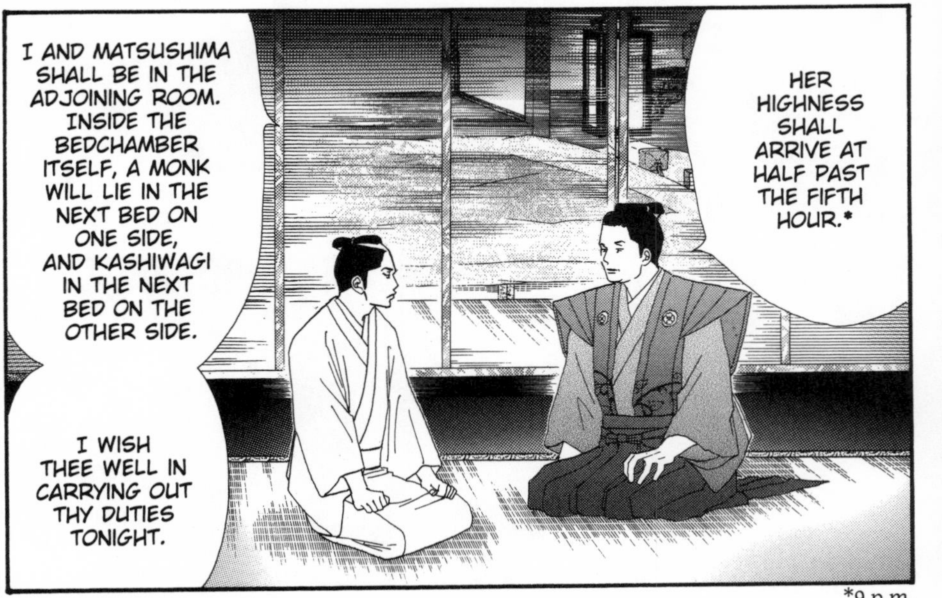
HER HIGHNESS SHALL ARRIVE AT HALF PAST THE FIFTH HOUR.*
I AND MATSUSHIMA SHALL BE IN THE ADJOINING ROOM. INSIDE THE BEDCHAMBER ITSELF, A MONK WILL LIE IN THE NEXT BED ON ONE SIDE, AND KASHIWAGI IN THE NEXT BED ON THE OTHER SIDE.
I WISH THEE WELL IN CARRYING OUT THY DUTIES TONIGHT.

*9 p.m.

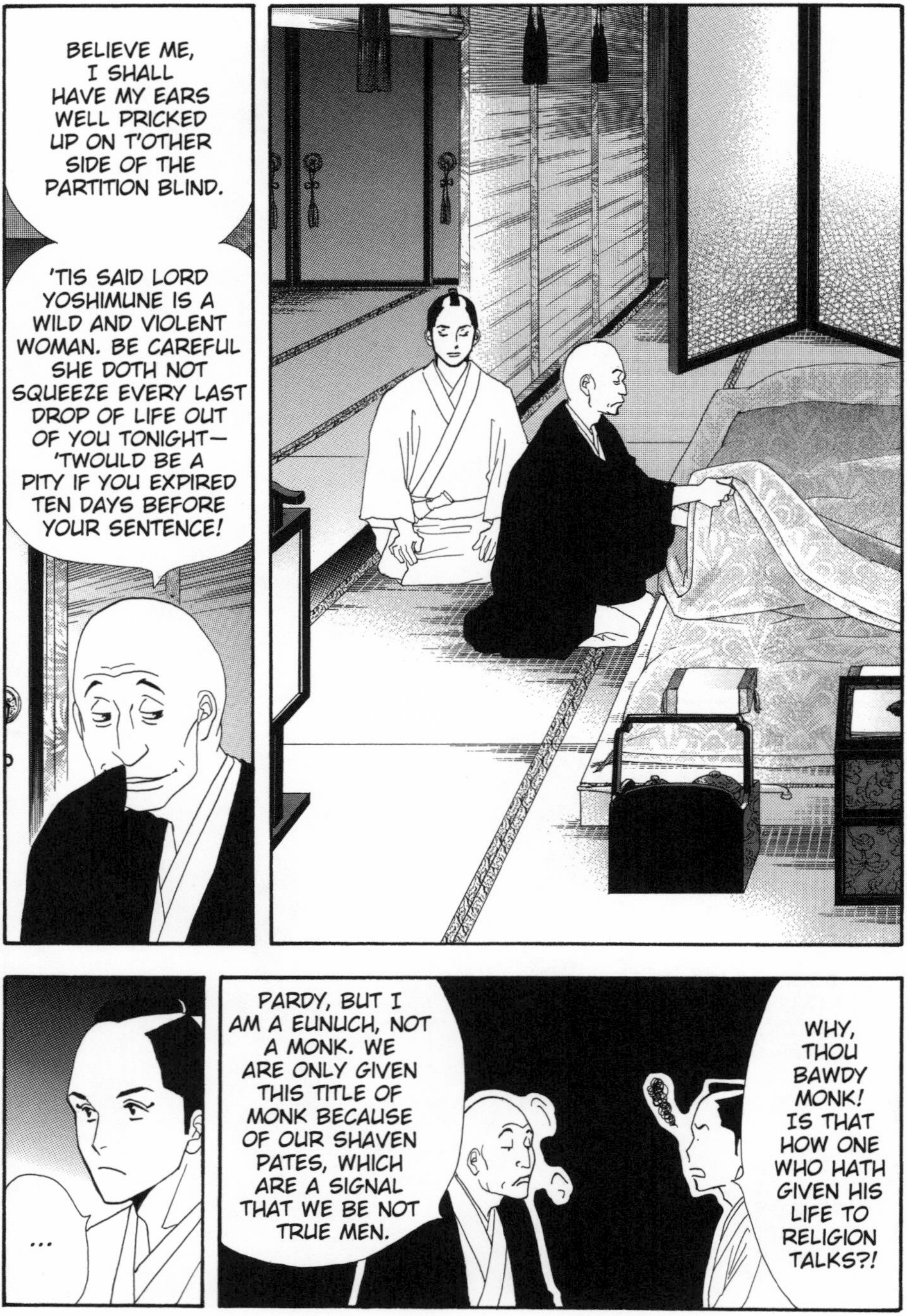
BELIEVE ME, I SHALL HAVE MY EARS WELL PRICKED UP ON T'OTHER SIDE OF THE PARTITION BLIND.
'TIS SAID LORD YOSHIMUNE IS A WILD AND VIOLENT WOMAN. BE CAREFUL SHE DOTH NOT SQUEEZE EVERY LAST DROP OF LIFE OUT OF YOU TONIGHT—'TWOULD BE A PITY IF YOU EXPIRED TEN DAYS BEFORE YOUR SENTENCE!
WHY, THOU BAWDY MONK! IS THAT HOW ONE WHO HATH GIVEN HIS LIFE TO RELIGION TALKS?!
PARDY, BUT I AM A EUNUCH, NOT A MONK. WE ARE ONLY GIVEN THIS TITLE OF MONK BECAUSE OF OUR SHAVEN PATES, WHICH ARE A SIGNAL THAT WE BE NOT TRUE MEN.
...

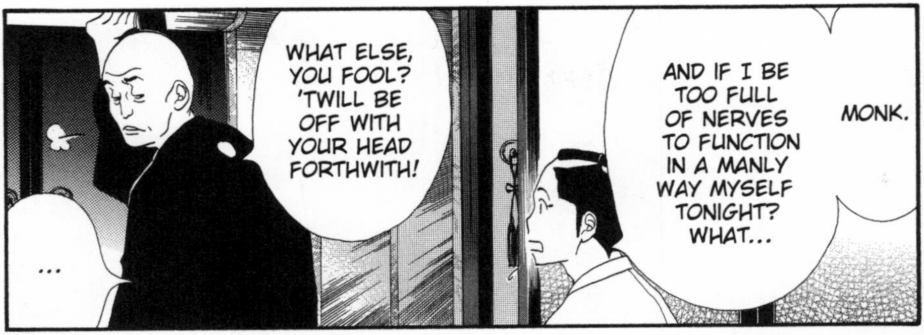
AND IF I BE TOO FULL OF NERVES TO FUNCTION IN A MANLY WAY MYSELF TONIGHT? WHAT...
MONK.
WHAT ELSE, YOU FOOL? 'TWILL BE OFF WITH YOUR HEAD FORTHWITH!
...

About half an hour later, Yoshimune entered the Inner Chambers from the Shogun's Quarters, made her way down the Passage of the Bells, stepped into the antechamber, and then appeared in the bedchamber itself.

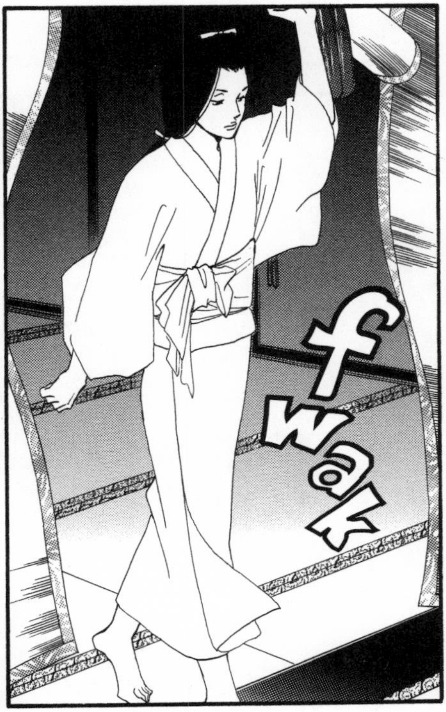
fwak

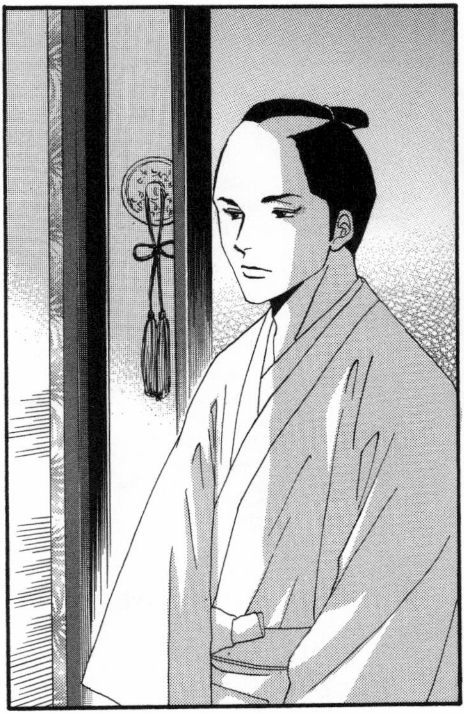

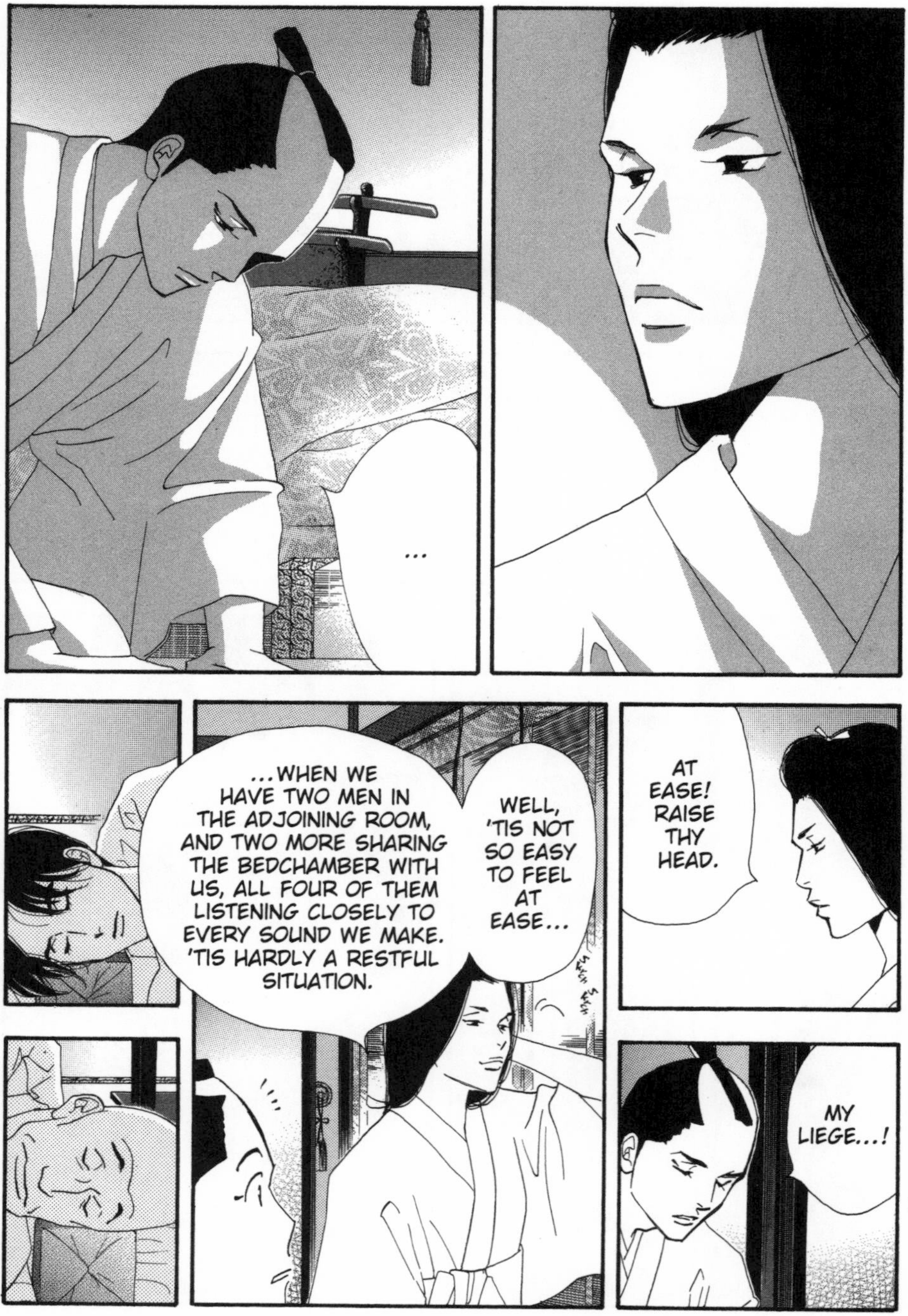
...
AT EASE! RAISE THY HEAD.
MY LIEGE...!
WELL, 'TIS NOT SO EASY TO FEEL AT EASE...
...WHEN WE HAVE TWO MEN IN THE ADJOINING ROOM, AND TWO MORE SHARING THE BEDCHAMBER WITH US, ALL FOUR OF THEM LISTENING CLOSELY TO EVERY SOUND WE MAKE. 'TIS HARDLY A RESTFUL SITUATION.

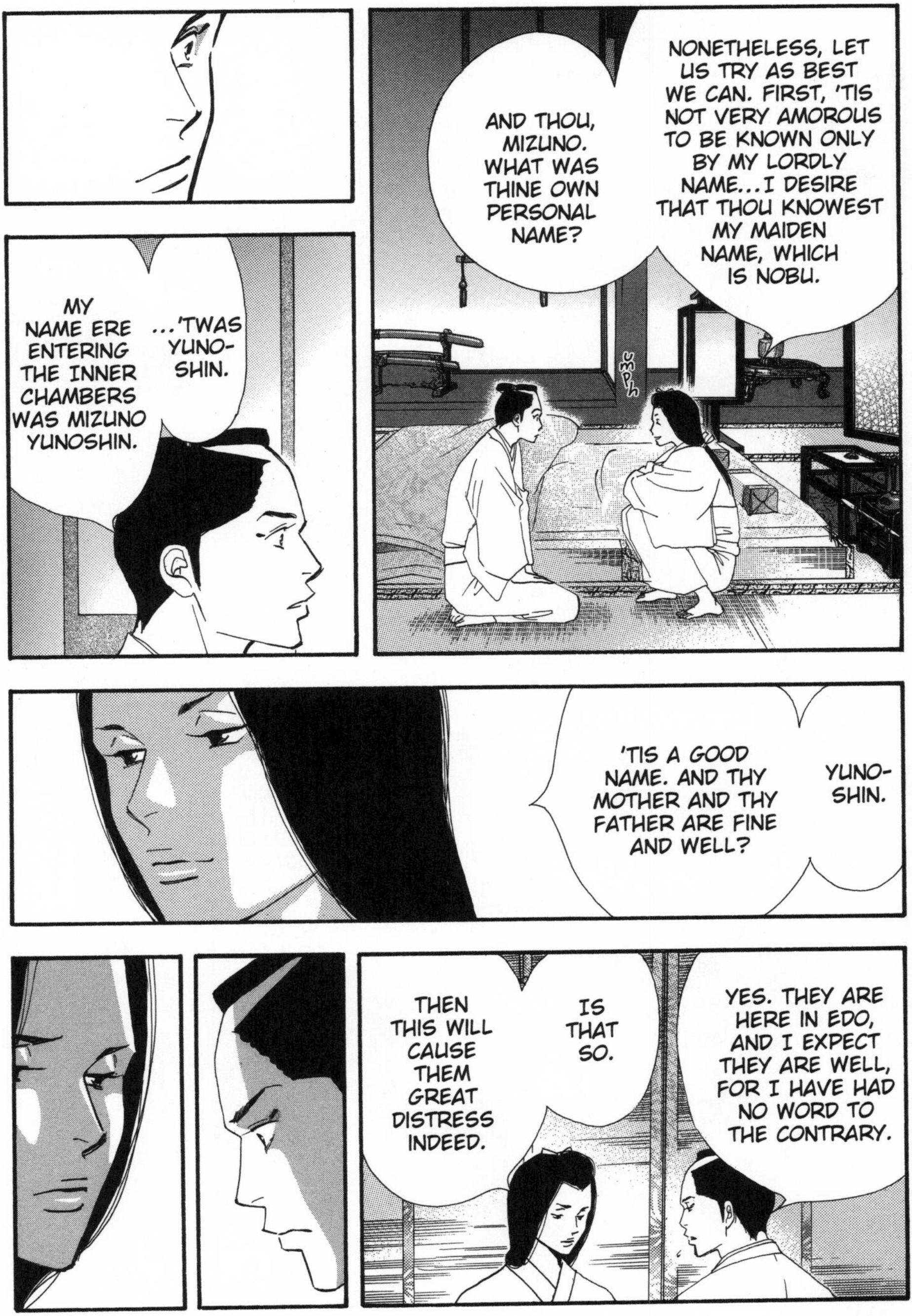
NONETHELESS, LET US TRY AS BEST WE CAN. FIRST, 'TIS NOT VERY AMOROUS TO BE KNOWN ONLY BY MY LORDLY NAME...I DESIRE THAT THOU KNOWEST MY MAIDEN NAME, WHICH IS NOBU.
AND THOU, MIZUNO. WHAT WAS THINE OWN PERSONAL NAME?
umph
MY NAME ERE ENTERING THE INNER CHAMBERS WAS MIZUNO YUNOSHIN.
...'TWAS YUNO-SHIN.
YUNO-SHIN.
'TIS A GOOD NAME. AND THY MOTHER AND THY FATHER ARE FINE AND WELL?
YES. THEY ARE HERE IN EDO, AND I EXPECT THEY ARE WELL, FOR I HAVE HAD NO WORD TO THE CONTRARY.
IS THAT SO.
THEN THIS WILL CAUSE THEM GREAT DISTRESS INDEED.

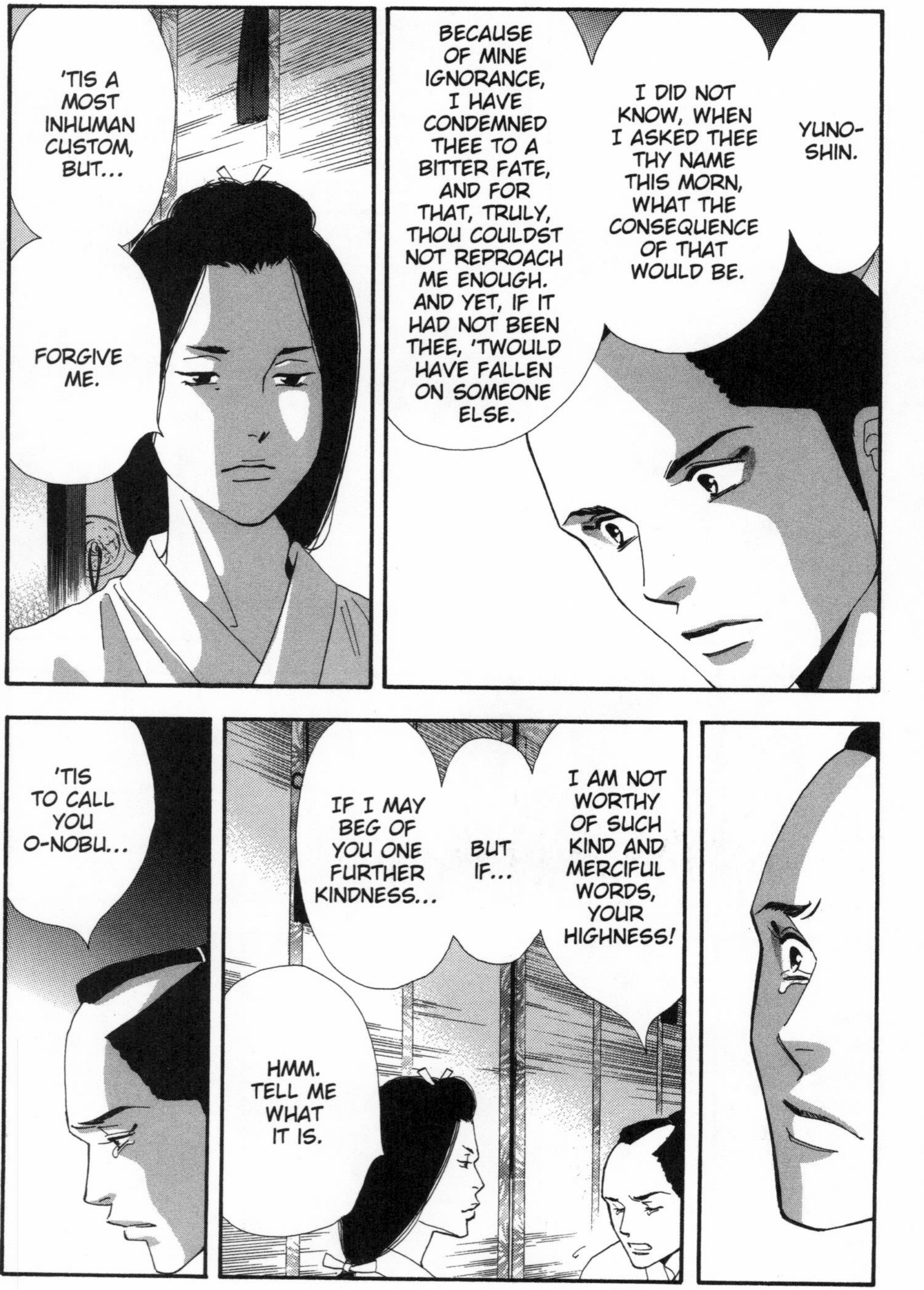
YUNO-SHIN.
I DID NOT KNOW, WHEN I ASKED THEE THY NAME THIS MORN, WHAT THE CONSEQUENCE OF THAT WOULD BE.
BECAUSE OF MINE IGNORANCE, I HAVE CONDEMNED THEE TO A BITTER FATE, AND FOR THAT, TRULY, THOU COULDST NOT REPROACH ME ENOUGH. AND YET, IF IT HAD NOT BEEN THEE, 'TWOULD HAVE FALLEN ON SOMEONE ELSE.
'TIS A MOST INHUMAN CUSTOM, BUT...
FORGIVE ME.
I AM NOT WORTHY OF SUCH KIND AND MERCIFUL WORDS, YOUR HIGHNESS!
BUT IF...
IF I MAY BEG OF YOU ONE FURTHER KINDNESS...
HMM. TELL ME WHAT IT IS.
'TIS TO CALL YOU O-NOBU...

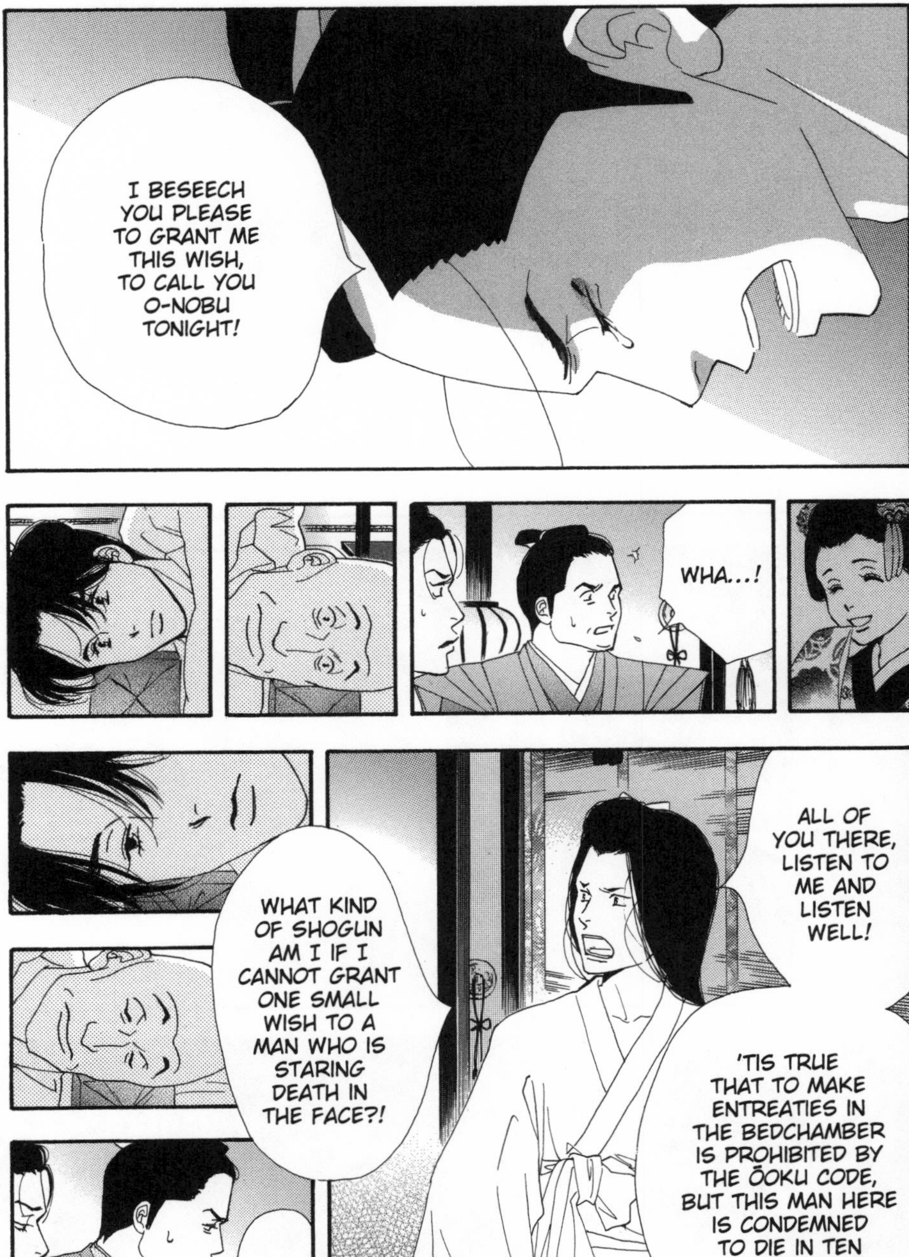
I BESEECH YOU PLEASE TO GRANT ME THIS WISH, TO CALL YOU O-NOBU TONIGHT!
WHA...!
ALL OF YOU THERE, LISTEN TO ME AND LISTEN WELL!
'TIS TRUE THAT TO MAKE ENTREATIES IN THE BEDCHAMBER IS PROHIBITED BY THE ŌOKU CODE, BUT THIS MAN HERE IS CONDEMNED TO DIE IN TEN DAYS' TIME!
WHAT KIND OF SHOGUN AM I IF I CANNOT GRANT ONE SMALL WISH TO A MAN WHO IS STARING DEATH IN THE FACE?!
...

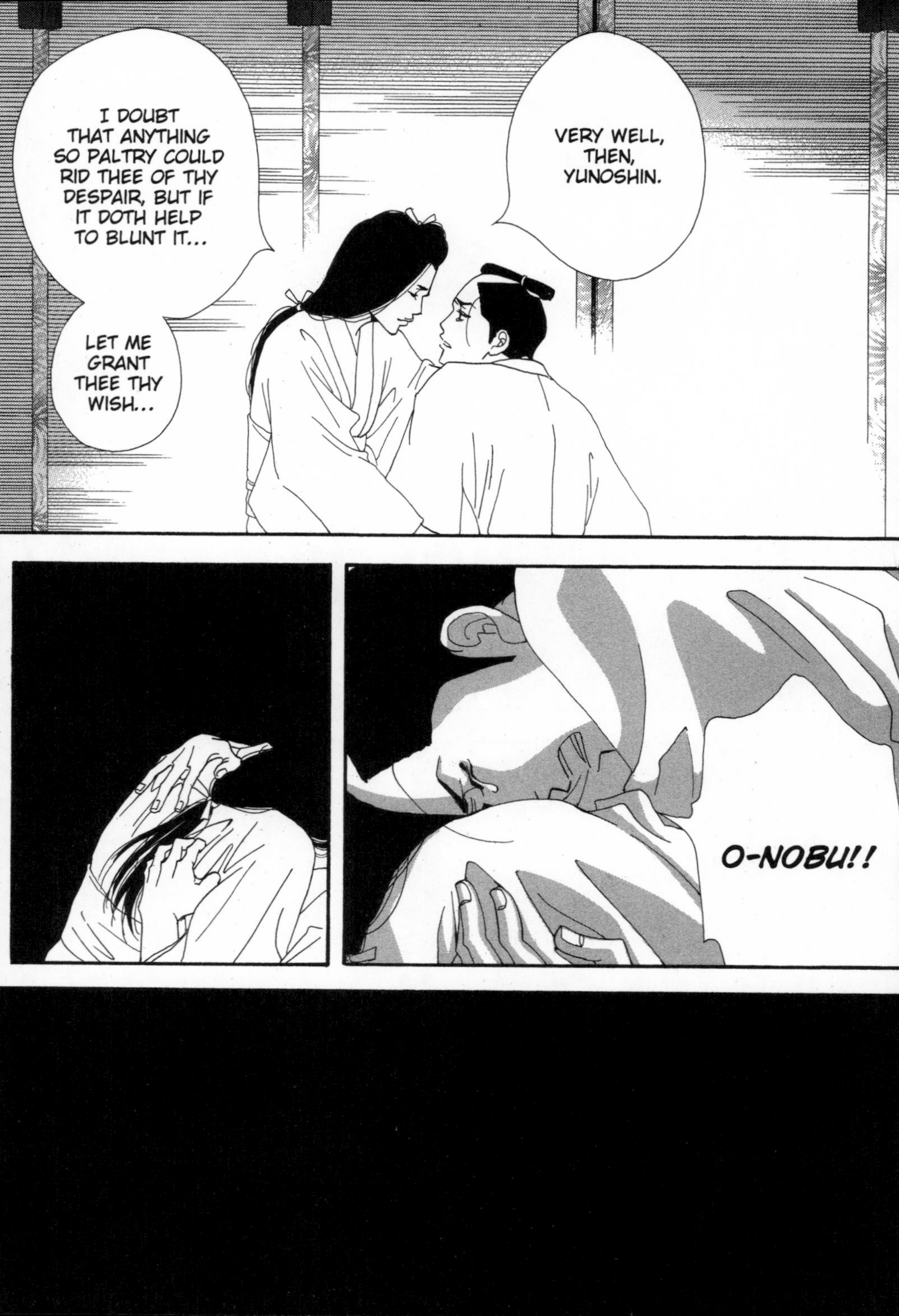
VERY WELL, THEN, YUNOSHIN.
I DOUBT THAT ANYTHING SO PALTRY COULD RID THEE OF THY DESPAIR, BUT IF IT DOTH HELP TO BLUNT IT...
LET ME GRANT THEE THY WISH...
O-NOBU!!

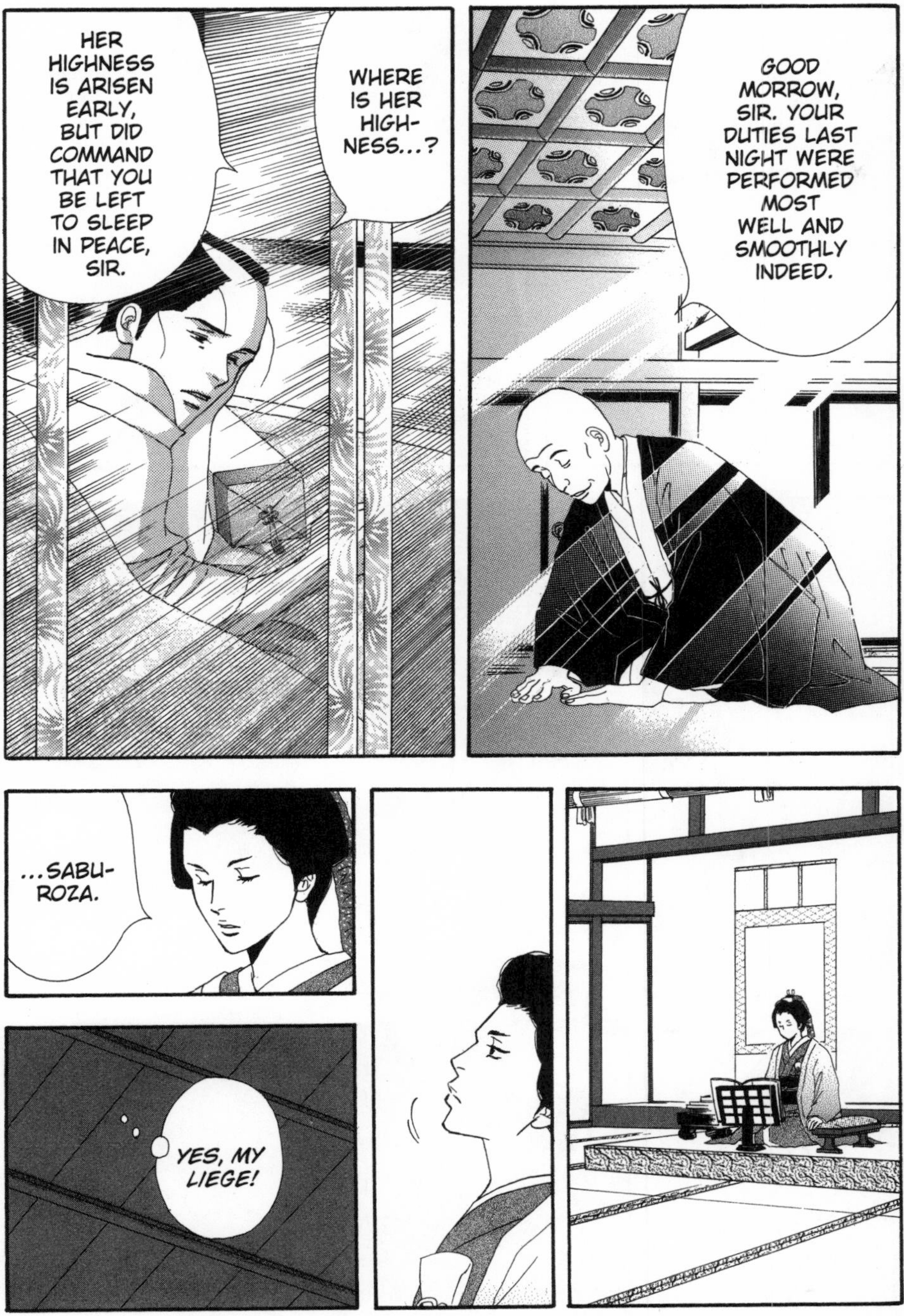
GOOD MORROW, SIR. YOUR DUTIES LAST NIGHT WERE PERFORMED MOST WELL AND SMOOTHLY INDEED.
WHERE IS HER HIGH-NESS...?
HER HIGHNESS IS ARISEN EARLY, BUT DID COMMAND THAT YOU BE LEFT TO SLEEP IN PEACE, SIR.
...SABU-ROZA.
YES, MY LIEGE!

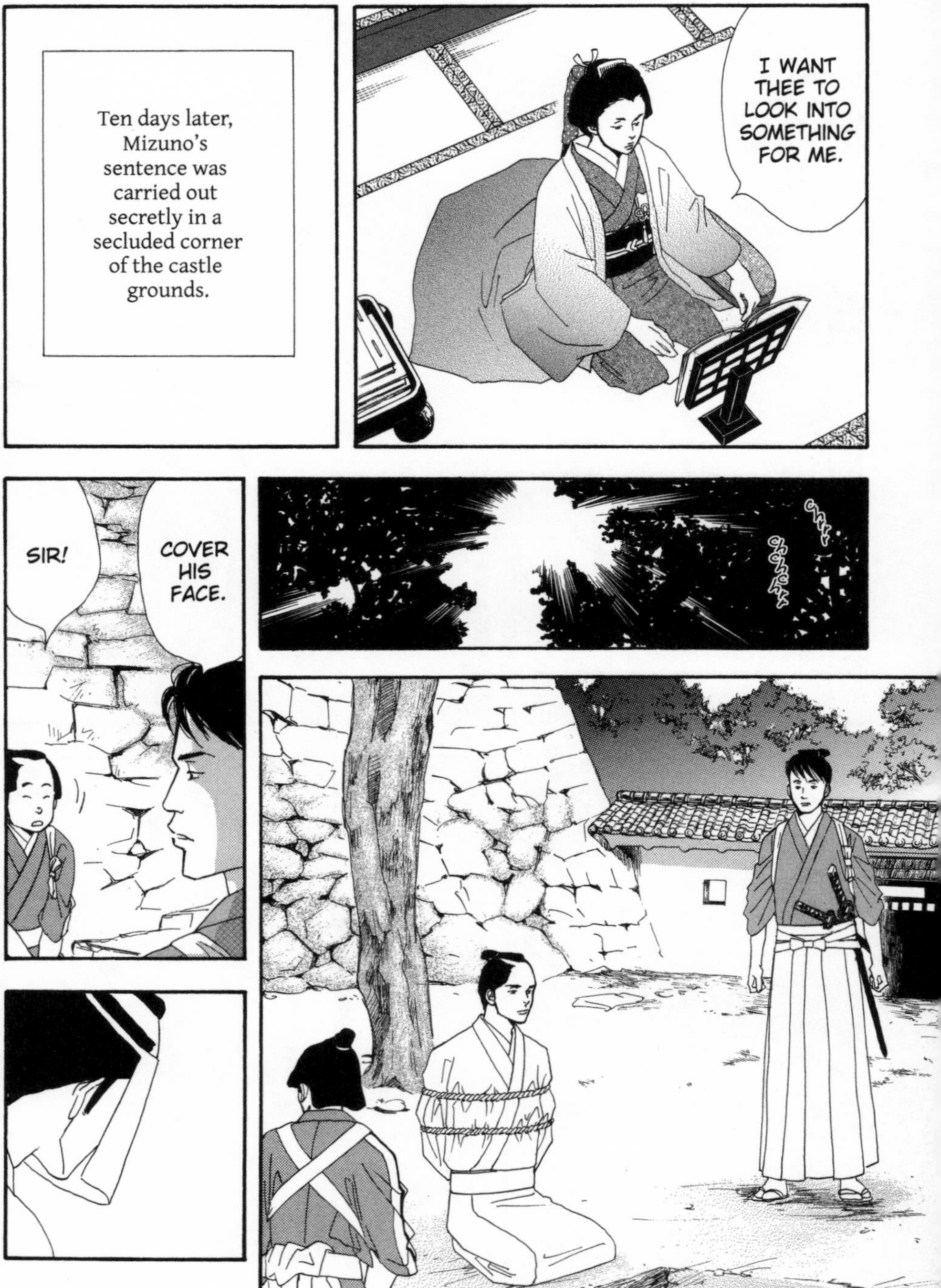
I WANT THEE TO LOOK INTO SOMETHING FOR ME.
Ten days later, Mizuno's sentence was carried out secretly in a secluded corner of the castle grounds.
chrrr
chchchrr
COVER HIS FACE.
SIR!

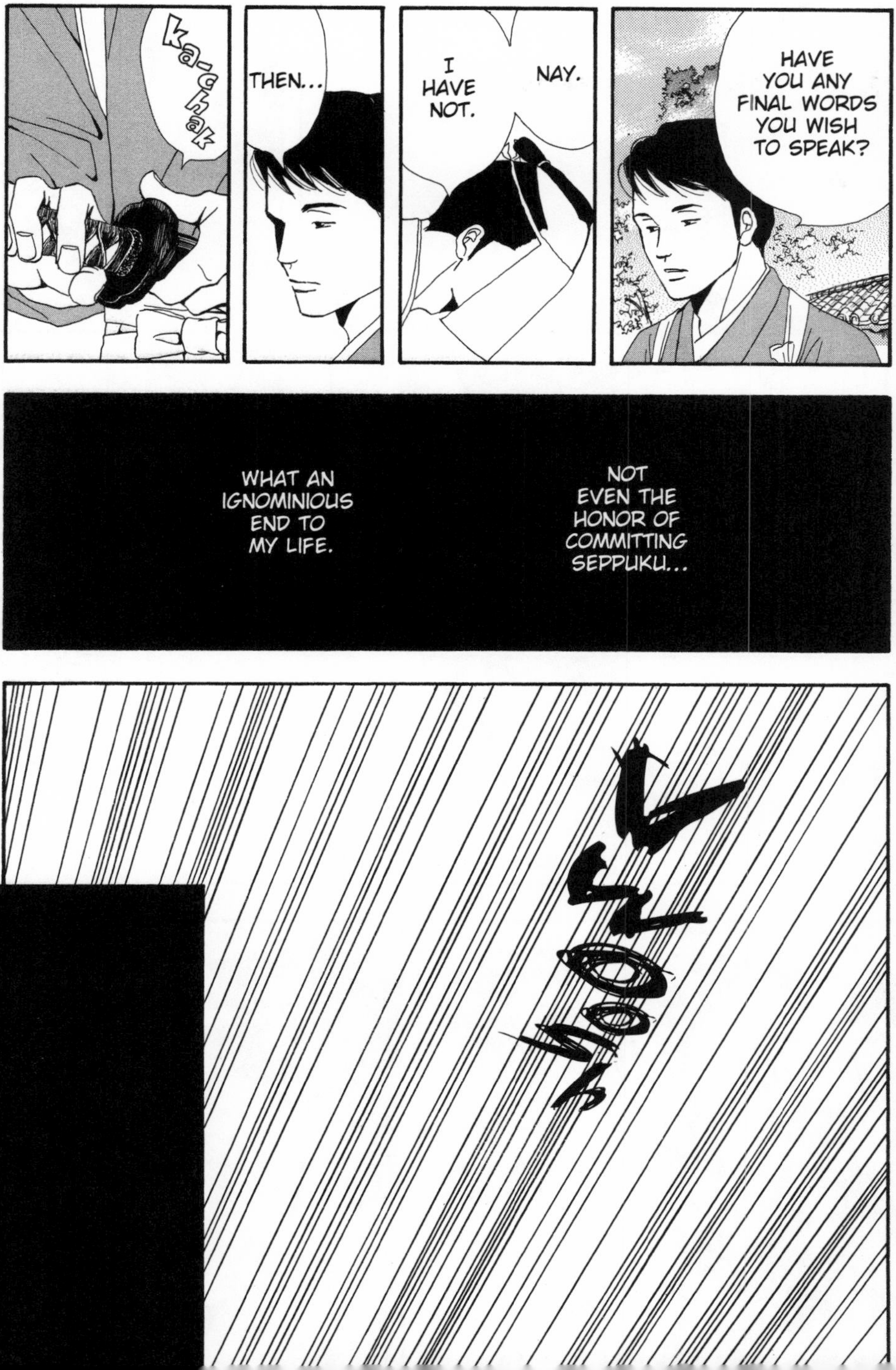
HAVE YOU ANY FINAL WORDS YOU WISH TO SPEAK?
NAY.
I HAVE NOT.
THEN...
ka-chak
NOT EVEN THE HONOR OF COMMITTING SEPPUKU...
WHAT AN IGNOMINIOUS END TO MY LIFE.
whoosh

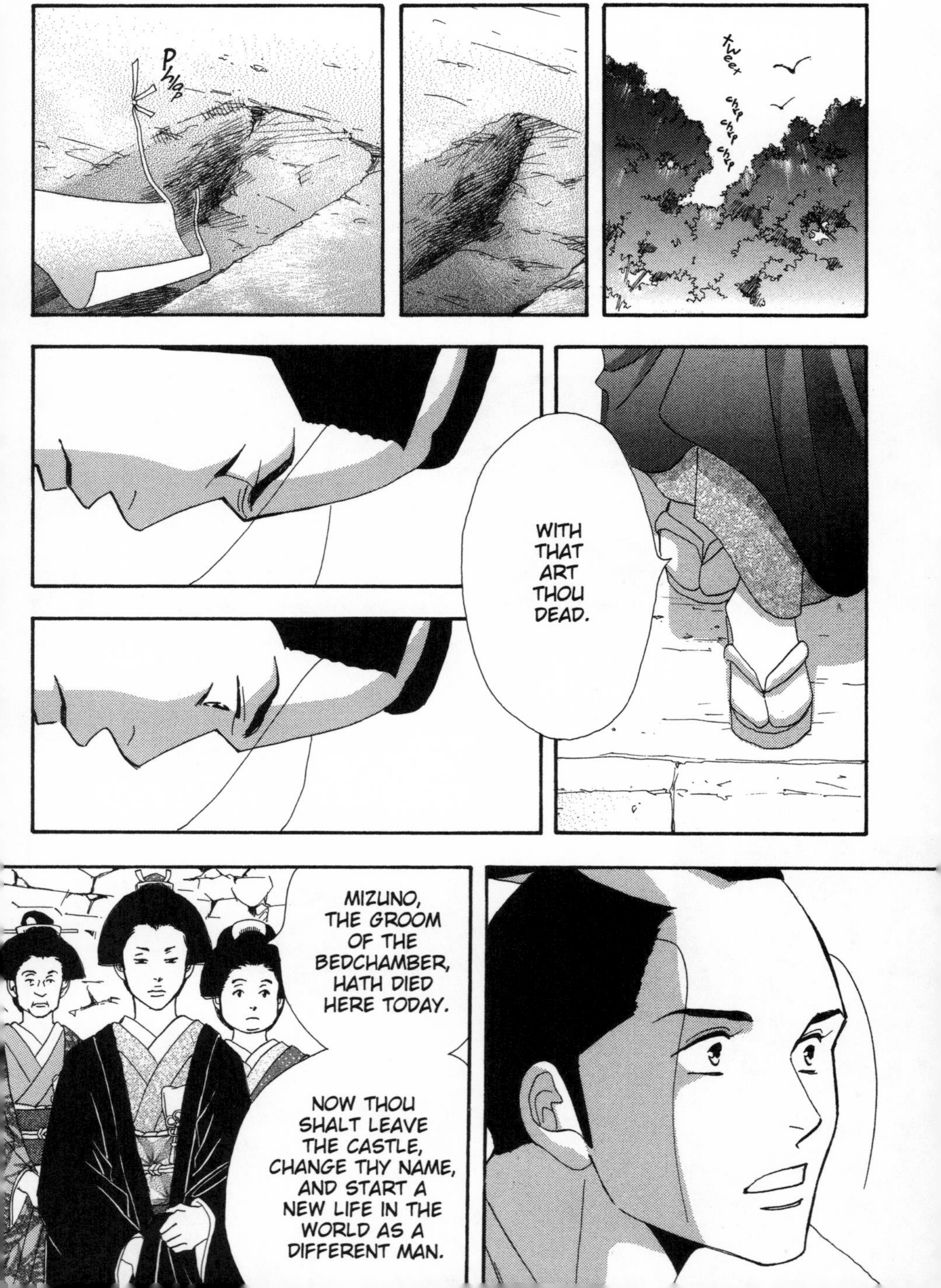
tweet
chep chep chep
Phlap
WITH THAT ART THOU DEAD.
MIZUNO, THE GROOM OF THE BEDCHAMBER, HATH DIED HERE TODAY.
NOW THOU SHALT LEAVE THE CASTLE, CHANGE THY NAME, AND START A NEW LIFE IN THE WORLD AS A DIFFERENT MAN.

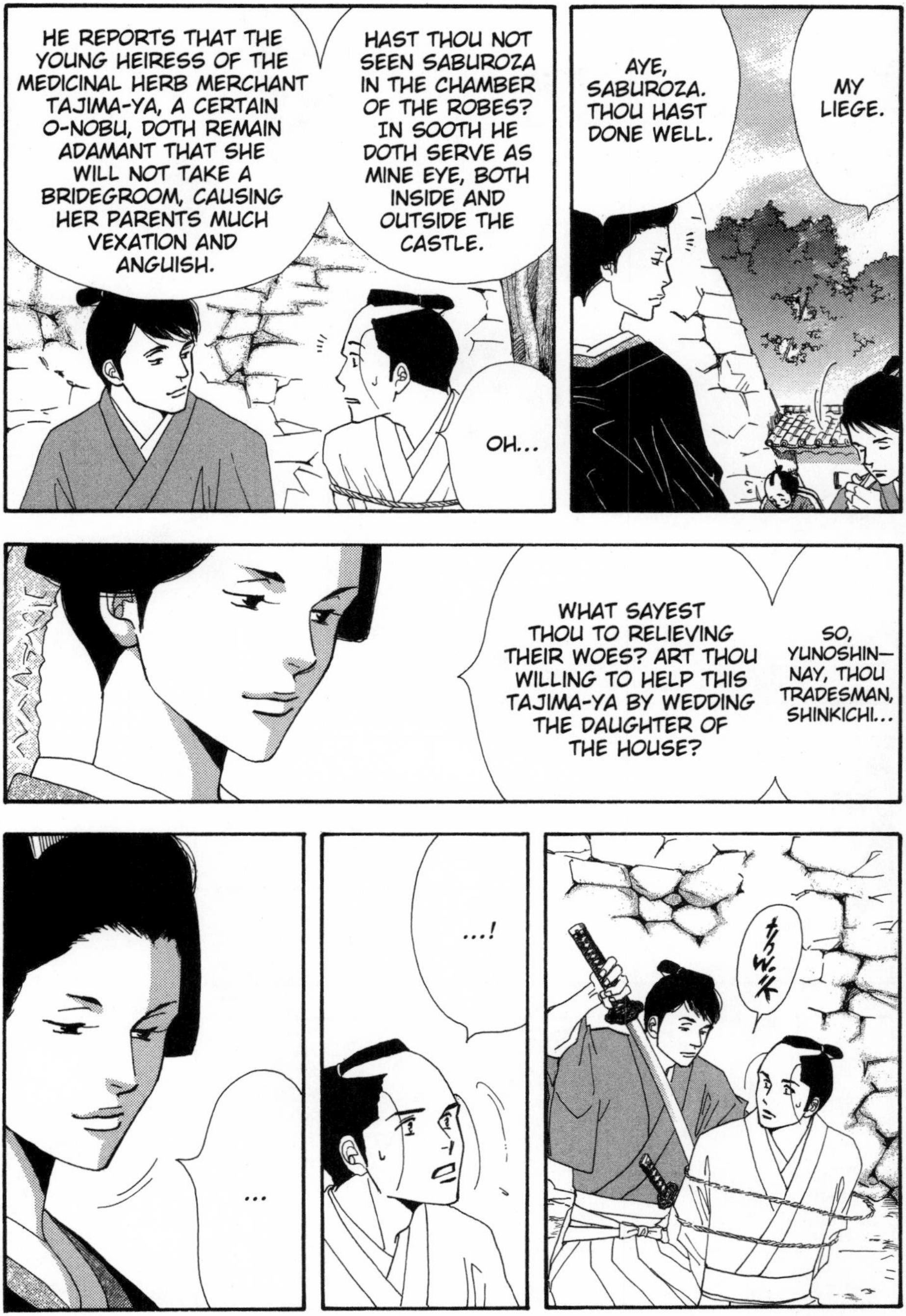
MY LIEGE.
AYE, SABUROZA. THOU HAST DONE WELL.
HAST THOU NOT SEEN SABUROZA IN THE CHAMBER OF THE ROBES? IN SOOTH HE DOTH SERVE AS MINE EYE, BOTH INSIDE AND OUTSIDE THE CASTLE.
HE REPORTS THAT THE YOUNG HEIRESS OF THE MEDICINAL HERB MERCHANT TAJIMA-YA, A CERTAIN O-NOBU, DOTH REMAIN ADAMANT THAT SHE WILL NOT TAKE A BRIDEGROOM, CAUSING HER PARENTS MUCH VEXATION AND ANGUISH.
OH...
SO, YUNOSHIN— NAY, THOU TRADESMAN, SHINKICHI...
WHAT SAYEST THOU TO RELIEVING THEIR WOES? ART THOU WILLING TO HELP THIS TAJIMA-YA BY WEDDING THE DAUGHTER OF THE HOUSE?
...!
...

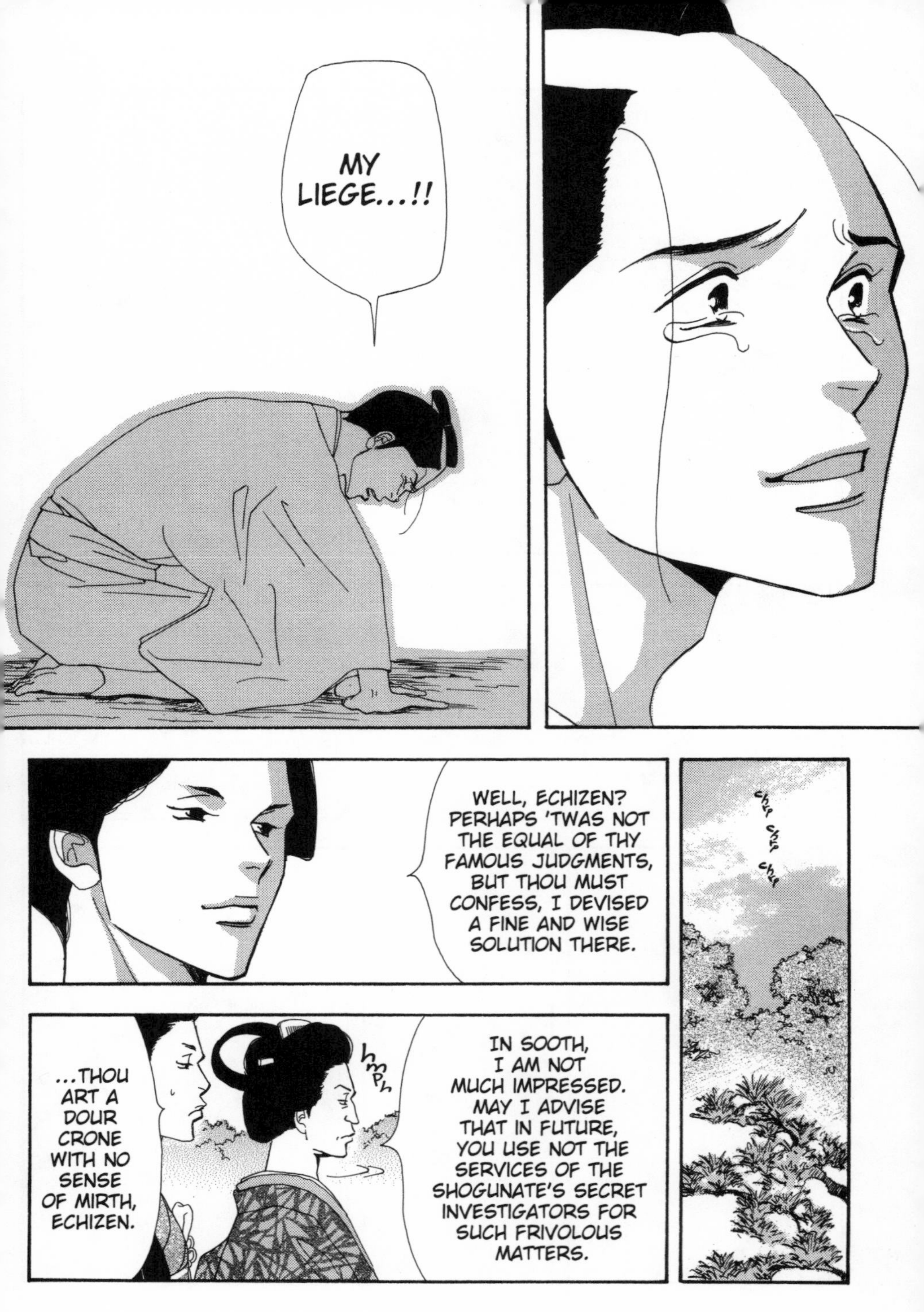
MY LIEGE...!!
WELL, ECHIZEN? PERHAPS 'TWAS NOT THE EQUAL OF THY FAMOUS JUDGMENTS, BUT THOU MUST CONFESS, I DEVISED A FINE AND WISE SOLUTION THERE.
IN SOOTH, I AM NOT MUCH IMPRESSED. MAY I ADVISE THAT IN FUTURE, YOU USE NOT THE SERVICES OF THE SHOGUNATE'S SECRET INVESTIGATORS FOR SUCH FRIVOLOUS MATTERS.
hmph
...THOU ART A DOUR CRONE WITH NO SENSE OF MIRTH, ECHIZEN.

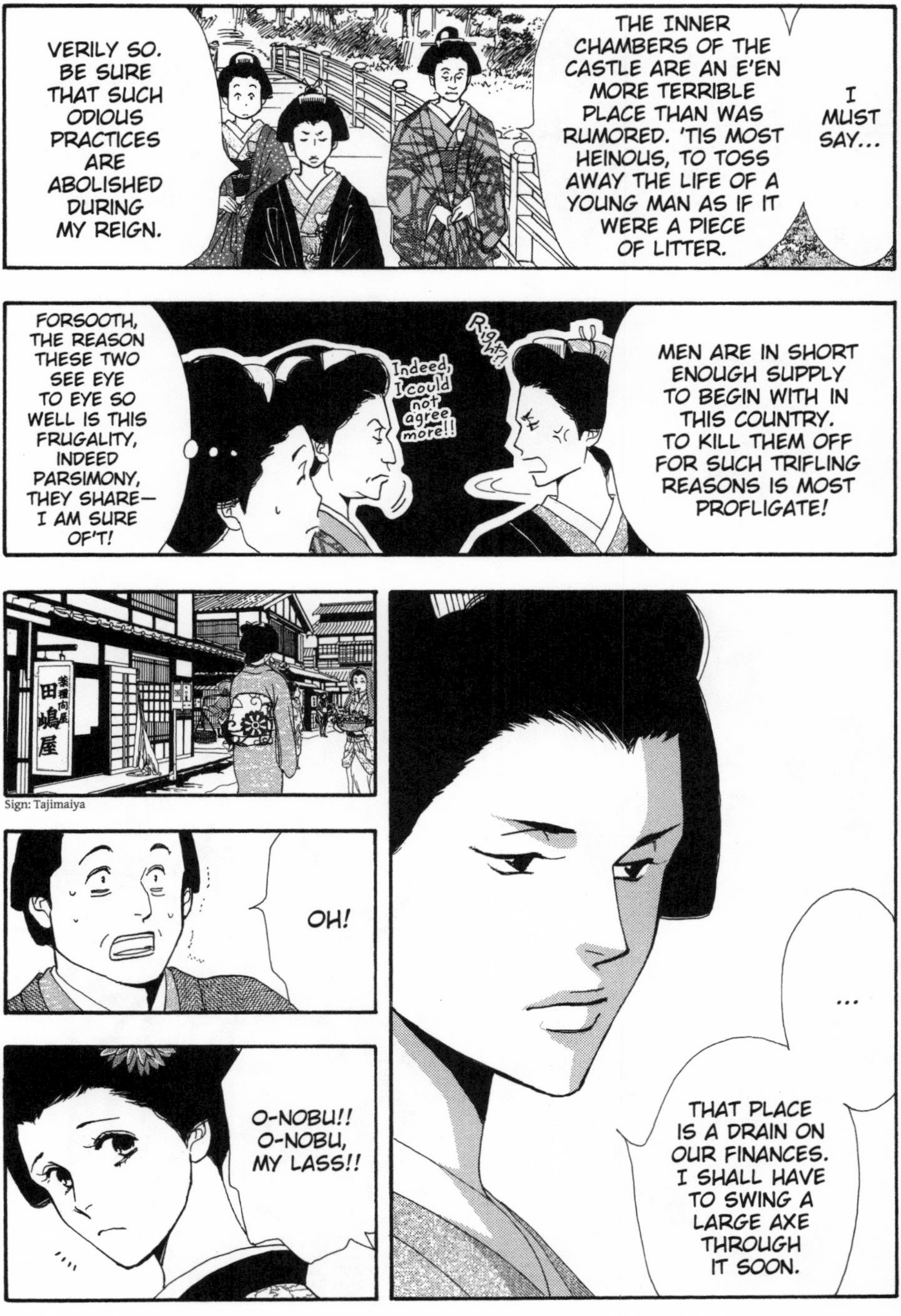
I MUST SAY...
THE INNER CHAMBERS OF THE CASTLE ARE AN E'EN MORE TERRIBLE PLACE THAN WAS RUMORED. 'TIS MOST HEINOUS, TO TOSS AWAY THE LIFE OF A YOUNG MAN AS IF IT WERE A PIECE OF LITTER.
VERILY SO. BE SURE THAT SUCH ODIOUS PRACTICES ARE ABOLISHED DURING MY REIGN.
MEN ARE IN SHORT ENOUGH SUPPLY TO BEGIN WITH IN THIS COUNTRY. TO KILL THEM OFF FOR SUCH TRIFLING REASONS IS MOST PROFLIGATE!
Right!
Indeed, I could not agree more!!
FORSOOTH, THE REASON THESE TWO SEE EYE TO EYE SO WELL IS THIS FRUGALITY, INDEED PARSIMONY, THEY SHARE— I AM SURE OF'T!
...
THAT PLACE IS A DRAIN ON OUR FINANCES. I SHALL HAVE TO SWING A LARGE AXE THROUGH IT SOON.
OH!
O-NOBU!! O-NOBU, MY LASS!!

Sign: Tajimaiya

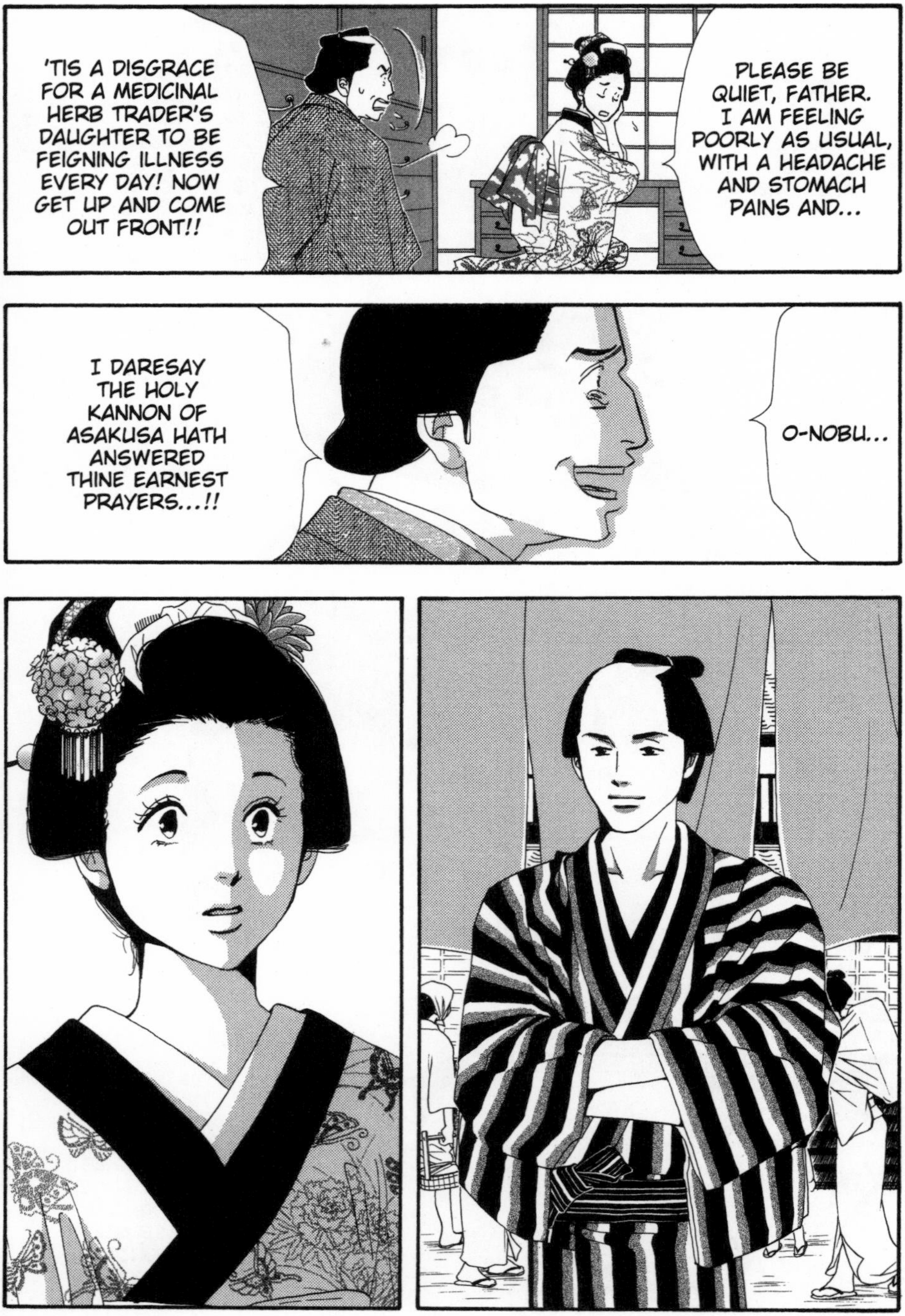
PLEASE BE QUIET, FATHER. I AM FEELING POORLY AS USUAL, WITH A HEADACHE AND STOMACH PAINS AND...
'TIS A DISGRACE FOR A MEDICINAL HERB TRADER'S DAUGHTER TO BE FEIGNING ILLNESS EVERY DAY! NOW GET UP AND COME OUT FRONT!!
O-NOBU...
I DARESAY THE HOLY KANNON OF ASAKUSA HATH ANSWERED THINE EARNEST PRAYERS...!!

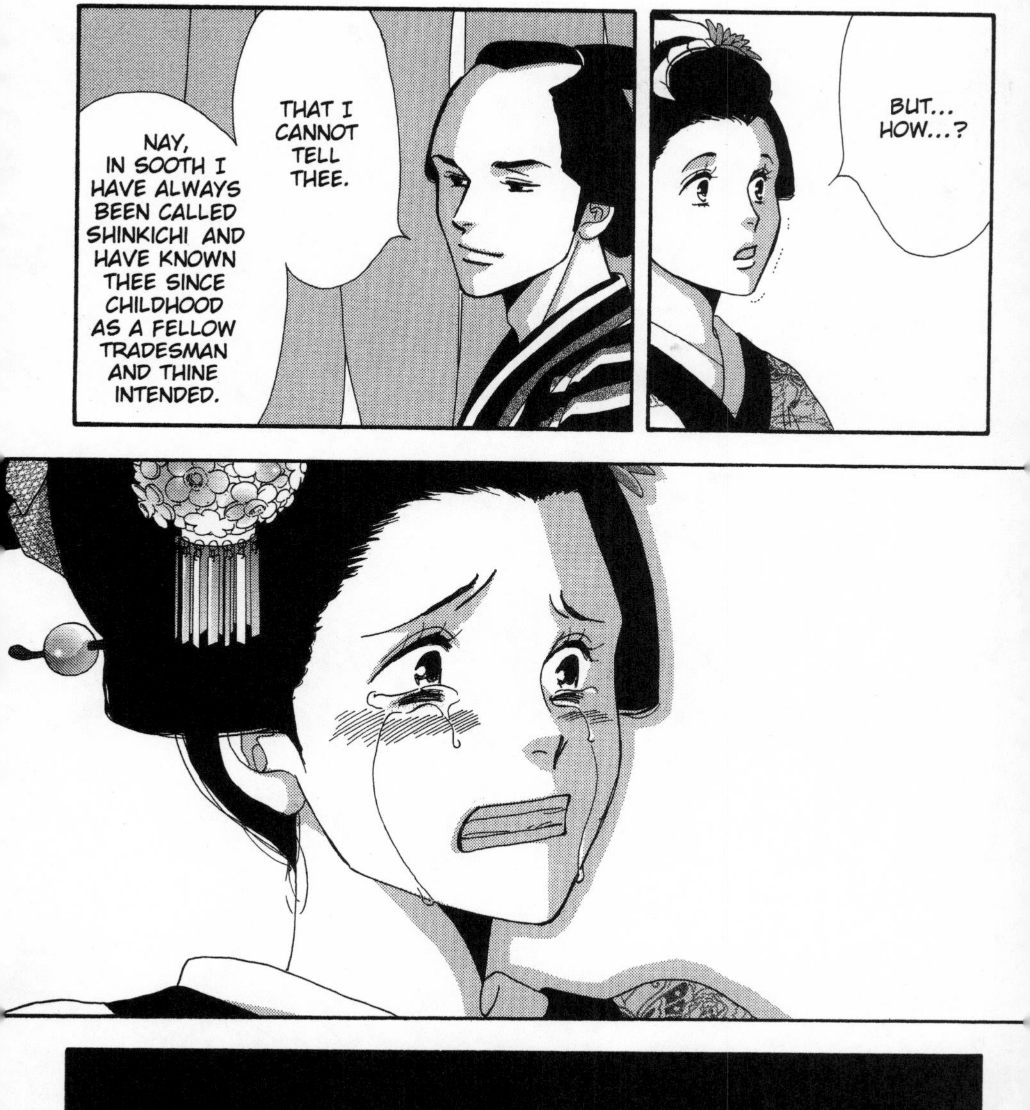
BUT... HOW...?
THAT I CANNOT TELL THEE.
NAY, IN SOOTH I HAVE ALWAYS BEEN CALLED SHINKICHI AND HAVE KNOWN THEE SINCE CHILDHOOD AS A FELLOW TRADESMAN AND THINE INTENDED.
The Inner Chambers' records for this day state only that "Mizuno, a Groom of the Bedchamber, was suddenly taken ill and died."

Ōoku

THE INNER CHAMBERS

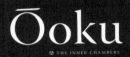

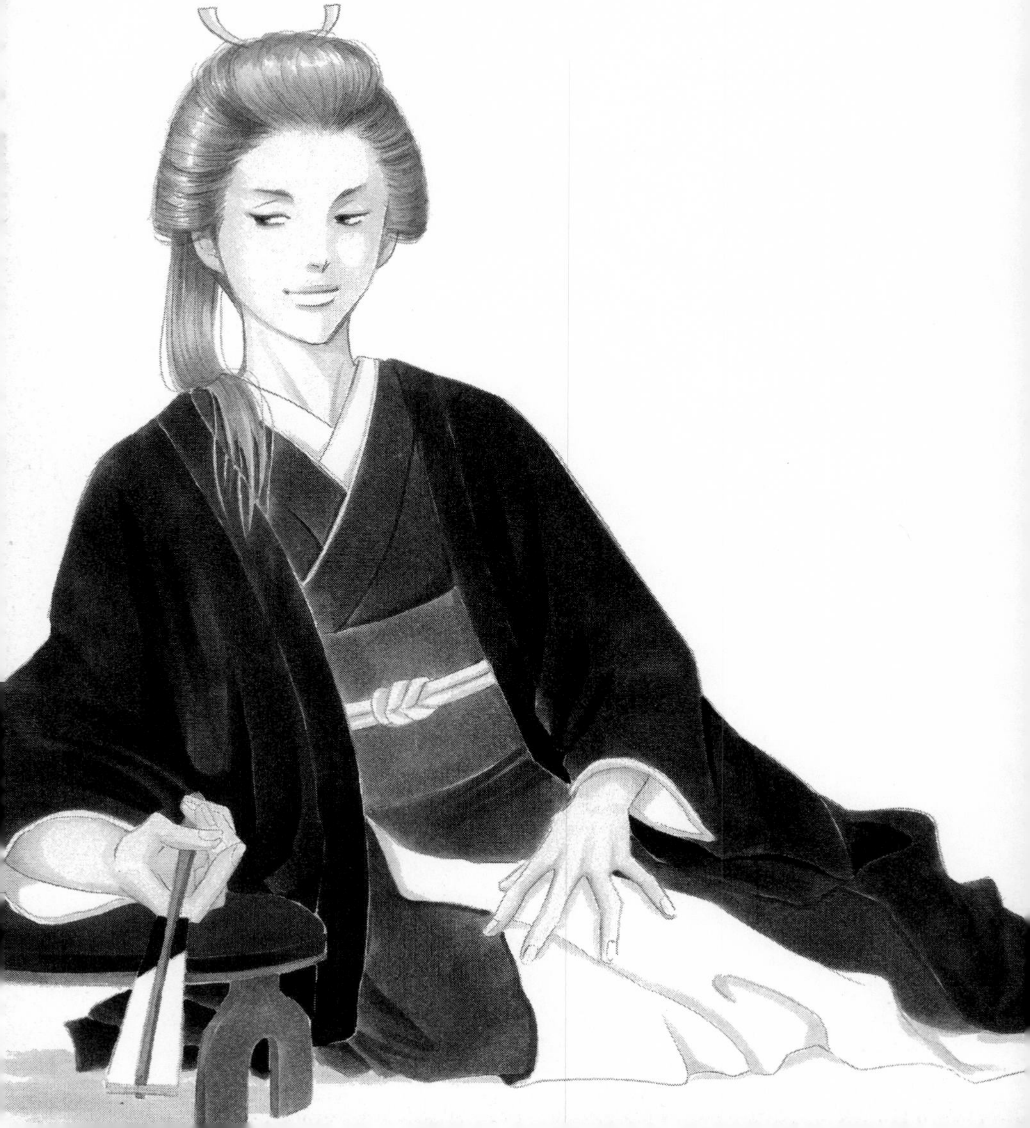

Ōoku

THE INNER CHAMBERS

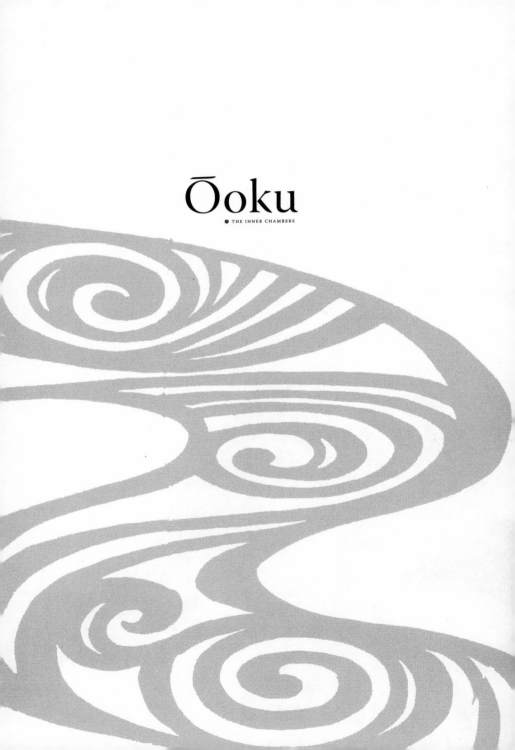

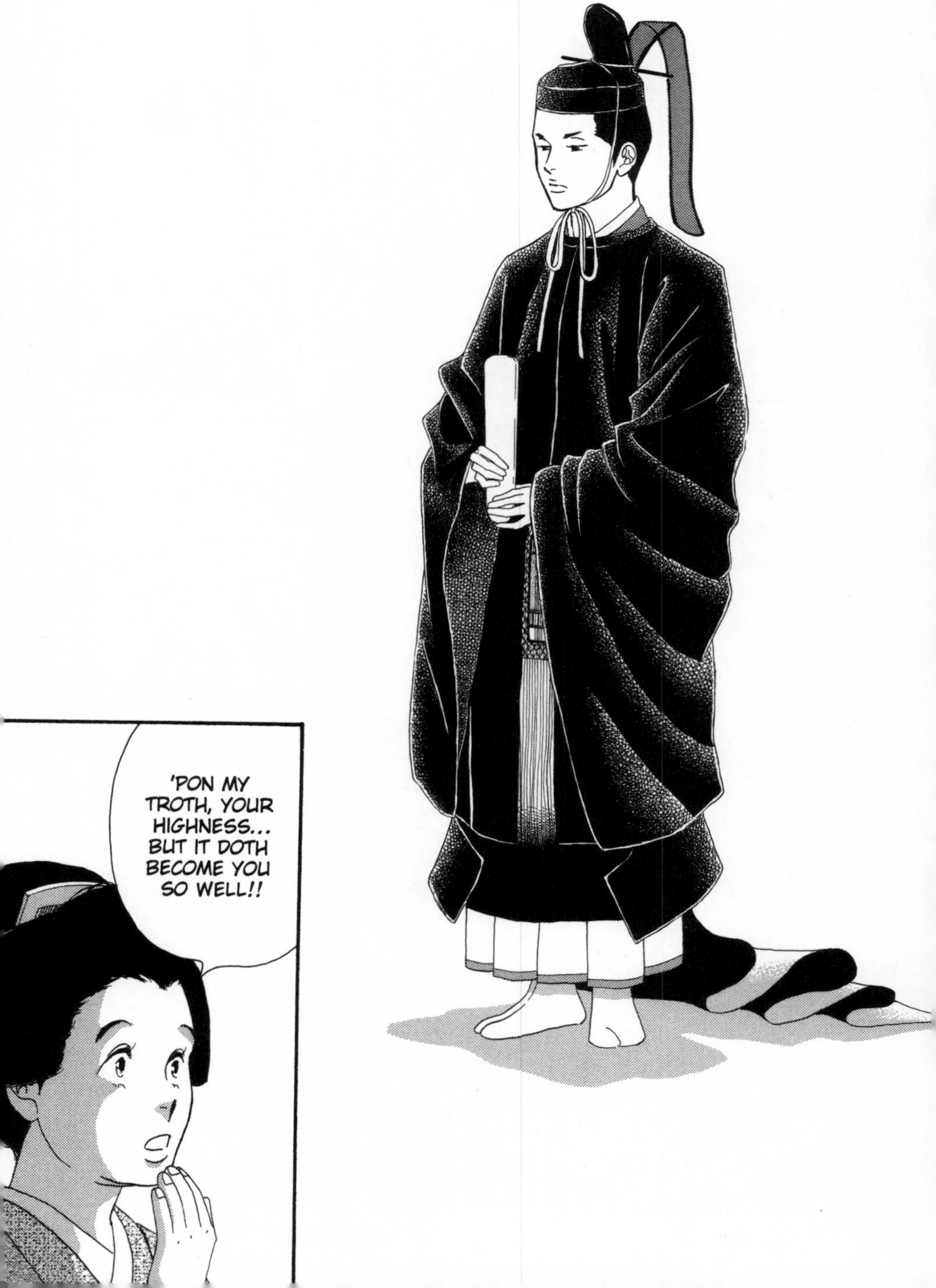
'PON MY TROTH, YOUR HIGHNESS... BUT IT DOTH BECOME YOU SO WELL!!

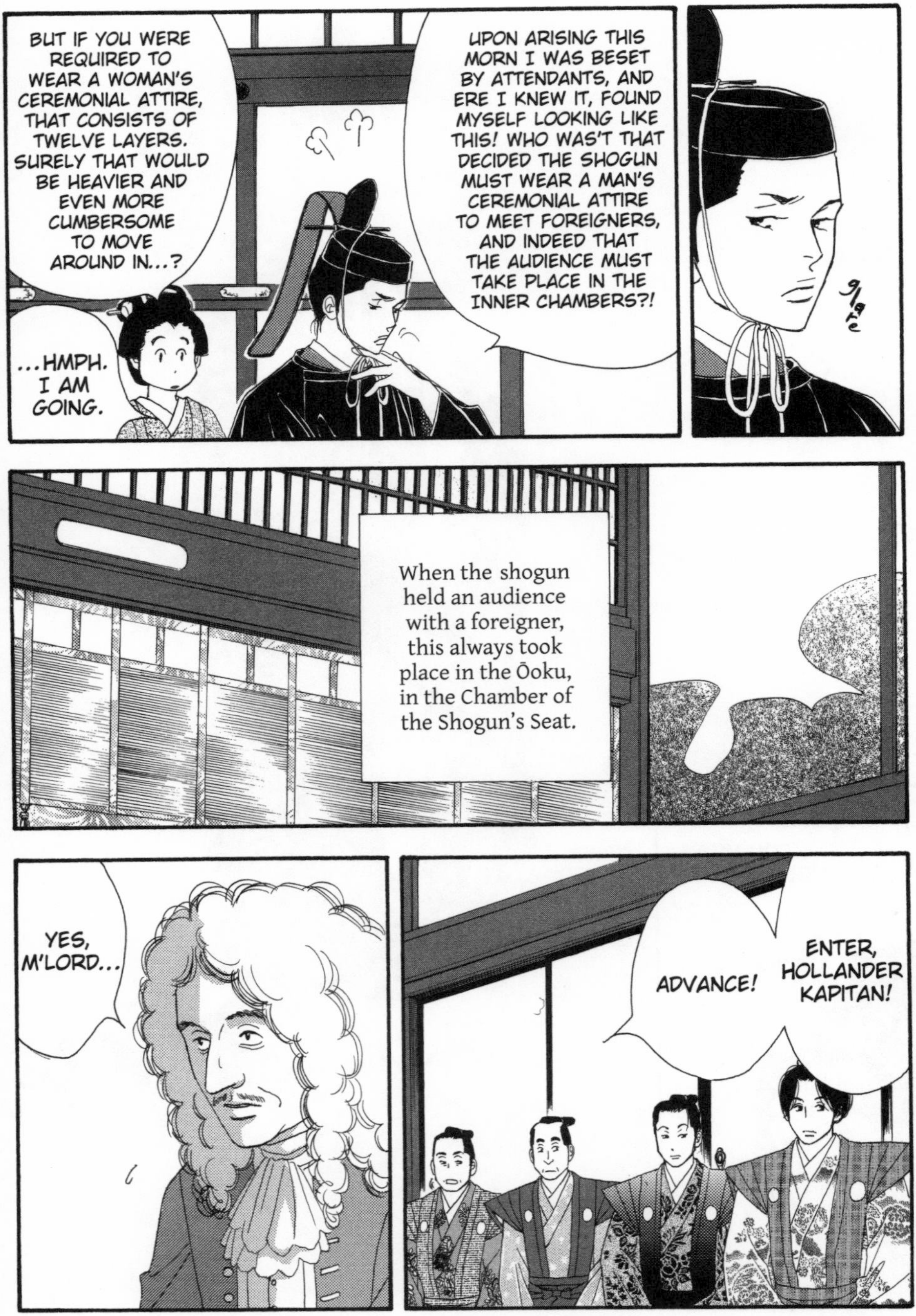
glare
UPON ARISING THIS MORN I WAS BESET BY ATTENDANTS, AND ERE I KNEW IT, FOUND MYSELF LOOKING LIKE THIS! WHO WAS'T THAT DECIDED THE SHOGUN MUST WEAR A MAN'S CEREMONIAL ATTIRE TO MEET FOREIGNERS, AND INDEED THAT THE AUDIENCE MUST TAKE PLACE IN THE INNER CHAMBERS?!
BUT IF YOU WERE REQUIRED TO WEAR A WOMAN'S CEREMONIAL ATTIRE, THAT CONSISTS OF TWELVE LAYERS. SURELY THAT WOULD BE HEAVIER AND EVEN MORE CUMBERSOME TO MOVE AROUND IN...?
...HMPH. I AM GOING.
When the shogun held an audience with a foreigner, this always took place in the Ōoku, in the Chamber of the Shogun's Seat.
ENTER, HOLLANDER KAPITAN!
ADVANCE!
YES, M'LORD...

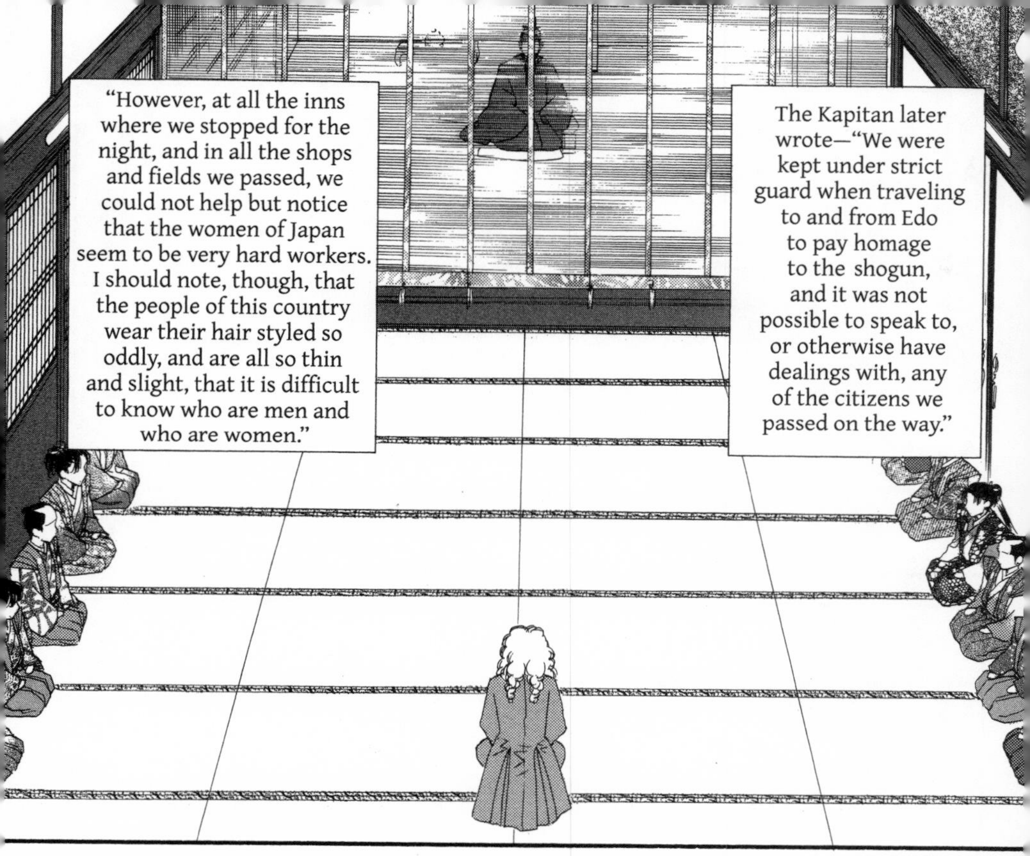
The Kapitan later wrote—"We were kept under strict guard when traveling to and from Edo to pay homage to the shogun, and it was not possible to speak to, or otherwise have dealings with, any of the citizens we passed on the way."
"However, at all the inns where we stopped for the night, and in all the shops and fields we passed, we could not help but notice that the women of Japan seem to be very hard workers. I should note, though, that the people of this country wear their hair styled so oddly, and are all so thin and slight, that it is difficult to know who are men and who are women."

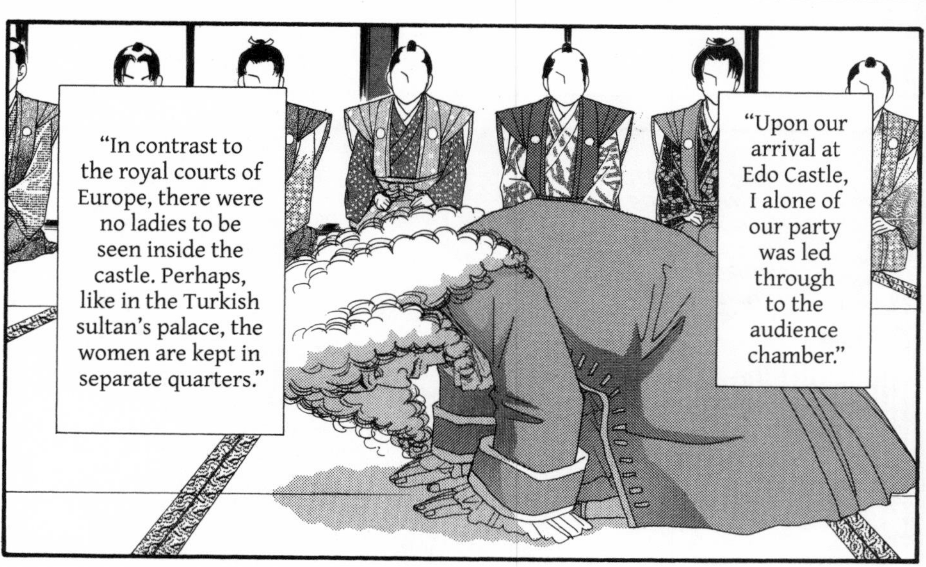
"Upon our arrival at Edo Castle, I alone of our party was led through to the audience chamber."
"In contrast to the royal courts of Europe, there were no ladies to be seen inside the castle. Perhaps, like in the Turkish sultan's palace, the women are kept in separate quarters."

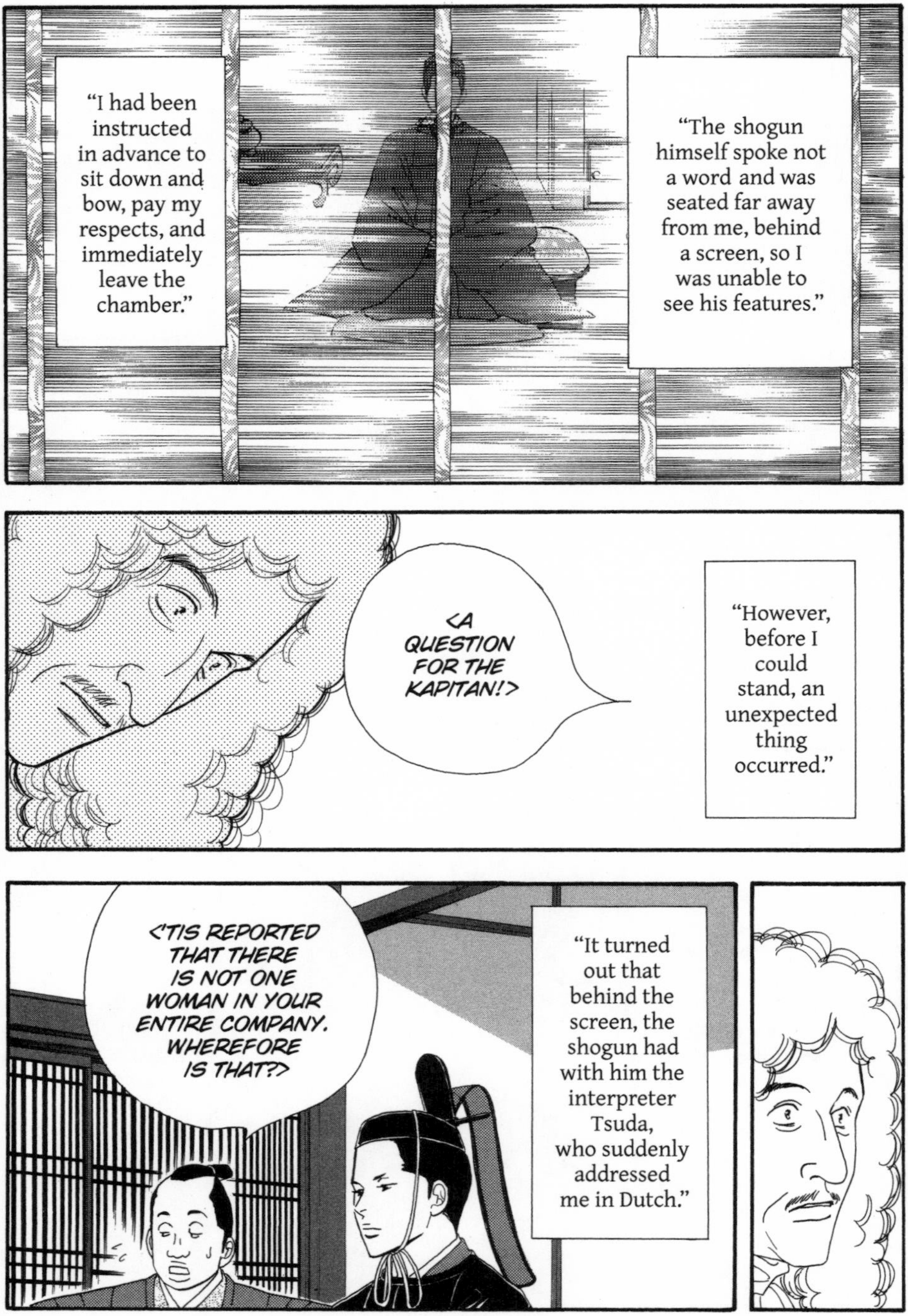
"The shogun himself spoke not a word and was seated far away from me, behind a screen, so I was unable to see his features."
"I had been instructed in advance to sit down and bow, pay my respects, and immediately leave the chamber."
"However, before I could stand, an unexpected thing occurred."
<A QUESTION FOR THE KAPITAN!>
"It turned out that behind the screen, the shogun had with him the interpreter Tsuda, who suddenly addressed me in Dutch."
<'TIS REPORTED THAT THERE IS NOT ONE WOMAN IN YOUR ENTIRE COMPANY. WHEREFORE IS THAT?>

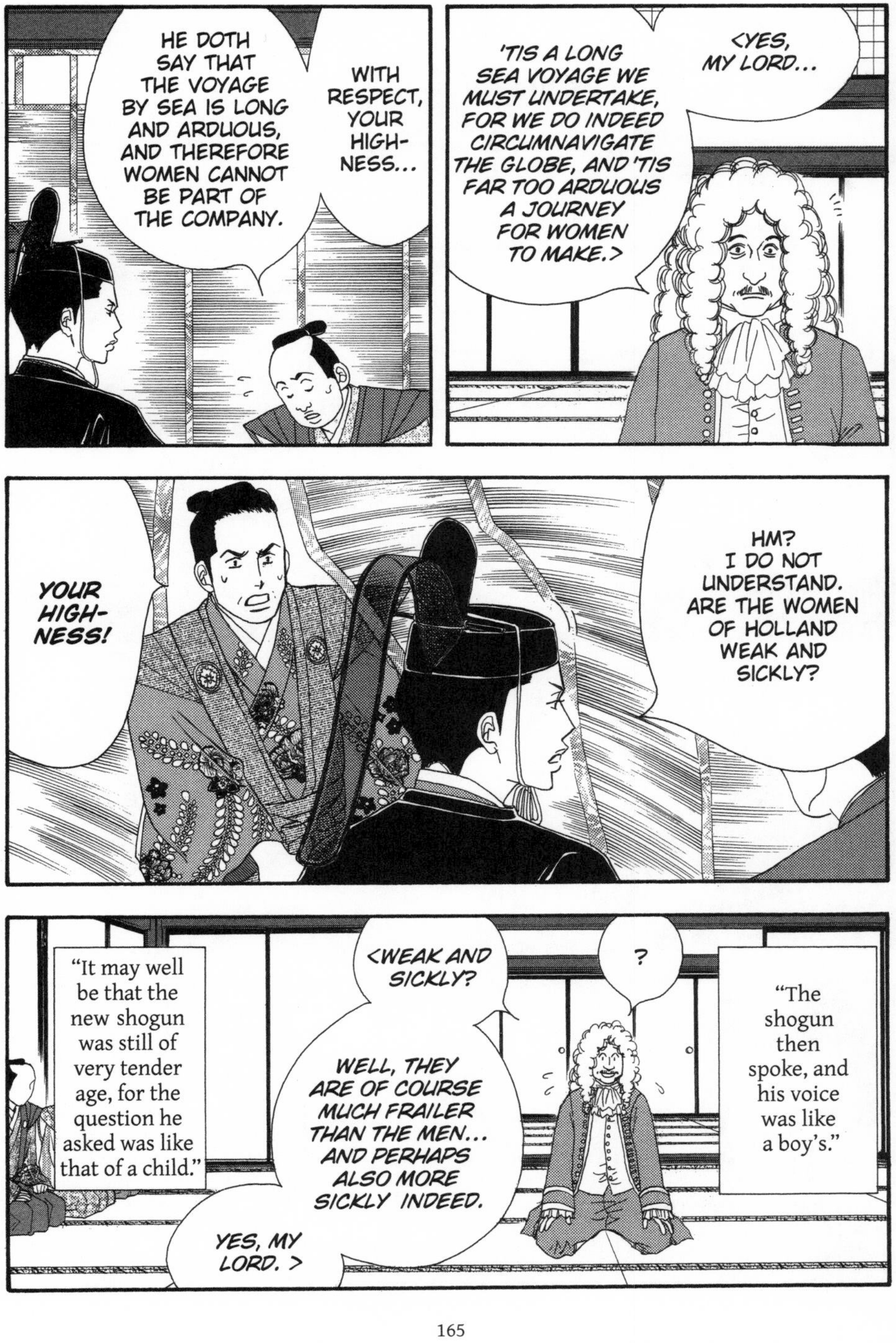
<YES, MY LORD…
'TIS A LONG SEA VOYAGE WE MUST UNDERTAKE, FOR WE DO INDEED CIRCUMNAVIGATE THE GLOBE, AND 'TIS FAR TOO ARDUOUS A JOURNEY FOR WOMEN TO MAKE.>
WITH RESPECT, YOUR HIGHNESS…
HE DOTH SAY THAT THE VOYAGE BY SEA IS LONG AND ARDUOUS, AND THEREFORE WOMEN CANNOT BE PART OF THE COMPANY.
HM? I DO NOT UNDERSTAND. ARE THE WOMEN OF HOLLAND WEAK AND SICKLY?
YOUR HIGHNESS!
"The shogun then spoke, and his voice was like a boy's."
?
<WEAK AND SICKLY?
WELL, THEY ARE OF COURSE MUCH FRAILER THAN THE MEN… AND PERHAPS ALSO MORE SICKLY INDEED.
YES, MY LORD.>
"It may well be that the new shogun was still of very tender age, for the question he asked was like that of a child."

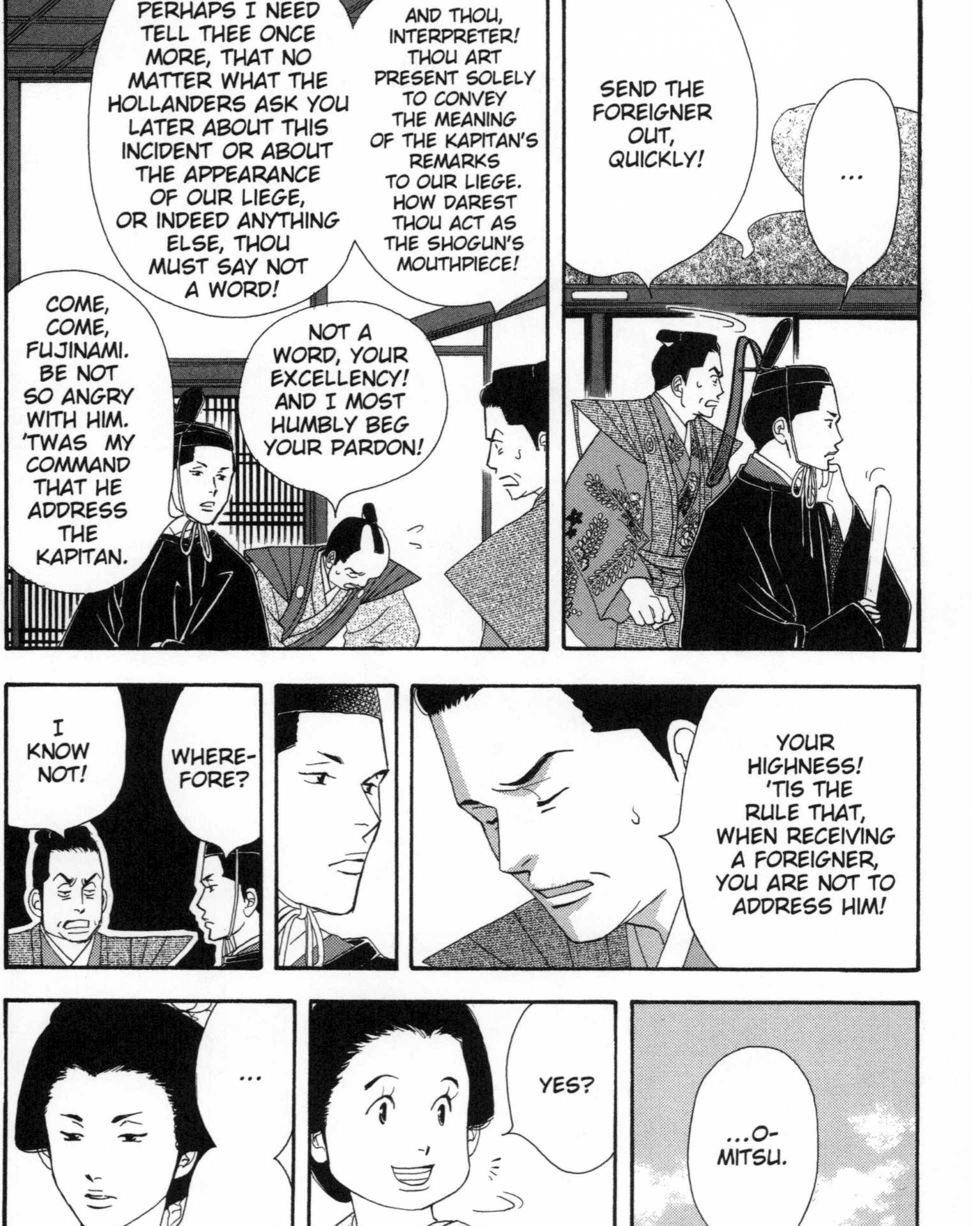
SEND THE FOREIGNER OUT, QUICKLY!
...
AND THOU, INTERPRETER! THOU ART PRESENT SOLELY TO CONVEY THE MEANING OF THE KAPITAN'S REMARKS TO OUR LIEGE. HOW DAREST THOU ACT AS THE SHOGUN'S MOUTHPIECE!
PERHAPS I NEED TELL THEE ONCE MORE, THAT NO MATTER WHAT THE HOLLANDERS ASK YOU LATER ABOUT THIS INCIDENT OR ABOUT THE APPEARANCE OF OUR LIEGE, OR INDEED ANYTHING ELSE, THOU MUST SAY NOT A WORD!
NOT A WORD, YOUR EXCELLENCY! AND I MOST HUMBLY BEG YOUR PARDON!
COME, COME, FUJINAMI. BE NOT SO ANGRY WITH HIM. 'TWAS MY COMMAND THAT HE ADDRESS THE KAPITAN.
YOUR HIGHNESS! 'TIS THE RULE THAT, WHEN RECEIVING A FOREIGNER, YOU ARE NOT TO ADDRESS HIM!
WHERE-FORE?
I KNOW NOT!
...O-MITSU.
YES?
...
HISAMICHI.

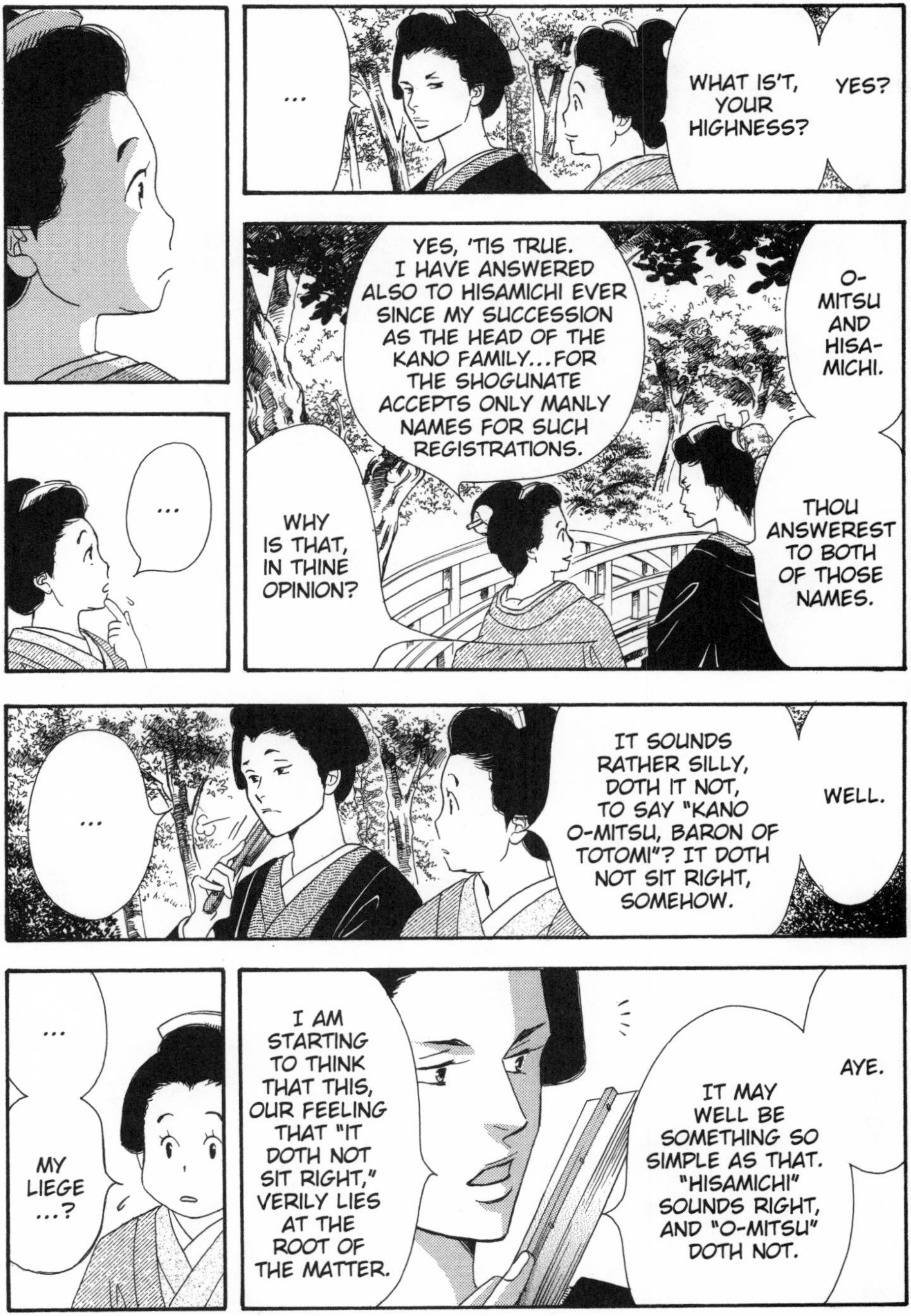
YES?
WHAT IS'T, YOUR HIGHNESS?
...
O-MITSU AND HISA-MICHI.
THOU ANSWEREST TO BOTH OF THOSE NAMES.
YES, 'TIS TRUE. I HAVE ANSWERED ALSO TO HISAMICHI EVER SINCE MY SUCCESSION AS THE HEAD OF THE KANO FAMILY...FOR THE SHOGUNATE ACCEPTS ONLY MANLY NAMES FOR SUCH REGISTRATIONS.
WHY IS THAT, IN THINE OPINION?
...
WELL.
IT SOUNDS RATHER SILLY, DOTH IT NOT, TO SAY "KANO O-MITSU, BARON OF TOTOMI"? IT DOTH NOT SIT RIGHT, SOMEHOW.
...
AYE.
IT MAY WELL BE SOMETHING SO SIMPLE AS THAT. "HISAMICHI" SOUNDS RIGHT, AND "O-MITSU" DOTH NOT.
I AM STARTING TO THINK THAT THIS, OUR FEELING THAT "IT DOTH NOT SIT RIGHT," VERILY LIES AT THE ROOT OF THE MATTER.
...
MY LIEGE ...?

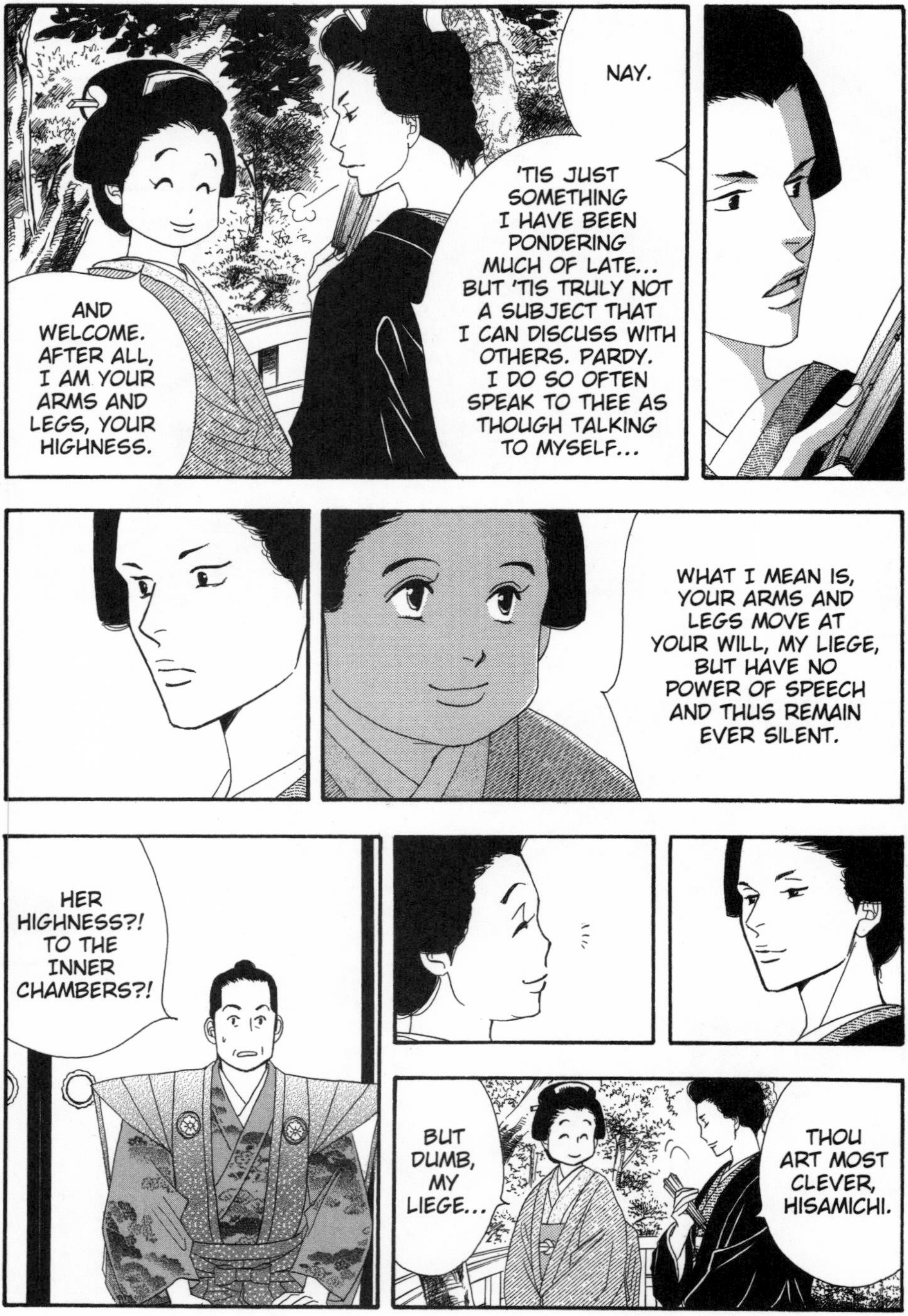
NAY.
'TIS JUST SOMETHING I HAVE BEEN PONDERING MUCH OF LATE... BUT 'TIS TRULY NOT A SUBJECT THAT I CAN DISCUSS WITH OTHERS. PARDY. I DO SO OFTEN SPEAK TO THEE AS THOUGH TALKING TO MYSELF...
AND WELCOME. AFTER ALL, I AM YOUR ARMS AND LEGS, YOUR HIGHNESS.
WHAT I MEAN IS, YOUR ARMS AND LEGS MOVE AT YOUR WILL, MY LIEGE, BUT HAVE NO POWER OF SPEECH AND THUS REMAIN EVER SILENT.
THOU ART MOST CLEVER, HISAMICHI.
BUT DUMB, MY LIEGE...
HER HIGHNESS?! TO THE INNER CHAMBERS?!

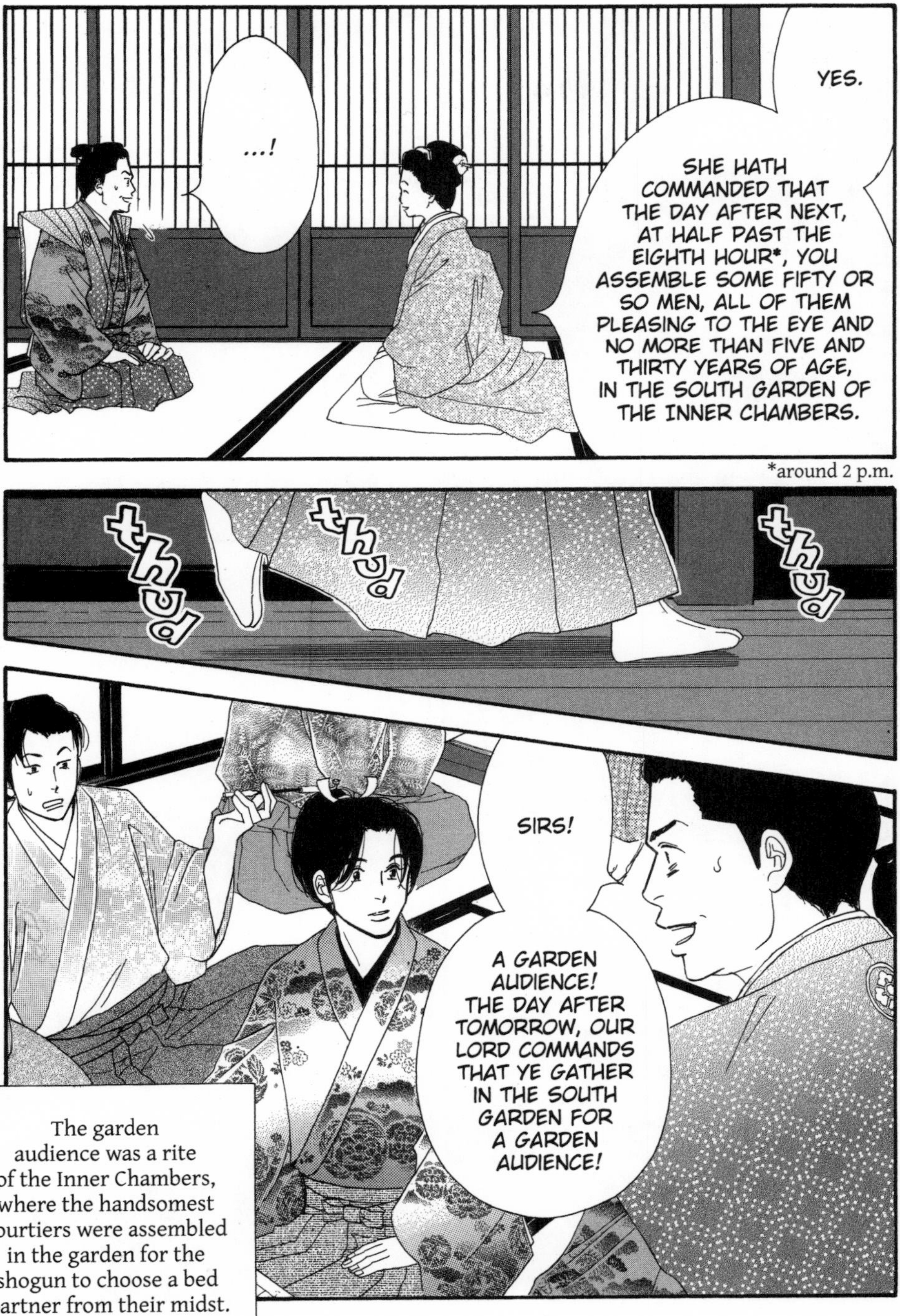
YES.
SHE HATH COMMANDED THAT THE DAY AFTER NEXT, AT HALF PAST THE EIGHTH HOUR*, YOU ASSEMBLE SOME FIFTY OR SO MEN, ALL OF THEM PLEASING TO THE EYE AND NO MORE THAN FIVE AND THIRTY YEARS OF AGE, IN THE SOUTH GARDEN OF THE INNER CHAMBERS.
...!
*around 2 p.m.
thud
thud
thud
SIRS!
A GARDEN AUDIENCE! THE DAY AFTER TOMORROW, OUR LORD COMMANDS THAT YE GATHER IN THE SOUTH GARDEN FOR A GARDEN AUDIENCE!
The garden audience was a rite of the Inner Chambers, where the handsomest courtiers were assembled in the garden for the shogun to choose a bed partner from their midst.

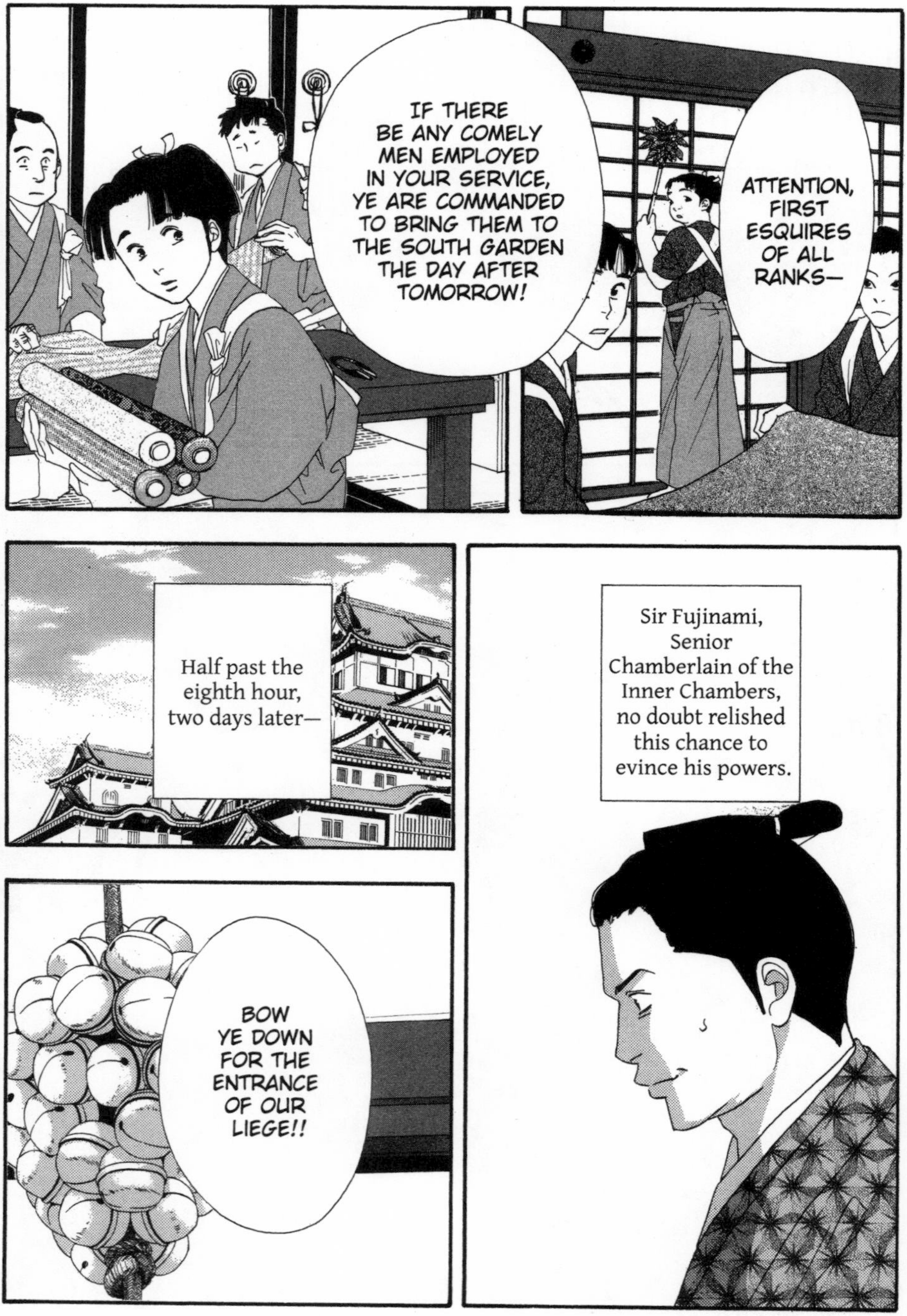
ATTENTION, FIRST ESQUIRES OF ALL RANKS—
IF THERE BE ANY COMELY MEN EMPLOYED IN YOUR SERVICE, YE ARE COMMANDED TO BRING THEM TO THE SOUTH GARDEN THE DAY AFTER TOMORROW!
Sir Fujinami, Senior Chamberlain of the Inner Chambers, no doubt relished this chance to evince his powers.
Half past the eighth hour, two days later—
BOW YE DOWN FOR THE ENTRANCE OF OUR LIEGE!!

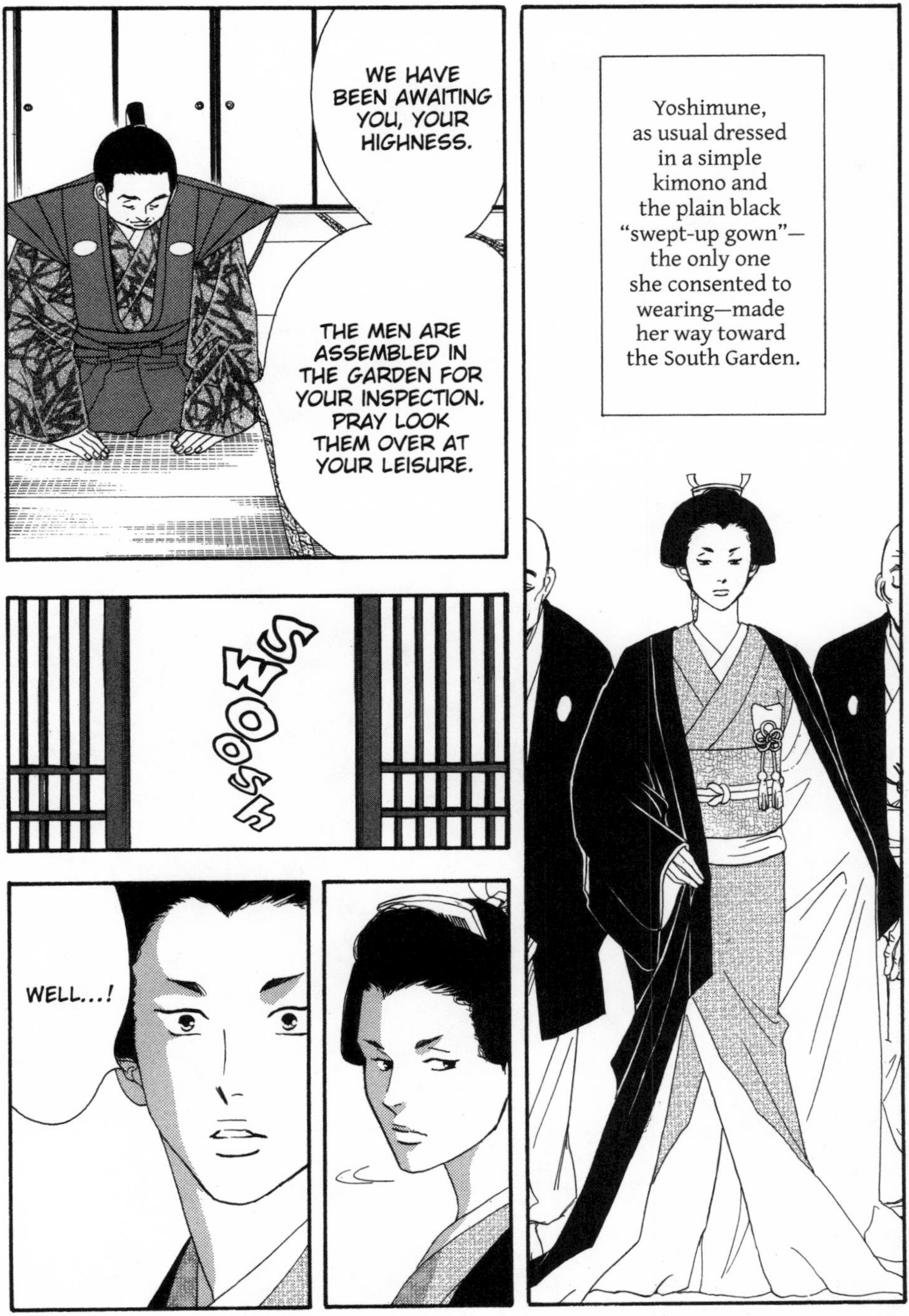
Yoshimune, as usual dressed in a simple kimono and the plain black "swept-up gown"—the only one she consented to wearing—made her way toward the South Garden.
WE HAVE BEEN AWAITING YOU, YOUR HIGHNESS.
THE MEN ARE ASSEMBLED IN THE GARDEN FOR YOUR INSPECTION. PRAY LOOK THEM OVER AT YOUR LEISURE.
SWOOSH
WELL...!

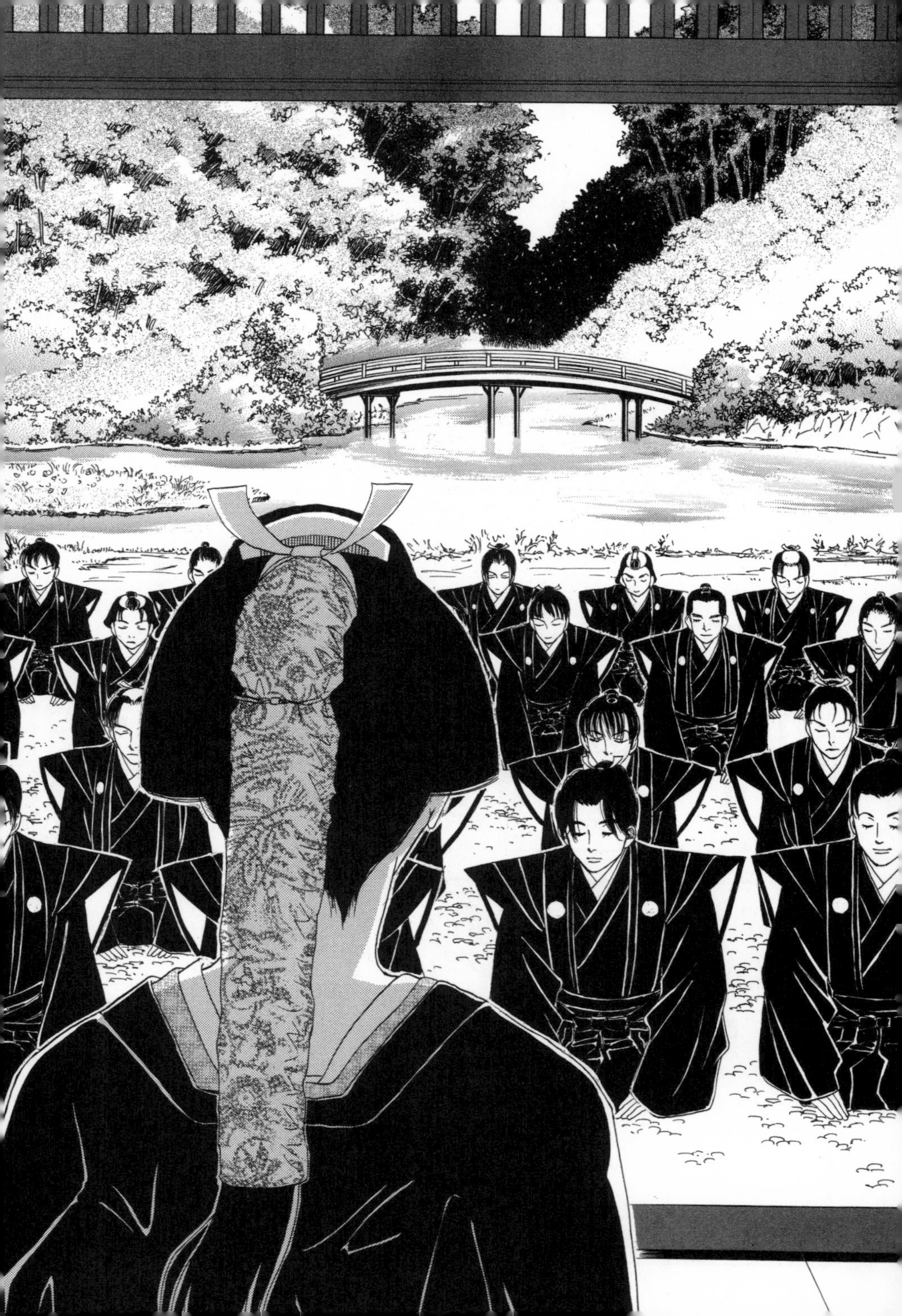

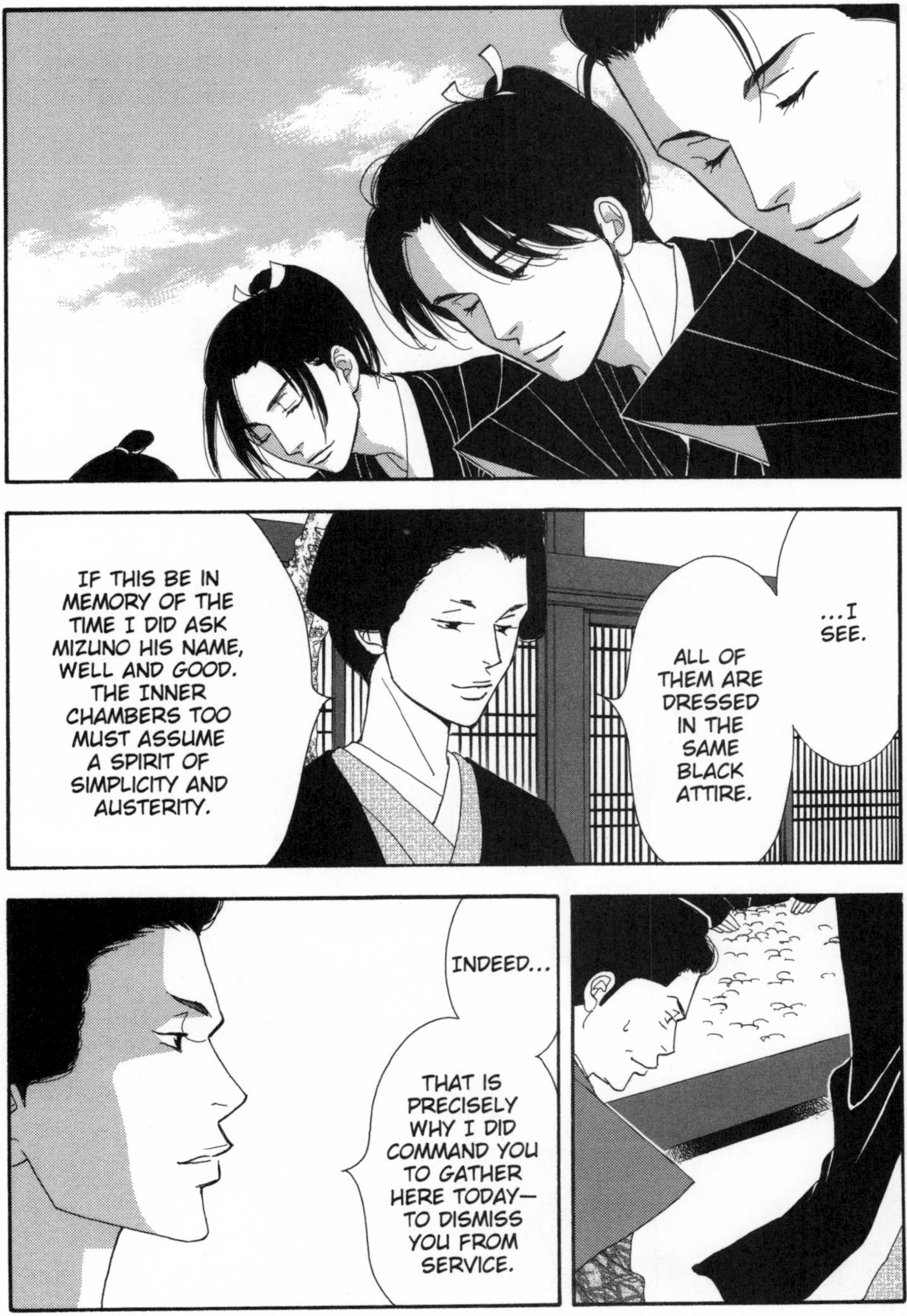
...I SEE.
ALL OF THEM ARE DRESSED IN THE SAME BLACK ATTIRE.
IF THIS BE IN MEMORY OF THE TIME I DID ASK MIZUNO HIS NAME, WELL AND GOOD. THE INNER CHAMBERS TOO MUST ASSUME A SPIRIT OF SIMPLICITY AND AUSTERITY.
INDEED...
THAT IS PRECISELY WHY I DID COMMAND YOU TO GATHER HERE TODAY— TO DISMISS YOU FROM SERVICE.

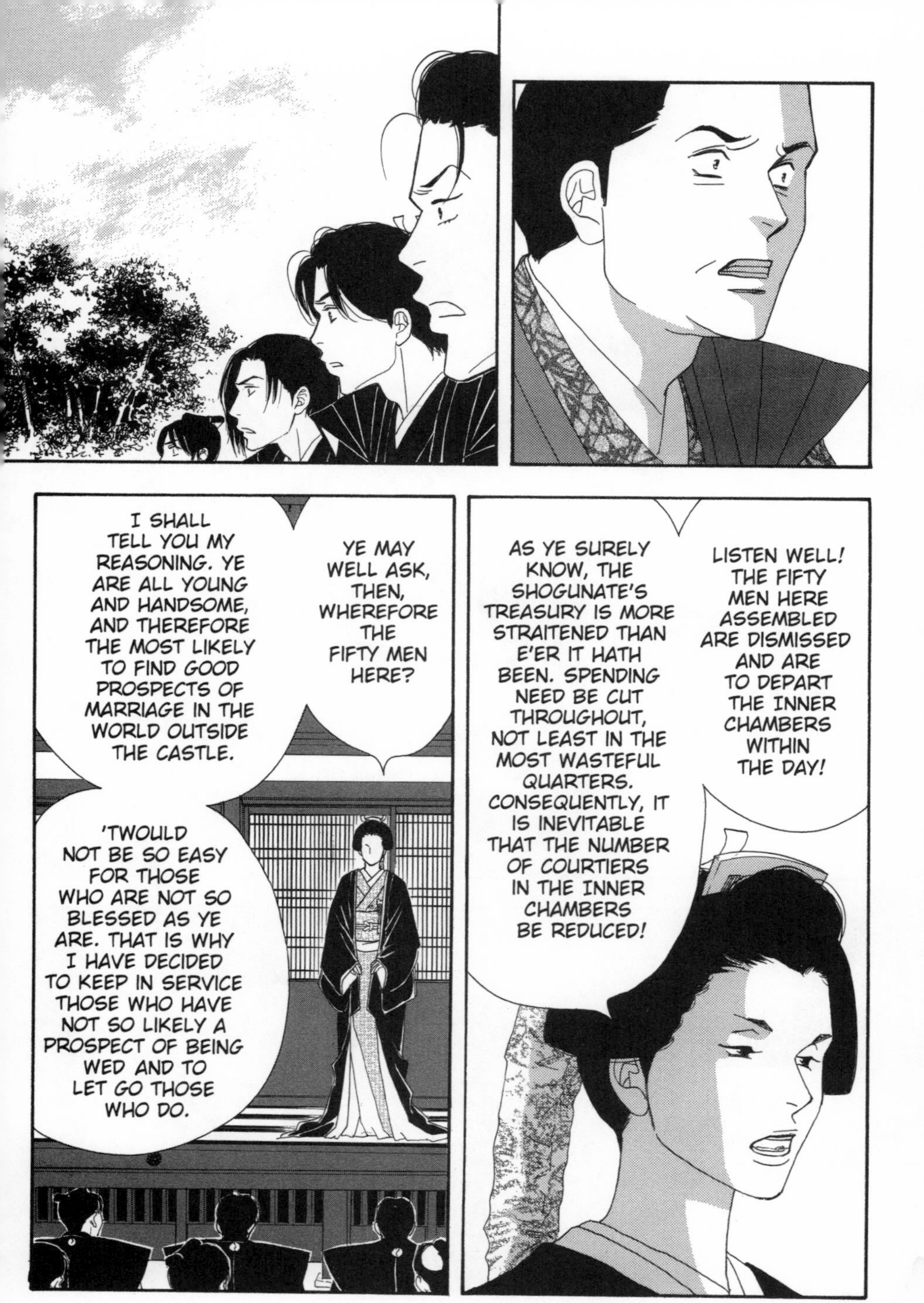
LISTEN WELL! THE FIFTY MEN HERE ASSEMBLED ARE DISMISSED AND ARE TO DEPART THE INNER CHAMBERS WITHIN THE DAY!
AS YE SURELY KNOW, THE SHOGUNATE'S TREASURY IS MORE STRAITENED THAN E'ER IT HATH BEEN. SPENDING NEED BE CUT THROUGHOUT, NOT LEAST IN THE MOST WASTEFUL QUARTERS. CONSEQUENTLY, IT IS INEVITABLE THAT THE NUMBER OF COURTIERS IN THE INNER CHAMBERS BE REDUCED!
YE MAY WELL ASK, THEN, WHEREFORE THE FIFTY MEN HERE?
I SHALL TELL YOU MY REASONING. YE ARE ALL YOUNG AND HANDSOME, AND THEREFORE THE MOST LIKELY TO FIND GOOD PROSPECTS OF MARRIAGE IN THE WORLD OUTSIDE THE CASTLE.
'TWOULD NOT BE SO EASY FOR THOSE WHO ARE NOT SO BLESSED AS YE ARE. THAT IS WHY I HAVE DECIDED TO KEEP IN SERVICE THOSE WHO HAVE NOT SO LIKELY A PROSPECT OF BEING WED AND TO LET GO THOSE WHO DO.

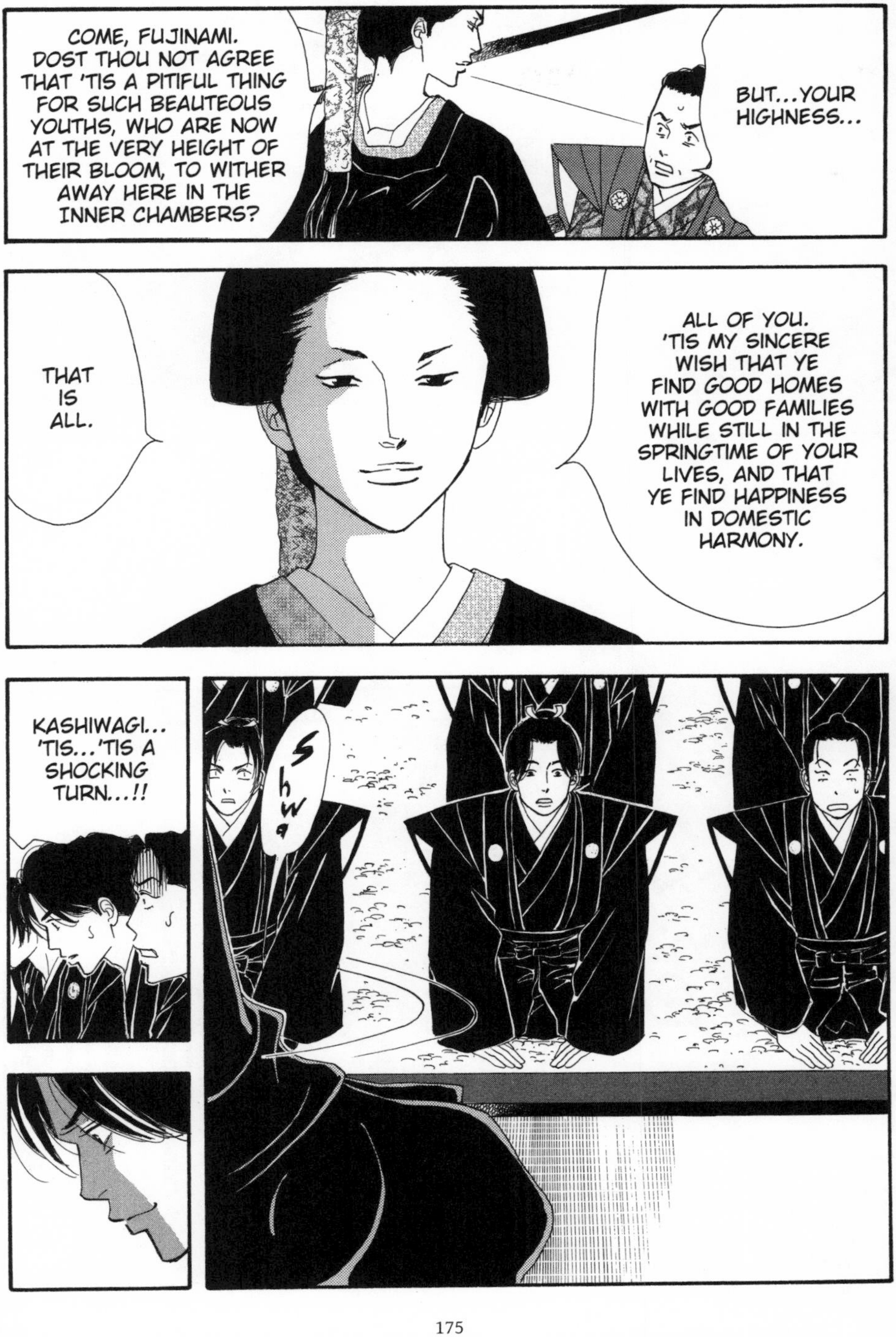
BUT...YOUR HIGHNESS...
COME, FUJINAMI. DOST THOU NOT AGREE THAT 'TIS A PITIFUL THING FOR SUCH BEAUTEOUS YOUTHS, WHO ARE NOW AT THE VERY HEIGHT OF THEIR BLOOM, TO WITHER AWAY HERE IN THE INNER CHAMBERS?
ALL OF YOU. 'TIS MY SINCERE WISH THAT YE FIND GOOD HOMES WITH GOOD FAMILIES WHILE STILL IN THE SPRINGTIME OF YOUR LIVES, AND THAT YE FIND HAPPINESS IN DOMESTIC HARMONY.
THAT IS ALL.
Shwa
KASHIWAGI... 'TIS...'TIS A SHOCKING TURN...!!

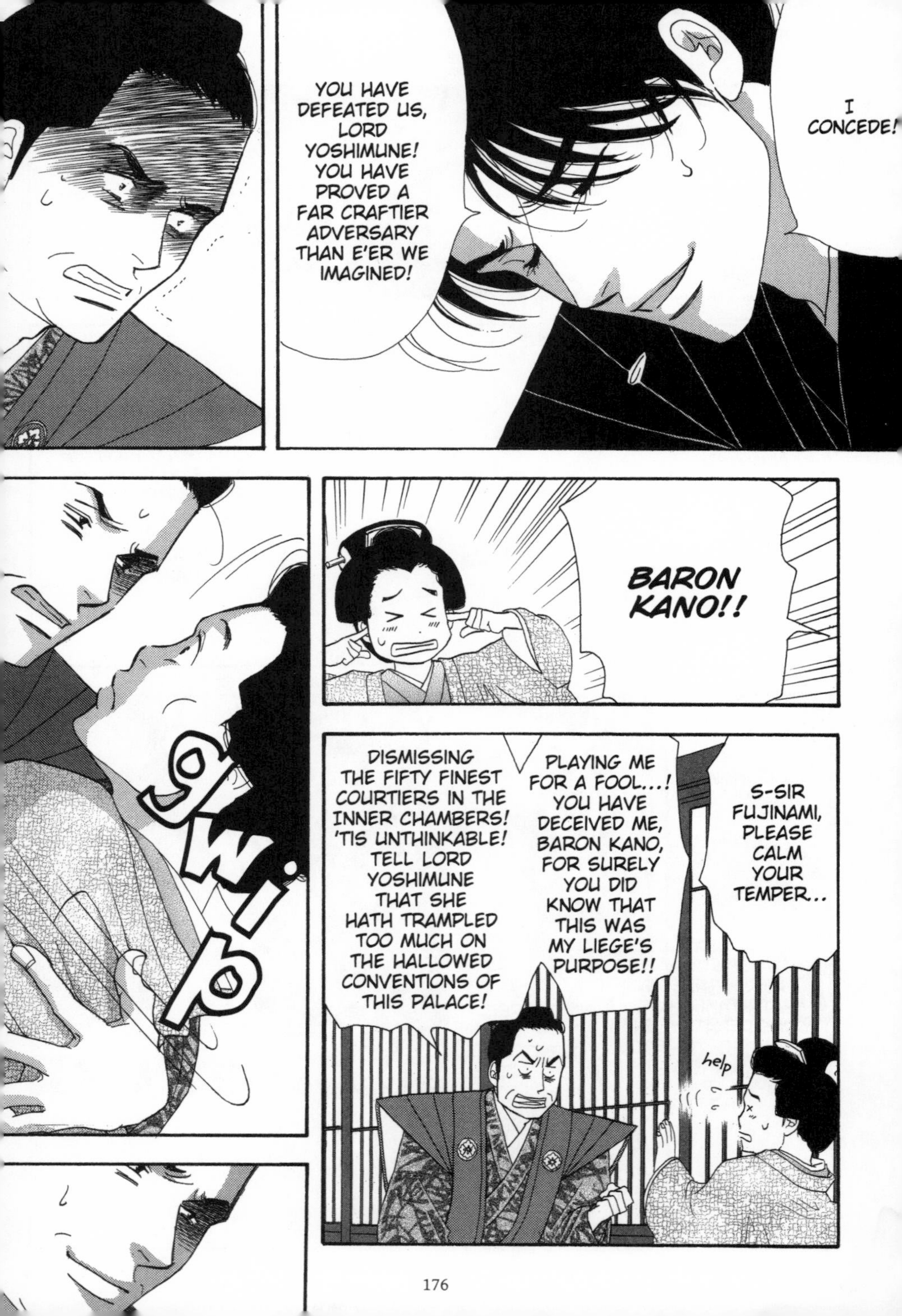
I CONCEDE!
YOU HAVE DEFEATED US, LORD YOSHIMUNE! YOU HAVE PROVED A FAR CRAFTIER ADVERSARY THAN E'ER WE IMAGINED!
BARON KANO!!
S-SIR FUJINAMI, PLEASE CALM YOUR TEMPER...
PLAYING ME FOR A FOOL...! YOU HAVE DECEIVED ME, BARON KANO, FOR SURELY YOU DID KNOW THAT THIS WAS MY LIEGE'S PURPOSE!!
DISMISSING THE FIFTY FINEST COURTIERS IN THE INNER CHAMBERS! 'TIS UNTHINKABLE! TELL LORD YOSHIMUNE THAT SHE HATH TRAMPLED TOO MUCH ON THE HALLOWED CONVENTIONS OF THIS PALACE!
help
gwip

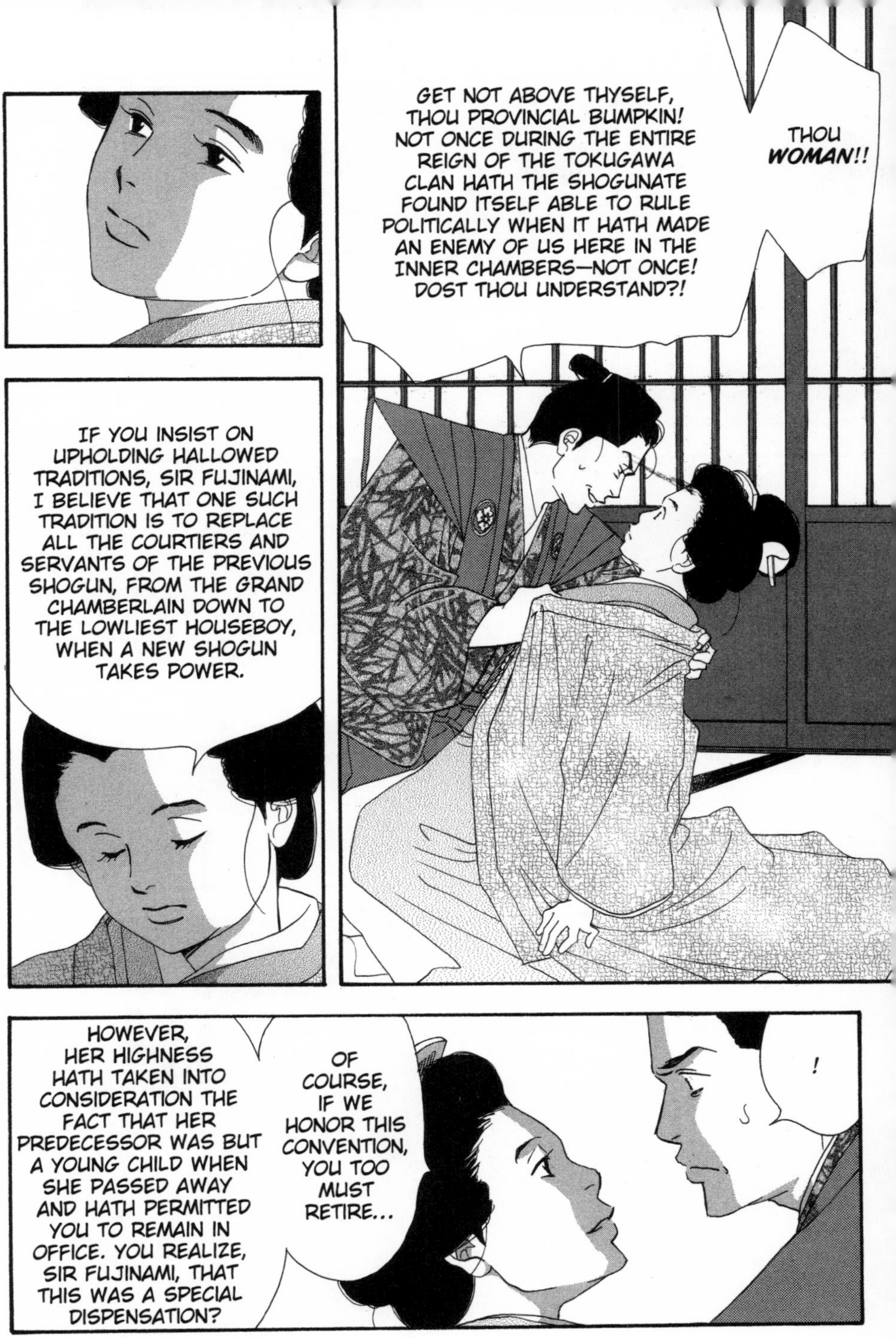
THOU *WOMAN*!!
GET NOT ABOVE THYSELF, THOU PROVINCIAL BUMPKIN! NOT ONCE DURING THE ENTIRE REIGN OF THE TOKUGAWA CLAN HATH THE SHOGUNATE FOUND ITSELF ABLE TO RULE POLITICALLY WHEN IT HATH MADE AN ENEMY OF US HERE IN THE INNER CHAMBERS—NOT ONCE! DOST THOU UNDERSTAND?!
IF YOU INSIST ON UPHOLDING HALLOWED TRADITIONS, SIR FUJINAMI, I BELIEVE THAT ONE SUCH TRADITION IS TO REPLACE ALL THE COURTIERS AND SERVANTS OF THE PREVIOUS SHOGUN, FROM THE GRAND CHAMBERLAIN DOWN TO THE LOWLIEST HOUSEBOY, WHEN A NEW SHOGUN TAKES POWER.
!
OF COURSE, IF WE HONOR THIS CONVENTION, YOU TOO MUST RETIRE...
HOWEVER, HER HIGHNESS HATH TAKEN INTO CONSIDERATION THE FACT THAT HER PREDECESSOR WAS BUT A YOUNG CHILD WHEN SHE PASSED AWAY AND HATH PERMITTED YOU TO REMAIN IN OFFICE. YOU REALIZE, SIR FUJINAMI, THAT THIS WAS A SPECIAL DISPENSATION?

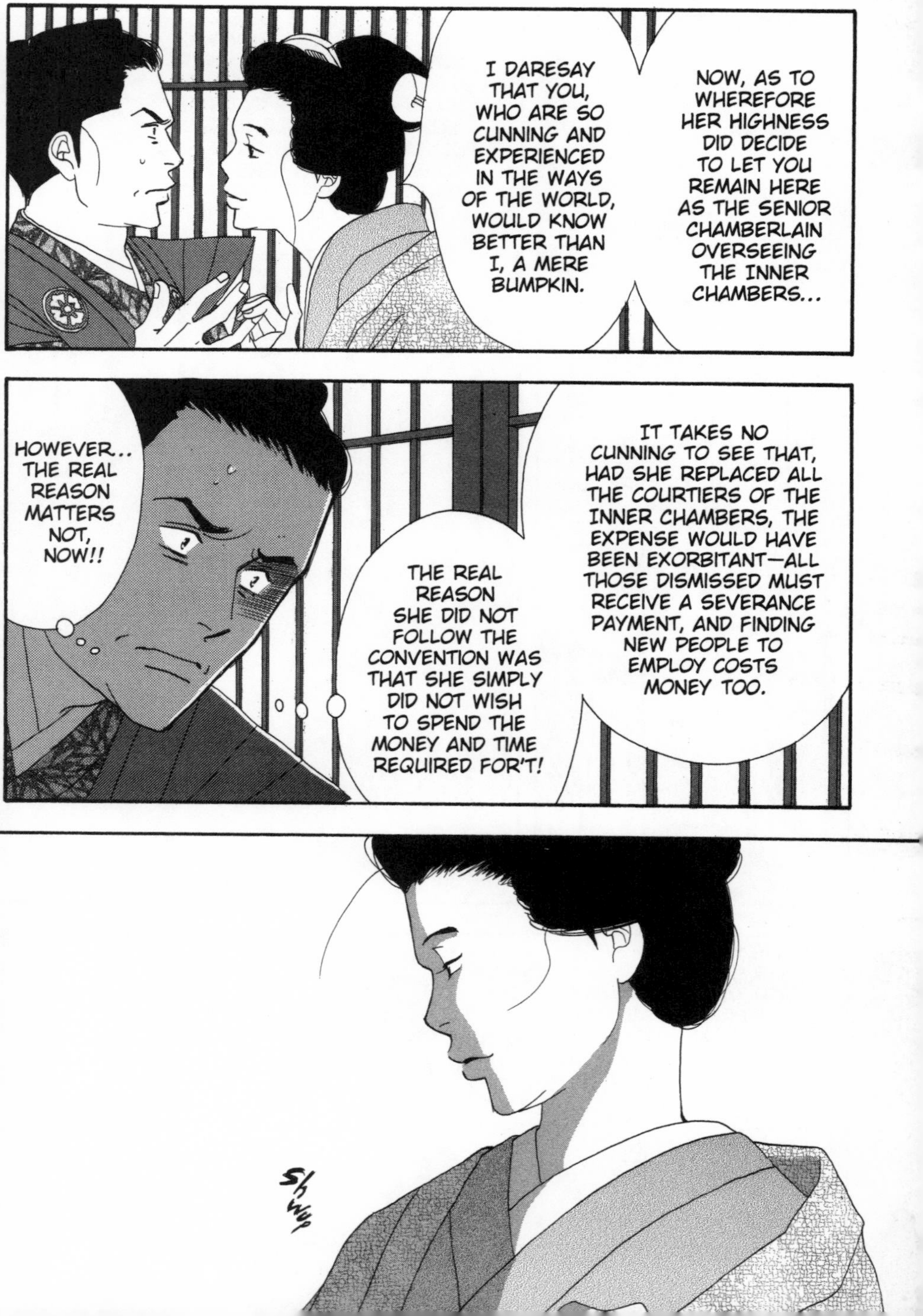
NOW, AS TO WHEREFORE HER HIGHNESS DID DECIDE TO LET YOU REMAIN HERE AS THE SENIOR CHAMBERLAIN OVERSEEING THE INNER CHAMBERS...
I DARESAY THAT YOU, WHO ARE SO CUNNING AND EXPERIENCED IN THE WAYS OF THE WORLD, WOULD KNOW BETTER THAN I, A MERE BUMPKIN.
IT TAKES NO CUNNING TO SEE THAT, HAD SHE REPLACED ALL THE COURTIERS OF THE INNER CHAMBERS, THE EXPENSE WOULD HAVE BEEN EXORBITANT—ALL THOSE DISMISSED MUST RECEIVE A SEVERANCE PAYMENT, AND FINDING NEW PEOPLE TO EMPLOY COSTS MONEY TOO.
THE REAL REASON SHE DID NOT FOLLOW THE CONVENTION WAS THAT SHE SIMPLY DID NOT WISH TO SPEND THE MONEY AND TIME REQUIRED FOR'T!
HOWEVER.. THE REAL REASON MATTERS NOT, NOW!!
Shwup

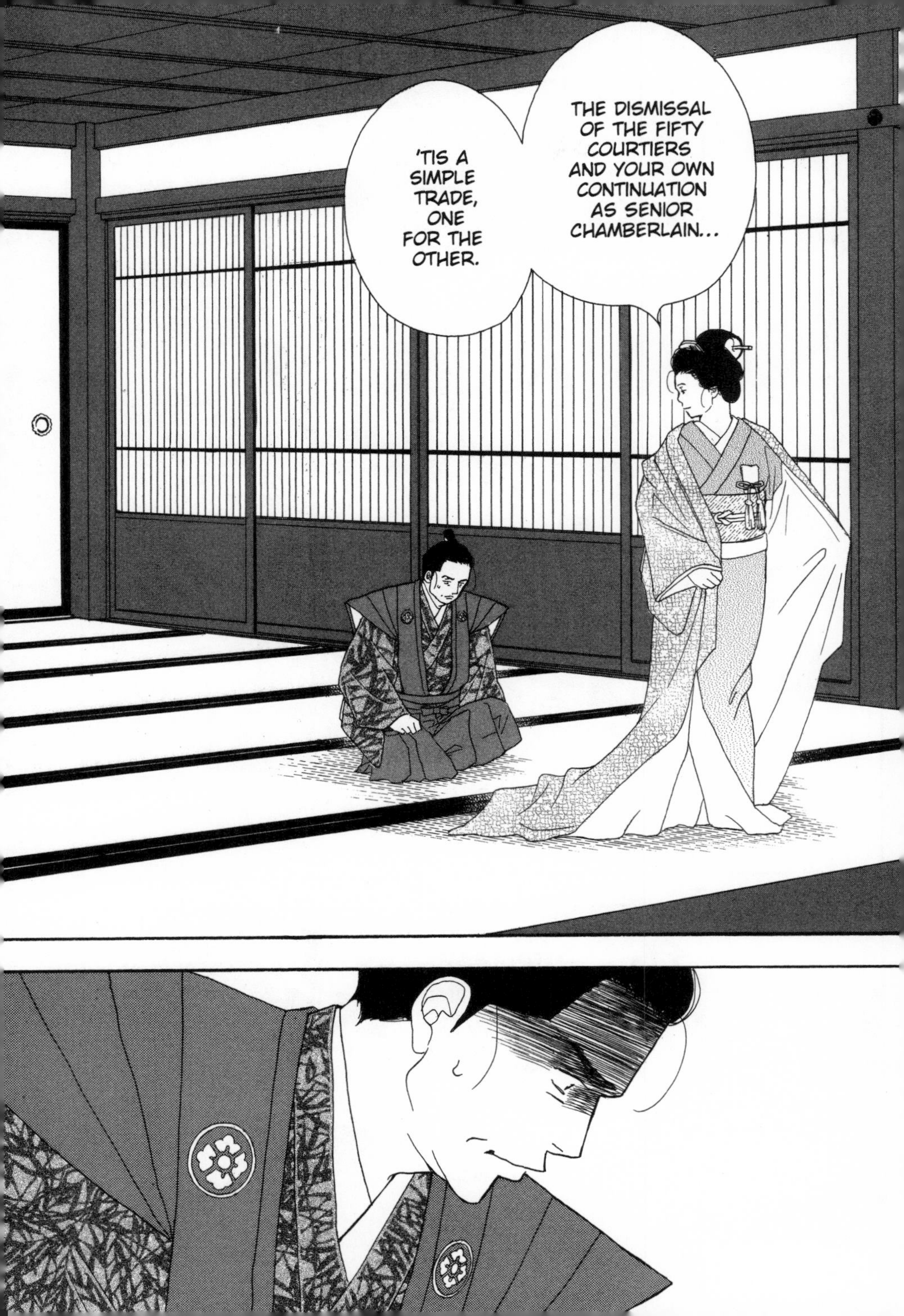
THE DISMISSAL OF THE FIFTY COURTIERS AND YOUR OWN CONTINUATION AS SENIOR CHAMBERLAIN...
'TIS A SIMPLE TRADE, ONE FOR THE OTHER.

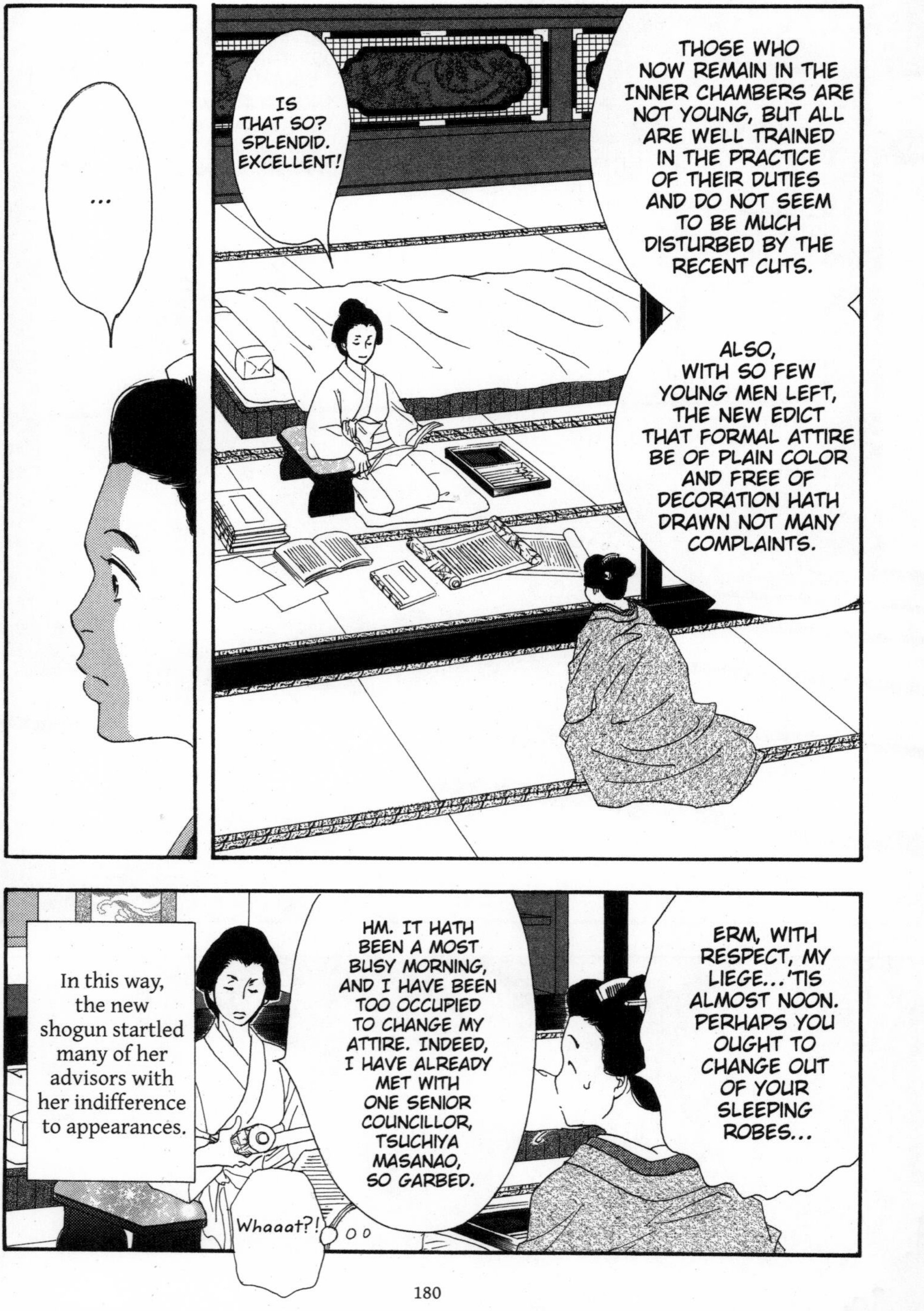
THOSE WHO NOW REMAIN IN THE INNER CHAMBERS ARE NOT YOUNG, BUT ALL ARE WELL TRAINED IN THE PRACTICE OF THEIR DUTIES AND DO NOT SEEM TO BE MUCH DISTURBED BY THE RECENT CUTS.
ALSO, WITH SO FEW YOUNG MEN LEFT, THE NEW EDICT THAT FORMAL ATTIRE BE OF PLAIN COLOR AND FREE OF DECORATION HATH DRAWN NOT MANY COMPLAINTS.
IS THAT SO? SPLENDID. EXCELLENT!
...
ERM, WITH RESPECT, MY LIEGE...'TIS ALMOST NOON. PERHAPS YOU OUGHT TO CHANGE OUT OF YOUR SLEEPING ROBES...
HM. IT HATH BEEN A MOST BUSY MORNING, AND I HAVE BEEN TOO OCCUPIED TO CHANGE MY ATTIRE. INDEED, I HAVE ALREADY MET WITH ONE SENIOR COUNCILLOR, TSUCHIYA MASANAO, SO GARBED.
In this way, the new shogun startled many of her advisors with her indifference to appearances.
Whaaat?!

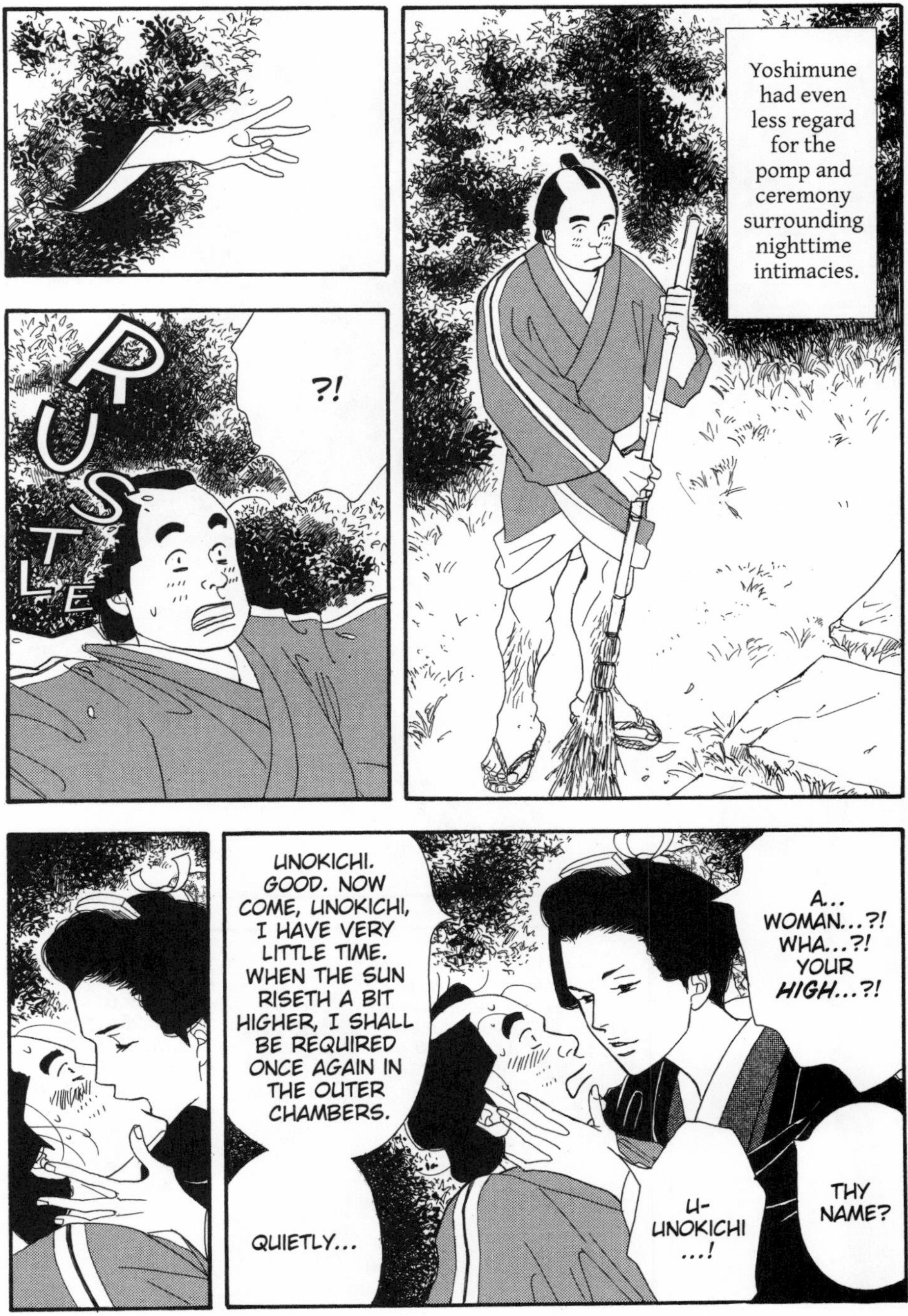
Yoshimune had even less regard for the pomp and ceremony surrounding nighttime intimacies.
RUSTLE
?!
A... WOMAN...?! WHA...?! YOUR *HIGH*...?!
THY NAME?
U-UNOKICHI ...!
UNOKICHI. GOOD. NOW COME, UNOKICHI, I HAVE VERY LITTLE TIME. WHEN THE SUN RISETH A BIT HIGHER, I SHALL BE REQUIRED ONCE AGAIN IN THE OUTER CHAMBERS.
QUIETLY...

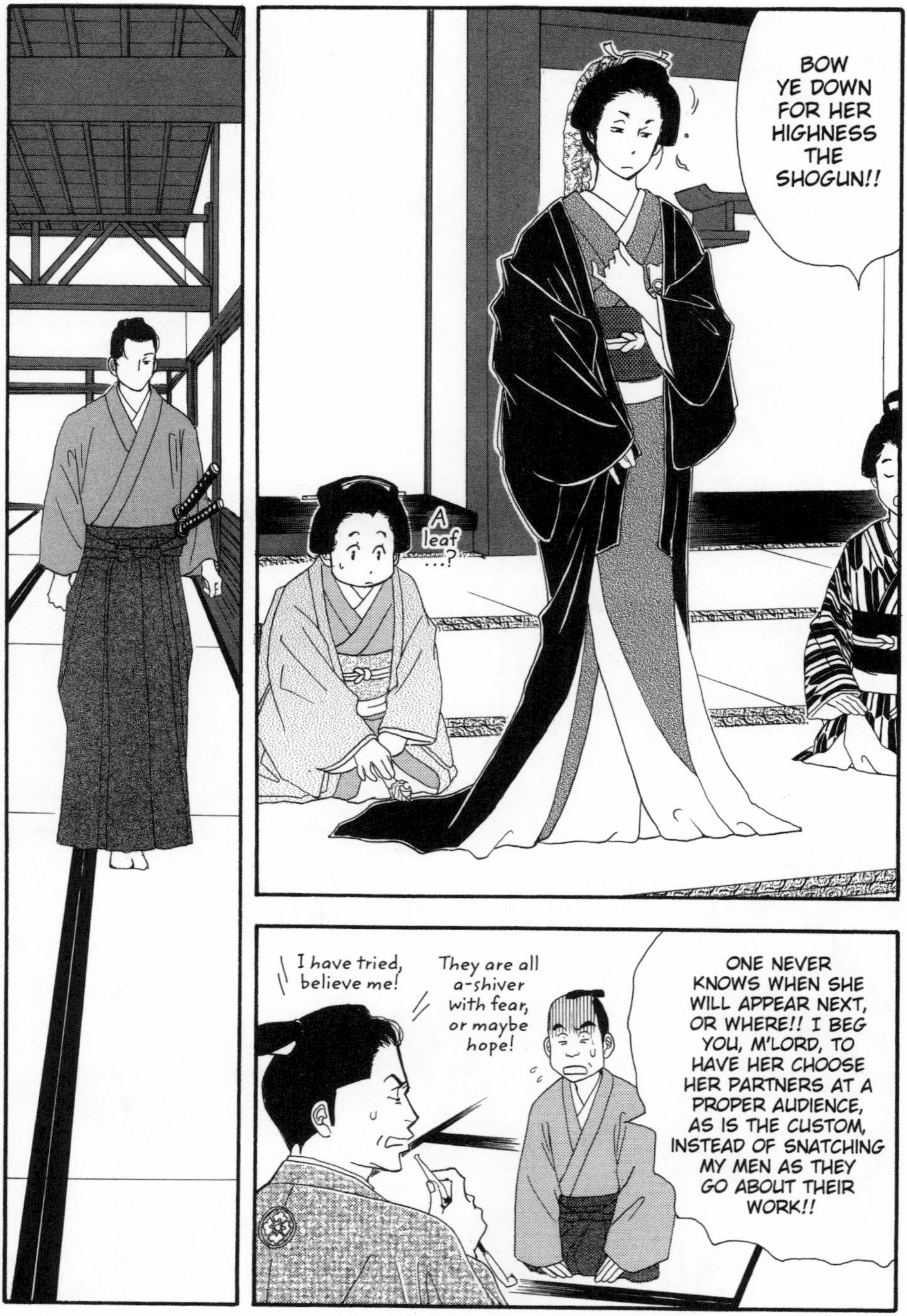
BOW YE DOWN FOR HER HIGHNESS THE SHOGUN!!
A leaf...?
ONE NEVER KNOWS WHEN SHE WILL APPEAR NEXT, OR WHERE!! I BEG YOU, M'LORD, TO HAVE HER CHOOSE HER PARTNERS AT A PROPER AUDIENCE, AS IS THE CUSTOM, INSTEAD OF SNATCHING MY MEN AS THEY GO ABOUT THEIR WORK!!
They are all a-shiver with fear, or maybe hope!
I have tried, believe me!

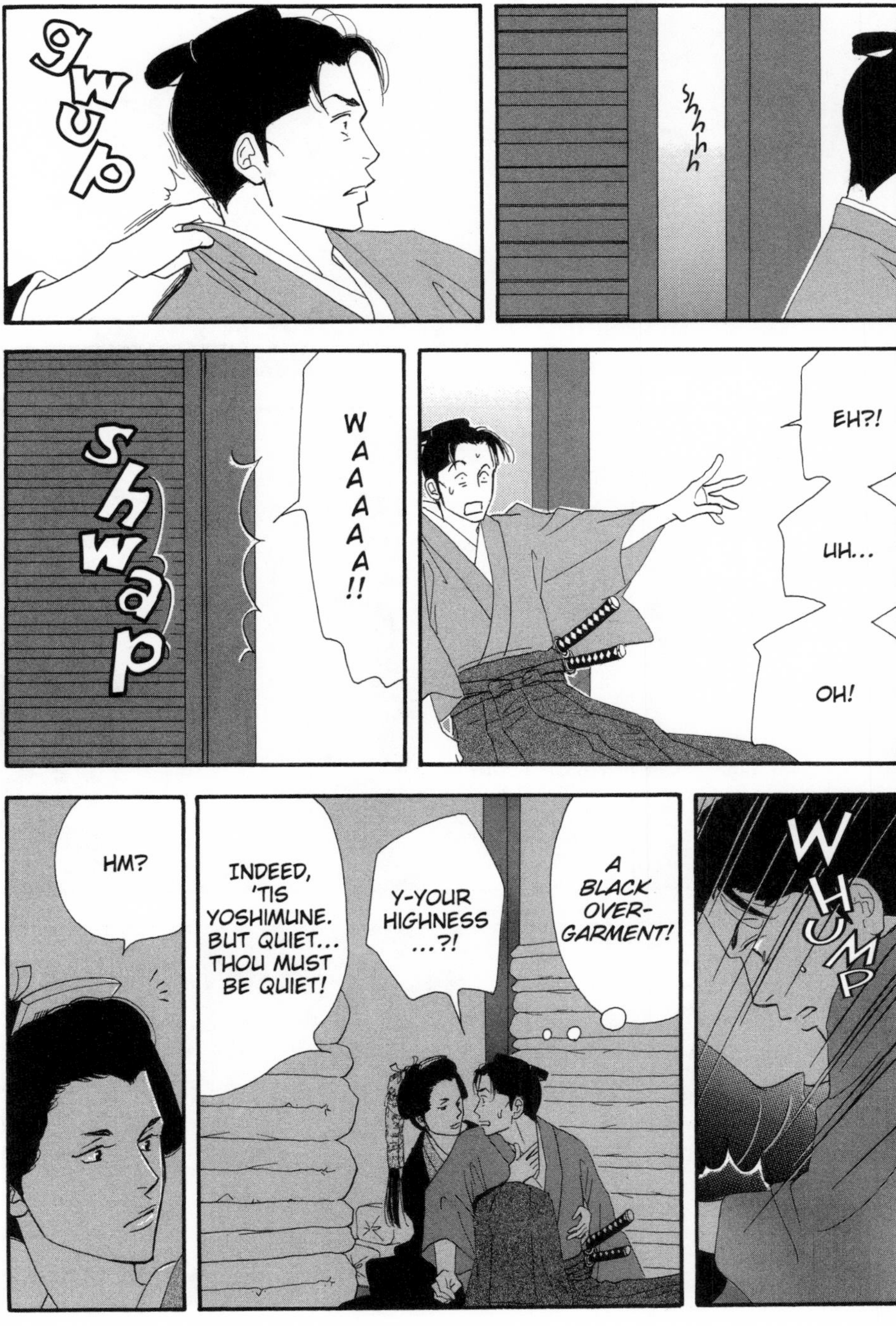
shhhh
gwup
EH?!
UH...
OH!
WAAAAAA!!
shwap
WHUMP
A BLACK OVER-GARMENT!
Y-YOUR HIGHNESS ...?!
INDEED, 'TIS YOSHIMUNE. BUT QUIET... THOU MUST BE QUIET!
HM?

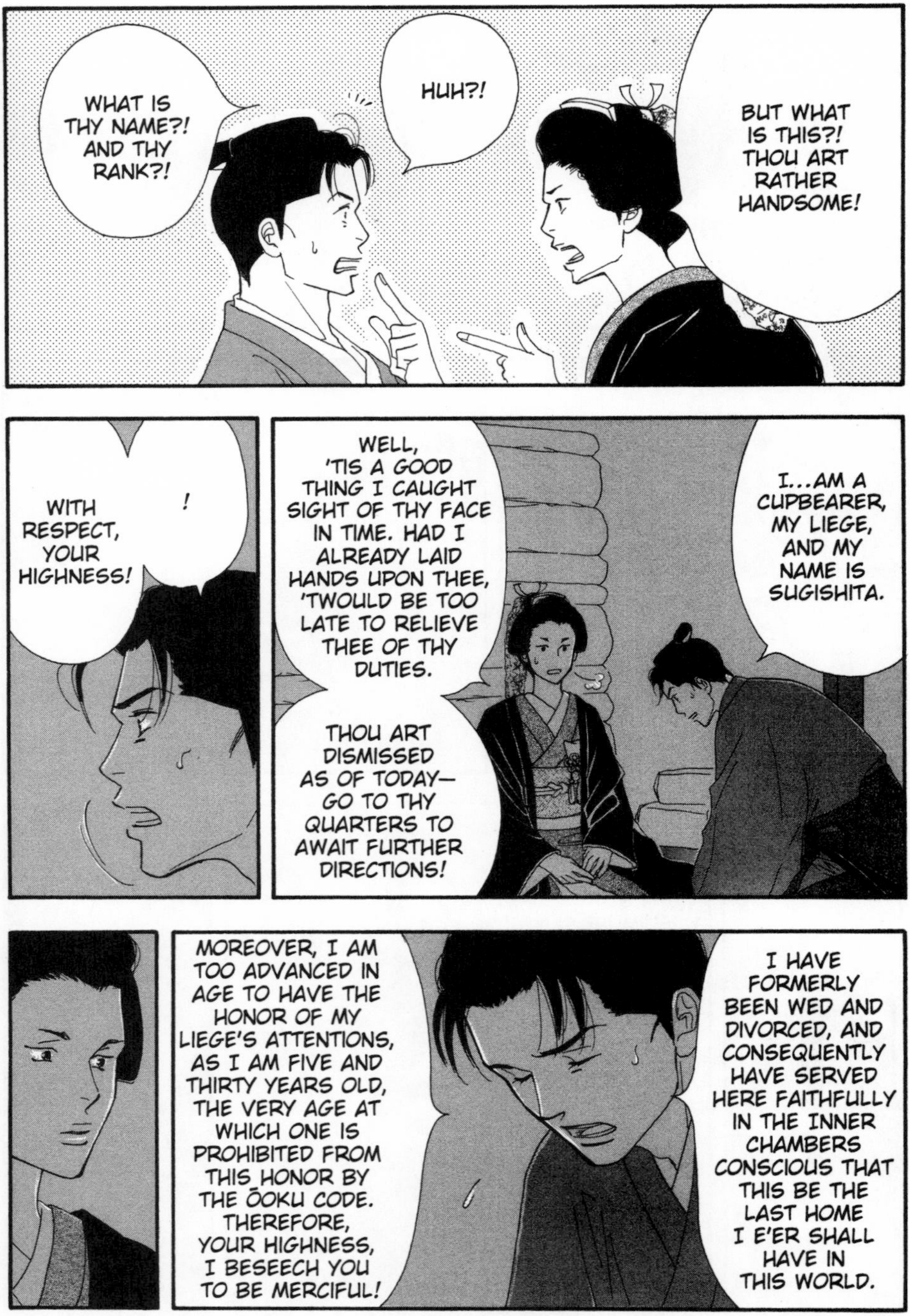
BUT WHAT IS THIS?! THOU ART RATHER HANDSOME!
HUH?!
WHAT IS THY NAME?! AND THY RANK?!
I...AM A CUPBEARER, MY LIEGE, AND MY NAME IS SUGISHITA.
WELL, 'TIS A GOOD THING I CAUGHT SIGHT OF THY FACE IN TIME. HAD I ALREADY LAID HANDS UPON THEE, 'TWOULD BE TOO LATE TO RELIEVE THEE OF THY DUTIES.
THOU ART DISMISSED AS OF TODAY—GO TO THY QUARTERS TO AWAIT FURTHER DIRECTIONS!
!
WITH RESPECT, YOUR HIGHNESS!
I HAVE FORMERLY BEEN WED AND DIVORCED, AND CONSEQUENTLY HAVE SERVED HERE FAITHFULLY IN THE INNER CHAMBERS CONSCIOUS THAT THIS BE THE LAST HOME I E'ER SHALL HAVE IN THIS WORLD.
MOREOVER, I AM TOO ADVANCED IN AGE TO HAVE THE HONOR OF MY LIEGE'S ATTENTIONS, AS I AM FIVE AND THIRTY YEARS OLD, THE VERY AGE AT WHICH ONE IS PROHIBITED FROM THIS HONOR BY THE ŌOKU CODE. THEREFORE, YOUR HIGHNESS, I BESEECH YOU TO BE MERCIFUL!

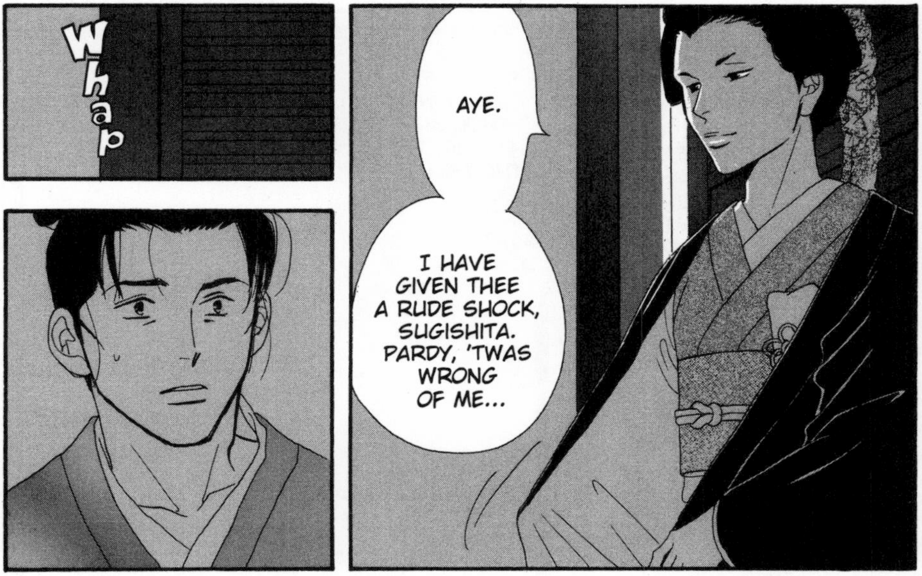
AYE.
I HAVE GIVEN THEE A RUDE SHOCK, SUGISHITA. PARDY, 'TWAS WRONG OF ME...
Whap

A day or two later, Sugishita was summoned to Sir Fujinami's chambers.

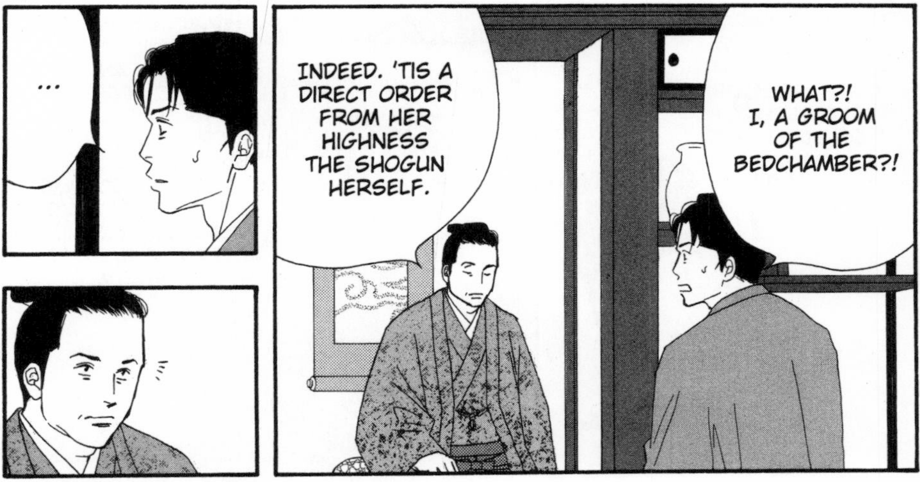
WHAT?! I, A GROOM OF THE BEDCHAMBER?!
INDEED. 'TIS A DIRECT ORDER FROM HER HIGHNESS THE SHOGUN HERSELF.
...

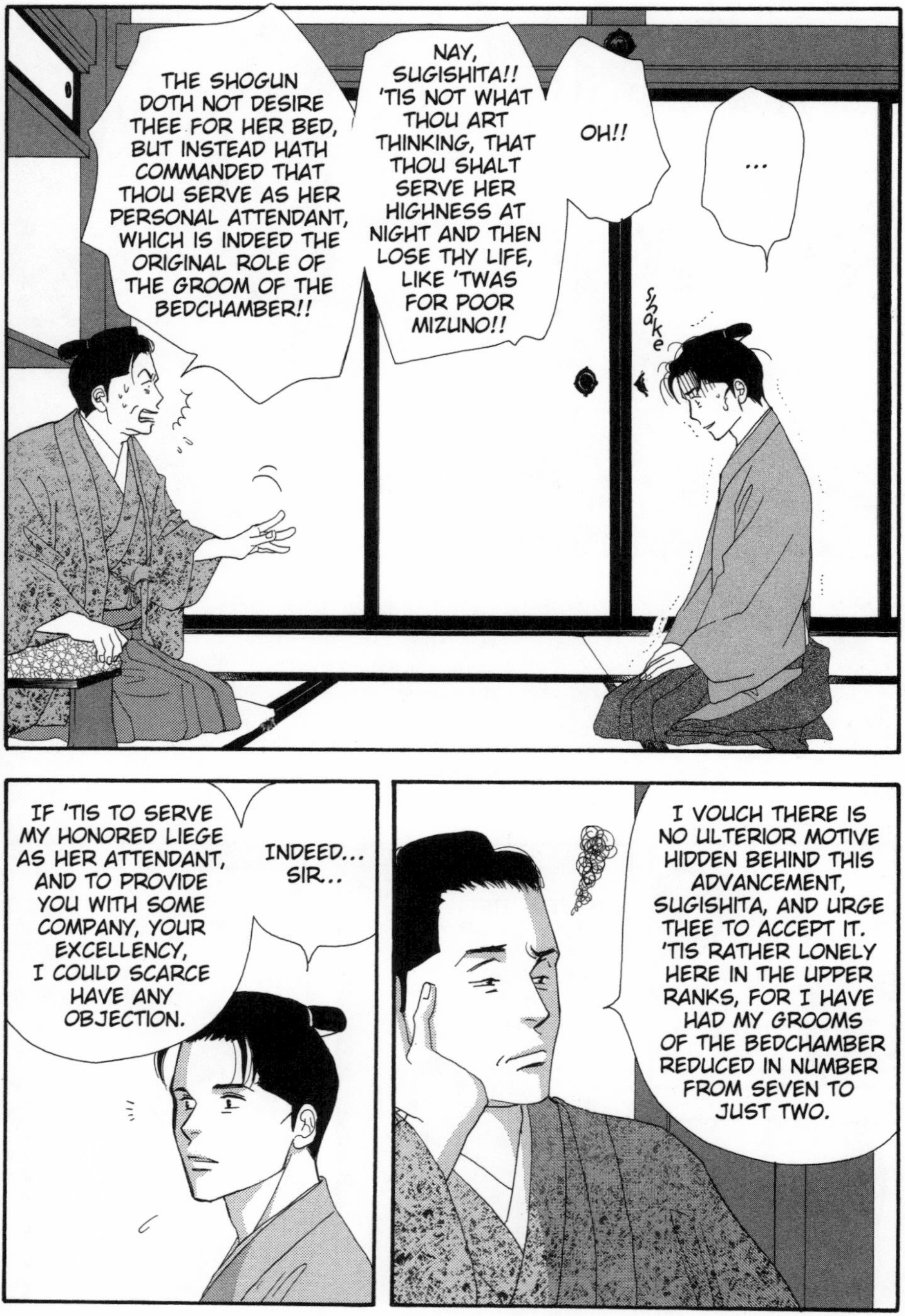
...
OH!!
NAY, SUGISHITA!! 'TIS NOT WHAT THOU ART THINKING, THAT THOU SHALT SERVE HER HIGHNESS AT NIGHT AND THEN LOSE THY LIFE, LIKE 'TWAS FOR POOR MIZUNO!!
shake
THE SHOGUN DOTH NOT DESIRE THEE FOR HER BED, BUT INSTEAD HATH COMMANDED THAT THOU SERVE AS HER PERSONAL ATTENDANT, WHICH IS INDEED THE ORIGINAL ROLE OF THE GROOM OF THE BEDCHAMBER!!
I VOUCH THERE IS NO ULTERIOR MOTIVE HIDDEN BEHIND THIS ADVANCEMENT, SUGISHITA, AND URGE THEE TO ACCEPT IT. 'TIS RATHER LONELY HERE IN THE UPPER RANKS, FOR I HAVE HAD MY GROOMS OF THE BEDCHAMBER REDUCED IN NUMBER FROM SEVEN TO JUST TWO.
INDEED... SIR...
IF 'TIS TO SERVE MY HONORED LIEGE AS HER ATTENDANT, AND TO PROVIDE YOU WITH SOME COMPANY, YOUR EXCELLENCY, I COULD SCARCE HAVE ANY OBJECTION.

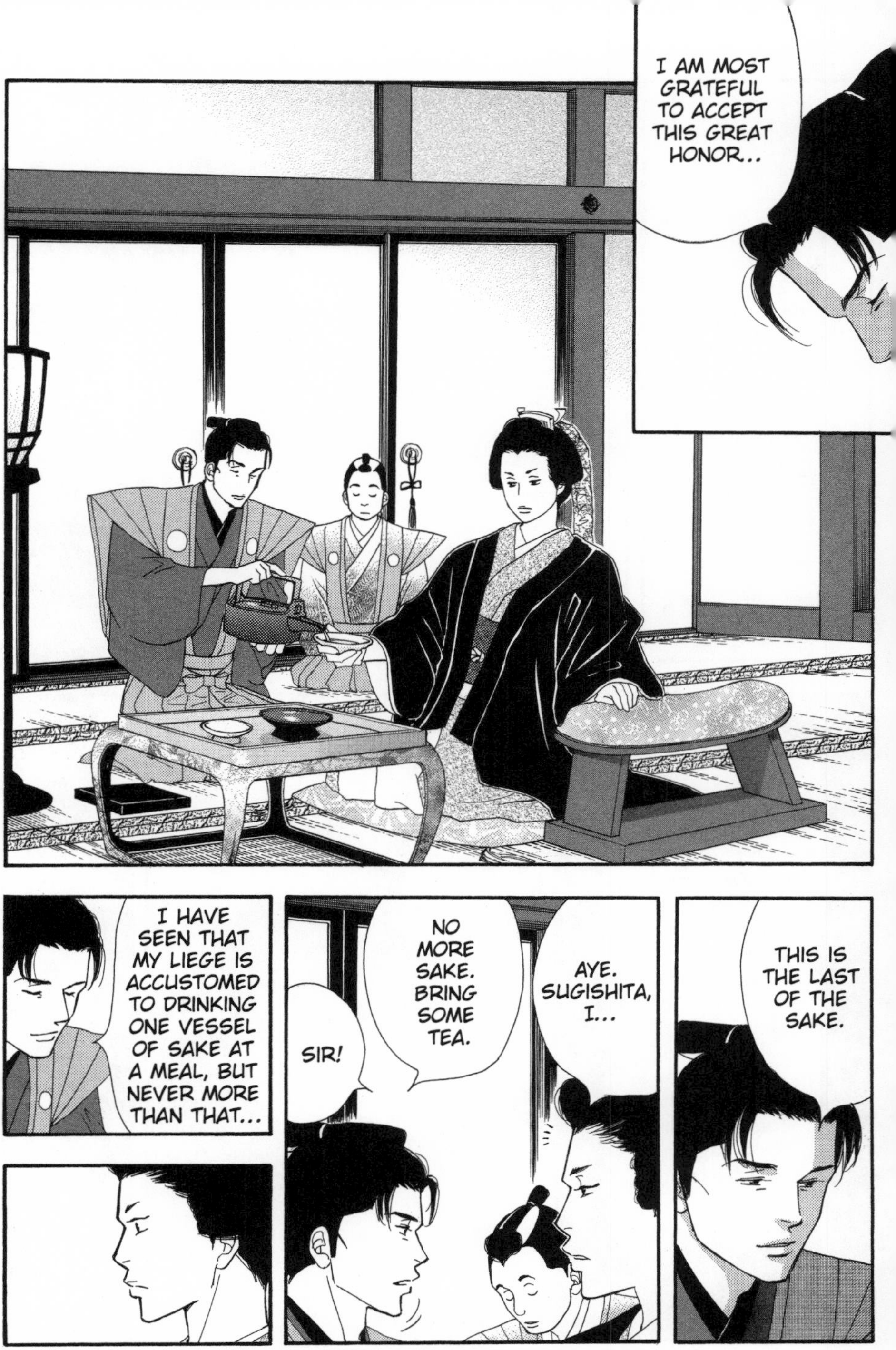
I AM MOST GRATEFUL TO ACCEPT THIS GREAT HONOR..
THIS IS THE LAST OF THE SAKE.
AYE. SUGISHITA, I...
NO MORE SAKE. BRING SOME TEA.
SIR!
I HAVE SEEN THAT MY LIEGE IS ACCUSTOMED TO DRINKING ONE VESSEL OF SAKE AT A MEAL, BUT NEVER MORE THAN THAT...

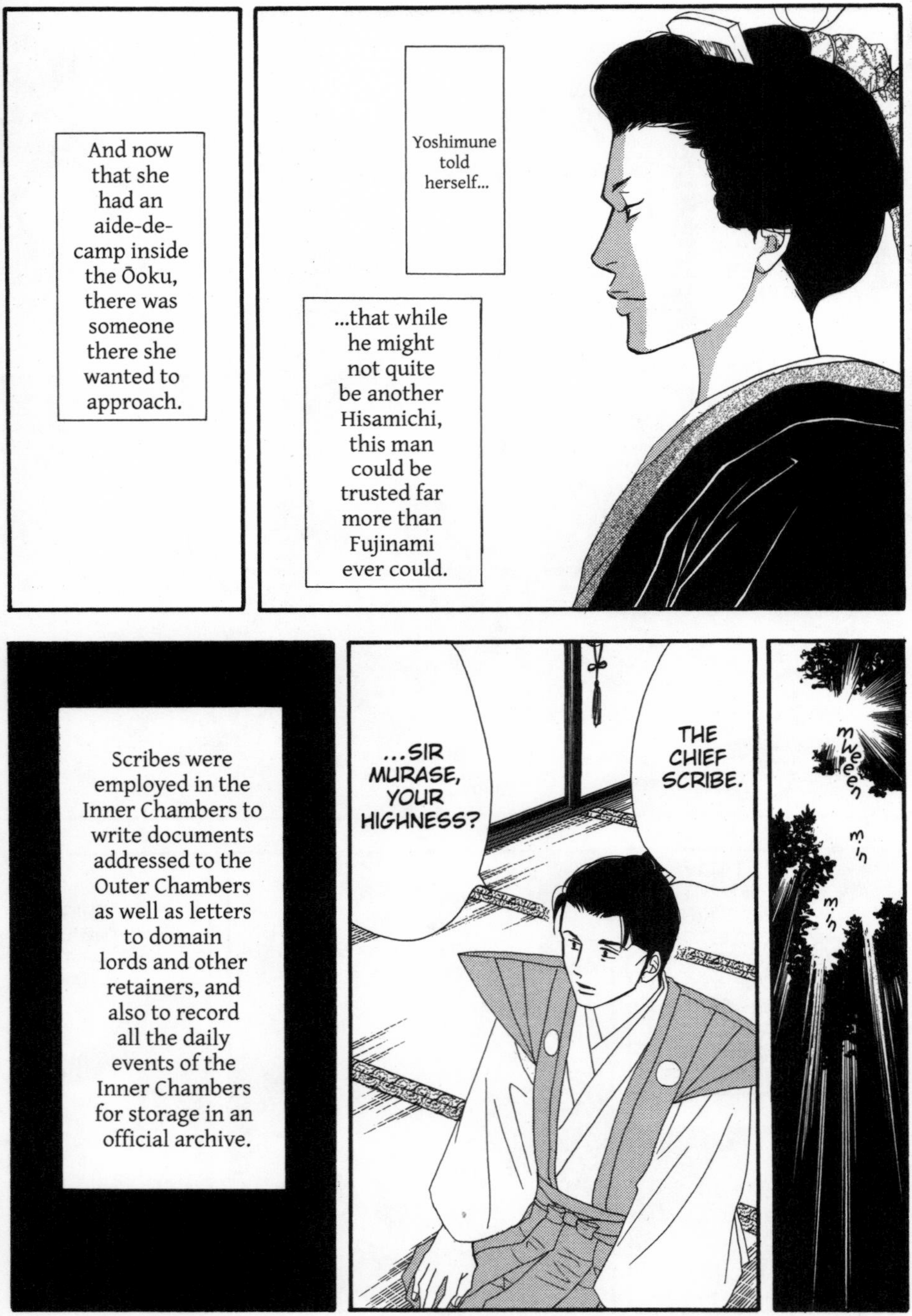
Yoshimune told herself...
...that while he might not quite be another Hisamichi, this man could be trusted far more than Fujinami ever could.
And now that she had an aide-de-camp inside the Ōoku, there was someone there she wanted to approach.
mween
min
min
THE CHIEF SCRIBE.
...SIR MURASE, YOUR HIGHNESS?
Scribes were employed in the Inner Chambers to write documents addressed to the Outer Chambers as well as letters to domain lords and other retainers, and also to record all the daily events of the Inner Chambers for storage in an official archive.

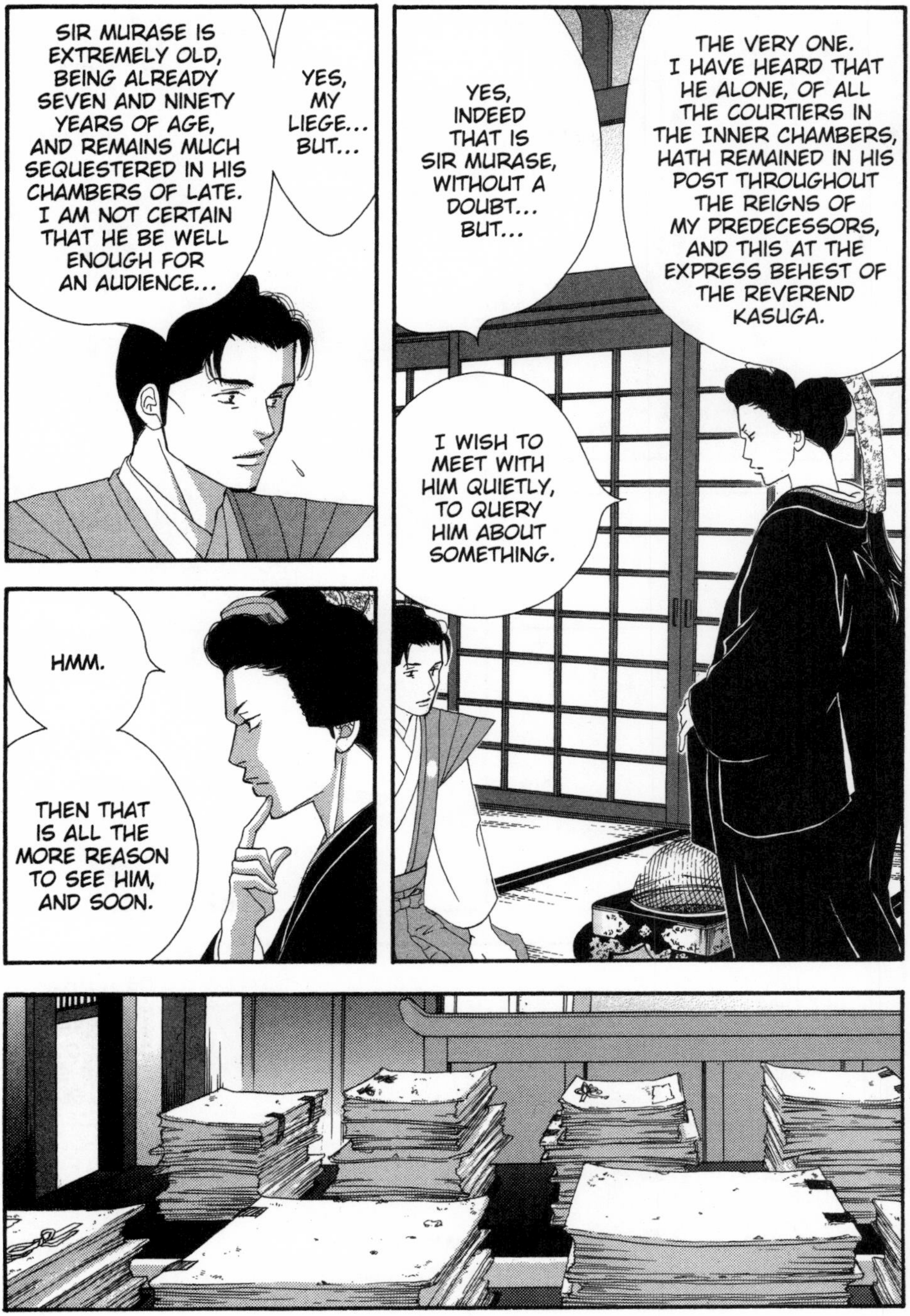
THE VERY ONE. I HAVE HEARD THAT HE ALONE, OF ALL THE COURTIERS IN THE INNER CHAMBERS, HATH REMAINED IN HIS POST THROUGHOUT THE REIGNS OF MY PREDECESSORS, AND THIS AT THE EXPRESS BEHEST OF THE REVEREND KASUGA.
YES, INDEED THAT IS SIR MURASE, WITHOUT A DOUBT... BUT...
I WISH TO MEET WITH HIM QUIETLY, TO QUERY HIM ABOUT SOMETHING.
YES, MY LIEGE... BUT...
SIR MURASE IS EXTREMELY OLD, BEING ALREADY SEVEN AND NINETY YEARS OF AGE, AND REMAINS MUCH SEQUESTERED IN HIS CHAMBERS OF LATE. I AM NOT CERTAIN THAT HE BE WELL ENOUGH FOR AN AUDIENCE...
HMM.
THEN THAT IS ALL THE MORE REASON TO SEE HIM, AND SOON.

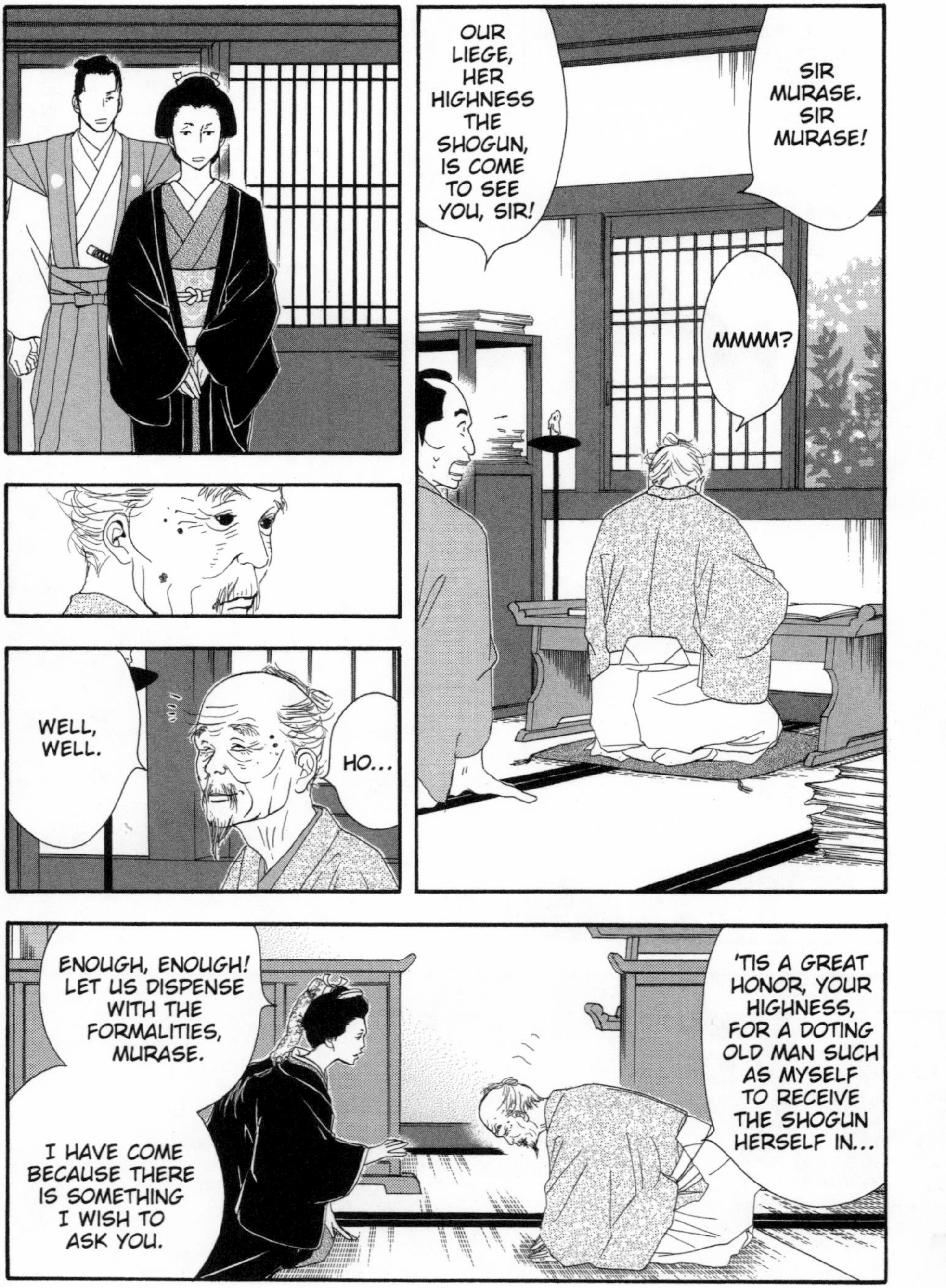
SIR MURASE. SIR MURASE!
OUR LIEGE, HER HIGHNESS THE SHOGUN, IS COME TO SEE YOU, SIR!
MMMM?
HO...
WELL, WELL.
'TIS A GREAT HONOR, YOUR HIGHNESS, FOR A DOTING OLD MAN SUCH AS MYSELF TO RECEIVE THE SHOGUN HERSELF IN...
ENOUGH, ENOUGH! LET US DISPENSE WITH THE FORMALITIES, MURASE.
I HAVE COME BECAUSE THERE IS SOMETHING I WISH TO ASK YOU.

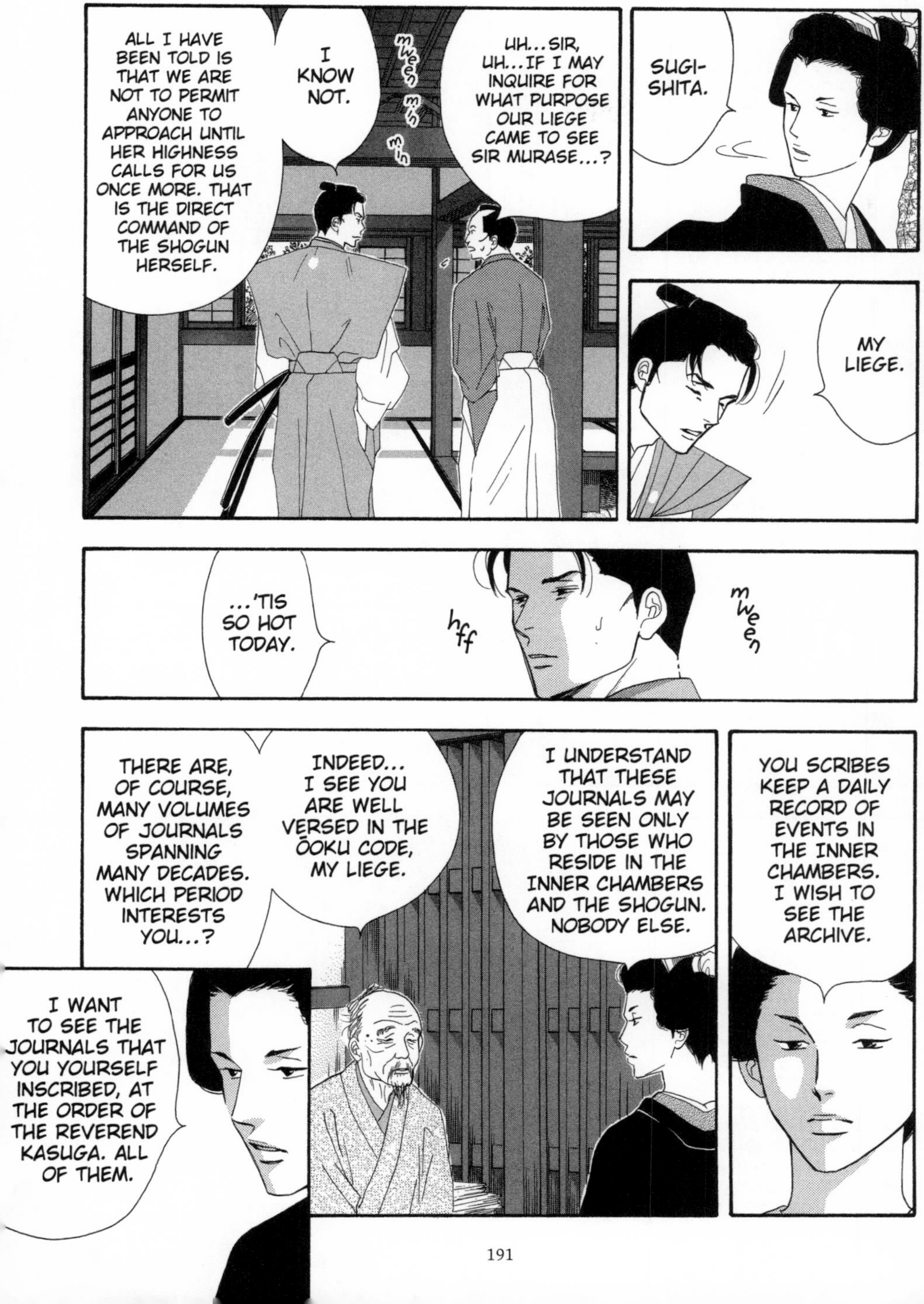
SUGI-SHITA.
MY LIEGE.
UH...SIR, UH...IF I MAY INQUIRE FOR WHAT PURPOSE OUR LIEGE CAME TO SEE SIR MURASE...?
mween min min
I KNOW NOT.
ALL I HAVE BEEN TOLD IS THAT WE ARE NOT TO PERMIT ANYONE TO APPROACH UNTIL HER HIGHNESS CALLS FOR US ONCE MORE. THAT IS THE DIRECT COMMAND OF THE SHOGUN HERSELF.
mween
hff
...'TIS SO HOT TODAY.
YOU SCRIBES KEEP A DAILY RECORD OF EVENTS IN THE INNER CHAMBERS. I WISH TO SEE THE ARCHIVE.
I UNDERSTAND THAT THESE JOURNALS MAY BE SEEN ONLY BY THOSE WHO RESIDE IN THE INNER CHAMBERS AND THE SHOGUN. NOBODY ELSE.
INDEED... I SEE YOU ARE WELL VERSED IN THE ŌOKU CODE, MY LIEGE.
THERE ARE, OF COURSE, MANY VOLUMES OF JOURNALS SPANNING MANY DECADES. WHICH PERIOD INTERESTS YOU...?
I WANT TO SEE THE JOURNALS THAT YOU YOURSELF INSCRIBED, AT THE ORDER OF THE REVEREND KASUGA. ALL OF THEM.

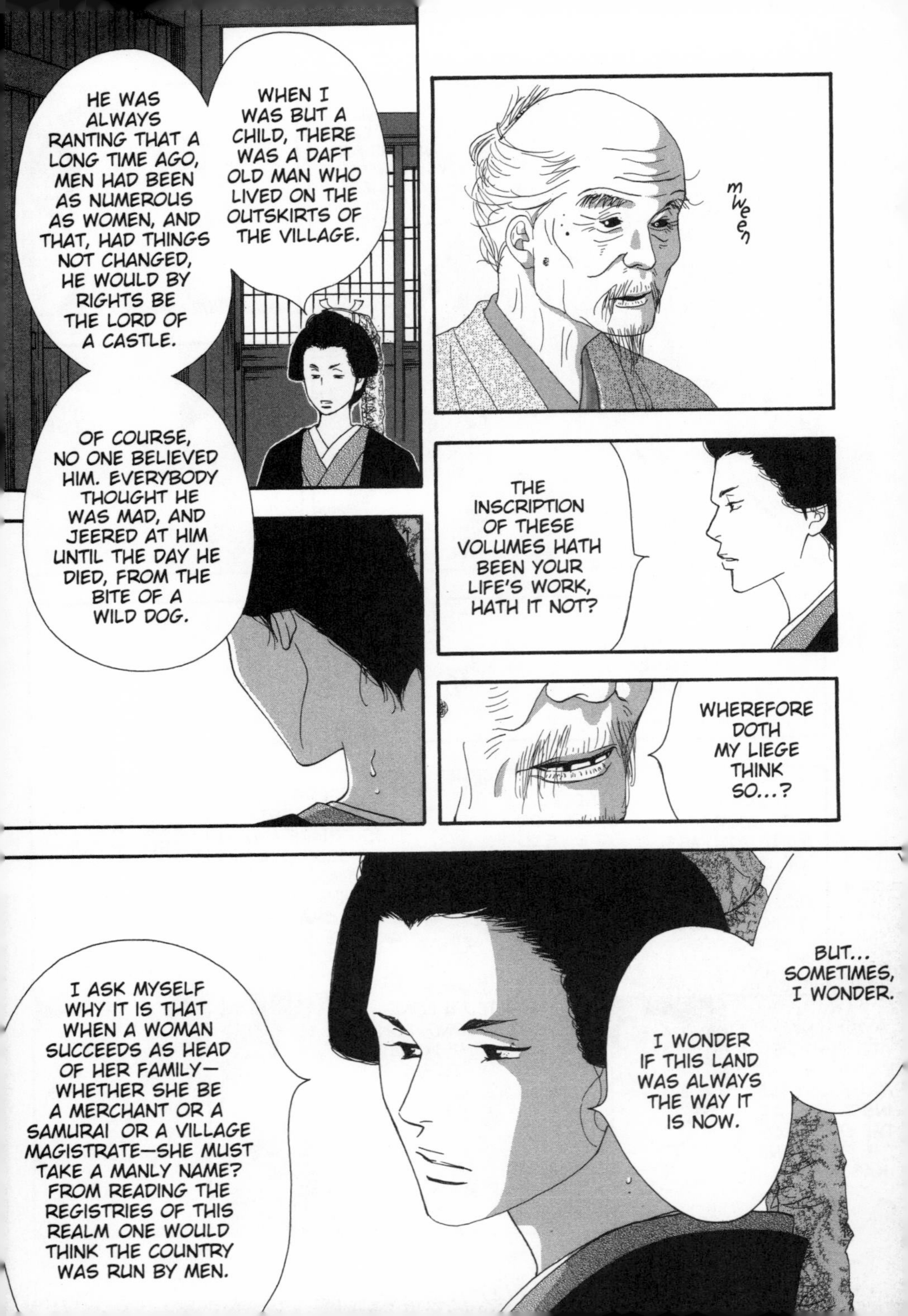
mween
WHEN I WAS BUT A CHILD, THERE WAS A DAFT OLD MAN WHO LIVED ON THE OUTSKIRTS OF THE VILLAGE.
HE WAS ALWAYS RANTING THAT A LONG TIME AGO, MEN HAD BEEN AS NUMEROUS AS WOMEN, AND THAT, HAD THINGS NOT CHANGED, HE WOULD BY RIGHTS BE THE LORD OF A CASTLE.
OF COURSE, NO ONE BELIEVED HIM. EVERYBODY THOUGHT HE WAS MAD, AND JEERED AT HIM UNTIL THE DAY HE DIED, FROM THE BITE OF A WILD DOG.
THE INSCRIPTION OF THESE VOLUMES HATH BEEN YOUR LIFE'S WORK, HATH IT NOT?
WHEREFORE DOTH MY LIEGE THINK SO...?
BUT... SOMETIMES, I WONDER.
I WONDER IF THIS LAND WAS ALWAYS THE WAY IT IS NOW.
I ASK MYSELF WHY IT IS THAT WHEN A WOMAN SUCCEEDS AS HEAD OF HER FAMILY—WHETHER SHE BE A MERCHANT OR A SAMURAI OR A VILLAGE MAGISTRATE—SHE MUST TAKE A MANLY NAME? FROM READING THE REGISTRIES OF THIS REALM ONE WOULD THINK THE COUNTRY WAS RUN BY MEN.

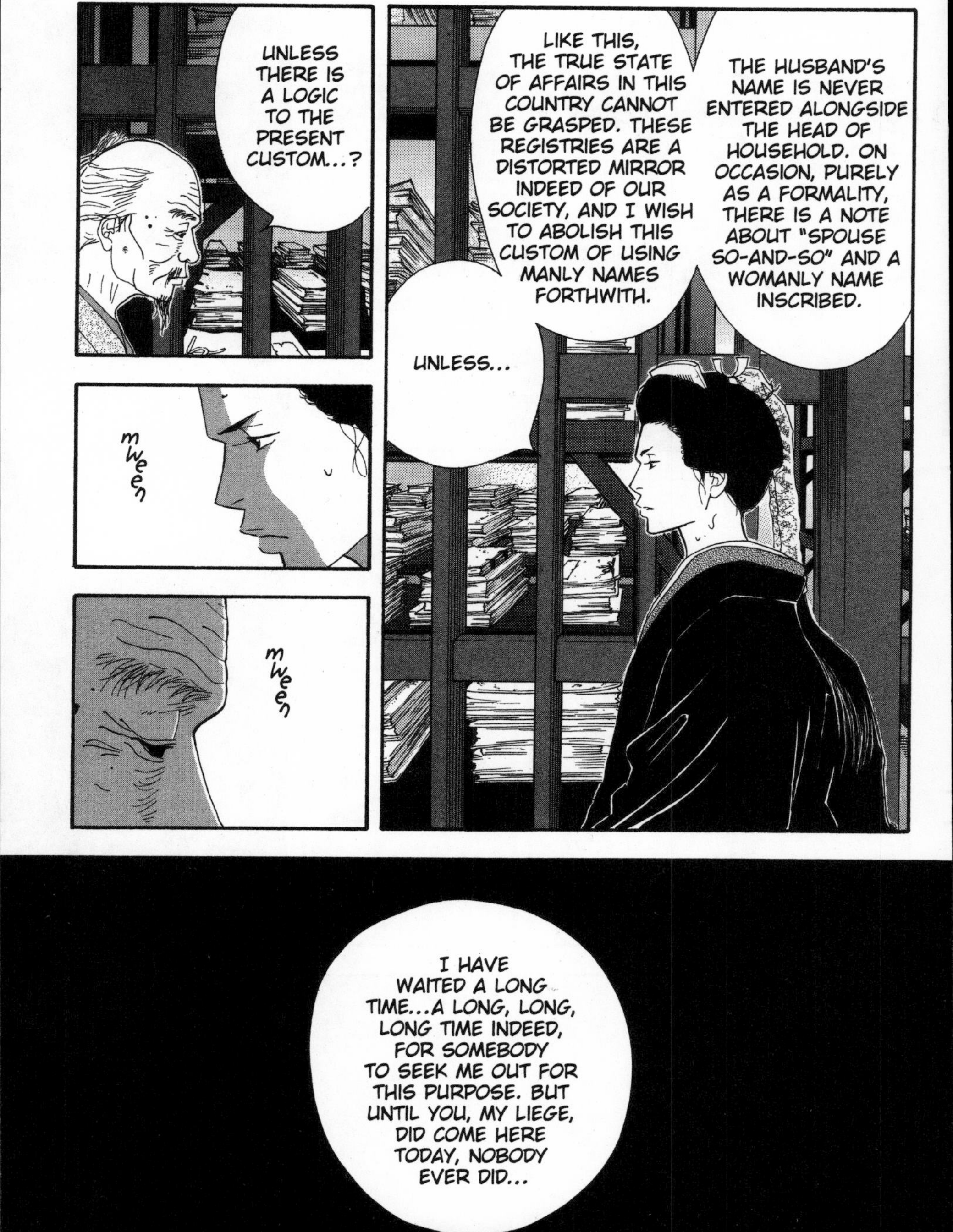
THE HUSBAND'S NAME IS NEVER ENTERED ALONGSIDE THE HEAD OF HOUSEHOLD. ON OCCASION, PURELY AS A FORMALITY, THERE IS A NOTE ABOUT "SPOUSE SO-AND-SO" AND A WOMANLY NAME INSCRIBED.
LIKE THIS, THE TRUE STATE OF AFFAIRS IN THIS COUNTRY CANNOT BE GRASPED. THESE REGISTRIES ARE A DISTORTED MIRROR INDEED OF OUR SOCIETY, AND I WISH TO ABOLISH THIS CUSTOM OF USING MANLY NAMES FORTHWITH.
UNLESS...
UNLESS THERE IS A LOGIC TO THE PRESENT CUSTOM...?
mween
mween
I HAVE WAITED A LONG TIME...A LONG, LONG, LONG TIME INDEED, FOR SOMEBODY TO SEEK ME OUT FOR THIS PURPOSE. BUT UNTIL YOU, MY LIEGE, DID COME HERE TODAY, NOBODY EVER DID...

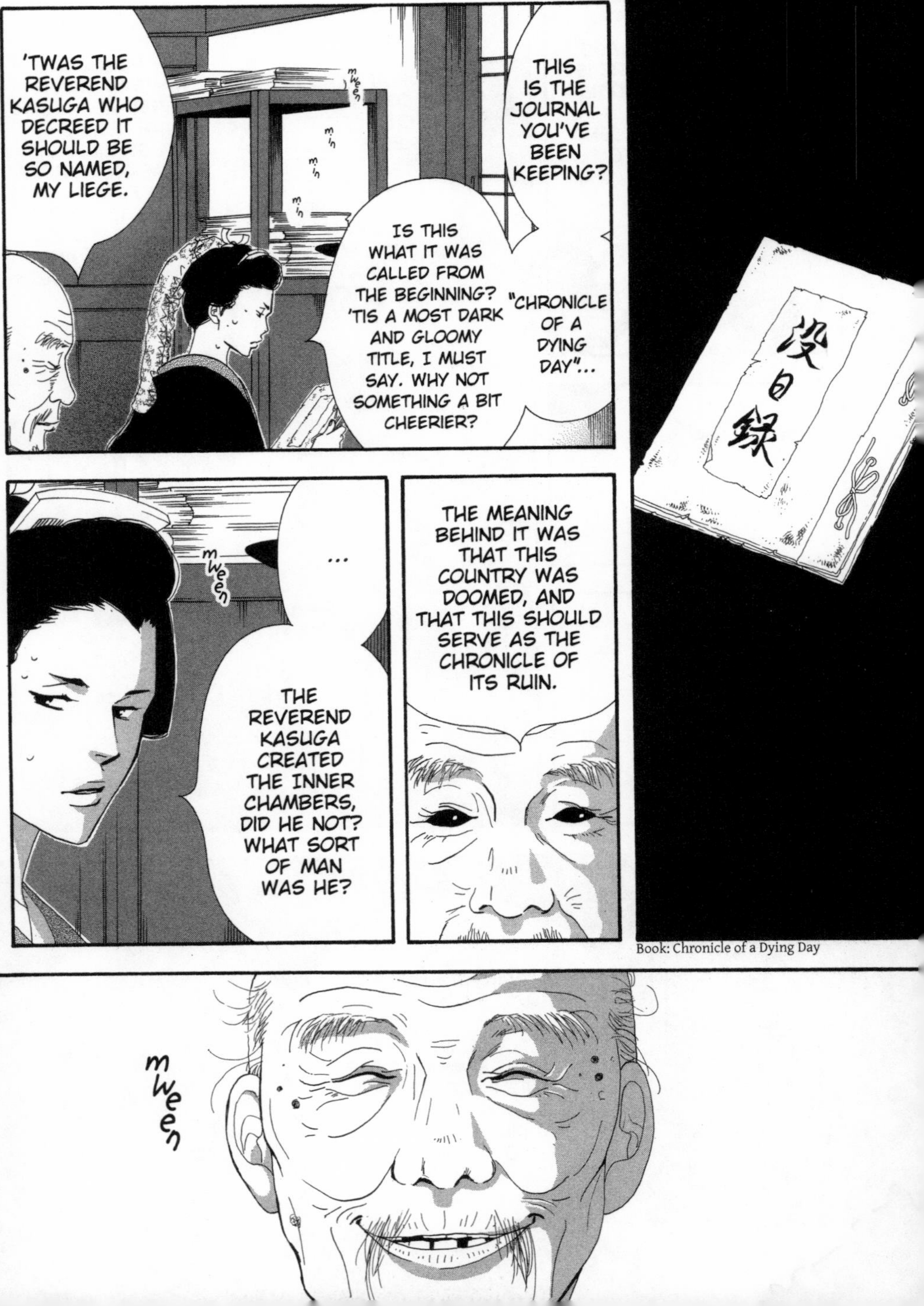
没日録
THIS IS THE JOURNAL YOU'VE BEEN KEEPING?
"CHRONICLE OF A DYING DAY"...
IS THIS WHAT IT WAS CALLED FROM THE BEGINNING? 'TIS A MOST DARK AND GLOOMY TITLE, I MUST SAY. WHY NOT SOMETHING A BIT CHEERIER?
'TWAS THE REVEREND KASUGA WHO DECREED IT SHOULD BE SO NAMED, MY LIEGE.
mween
min
min
min
THE MEANING BEHIND IT WAS THAT THIS COUNTRY WAS DOOMED, AND THAT THIS SHOULD SERVE AS THE CHRONICLE OF ITS RUIN.
...
THE REVEREND KASUGA CREATED THE INNER CHAMBERS, DID HE NOT? WHAT SORT OF MAN WAS HE?
mween
mween
Book: Chronicle of a Dying Day

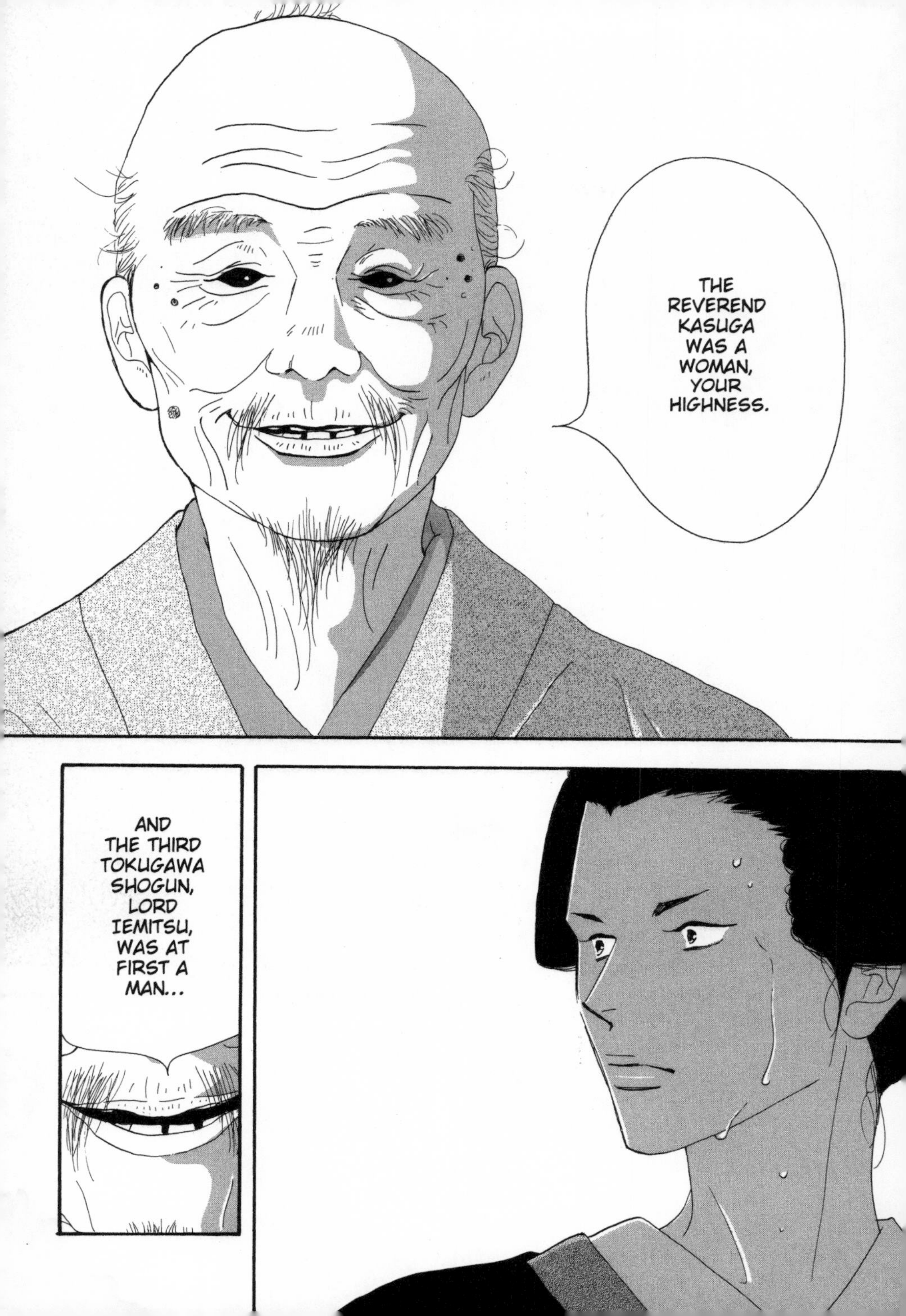
THE REVEREND KASUGA WAS A WOMAN, YOUR HIGHNESS.
AND THE THIRD TOKUGAWA SHOGUN, LORD IEMITSU, WAS AT FIRST A MAN...

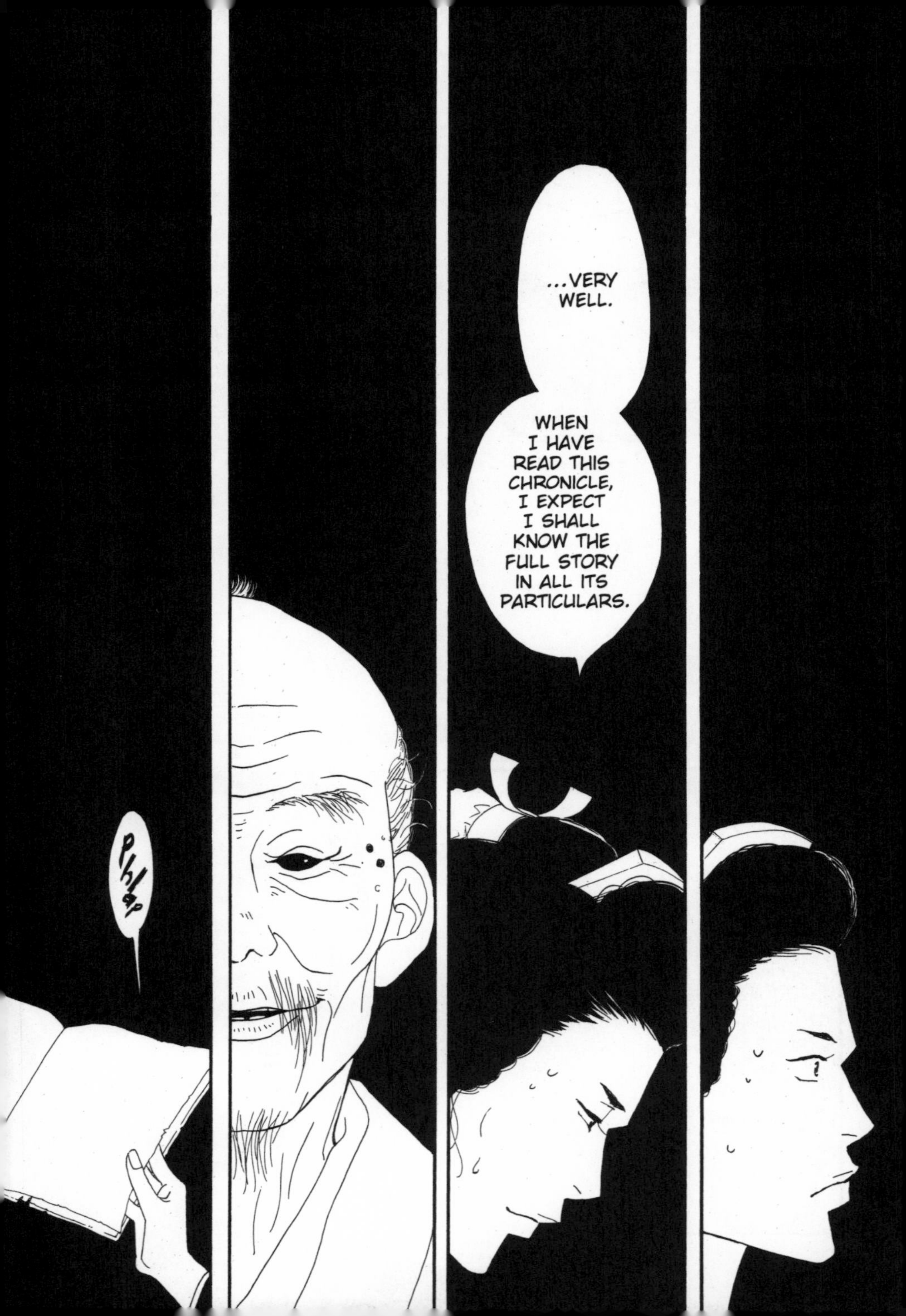
...VERY WELL.
WHEN I HAVE READ THIS CHRONICLE, I EXPECT I SHALL KNOW THE FULL STORY IN ALL ITS PARTICULARS.
Phlap

Ōoku: The Inner Chambers

VOLUME 1 · END NOTES

by Akemi Wegmüller

Page 9, panel 1 · EDO CASTLE

Edo Castle was the seat of the Tokugawa Shogunate. Its core, the *honmaru*, consisted of three sections: the *Omote* (Outer Chambers, literally "front" or "exterior") housed the government bureaucracy and reception halls, the *Naka-oku* (Shogun's Quarters, literally "middle interior") was the shogun's personal chambers, and the *Ōoku* (Inner Chambers, literally "great or deep interior") was the women's quarters. While the Outer Chambers and the Shogun's Quarters were connected, or in fact two parts of the same large complex, the Inner Chambers were separate. Their only connection to the rest of the palace was the Passage of the Bells, a corridor lined with bells that led from the Shogun's Quarters, where it was guarded by a locked door. The bells, fixed to a long rope lining the corridor, were rung to announce when the shogun was entering or leaving.

Page 9, panel 1 · ŌOKU

The Ōoku itself consisted of numerous buildings, but the whole complex was basically divided into three large areas: The *Goten-muki* (Palace) housed the shogun's bedchamber; the personal apartments of the shogun's wife, concubines, and children; the chamber where all their robes were sewn; and attendants' stations. The *Hiroshiki-muki* (Great Chamber) housed the Ōoku offices and actually had male (in this manga, female) officials working in it. Lastly, the *Nagatsubone-muki* (Courtiers' Quarters, literally "long buildings"), a series of long two story buildings divided into apartments, called "wings" in this manga, housed the courtiers. The first wing housed the Chamberlains, the second wing the next highest ranks, the third wing those below, and so on, and there was even a wing with servants' quarters. The entire Ōoku complex had only one exit, which led from the Hiroshiki-muki to one of the castle gates. Because the Hiroshiki-muki had both this exit and the male officials in it, it was closed off from the rest of the complex by two entrances. One entrance, the *O-jō-guchi* (Entrance of the Lock) led to the palace, while the other, the *Nanatsu-guchi* (Entrance of the Seventh Hour) led to the Courtiers' Quarters. The latter was so called because it was locked every day at the seventh afternoon hour, roughly four p.m. (it was opened at the fifth morning hour, roughly eight a.m.). The only other entrance was the *Ue-no-O-jō-guchi* (High or Upper Entrance of the Lock) at the end of the Passage of the Bells.

Page 15, panel 1 · KANTO REGION

The central eastern region of Honshu, the largest of the Japanese islands, that encompasses Tokyo, Kanagawa, Saitama, Gunma, Tochigi, Ibaraki, and Chiba prefectures. During the Edo period, it was the center of the feudal power system. Kansai, which includes Kyoto and Osaka, is further west and was the nation's power center for much of Japan's history until the Edo period. The emperor and the aristocracy continued to reside in Kyoto throughout the Edo period.

Page 17, panel 1 · SHOGUN

Shogun was a military rank akin to "general of the armies," but in actuality during the Edo period the shogun was the ruler of Japan and the emperor only nominally the sovereign. The emperor resided in the imperial court in Kyoto, and daughters of the imperial family were often married into the Tokugawa clan to strengthen political ties, but the real power was indisputably in the shogun's hands.

Page 22, panel 1 · FOURTH MONTH OF THE SIXTH YEAR OF SHOTOKU

The dates used in this manga refer to the lunar calendar used in the pre-modern period for days and months and imperial era names for years. Likewise, time in those days was measured very differently: Day and night were each divided into six equal measures of roughly two hours each, which were then divided into two halves of about an hour each. But since summer days are longer and winter nights are longer, these "hours" were rather elastic and changed with the seasons.

Page 23, panel 1 · FENCING

Classical Japanese fencing is called *kenjutsu,* literally "the art of the sword."

Page 25, panel 6 · HATAMOTO

Hatamoto belong to the samurai class and are direct retainers of the shogunate. The term literally means "at the base of the flag" and refers to the position of military commander in charge of defending the army camp and flag. The most important characteristic of the hatamoto class is that they are able to have an audience with the shogun.

Page 27, panel 3 · BARON OF HIZEN

The original Japanese title is *hizen-no-kami. Kami* is one of the daimyo (or lordly) ranks and is often translated as "lord." However, in *Ōoku* the term "lord" is reserved for aristocrats who administer to domains, such as Yoshimune.

Page 27, panel 3 · COMMISSIONER OF TEMPLES AND SHRINES

Jisha bugyo in Japanese. It was a high-ranking office of the Tokugawa bureaucracy and thus a favorable match. There were only four of them at one time for the whole country.

Page 29, panel 3 · ADOPTION

In Japan, adoption was not reserved for children. A family lacking a son would sometimes adopt a grown man, who would take on the family name. Sometimes the adoptee would marry into the family, but this was not necessary.

Page 41, panel 4 · MIZUNO

Literally means "water field."

Page 43, panel 2 · OUR CURRENT SHOGUN

Ienobu (shown on p. 17) died in 1712 and was succeeded by her daughter, Ietsugu.

Page 45, panel 3 · LATEST STYLE IN EDO

Yunoshin is an *Edokko* (literally "child of Edo," someone who is born and raised in Edo). His awareness of fashions, his love of subtle and somber colors and patterns, his quick and zingy speech rhythms, his vocabulary and his general sharpness of wit, tongue, taste, and temper are all very typical of the Edokko. Edo is the region now known as Tokyo.

Page 47, panel 1 · HAKAMA

A Japanese garment tied at the waist and worn over kimono. Divided hakama resemble pants in that they have two separate legs and were worn when riding horses. The undivided hakama do not have separate legs.

Page 47, panel 1 · PERMITTED TO WEAR SWORDS

In the world outside the Ōoku, all samurai are permitted to wear swords, but merchants, farmers, and other classes are not.

Page 56, panel 1 · SEPPUKU

A Japanese ritual suicide by disembowelment. Originally, only samurai were allowed to practice it—either to die with honor before falling into the hands of enemies or to restore honor after having committed some disgrace. Seppuku is also known as *harakiri*.

Page 58, panel 3 · KEEP THEIR FORELOCKS

A tonsure is the sign of manhood; forelocks are shaved off when boys have come of age. By keeping their forelocks, they are stressing their youth and boyishness.

Page 63, panel 4 · DOJO

A training hall for martial arts such as kendo, it literally means "place of the way."

Page 75, panel 1 · GOKENIN

Gokenin belong to the samurai class and are also direct retainers of the shogunate, but are of lower rank than hatamoto and therefore are not permitted to have audiences with the shogun.

Page 81, panel 1 · CINTAMANI PATTERN

A popular fabric pattern in Eastern countries. The circles represent pearls (the cintamani jewel, or wish-fulfilling jewel of Buddhist origin), and the radiating lines represent fire or waves.

Page 81, panel 1 · SWEPT-UP GOWN

Refers to the way the garment must be lifted up to walk. When this garment is worn by noble women, it is called a *kaidori*.

Page 81, panel 1 · NERINUKI

A fabric weave where the warp is raw silk thread and the weft is scoured silk yarn.

Page 81, panel 2 · UCHIKAKE

Another term for "swept-up gown," but used for women of the samurai class.

Page 96, panel 1 · FORMAL ATTIRE

This refers to the *kamishimo*, which literally means "upper and lower" and is an ensemble that goes over the kimono for formal occasions. The upper section is a sleeveless robe with wide, starched shoulders, and the lower section is an undivided hakama.

Page 156, panel 4 · ECHIZEN

A historical figure, Ōoka Echizen-no-kami Tadasuke (also known as Ōoka Echizen) was a renowned judge appointed commissioner of Edo by the shogun Yoshimune.

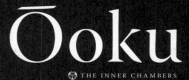

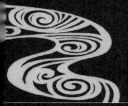

Ōoku

THE INNER CHAMBERS

Ōoku: The Inner Chambers
Vol. 1

Story and Art by Fumi Yoshinaga

Translation & Adaptation/Akemi Wegmüller
Touch-up Art & Lettering/Monlisa De Asis
Design/Frances O. Liddell
Editor/Pancha Diaz

VP, Production/Alvin Lu
VP, Sales & Product Marketing/Gonzalo Ferreyra
VP, Creative/Linda Espinosa
Publisher/Hyoe Narita

Printed in the U.S.A.

Published by VIZ Media, LLC
P.O. Box 77010
San Francisco, CA 94107

10 9 8 7 6 5 4 3 2
First printing, August 2009
Second printing, April 2010

www.viz.com

CREATOR BIOGRAPHY

FUMI YOSHINAGA

Fumi Yoshinaga is a Tokyo-born manga creator who de-
buted in 1994 with *Tsuki to Sandaru* (*The Moon and the
Sandals*). Yoshinaga has won numerous awards, includ-
ing the 2009 Osamu Tezuka Cultural Prize for *Ōoku*,
the 2002 Kodansha Manga Award for her series *Antique
Bakery*, and the 2006 Japan Media Arts Festival Excel-
lence Award for *Ōoku*. She was also nominated for the
2008 Eisner Award for Best Writer/Artist.

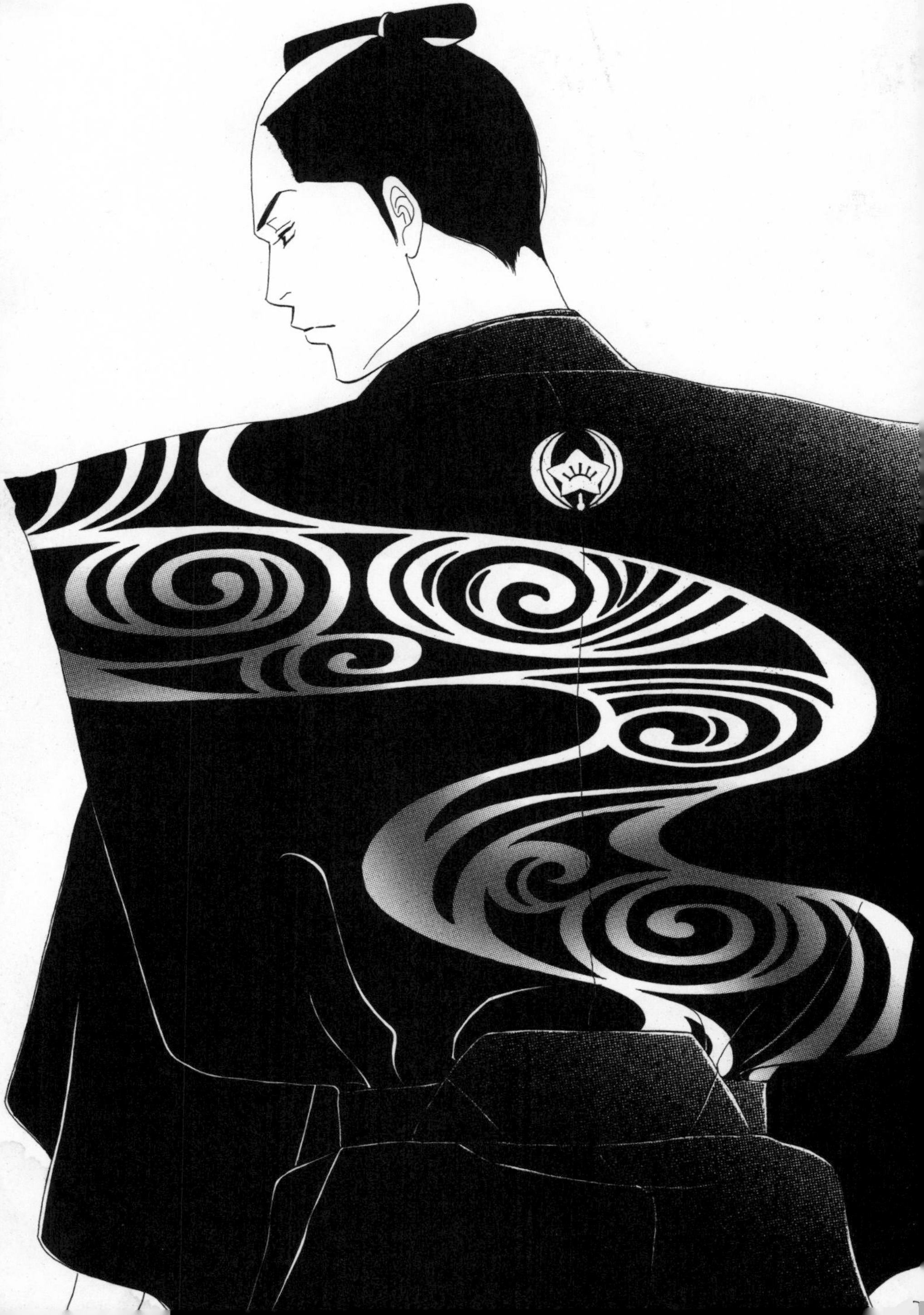

THIS IS THE LAST PAGE.

Ōoku: The Inner Chambers has been printed in the original Japanese format in order to preserve the orientation of the original artwork.

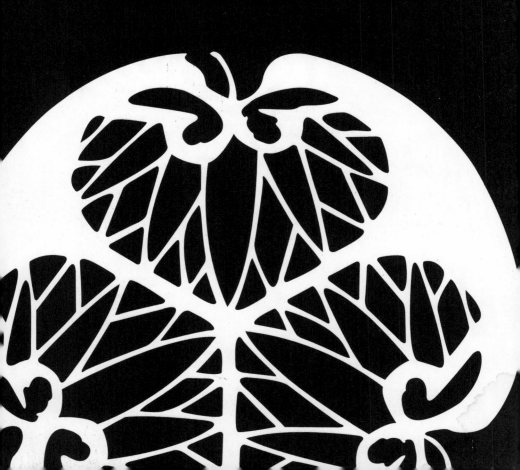